Second Edition

A Systems Approach to Small Group Interaction

STEWART L. TUBBS

Boise State University

Random House   New York

Second Edition

9876

Copyright © 1978, 1984 by Newbery Award Records, Inc.

Manufactured in the United States of America

Library of Congress Cataloging in Publication Data

Tubbs, Stewart L., 1943–
    A systems approach to small group interaction.

    Bibliography: p.
    Includes index.
    1. Work groups.   2. Small groups.   3. Organizational behavior. I. Title.
HD66.T82   1983   302.3′4   83-6399
ISBN 0-394-34993-8

To the memory of
my father and mother

Preface

It has been over ten years since I began the first edition of this book. Much has changed in our society since 1970. One of the changes has been the vastly increased use of groups as a mechanism to bring about change. Group problem solving and decision making is a growth industry!

This edition remains fundamentally the same in that it applies a systems approach to the study of small groups. However, this edition also contains many changes. After receiving responses from hundreds of student readers of the first edition. I have modified the book in the following ways:

1. More than half the cases in the book are new.

2. The cases have been changed from being descriptive to stating a problem that students can themselves discuss. The student discussion of the case can become the subject of further analysis.

3. Five of the readings following the chapters are new, reflecting more up-to-date applications of the text material.

4. The exercises have been placed immediately after each chapter, rather than following the readings. This should facilitate their use.

5. New exercises have been added to promote more student participation and involvement.

6. Chapter 1 has new material on system analysis.

7. Chapter 2 has a more streamlined treatment of personality.

8. Chapters 3 and 7 have new material on the rise of quality circles (small groups) to improve productivity and to facilitate change in organizations. Also, the material on encounter groups has been reduced.

9. Chapter 4 has a new section on contingency theories of leadership.

10. Chapter 6 has an expanded section on conflict resolution.

All of these changes were made to make the book more usable. This book will help you become more effective in your small group behavior. However, reading a book on this subject is like reading a book on baseball. You have to go out and practice to really see improvement.

Finally, I would like to thank Dr. Gale Richards of Arizona State University for his valuable assistance in reviewing this revision.

Boise, Idaho   S.L.T.
August 1983

Preface
to the
First Edition

A great deal of recent research suggests that those individuals who are educated in small group theory and methods will get better results from their groups. Additional research shows that improving communication in small groups improves the end results or consequences of group activities. In other words, groups potentially can be stimulating, productive, and enjoyable. This book is devoted to helping you achieve these positive results in groups to which you belong.

On the other hand, many people feel that groups are just time wasters. In many task-oriented groups there is the real problem of getting sidetracked. In fact, Berg (1967) found that the 124 groups he studied pursued their discussion topic for an average of only 58 seconds at a time before getting off onto some other topic. Small wonder that one student elected to lead a group described his job as "chairman of the bored." This book should help you get better results than you have been getting in your groups.

Typically, small group books tend to fall into one of three types: (1) those that emphasize traditional problem-solving methods; (2) those that emphasize interpersonal relations and personal growth; and (3) those that emphasize theory and research while paying little attention to small group skill development. This book integrates all three of these approaches. Its approach is a synthesis of emphases on both theory and research as well as on skill development. This book integrates all three of these approaches. Its approach is a synthesis of emphases on both theory and research as well as on skill development, and is in line with the current emphasis on career-oriented education in which students should expect to increase their small group skills competency as well as their intellectual development. Neither is much good without the other. This approach is consistent with John Gardner's philosophy:

> The society which scorns excellence in plumbing because plumbing is a humble activity and tolerates shoddiness in philosophy because it is an exalted activity will have neither good plumbing nor good philosophy. Neither its pipes nor its theories will hold water.

The major concept of this book is the small group as an open system of simultaneously interacting forces. These forces include: (1) relevant background factors of the group members, (2) the internal influences or group processes, and (3) the consequences of the interaction of these factors. The open systems model serves as an organizing framework for the book. Chapter 1 describes the group phenomenon and explains the model. Chapter 2 deals with the background factors of group members which are relevant to their behavior in the group. Chapter 3 describes the environment and structure of the group. Chapter 4 deals with status, power, leadership, and social influence processes. Chapter 5 outlines several communication variables that are relevant to group behavior. Chapter 6 focuses on methods of decision making and conflict resolution. The final chapter explains the possible consequences of small group interaction.

The format of this book is unique for a small group book. Each chapter begins with a real-life case study that illustrates the principles discussed in the chapter. Each chapter includes two carefully selected readings that elaborate on one or more of the topics discussed in the chapter. The readings supplement and reinforce the text material. Exercises designed for student involvement and skill development follow the readings for the chapter.

This book integrates a number of diverse theories and techniques through a unifying conceptual scheme called systems theory. During the preparation of this book, hundreds of students were surveyed to determine those topics which are most often mentioned by students, and by professors, as being most worthy of inclusion.

This book has resulted from the efforts of a number of individuals. I thank the following people for helping with the book at various stages: Dr. John Baird, General Motors Institute; Dr. Gary Schwendiman, University of Nebraska; Dr. Keith Williamson, Temple University; and of course Scotty Lucasse, our secretary/editor extraordinaire.

Flint, Michigan   S.L.T.
October 1977

Contents

1
What Is Small Group Interaction?
1

2
Relevant Background Factors
43

3

Internal Influences

Group Circumstances and Structure

93

4

Internal Influences

Leadership and Social Influence Processes

149

5

Internal Influences

Communication Processes

211

6

Internal Influences

Conflict Resolution and Decision-Making Processes

269

7

Consequences

321

References
367

Index
383

1

What Is Small Group Interaction?

CASE STUDY*

Scene: The 14th floor of the General Motors Building in Detroit, where GM's executives make the Corporation's major decisions.

    Subject: Whether Cadillac should develop and produce a smaller model to compete more effectively against luxury imports and to also hedge against energy shortages, and if so, to decide which package would be best to do the job.

    Conversation, as related by Robert J. Templin, Cadillac's chief engineer:

> They were not speaking with one voice. We had, as always, a difference of opinion. There were those who felt that the car we conceived was too small, and they were nervous about even getting into this size car for fear of what impact it might have on the full-size buyers — that it would some-how degree or disillusion them. And they just didn't feel that Cadillac should be offering two sizes of cars.

> Now there was the other camp that pretty much said that we don't know what the right size of car is and Cadillac sure as hell better have both sizes and see what the customer tells us. We [at Cadillac] certainly sided with that approach because we felt that it was a risk we had to take; we had to play that card and see what the heck happened.

    Core of the dispute was the car's width, a key parameter because this also determines all other dimensions and thus weight. Cadillac aimed at a package approximately 72 in. wide — 8 in. narrower than its standard de Ville and about the same width as GM's compacts. This enabled engineers to shave more than 2 ft. from the full-size Cadillac and to put Seville on a 114-in. wheelbase, only 3 in. longer than the Corporation's compacts.

    But Edward N. Cole, GM president until his retirement, argued against the slimmer package. He wanted a 76-in. width equaling that of GM's intermediate cars. This, of course, would have increased all of the proposed car's dimensions and its weight. And besides, Cadillac thought 76 in. was too close to the 80-in. wide full-size cars it builds.

    Mr. Templin recalls the dispute:

> Some of the people downtown, particularly Mr. Cole, felt that we ought to go bigger, ought to be wider. The discussions got pretty intense on that particular point, so we did a styling exercise based on the 72-in. width

---

* From David C. Smith, 1975. "The New Small Seville: Cadillac's King-Size Gamble." *Wards Auto World* **11**: 23-28. Copyright © 1975 Ward's Auto World Magazine. Reprinted with permission.

and presented it for management approval. I had been there (as Cadillac chief engineer) almost a year, and that was the longest year I've ever lived. I could see my career ending when we made that presentation because the two camps were very, very vocal, and I was right in the middle.

There'd been increasing interest in developing a smaller Cadillac and dealer reaction to a small Cadillac was generally favorable.

With the deepening energy crisis, Mr. Templin recalls,

I had a real strong feeling in my bones that we had better be ready to face this energy thing even before the boycott and the embargo, so I proceeded to do what I could to get the program off the ground and Bob Lund was 100 percent in sympathy with that.

Because the German-made GM Opel Diplomat was "convenient to rework," Cadillac tried several prototypes and proposals based on this car. One was equipped with front-wheel drive (FWD) which Cadillac originally wanted but was forced to abandon because of high tooling costs. FWD used in the Cadillac Eldorado is simply too wide to be adapted to Seville. One prototype featured a 3-rotor rotary engine which ran "dead smooth," as Mr. Templin describes it. But Cadillac would have had to use Chevrolet's rotary engine components. When Chevy encountered fuel and emission hangups and slowed its rotary program, Cadillac decided upon a conventional 350-cu. in. V-8 supplied by Oldsmobile.

Meantime, numerous body, suspension and drivetrain combinations were tried.

At one point, for example, Cadillac considered bringing Opel bodies to the United States where they'd be mated to Cadillac's own sheet metal, chassis, and drive trains. Because European body-building techniques are different from those in the United States, this plan was scrapped as economically unfeasible. "We really went into this thing deep, but when you added it all up, it must have looked like it wouldn't fly," says Mr. Templin.

Cadillac also looked at bodies and stampings produced by GM-Holden's Pty. Ltd. in Australia, but that idea was ruled out because these cars have right-hand drive and this would have meant costly redesigning and retooling for United States use.

In the end, Cadillac turned to design studios at the GM Technical Center in Warren, Mich., to develop a styling prototype. "We told them we wanted to do a car that was basically 72 in. wide and 204 in. long and that we wanted the best seating package in there we could get," says Mr. Templin. The first approach also included front drive, but when that was ruled out, the only significant change was to move the back wheels 2 in. farther back. "Other than that, the car didn't really change from the original clay [model]," he says.

It was this car that Messrs. Templin and Lund showed to GM's top management. D-day was Dec. 21, and the decision was not reached easily. President Cole and his supporters remained adamant in opposing the design. Board Chairman Richard C. Gerstenberg led the group of supporters. The 72-in.-wide car finally got the nod. "We got out of that meeting around 7 o'clock at night, just soaking wet. It was a pretty intense discussion," Mr. Templin recalls.

GM and the entire auto industry closed down for the traditional Christmas holiday that same day — Dec. 21 — and remained closed until after New Year's Day. But Cadillac was so excited about the go-ahead that some people worked during the holidays, "and by the end of January, we were so far into the car that we almost couldn't stop," says Mr. Templin. "We knew what we wanted to do and we jumped into it with both feet."

One reason Cadillac could move quickly was that its engineers and GM's Tech Center designers already had a sizeable head start. "We were so anxious to get this car, we were working on it like it was approved even before it was," says Mr. Templin. "We figured if we got shot down, we'd just scrap the stuff and start over whichever way it went."

Their advance work was relatively free of upper management involvement because the project was controversial and many doubted the car would "ever hit the street; they really didn't think it would live," he adds.

1. *What do you think were the strengths or weaknesses of the group in this case?*

2. *What would you do differently if you were in this group?*

I
n 1973 a small group of men conducted a problem-solving discussion that has had worldwide impact. That small group consisted of sheiks from the oil-rich countries of the Middle East. This group later expanded and became known as the Organization of Petroleum Exporting Countries or, more commonly, OPEC. The oil ministers' discussions and the decisions following have revolutionized the American way of life. Due to rapid price rises in oil, Americans became more energy conscious than ever. This change triggered a massive population shift from the northeast to the southwest quadrant of the country. Perhaps no individual industry was influenced more dramatically by the new energy prices than the auto industry. The preceding case study is one

FRANK AND ERNEST by Bob Thaves

SINCE WE JUST INVENTED MEETINGS, I ASSUME THERE ISN'T ANY OLD BUSINESS....

THAVES 9-16

Reprinted by permission. © 1980 NEA, Inc.

example of hundreds of changes in product development brought on by the OPEC pricing decisions.

These two small group examples (OPEC and General Motors) also illustrate the systems approach to studying small group interaction. The systems approach encourages us to realize that events in one part of the world system (namely OPEC's decision on oil pricing) often influence other events in the total system (GM's decision to downsize its cars). Further events, like consumers' decisions not to use so much gas and oil, then resulted in an oil surplus, resulting in more gradual price increases from OPEC. Thus the influence is a reciprocal process. However, analyzing several levels of systems is beyond the scope of this book. Instead let us concentrate on analyzing one group discussion in an attempt to learn how to improve our own personal effectiveness in groups.

In the preceding account of a top-level executive decision-making discussion we see illustrated many principles of small-group interaction that you will be encountering in this book. The auto executives' discussion group includes people with different personalities, ages, attitudes, and levels of status. It shows a problem-solving group with a specific task being accomplished within a given situation and setting that affect the way the group members behave. It describes the style of communication, and considerable conflict of ideas. The consequences of these meetings include a solution to the problem, information sharing among committee members, coordination of the members' efforts, increased commitment to the decision, and a multimillion-dollar level of risk taking. All of these topics will be dealt with in some detail throughout the book.

Just in case you are wondering how typical these stories of group decision making are, Goldhaber (1974, p. 214) states:

Tillman (1960) found that 94 percent of organizations with more than 10,000 employees had formal committees. Kriesberg (1950) reported that executives typically spend an average of 10 hours per week in formal committee meetings. My own research at the University of New Mexico (Goldhaber 1971) showed that the average tenured faculty member served on one college committee, two to three departmental committees, one university standing committee and two to three sub-committees *simultaneously* (in addition to attending departmental, college, and university faculty meetings). The number of hours per week spent in committees and other regularly scheduled meetings (by tenured faculty) was 11. When nonscheduled and informal meetings are added on, it is easy to understand why faculty members reported that they were "tired" of all the committee assignments. One faculty member reported that he barely had time left to prepare for his classes.

Goldhaber (1974) also reported that a survey of 25 organizations revealed that most managers felt that meetings were a waste of time, since they often took too long and accomplished too little. This is reminiscent of one of Parkinson's (1957) tongue-in-cheek laws called the Law of Triviality, which states that the amount of time spent in committee discussion is inversely proportional to the sum (of money) involved. Thus, in some cases, a multimillion-dollar decision may be dismissed rather quickly due to the fact that most people don't understand much about its complexities, while relatively inexpensive items are debated at length since they are concrete enough to be understood by all.

A survey made by Executive Standards, a management consulting firm, and reported by Connecticut General Life Insurance Company (1975) showed that the average executive spends almost 700 hours a year in meetings. That averages out to almost two out of every five working days that are totally consumed in meetings. One Ford Motor Company division improved their meetings by requiring committee members to report in writing to the division general manager any meeting lasting over one hour. In addition, each member was encouraged to indicate whether he or she thought the meeting was worth the time involved. This plan resulted in shorter meetings, better agendas, and an increased sense of responsibility on the part of the committee chairperson.

On the other hand, while meetings may be time-consuming, the potential strength of the group seems to have been borne out by the recent innovations at Trans World Airlines and Sears, Roebuck. In one week, both giant corporations drastically altered their top management structure by eliminating the corporate chief executive's position for one person and replacing it with the so-called office of the chairman. This position is shared by a group of between three and five top corporate officials. This form of team top management has been used for some time by other firms such as General Electric, IT&T, Morgan Guaranty Trust Co., Honeywell, Armco Steel, and Associated Dry Goods (*Time* 1976).

The system appears to offer several advantages. It allows for greater continuity in leadership as older executives retire and are replaced one at a time. Greater flexibility is allowed, since the company's top executives can be in more than one place at a time. Finally, company officials tend to become less inhibited in pushing for important innovations. (See Chapter 7 for a discussion of the "risky-shift" phenomenon in groups.)

BERRY'S WORLD

"Let's not get into anything too heavy today.
I'm suffering from interpersonal overload!"

Reprinted by permission. © 1979 NEA. Inc.

The extensive use of committees is by no means limited to the United States. Moseley (1974) writes that the Russians have begun to use committees extensively (from the Communist party central committee on down). He states: "A survey of 1,235 heads of large Soviet industrial enterprises showed that many of them spend much of their day in conference. It said the director, chief engineer, and other officials of one plant in the Ukraine hold an average of 71 conferences a month" (better than two a day).

In Red China, Tavris (1974, p. 48) found that the so-called Speak Bitterness Revolution consists primarily of women's encounter groups designed to increase their level of liberation and equality in Chinese society. Meetings are used so much to bring about attitude change that the Chinese have developed a saying, "Under the Kuomintang, a plague of taxes; under the Communists, a plague of meetings." Similarly, Streigel (1975) reported that women's consciousness-raising groups have become a major institution in the United States as a vehicle for promoting the women's movement.

Because discussions and meetings are so prevalent in all aspects of society, it seems well worth the effort to learn more effective ways of interacting in small groups. Several studies by Burke and Bennis (1961), Larson and Gratz (1970), Mosvick (1971), and Weaver (1971) have shown that courses in small group interaction do bring about higher levels of personal competence in small group methods. After reading this book, you should be able to get more out of your small group experiences than you did in the past. However, no one can improve communication skills simply by reading a book. At the end of each chapter you will find a number of small group activities that should help you gain experience as well as intellectual growth.

At the end of each chapter you will find two supplemental reading selections. These are designed to add depth and breadth to the discussion in the text material. For example, see the article at the end of this chapter by Norman Maier for a discussion of the inherent strengths and weaknesses associated with the use of groups.

A DEFINITION

Just what is meant by the term *small group interaction?* This question is more complicated than you might think. For one thing, what is a group? Shaw (1976) has identified six different ways in which we can identify a group. They are (1) in terms of perceptions (do members make an impression on others?), (2) in terms of motivation (is the group membership rewarding?), (3) in terms of goals (working together for a purpose), (4) in terms of organization (each person has some organized role to play — such as moderator, note taker, etc.), (5) in terms of interdependency (each person is somewhat dependent on the others), and (6) in terms of *interaction* (the group is small enough to allow face-to-face communication among members). To summarize, a group is a collection of individuals who influence one another, derive some satisfaction from maintaining membership in the group, interact for some purpose, assume specialized roles, are dependent on one another, and communicate face to face.

Shaw (1976) states that small-group communication can be considered as virtually synonymous with interaction. Other authors have taken a similar position on this issue. Thibaut and Kelley (1959, p. 10) put it this way:

> The essence of any interpersonal relationship is interaction. . . . By interaction it is meant that they emit behavior in each other's

presence, they create products for each other, or they communicate with each other.

Berelson and Steiner (1964, p. 326) go into a bit more detail when they write that *interaction*

> is a generic term for the exchange . . . between people. Usually inter-action is direct communication — mainly talking and listening — but it can also include gestures, glances, nods or shakes of the head, pats on the back, frowns, caresses or slaps, and any other way in which meanings can be transmitted from one person to another and back again . . . "interaction" refers to communication in its broadest sense.

If we employ the term *group* as defined above, small group interaction may be defined as *the process by which three or more members of a group exchange verbal and nonverbal messages in an attempt to influence one another*. This definition incorporates the views of Thibaut and Kelley (1959), Berelson and Steiner (1964), and Shaw (1976), among others.

CONCEPTUAL ORIENTATIONS

Small group interaction is very complicated and involves a large number of factors that act and interact simultaneously. In addition, these factors are in a continual state of flux. Think of the difficulty of trying to describe and analyze all the behaviors that occur at just one party! We have all been to parties that generate far more reactions than we would have thought. One entire book (Pettinger 1964) was devoted to the *first five minutes* of inter-action in one communicate situation. This prompted one friend to specu-late that, at that rate, a *one-hour* discussion would require a 12-volume series! The point is that any attempt to provide a conceptual orientation to small group interaction or any social process must be highly simplified.

MILLS'S MODELS

Mills (1967) identified six models for studying and analyzing small groups. They are (1) the quasi-mechanical model, (2) the organismic model, (3) the conflict model, (4) the equilibrium model, (5) the structural-functional model, and (6) the cybernetic-growth model. Each of these models offers a different perspective from which to view small group processes. Each model is based upon certain assumptions that affect the questions we ask about group behavior as well as the answers we are likely to obtain.

The *quasi-mechanical model* assumes that a group is like a machine. All behavioral acts in a group are seen as functions that can be categorized. Each functional act (e.g., a question) calls for a reaction (e.g., an answer). All actions and reactions are quantifiable and may be added, subtracted, multiplied, or divided in such a way to mathematically represent the dynamics of the group. Bales's (1950, 1970) work as described in Chapter 4 is an example of such an approach. Group behavior is considered to follow universal and unchanging laws. This model also assumes that people are merely interchangeable parts in the system, and that all problem-solving groups will exhibit many of the same behaviors. Mills (1967) criticizes the quasi-mechanical model for not telling us much about group discussion and for not being very relevant in its application.

The *organismic model* assumes that groups are like biological organisms. That is, they have a period of formation (birth), a life cycle, and eventually a death. Different people in the group become differentiated in their behaviors (e.g., task leader, recorder, social leader) just as bodily systems carry on different functions (e.g., digestive, respiratory, muscular). The emphasis is upon the group's *natural* evolution and development. Thus natural, ongoing, real-life groups are more often the object of study than artificial, zero-history groups created for the purpose of a laboratory study. Thus this model severely reduces the methods for studying groups that might otherwise be employed.

The *conflict model* assumes that the small group is a context for an endless series of conflicts. All members of groups have to face the conflict of being truly independent versus conforming to some extent to the group norms and expectations. Also, since there are many groups to affiliate with, individuals feel conflict in deciding which group to join. The person with several bids from fraternities is a classic example — the choice is difficult to make. Within the group, differences of opinion are a continual source of potential conflict. Conflicts arise between groups as well. Mills (1967) argues that this model is too limited in that it tends to overlook all the socially binding (cohesive) factors in favor of the socially divisive factors. It is too one-sided.

The *equilibrium model* assumes that groups and group members have a need to maintain some sort of balance or equilibrium — for example, that conflicts between group members tend to be followed by attempts to smooth over hard feelings and return to a state of interpersonal harmony. Several equilibrium models have been developed. The first was Heider's balance theory, which is described in Chapter 2. Although the equilibrium models give us insight on a relatively simple level of analysis, when all the important elements are considered, the model is too limited to be able to explain much. For example, if I have an attitude toward a friend (positive) and he says something I don't like (negative), I can resolve this by agreeing with him or disliking him. But what if I forgive his comment, even though I still disagree with him on that issue, and continue to like him and agree with him on lots of other issues?

The *structural-functional model* assumes that the group is a goal-seeking system that is constantly adapting to meet new demands. It assumes that goal attainment is the primary source of satisfaction to its members. It also assumes that some members will take on the function of keeping the group functioning. These so-called group-maintenance functions will serve to keep interpersonal relations from breaking down so that the group would cease functioning. The model is one of the better ones available because it includes the role of learning, by which groups can survive by adapting to the demand for new behaviors.

The *cybernetic-growth model* shifts the emphasis from group survival to group growth. This model assumes the existence of group agents that help the group adapt to new information (or feedback). Thus growth and development are attained by the group's responding to feedback from its earlier performance. Three types of feedback, (1) goal seeking, (2) group restructuring, and (3) self-awareness, are required to help the group grow and develop. Mills (1967, p. 20) uses the example of the quarterback of a football team to illustrate the three types of feedback:

> He reads the weakness in other teams' defenses and tries to capitalize on them (goal seeking); due to unforeseen circumstances, he may have to revise the pre-game strategy, trying out one modification after the other (internal re-arrangement); and on each play he assesses the developing weaknesses or strengths in his team, and, in general, the present state and condition of his team (consciousness). Since he can act on his ideas — observe the effects of his action and therefore test them — he is in a position to learn to direct his team. Through self-monitoring, self-steering, and testing these processes, he is able to increase his capabilities for self-determination.

Mills argues convincingly that this model is strong in that it helps us identify the important factors or variables that lead to growth on the part of the group as well as on the part of the individual members. A partial list of potential end results of group growth for individual members includes the following (Mills 1967, p. 22):

Indicators of a Person's Capacity to Grow

1. *Adaptation*
   a. Receptivity to a wider range of information about himself, others, his groups, his and other societies, and the physical environment
   b. Receptivity to new freedoms, responsibilities, and obligations — to new roles
   c. Flexibility in modifying his ideas, beliefs, personal norms, and emotional attachments without loss of intellectual or moral integrity

2. *Goal-attainment*
   a. Capacity to postpone immediate gratification, and to conceive of and evaluate an increasing number of avenues for gratification

    b. Capacity to decommit himself from one goal, and to recommit himself to new and additional goals, and to learn how to attain them

3. *Integration*

    a. Capacity to perform in an expanded repertoire of roles and variety of social relations without suffering diffusion of his identity

4. *Pattern-maintenance and extension*

    a. Capacity for deeper emotional involvement with others without surrendering his self

    b. Increasing ability to convey his experience, learning, and capabilities to others

THE SYSTEMS PERSPECTIVE

Although the six models just described have a number of worthwhile characteristics, a seventh model that synthesizes elements of the first six seems to be even more appropriate for conceptualizing small group interaction. The remainder of this book is organized around the idea that small group interaction can most adequately be thought of as occurring in a system of interdependent forces, each of which can be analyzed and set in the perspective of other forces. This idea represents a so-called general systems method of thinking about small groups. Seiler (1967, p. 4) describes the systems method of analysis as emphasizing "the notions of multiple causation and the complex interrelation of forces." In other words, it is a way of thinking about behavior that avoids the idea that complex behaviors in groups result from a single cause.

Several critics of the small group field (Bormann 1970; Mortenson 1970; Gouran 1973) agree that we need some conceptual framework to help us understand the ways in which the huge number of small group variables fit together. It is a little like having a box of puzzle pieces with no picture or model to help us see how they are supposed to fit together. With this in mind, let us turn to a general systems model of small group interaction that should help clarify some of these conceptual problems. The model (Fig. 1.1) is meant to suggest the relationships among a number of the variables frequently discussed in the small group literature.

Because Chapters 2 through 7 discuss the elements in the model in greater detail, the analysis at this point will be relatively brief. The model identifies three categories of variables. First, *relevant background factors* refers to attributes within the individual participants that existed prior to the group's formation and that will endure in some modified form after the group no longer exists. These background factors, such as personality,

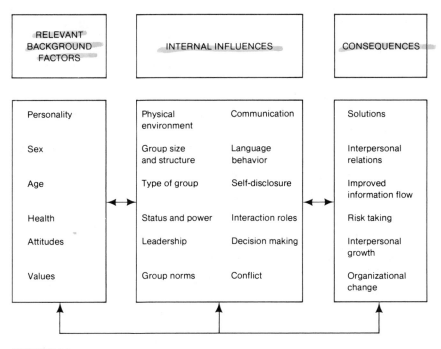

FIGURE 1.1
The Tubbs model of small group interaction.

attitudes, and values, influence the group's functioning; in turn, the group process modifies the background factors. For example, the case study at the beginning of this chapter indicated the strong conflict between the GM top executives, whose differing attitudes caused a great deal of research and discussion as to just how small to make the Cadillac Seville. From what we can tell, this group was all male, and the group members by virtue of their high-level positions probably held similar values about a lot of issues related to this topic of discussion. For example, you would not expect anyone in this group to launch off into a tirade against the corrupt profit-mongering characteristics of big business. As a result of the group members' similarities in age, sex, attitudes, and values, we would expect a great deal less conflict in this group than we might expect if we added a few members who differed on these factors.

The second set of variables in the model is referred to as *internal influences.* These influences include (among others) the type of group, the style of leadership used, and the language behavior, interaction roles, and decision style employed by the group. Each of these factors may be varied to change the nature and functioning of the group. For example, think how different the discussion in the Cadillac case would be if we had a group of only three people conducting an encounter group on a secluded beach where the group norm was to enjoy and to live for the moment! It is obvious that as these internal influences vary, the nature of the group's accomplishments vary.

The third set of variables in the systems model is the *consequences* of small group interaction. Consequences will obviously vary with the background of the participants, as well as with the nature of the internal influences. Consequences may include solutions to problems, interpersonal relations among group members, the amount and quality of information sharing, the level of risk taking, the amount of interpersonal growth of participants, and possibly the amount of change in any larger organization of which the group may be a part. The consequences are the outputs of the group's activities. They are the raison d'être of a group, the reason the group is formed in the first place.

Finally, as suggested by the open systems model, the consequences or outputs of the group are fed back into the system through the feedback loop. Katz and Kahn (1966, p. 17) describe an open system this way: "Activities can be examined in relation to the *energic input* into the system, the *transformation of energies within the system,* and the *resulting product or energic output.* "(Italics added.) They also say (p. 16) that "our theoretical model for the understanding of [social] organizations is that of an input-output system in which the energic return from the output reactivates the system."

Let's look at it in less theoretical terms. A highly successful baseball team develops a renewed sense of energy from having a winning season. This energy is reinvested in the team by new attitudes of becoming even more successful, admiring each other more, and so forth. This new energy and motivation level may allow the team members to enjoy a higher level of status, a new and more democratic style of leadership, and a more plush physical environment within which to work or live. This entire process of multiple causation is indicated by the two-headed arrows in the model (Fig. 1.1). Keep in mind that the model appears to be static, like a photograph. But in reality, small group behaviors should be modeled by a movie with each of the parts *moving* in relation to the others.

Different levels of systems analysis and the type of system studied include:

□ Astronomy — universal systems

□ Ecology — planetary systems

□ Political science — political systems

□ Sociology — social systems

□ Psychology — human systems

□ Physiology — organ systems

□ Molecular biology — microscopic systems

General systems theory has been applied to many different fields of study, including biology, engineering, mathematics, and psychiatry. Systems analysis has become a particularly popular way of analyzing human behavior in organizations and has been written about in several sources (Katz and Kahn 1966; Seiler 1967; Kast and Rosenzweig 1970; Huse and Bowditch 1973). Communication scholars have paid relatively little attention to the application of systems theory to the communication field. Ruben (1972, p. 135) states: "Of the growing number of basic human communication books, I am familiar with only two, *Communication and Communication Systems* [Thayer 1968] and *Pragmatics of Human Communication* [Watzlawick *et al.* 1967] which utilize an integrated system framework as an approach to human communication." In addition to these, a third book has now been added that applies systems theory concepts to human communication (Ruben and Kim 1975). However, no other book currently available applies a systems theory analysis to small group communication.

With some of this background in mind, let us look briefly at five general systems concepts that apply to small group communication and are suggested by our general systems model.

Input   Input refers to the raw material of small group interaction. It includes all six of the relevant background factors depicted in the model. It also includes information that the group receives from outside the group. For example, a problem-solving group in the midst of a discussion may notice that they are running short on time. This new informational input will probably influence the group to change their procedures (e.g., stop talking about side issues) and focus more directly or efficiently on solving the problem at hand.

A system that has inputs from outside is called an *open system*. An open system is said to interact with its environment, in contrast to remaining isolated. Gross (1964, p. 113) identifies four phenomena characteristic of open systems:

1. entries and exits, which transform outsiders into members and members into outsiders;

2. multiple membership, which results in members' loyalties to outside groups;

3. resource exchange, which involves the absorption of inputs in the production process and in the delivery of output produced; and

4. mutual or reciprocal influence on the part of both members and outsiders.

Anyone who has ever felt torn between loyalty to two different groups will easily be able to understand the relevance of Gross's four points.

Throughput   Throughput refers to the internal influences depicted in our model. It means all of the actual verbal and nonverbal behaviors that occur in the course of a group discussion. It includes the process of creating and modifying ideas in the course of a discussion. Throughput is the heart and in some cases the entirety of what most small group communication books discuss. Chapters 3 through 6 will discuss these variables in detail.

Output   Output is referred to in the consequences section of our model. These are sometimes called the end results of group interaction. However, as we shall soon see, end results imply a beginning and an end, which is somewhat misleading, because groups often have an ongoing life history during which these outputs or consequences are continually being modified on the basis of continuing interaction. Chapter 7 is devoted to discussing the consequences or outputs of small group interaction.

Cycles   Often the outputs of group interaction are fed back to the group and become inputs for future interactions. For example, a severe personality conflict in one meeting (of a group) may reduce the level of cohesiveness or interpersonal closeness of group members. As a result some members may refuse to attend future meetings, some may attend but will not participate as openly, or some may try harder the next time to be more diplomatic in their remarks in order to avoid a recurrence of the conflict. The arrows at the bottom of our model (Fig. 1.1) indicate what is commonly called a feedback loop. This loop represents the cyclical and ongoing nature of group processes and also implies that the process does not begin and end anew with each group meeting but instead builds on all the past experiences of each group member.

Equifinality   You have undoubtedly heard the expression, "There is more than one way to skin a cat." This expression captures part of what is meant by the term *equifinality*. This concept means that, although two groups may have different members, leadership styles, decision-making methods, and so on, they may still arrive at the same solution to a given problem. There is an incredibly large number of combinations of all the variables in our small group model. These combinations may in some cases interact in such a way as to produce the same group consequences but from dramatically different processes. Conversely, two groups may attempt to use the same procedures but end up with different outcomes. Thus equifinality refers to the unpredictability and potential for adaptation that groups possess.

For those readers who are fairly familiar with small group literature, a synthesis of different small group models is offered in Fig. 1.2. You will note the considerable similarity of conceptual approaches that span more than thirty years of writing. Note, however, that the present model is the only one that explicitly emphasizes the dynamic and simultaneous interaction of all the component parts.

Homans (1950)	External system		Internal system	
Stogdill (1959)	Member inputs	Mediating variables	Resultant variables	
Thibaut and Kelley (1959)	Exogenous variables	Endogenous variables	Resultant variables	
McGrath and Altman (1966)	Properties of group members	Conditions imposed on group	Interaction process	Performance
Kibler and Barker (1969)	Antecedents	Messages	Consequences	
Fisher (1971)	Inputs	Mediating variables	Outputs	
Gouran (1973)	Context of communication	Communication behaviors	Group outcomes	
Tubbs (1984)	Relevant background factors	Internal influences	Consequences	

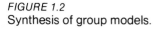

FIGURE 1.2
Synthesis of group models.

SUMMARY

This chapter began with a real-life example of a problem-solving small group. From there we noted that groups are a pervasive part of each of our lives and that small groups are a basic institution in societies all over the world. Next, some key definitions were discussed, along with six theoretical models for small group analysis. Finally, a general systems model was offered as an organizing framework for the analysis of small group interaction. This framework also serves as an outline for the remainder of this book. In the next six chapters and the accompanying readings, each part of the model will be discussed in greater detail. Chapter 2 covers *relevant background factors,* Chapters 3 through 6 are devoted to *internal influences,* and Chapter 7 deals with the *consequences* of small group interaction.

Exercises

1. First Impressions

Each person in the class should introduce himself or herself. Class members should feel free to ask each person questions to get a more complete impression. After the introductions, each person should write down some first impressions of the other class members (if you each display a large name card this is much easier). Those who want to may share their first impressions with the class. Then reactions to those impressions may also be shared and discussed.

2. Interpersonal Perceptions

Separate into groups of five and fill out the Preliminary Scale of Interpersonal Perceptions on each of the other four group members. Pass the completed scales to each person in the group. Examine the feedback you get and discuss these with the others in the group. You may want to share with one another the behaviors that led to these perceptions.

PRELIMINARY SCALE OF INTERPERSONAL PERCEPTIONS

Group Member's Name _____

On the scale below each question, circle the number that best describes the way you see this person's participation in group discussion. Try to distinguish between those areas where the person rates high and those where he/she rates less well.

1. How well does this person understand himself/herself in relation to this group? (Circle one numeral)

5	4	3	2	1
He/she has a very good understanding				He/she has very little understanding

2. How effective do you think this person is in contributing ideas, insights, and suggestions that help the group solve problems and achieve its goals? (Circle one numeral)

5	4	3	2	1
He/she is exceptionally effective				He/she is very ineffective

3. How effective do you think this person is in performing functions that build the group and keep it working well? (Circle one numeral)

5	4	3	2	1
He/she is exceptionally effective				He/she is very ineffective

4. In your opinion, how able is this person to express himself/herself freely and comfortably in the group? (Circle one numeral)

5	4	3	2	1

He/she is exceptionally   He/she is very
free and comfortable   restricted and tense

5. To what extent do you feel that this person really understands your ideas and feelings? (Circle one numeral)

5	4	3	2	1

He/she has a very   He/she has very
good understanding   little understanding

3. Group Consensus Activity

Form into groups of five, and then read and discuss the following article on cloning. As an agenda, try to answer the questions that follow the article.

---

*SCIENTISTS REPORT CLONING OF MOUSE — A FIRST FOR MAMMALS**

By WALTER SULLIVAN, The New York Times

NEW YORK — Scientists in Switzerland have reported the first authenticated cloning of a mammal. Using cells from mouse embryos, they say they have produced three mice that are genetically identical to the original embryos.

Cloning is the production of a plant or animal identical with one from which a cell or cell nucleus has been taken and activated to become a complete organism. In plants, the procedure, using a cutting, is relatively routine. Cloning has been performed to a limited extent in frogs and other amphibians, but the possibility of cloning mammals had not previously been demonstrated.

The mice were cloned by taking nuclei from embryonic rather than adult cells, the scientists reported. Whether it will be possible to produce clones from adult mice or other adult mammals, including man, remains uncertain.

Some researchers hope to mass-produce prize livestock in this manner. Others believe such experiments can provide an understanding of the development of individuals from embryos to adults, including the origin of birth defects.

In the mouse experiments, each clone was produced by taking a nucleus obtained from a mouse embryo at an early stage of development and inserting it into a fertilized egg from another mouse. The original nuclear material in that egg was then extracted, leaving only the inserted nucleus.

The egg, after being cultured about four days, was placed in the womb of a mouse that then gave birth to an offspring with all the genetic features of the embryo from which the nucleus had been taken. The offspring bore no relationship to the mouse whose egg had been used or to the mother that bore it.

Two of the three mouse clones later produced seemingly normal offspring. The third died after seven weeks, but an autopsy revealed no abnormalities related to the cloning.

Earlier reports that mammals, and even a human being, had been cloned have never been authenticated or taken seriously by biologists.

The achievement shows that cloning, because it has been successfully performed in amphibians, is also possible with embryonic mammals, presumably including

---

humans. It also suggests that the ability of amphibians to regenerate body parts may not be entirely beyond reach in mammals. Regeneration would be possible if genetic information within the nuclei of cells of an adult could be reactivated to perform roles, such as producing a new limb or new individual, other than those assigned to that specialized cell.

The transplants of the nuclei were performed at the University of Geneva by Dr. Karl Illmensee and Dr. Peter C. Hoppe, who is from the Jackson Laboratory in Bar Harbor, Maine. Their work has been reported at several scientific meetings and will be described later this month in the journal Cell, published by the Massachusetts Institute of Technology in Cambridge, Mass.

As in earlier nuclear transplants, the nucleus was extracted by a glass tube, or pipette, honed to hairlike sharpness. Under observation with a microscope, the pipette, controlled by a mechanical micromanipulator, was inserted into a cell taken from a mouse embryo at an early stage of development (the spherical, or blastocyst, stage, reached a few days after fertilization).

The pipette was then inserted into an egg from another mouse so recently fertilized that the sperm nucleus had not yet joined with the egg nucleus. The pipette was then used to extract the two original nuclei.

Altogether, 542 transplants were performed. Of these, 363, including the three that produced live mice, were of nuclei derived from the inner cell mass of an embryo at the blastocyst stage. It is the inner cell mass that evolves into the fetus.

The remaining nuclei were from cells forming the outer part of the blastocyst sphere, or the trophectoderm. These cells normally evolve into such structures as the uterus and umbilical cord. Their nuclei were apparently incapable of being sufficiently activated within the egg to produce an individual.

Of the 363 transplants of nuclei from the inner cell mass, 142 survived the micromanipulation and were cultured in glass vessels. Of these, 96 subdivided at least once, and within four days 48 had developed into many-celled blastocysts.

Of these embryos, 16 that appeared normal were transferred into the wombs of five white mice prepared for pregnancy by hormone treatment. The embryos had developed from eggs taken from black mice, but the nuclei inserted into them were from mice colored either grey or agouti (the color of wild mice).

Specially prepared mice also received 44 embryos taken from white mice and not subject to nuclear transplants. The added embryos enabled the prepared mice to produce litters of normal size. They all become pregnant and gave birth to a total of 35 mice. All but the three mice recognized as clones were white. None had the black fur of the strain that provided the egg cells.

The three clones had the color of the strains from which the transplanted nuclei were derived. Two, a male and female, were gray. The third was an agouti female. Tiny samples of tissue were taken from the ear, tail and skin of these mice to be cultured for genetic screening. Enzymes from the mice were also analyzed as genetic markers.

In all respects the mice resembled the embryos from which the nuclei had been taken, rather than the egg donor or the mouse prepared for pregnancy.

What are the implications of this case for the cloning of humans? Would clones be human? Would they have souls? What rights should they have? Is it desirable to clone humans? What should be the U.S. policy toward the cloning of humans?

4. Ice-Breaking Exercises

Fill out the two forms that follow, and then get into groups of five or so and share answers. Later, you can discuss what you as a group experience from these exercises.

1. The person in the group I would like to get to know better is

2. The person in the group who seems to be most like myself is

3. The person in the group whom I would like to know, that I care and am concerned about, is

4. The person who has been the most helpful is

5. A person I would like to hitchhike around the country with is

6. A person I would trust to fold my parachute before jumping from an airplane is

7. A person I would like to have a deep discussion with is

8. A person I would like most to keep in touch with is

9. A person I would trust with my secrets is

10. A person whom I feel I know least well is

What other things would you like to say to someone in this group? Take a risk (be constructive).

What person in this group:

_____   1. Has the darkest eyes?

_____   2. Has the longest name?

_____   3. Could hide in the smallest place?

_____   4. Has the biggest hands?

_____   5. Has the oldest brother or sister?

_____   6. Can give the biggest smile?

_____   7. Can make the scariest face?

_____   8. Has the most brothers and sisters?

_____   9. Has the fewest brothers and sisters?

_____ **10.** Has the lightest hair?

_____ **11.** Has the most freckles?

_____ **12.** Can make the highest mark on the wall without jumping?

_____ **13.** Is wearing the most colors?

_____ **14.** Has the longest hair?

_____ **15.** Has the shortest name?

_____ **16.** Has lived in the most places?

_____ **17.** Has had the most pets?

_____ **18.** Can hum the lowest note?

_____ **19.** Has the smallest waist?

_____ **20.** Can stand on one foot for the longest time without holding on to something?

5. Group Decision Making

Separate into groups of five or so. Choose one of the cases described below, and decide as a group what you would do in the situation. Then discuss your group processes.

WHAT WOULD YOU DO?*

Every day, doctors, nurses, patients and patients' families face life-and-death decisions. There is rarely an obvious "right" choice; each of them is, in some way, bad. Here are some real cases that present painful alternatives. The choices made by those responsible — and the results of their actions — appear below.

1. Doctors at a university hospital examined a 10-year-old boy whose bone cancer of the upper arm had recurred in spite of radiation treatments. The physicians advised amputation of the limb and warned that without the operation, the child would almost certainly die. But the boy, an enthusiastic Little Leaguer, begged his parents and the doctors to let him keep his arm so that he could continue to play baseball.

2. A 7-year-old girl was suffering from a progressive neurological disease that had made her totally dependent on a respirator. She could talk and think normally, but the rest of her body functions were deteriorating rapidly and she was obviously in pain. Attempts to "wean" her from the respirator were unsuccessful, and doctors eventually realized it was unlikely she would ever recover. The parents, who were deeply religious, agonized over a decision about whether to turn off the machine.

3. A young woman, who was dying of multiple sclerosis, finally lapsed into an irreversible coma. She remained totally unresponsive for about a week, and her doctors agreed there was nothing more they could do to help her. One evening the patient, still comatose, began to gasp for breath. Her parents, who were sitting by the bedside, summoned the nurse and asked her to call a doctor.

4. A 6-year-old boy had severe renal failure in both kidneys; his best chance of survival would be a transplant from a sibling. Each of his two older sisters, 8 and 12, was willing to donate a kidney in an effort to save the boy. The risk to either girl — from the operation or from living with one kidney — was quite small. But common medical practice dictated that young donors should not be used, except in the case of a twin.

5. At the student-health service of a major university, a young man told his psychotherapist that he wanted to kill a young woman who lived nearby but who was then on a trip abroad. The therapist conferred with two colleagues, and, in a limited breach of professional confidentiality, informed the campus police; they picked up the student and detained him for questioning. Concluding that the youth was harmless, the police decided to release him after extracting a promise that he would not bother the woman he had spoken of murdering. The health service thought it unnecessary to take any further action.

---

1. The family decided against surgery. Now, nearly a year later, the boy is receiving radiation and chemotherapy — and playing baseball. Physicians say it is too soon to estimate his chances of recovery.

2. The physician asked the parents if they wanted to discover whether God wished the child to breathe on her own. The distraught couple agreed and, as they sat vigil, the respirator was removed; the child died about four hours later.

3. The nurse requested that the parents leave the room. Instead of summoning the doctor immediately, she waited until the patient had stopped breathing. Then she went, with a physician, to tell the parents that their daughter had died. "It was the hardest thing I ever did in my life," the nurse admits.

4. The doctors refused the sisters as donors, on the ground that they were too young to make a major medical decision that could affect their whole lives. The brother has survived for four years on dialysis.

5. Two months later, shortly after the woman's return, the student went to her home and killed her. Her parents sued the university — and won. The state supreme court ruled that the health service and the university had a "duty" to warn the girl of the threat on her life.

OVERVIEW OF READINGS

The systems model presented in Fig. 1.1 represented an attempt to show the interrelated nature of 24 variables relevant to the study of small group interaction (6 variables in each of the 4 columns in the model). Dorwin Cartwright's article shows how three variables fit together as he discusses the tremendous influence groups can have in changing people. The eight principles in the article are as relevant today as when he wrote them over thirty years ago. This fact helps to emphasize both the predictability and the importance of knowing group dynamics principles. It is also interesting to note that these principles also fit quite comfortably within the systems approach to studying small group interaction, which is the conceptual model around which this book is structured.

The article by Norman Maier offers a good synthesis of what we know are the basic strengths and weaknesses of small group interaction. He also shows that the strengths can be increased and the weaknesses decreased (that is, the consequences can be different), depending on the quality of group processes and the style of leadership used. Both of these articles help illustrate the way in which the systems model of small group interaction helps us understand the complicated relationships between and among these numerous variables.

Achieving Change in People: Some Applications of Group Dynamics Theory

Dorwin Cartwright

What principles of achieving change in people can we see emerging? To begin with the most general proposition, we may state that the behavior, attitudes, beliefs, and values of the individual are all firmly grounded in the groups to which he belongs. How aggressive or cooperative a person is, how much self-respect and self-confidence he has, how energetic and productive his work is, what he aspires to, what he believes to be true and good, whom he loves or hates, and what beliefs and prejudices he holds — all these characteristics are highly determined by the individual's group memberships. In a real sense, they are properties of groups and of the relationships between people. Whether they change or resist change will, therefore, be greatly influenced by the nature of these groups. Attempts to change them must be concerned with the dynamics of groups.

In examining more specifically how groups enter into the process of change, we find it useful to view groups in at least three different ways. In the first view, the group is seen as a source of influence over its members. Efforts to change behavior can be supported or blocked by pressures on members stemming from the group. To make constructive use of these pressures the group must be used *as a medium of change*. In the second view, the group itself becomes the *target of change*. To change the behavior of individuals it may be necessary to change the standards of the group, its style of leadership, its emotional atmosphere, or its stratification into cliques and hierarchies. Even

Dorwin Cartwright, "Achieving Change in People: Some Applications of Group Dynamics Theory" from *Human Relations*, Vol. 4, 1951. Reprinted by permission of Plenum Publishing Corporation.

though the goal may be to change the behavior of *individuals,* the target of change becomes the group. In the third view, it is recognized that many changes of behavior can be brought about only by the organized efforts of groups *as agents of change.* A committee to combat intolerance, a labor union, an employers association, a citizens group to increase the pay of teachers — any action group will be more or less effective depending upon the way it is organized, the satisfactions it provides to its members, the degree to which its goals are clear, and a host of other properties of the group.

An adequate social technology of change, then, requires at the very least a scientific understanding of groups viewed in each of these ways. We shall consider here only the first two aspects of the problem: the group as a medium of change and as a target of change.

THE GROUP AS A MEDIUM OF CHANGE

Principle No. 1. If the group is to be used effectively as a medium of change, those people who are to be changed and those who are to exert influence for change must have a strong sense of belonging to the same group.

Kurt Lewin described this principle well. "The normal gap between teacher and student, doctor and patient, social worker and public, can . . . be a real obstacle to acceptance of the advocated conduct." In other words, in spite of whatever status differences there might be between them, the teacher and the student have to feel as members of one group in matters involving their sense of values. The chances for reeducation seem to be increased whenever a strong we-feeling is created (5). Recent experiments by Preston and Heintz have demonstrated greater changes of opinions among members of discussion groups operating with participatory leadership than among those with supervisory leadership (12). The implications of this principle for classroom teaching are far-reaching. The same may be said of supervision in the factory, army, or hospital.

Principle No. 2. The more attractive the group is to its members the greater is the influence that the group can exert on its members.

This principle has been extensively documented by Festinger and his co-workers (4). They have been able to show in a variety of settings that in more cohesive groups there is a greater readiness of members to attempt to influence others, a greater readiness to be influenced by others, and stronger pressures toward conformity when conformity is a relevant matter for the group. Important for the practitioner wanting to make use of this principle is, of course, the question of how to increase the attractiveness of groups. This is a question with many answers. Suffice it to say that a group is more attractive the more it satisfies the needs of its members. We have been able to demonstrate experimentally an increase in group cohesiveness by increasing the liking of members for each other as persons, by increasing the perceived importance of the group goal, and by increasing the prestige of the group among other groups. Experienced group workers could add many other ways to this list.

Principle No. 3. In attempts to change attitudes, values, or behavior, the more relevant they are to the basis of attraction to the group, the greater will be the influence that the group can exert upon them.

I believe this principle gives a clue to some otherwise puzzling phenomena. How does it happen that a group, like a labor union, seems to be able to exert such strong discipline over its members in some matters (let us say in dealings with management), while it seems unable to exert nearly the same influence in other matters (let us say in political action)? If we examine why it is that members are attracted to the group, I believe we will find that a particular reason for belonging seems more related to some of the group's activities than to others. If a man joins a union mainly to keep his job and to improve his working conditions, he may be largely uninfluenced by the union's attempt to modify his attitudes toward national and international affairs. Groups differ tremendously in the range of matters that are relevant to them and hence over which they have influence. Much of the inefficiency of adult education could be reduced if more attention were paid to the need that influence attempts be appropriate to the groups in which they are made.

Principle No. 4. The greater the prestige of a group member in the eyes of the other members, the greater the influence he can exert.

Polansky, Lippitt, and Redl (11) have demonstrated this principle with great care and methodological ingenuity in a series of studies in children's summer camps. From a practical point of view it must be emphasized that the things giving prestige to a member may not be those characteristics most prized by the official management of the group. The most prestige-carrying member of a Sunday school class may not possess the characteristics most similar to the minister of the church. The teacher's pet may be a poor source of influence within a class. This principle is the basis for the common observation that the official leader and the actual leader of a group are often not the same individual.

Principle No. 5. Efforts to change individuals or subparts of a group which, if successful, would have the result of making them deviate from the norms of the group will encounter strong resistance.

During the past years a great deal of evidence has been accumulated showing the tremendous pressures which groups can exert upon members to conform to the group's norms. The price of deviation in most groups is rejection or even expulsion. If the member really wants to belong and be accepted, he cannot withstand this type of pressure. It is for this reason that efforts to change people by taking them from the group and giving them special training so often have disappointing results. This principle also accounts for the finding that people thus trained sometimes display increased tension, aggressiveness toward the group, or a tendency to form cults or cliques with others who have shared their training.

These five principles concerning the group as a medium of change would appear to have readiest application to groups created for the purpose of producing changes in people. They provide certain specifications for building effective training or therapy groups. They also point, however, to a difficulty in producing change in people in that they show how resistant an individual is to changing in any way contrary to group pressures and expectations. In order to achieve many kinds of changes in people, therefore, it is necessary to deal with the group as a target of change.

THE GROUP AS A TARGET OF CHANGE

Principle No. 6. Strong pressure for changes in the group can be established by creating a shared perception by members of the need for change, thus making the source of pressure for change lie within the group.

Marrow and French (9) reports a dramatic case-study which illustrates this principle quite well. A manufacturing concern had a policy against hiring women over 30 because it was believed that they were slower, more difficult to train, and more likely to be absent. The staff psychologist was able to present to management evidence that this belief was clearly unwarranted at least within their own company. The psychologist's facts, however, were rejected and ignored as a basis for action because they violated accepted beliefs. It was claimed that they went against the direct experience of the foremen. Then the psychologist hit upon a plan for achieving change which differed drastically from the usual one of argument, persuasion, and pressure. He proposed that management conduct its own analysis of the situation. With his help management collected all the facts which they believed were relevant to the problem. When the results were in they were now their own facts rather than those of some "outside" expert. Policy was immediately changed without further resistance. The important point here is that facts are not enough. The facts must be the accepted property of the group if they are to become an effective basis for change. There seems to be all the difference in the world in changes actually carried out between those cases in which a consulting firm is hired to do a study and present a report and those in which technical experts are asked to collaborate with the group in doing its own study.

Principle No. 7. Information relating to the need for change, plans for change, and consequences of change must be shared by all relevant people in the group.

Another way of stating this principle is to say that change of a group ordinarily requires the opening of communication channels. Newcomb (10) has shown how one of the first consequences of mistrust and hostility is the avoidance of communicating openly and freely about the things producing the tension. If you look closely at a pathological group (that is, one that has trouble making decisions or effecting coordinated efforts of its members), you will certainly find strong restraints in that group against communicating vital information among its members. Until these restraints are removed there can be little hope for any real and lasting changes in the group's functioning. In passing it should be pointed out that the removal of barriers to communication will ordinarily be accompanied by a sudden increase in the communication of hostility. The group may appear to be falling apart, and it will certainly be a painful experience to many of the members. This pain and the fear that things are getting out of hand often stop the process of change once begun.

Principle No. 8. Changes in one part of a group produce strain in other related parts which can be reduced only by eliminating the change or by bringing about readjustments in the related parts.

It is a common practice to undertake improvements in group functioning by providing training programs for certain classes of people in the organization. A training program for foremen, for nurses, for teachers, or for group workers is established. If the content of the training is relevant for organizational change, it must of necessity deal with the relationships these people have with other subgroups. If nurses in a hospital change their behavior significantly, it will affect their relations both with the patients and with the doctors. It is unrealistic to assume that both these groups will remain indifferent to any significant changes in this respect. In hierarchical structures this process is most clear. Lippitt has proposed on the basis of research and experience that in such organizations attempts at change should always involve three levels, one being the major target of change and the other two being the one above and the one below.

These eight principles represent a few of the basic propositions emerging from research in group dynamics. Since research is constantly going on and since it is the very nature of research to revise and reformulate our conceptions, we may be sure that these principles will have to be modified and improved as time goes by. In the meantime they may serve as guides in our endeavors to develop a scientifically based technology of social management.

In social technology, just as in physical technology, invention plays a crucial role. In both fields progress consists of the creation of new mechanisms for the accomplishment of certain goals. In both fields inventions arise in response to practical needs and are to be evaluated by how effectively they satisfy these needs. The relation of invention to scientific development is indirect but important. Inventions cannot proceed too far ahead of basic scientific development, nor should they be allowed to fall too far behind. They will be more effective the more they make good use of known principles of science, and they often make new developments in science possible. On the other hand, they are in no sense logical derivations from scientific principles.

I have taken this brief excursion into the theory of invention in order to make a final point. To many people "group dynamics" is known only for the social inventions which have developed in recent years in work with groups. Group dynamics is often thought of as certain techniques to be used with groups. Role playing, buzz groups, process observers, post-meeting reaction sheets, and feedback of group observations are devices popularly associated with the phrase "group dynamics." I trust that I have been able to show that group dynamics is more than a collection of gadgets. It certainly aspires to be a science as well as a technology.

This is not to underplay the importance of these inventions nor of the function of inventing. As inventions they are all mechanisms designed to help accomplish important goals. How effective they are will depend upon how skillfully they are used and how appropriate they are to the purposes to which they are put. Careful evaluative research must be the ultimate judge of their usefulness in comparison with alternative inventions. I believe that the principles enumerated in this paper indicate some of the specifications that social inventions in this field must meet.

REFERENCES

1. Cartwright, D. Some principles of mass persuasion: Selected findings of research on the sale of United States war bonds. *Human Relations*, 1949, 2(3), 253-67.

2. Cartwright, D. *The research center for group dynamics: A report of five years' activities and a view of future needs.* Ann Arbor: Institute for Social Research, 1950.

3. Coch, L. and French, J.T.P., Jr. Overcoming resistance to change. *Human Relations,* 1948, *1*(4), 512-32.

4. Festinger, L., *et al. Theory and experiment in social communication:* Collected papers. Ann Arbor: Institute for Social Research, 1950.

5. Lewin, K. *Resolving social conflicts,* p. 67. New York: Harper & Bros., 1951.

6. Lewin, K. *Field theory in social science,* pp. 229-36. New York: Harper & Bros., 1951.

7. Lewin, K., Lippitt, R., and White, R. K. Patterns of aggressive behavior in experimentally created "social climates." *Journal of Social Psychology,* 1939, *10,* 271-99.

8. Lippitt, R. *Training in Community Relations.* New York: Harper & Bros., 1949.

9. Marrow, A. J. and French, J.R.P., Jr. Changing a stereotype in industry. *Journal of Social Issues,* 1945, *1*(3), 33-37.

10. Newcomb, T. M. Autistic hostility and social reality. *Human Relations,* 1947, *1*(1), 69-86.

11. Polansky, N., Lippitt, R., and Redl, F. An investigation of behavioral contagion in groups. *Human Relations,* 1950, *3*(4), 319-48.

12. Preston, M. G. and Heintz, R. K. Effects of participatory vs. supervisory leadership on group judgment. *Journal of Abnormal and Social Psychology,* 1949, *44,* 345-55.

Assets and Liabilities in Group Problem Solving: The Need for an Integrative Function

Norman R. F. Maier

A number of investigations have raised the question of whether group problem solving is superior, inferior, or equal to individual problem solving. Evidence can be cited in support of each position so that the answer to this question remains ambiguous. Rather than pursue this generalized approach to the question, it seems more fruitful to explore the forces that influence problem solving under the two conditions (see reviews by Hoffman 1965; Kelley and Thibaut 1954). It is hoped that a better recognition of these forces will permit clarification of the varied dimensions of the problem-solving process, especially in groups.

The forces operating in such groups include some that are assets, some that are liabilities, and some that can be either assets or liabilities, depending upon the skills of the members, especially those of the discussion leader. Let us examine these sets of forces.

GROUP ASSETS

GREATER SUM TOTAL OF KNOWLEDGE AND INFORMATION

There is more information in a group than in any of its members. Thus problems that require the utilization of knowledge should give groups an advantage over individuals. Even if one member of the group (e.g., the leader) knows much

The research reported here was supported by Grant No. MH-02704 from the United States Public Health Service. Grateful acknowledgment is made for the constructive criticism of Melba Colgrove, Junie Janzen, Mara Julius, and James Thurber.

From *Psychological Review*, 1967, 74: 239-249. Copyright 1967 by the American Psychological Review. Reprinted by permission of the publisher.

more than anyone else, the limited unique knowledge of lesser-informed individuals could serve to fill in some gaps in knowledge. For example, a skilled machinist might contribute to an engineer's problem solving and an ordinary workman might supply information on how a new machine might be received by workers.

GREATER NUMBER OF APPROACHES TO A PROBLEM

It has been shown that individuals get into ruts in their thinking (Duncker 1945; Maier 1930; Wertheimer 1959). Many obstacles stand in the way of achieving a goal, and a solution must circumvent these. The individual is handicapped in that he tends to persist in his approach and thus fails to find another approach that might solve the problem in a simpler manner. Individuals in a group have the same failing, but the approaches in which they are persisting may be different. For example, one researcher may try to prevent the spread of a disease by making man immune to the germ, another by finding and destroying the carrier of the germ, and still another by altering the environment so as to kill the germ before it reaches man. There is no way of determining which approach will best achieve the desired goal, but undue persistence in any one will stifle new discoveries. Since group members do not have identical approaches, each can contribute by knocking others out of ruts of thinking.

PARTICIPATION IN PROBLEM SOLVING INCREASES ACCEPTANCE

Many problems require solutions that depend upon the support of others to be effective. Insofar as group problem solving permits participation and influence, it follows that more individuals accept solutions when a group solves the problem than when one person solves it. When one individual solves a problem he still has the task of persuading others. It follows, therefore, that when groups solve such problems, a greater number of persons accept and feel responsible for making the solution work. A low-quality solution that has good acceptance can be more effective than a higher quality solution that lacks acceptance.

BETTER COMPREHENSION OF THE DECISION

Decisions made by an individual, which are to be carried out by others, must be communicated from the decision-maker to the decision-executors. Thus individual problem solving often requires an additional stage — that of relaying the decision reached. Failure in this communication process detracts from the merits of the decision and can even cause its failure or create a problem of greater magnitude than the initial problem that was solved. Many organizational problems can be traced to inadequate communication of decisions made by superiors and transmitted to subordinates, who have the task of implementing the decision.

The chances for communication failures are greatly reduced when the individuals who must work together in executing the decision have participated in making it. They not only understand the solution because they saw it develop, but they are also aware of the several other alternatives that were considered and the reasons why they were discarded. The common assumption that decisions supplied by superiors are arbitrarily reached therefore disappears. A full knowledge of goals, obstacles, alternatives, and factual information is essential to communication, and this communication is maximized when the total problem-solving process is shared.

GROUP LIABILITIES

SOCIAL PRESSURE

Social pressure is a major force making for conformity. The desire to be a good group member and to be accepted tends to silence disagreement and favors consensus. Majority opinions tend to be accepted regardless of whether or not their objective quality is logically and scientifically sound. Problems requiring solutions based upon facts, regardless of feelings and wishes, can suffer in group problem-solving situations.

It has been shown (Maier and Solem 1952) that minority opinions in leaderless groups have little influence on the solution reached, even when these opinions are the correct ones. Reaching agreement in a group often is confused with finding the right answer, and it is for this reason that the dimensions of a decision's acceptance and its objective quality must be distinguished (Maier 1963).

VALENCE OF SOLUTIONS

When leaderless groups (made up of three or four persons) engage in problem solving, they propose a variety of solutions. Each solution may receive both critical and supportive comments, as well as descriptive and explorative comments from other participants. If the number of negative and positive comments for each solution are algebraically summed, each may be given a *valence index* (Hoffman and Maier 1964). The first solution that receives a positive valence value of 0.15 tends to be adopted to the satisfaction of all participants about 85 percent of the time, regardless of its quality. Higher quality solutions introduced after the critical value for one of the solutions has been reached have little chance of achieving real consideration. Once some degree of consensus is reached; the jelling process seems to proceed rather rapidly.

The critical valence value of 0.15 appears not to be greatly altered by the nature of the problem or the exact size of the group. Rather, it seems to designate a turning point between the idea-getting process and the decision-making process (idea evaluation). A solution's valence index is not a measure of the number of persons supporting the solution, since a vocal minority can build up a solution's valence by actively pushing it. In this sense, valence becomes an influence in addition to social pressure in determining an outcome.

Since a solution's valence is independent of its objective quality, this group factor becomes an important liability in group problem solving, even when the value of a decision depends upon objective criteria (facts and logic). It becomes a means whereby skilled manipulators can have more influence over the group process than their proportion of membership deserves.

INDIVIDUAL DOMINATION

In most leaderless groups a dominant individual emerges and captures more than his share of influence on the outcome. He can achieve this end through a greater degree of participation (valence), persuasive ability, or stubborn persistence (fatiguing the opposition). None of these factors is related to problem-solving ability, so that the best problem solver in the group may not have the influence to upgrade the quality of the group's solution (which he would have had if left to solve the problem by himself).

Hoffman and Maier (1967) found that the mere fact of appointing a leader causes this person to dominate a discussion. Thus, regardless of his problem-solving ability a leader tends to exert a major influence on the outcome of a discussion.

CONFLICTING SECONDARY GOAL: WINNING THE ARGUMENT

When groups are confronted with a problem, the initial goal is to obtain a solution. However, the appearance of several alternatives causes individuals to have preferences and once these emerge the desire to support a position is created. Converting those with neutral viewpoints and refuting those with opposed viewpoints now enter into the problem-solving process. More and more the goal becomes that of winning the decision rather than finding the best solution. This new goal is unrelated to the quality of the problem's solution and therefore can result in lowering the quality of the decision (Hoffman and Maier 1966).

FACTORS THAT SERVE AS ASSETS OR LIABILITIES, DEPENDING LARGELY UPON THE SKILL OF THE DISCUSSION LEADER

DISAGREEMENT

The fact that discussion may lead to disagreement can serve either to create hard feelings among members or lead to a resolution of conflict and hence to an innovative solution (Hoffman 1961; Hoffman, Harburg, and Maier, 1962; Hoffman and Maier 1961; Maier 1958, 1963; Maier and Hoffman 1965). The first of these outcomes of disagreement is a liability, especially with regard to the acceptance of solutions; while the second is an asset, particularly where innovation is desired. A leader can treat disagreement as undesirable and thereby reduce the probability of both hard feelings and innovation, or he can maximize disagreement and risk hard feelings in his attempts to achieve innovation. The skill of a leader requires his ability to create a climate for disagreement which will permit innovation without risking hard feelings. The leader's perception of disagreement is one of the critical factors in this skill area (Maier and Hoffman 1965). Others involve permissiveness (Maier 1953), delaying the reaching of a solution (Maier and Hoffman 1960b; Maier and Solem 1962), techniques for processing information and opinions (Maier 1963; Maier and Hoffman 1960b; Maier and Maier 1957), and techniques for separating idea-getting from idea-evaluation (Maier 1960, 1963; Osborn 1953).

CONFLICTING INTERESTS VERSUS MUTUAL INTERESTS

Disagreement in discussion may take many forms. Often participants disagree with one another with regard to solutions, but when issues are explored one finds that these conflicting solutions are designed to solve different problems. Before one can rightly expect agreement on a solution, there should be agreement on the nature of the problem. Even before this, there should be agreement on the goal, as well as on the various obstacles that prevent the goal from being reached. Once distinctions are made between goals, obstacles, and solutions (which represent ways of overcoming obstacles), one finds increased solving and less conflict (Hoffman and Maier 1959; Maier 1960, 1963; Maier and Solem 1962; Solem 1965).

Often there is also disagreement regarding whether the objective of a solution is to achieve quality or acceptance (Maier and Hoffman 1964b), and frequently separate problems, each having separate solutions so that a search for a single solution is impossible (Maier 1963). Communications often are inadequate because the discussion is not synchronized and each person is engaged in discussing a different aspect. Organizing discussion to synchronize the exploration of different aspects of the problem and to follow a systematic procedure increases solution quality (Maier and Hoffman 1960a; Maier and Maier 1957). The leadership function of influencing discussion procedure is quite distinct from the function of evaluating or contributing ideas (Maier 1950, 1953).

When the discussion leader aids in the separation of the several aspects of the problem-solving process and delays the solution-mindedness of the group (Maier 1958, 1963; Maier and Solem 1962), both solution quality and acceptance improve; when he hinders or fails to facilitate the isolation of these varied processes, he risks a deterioration in the group process (Solem 1965). His skill thus determines whether a discussion drifts toward conflicting interests or whether mutual interests are located. Cooperative problem solving can occur only after the mutual interests have been established and it is surprising how often they can be found when the discussion leader makes this his task. (Maier 1952, 1963; Maier and Hayes 1962).

RISK TAKING

Groups are more willing than individuals to reach decisions involving risks (Wallach and Kogan 1965; Wallach, Kogan, and Bem 1962). Taking risks is a factor in acceptance of change, but change may represent either a gain or a loss. The best guard against the latter outcome seems to be primarily a matter of a decision's quality. In a group situation this depends upon the leader's skill in utilizing the factors that represent group assets and avoiding those that make for liabilities.

TIME REQUIREMENTS

In general, more time is required for a group to reach a decision than for a single individual to reach one. Insofar as some problems require quick decisions, individual decisions are favored. In other situations acceptance and quality are requirements, but excessive time without sufficient returns also represents a loss. On the other hand, discussion can resolve conflicts, whereas reaching consensus has limited value (Wallach and Kogan 1965). The practice of hastening a meeting can prevent full discussion, but failure to move a discussion forward can lead to boredom and fatigue-type solutions, in which members agree merely to get out of the meeting. The effective utilization of discussion time (a delicate balance between permissiveness and control on the part of the leader), therefore, is needed to make the time factor an asset rather than a liability. Unskilled leaders tend to be too concerned with reaching a solution and therefore terminate a discussion before the group potential is achieved (Maier and Hoffman 1960b).

WHO CHANGES?

In reaching consensus or agreement, some members of a group must change. Persuasive forces do not operate in individual problem solving in the same way they operate in a group situation; hence, the changing of someone's mind is not an issue. In group situations, however, who changes can be an asset or a liability. If persons with the most constructive views are induced to change, the end-product suffers; whereas if persons with the least constructive point of view change the end-product is upgraded. The leader can upgrade the quality of a decision because of his opportunity to influence the majority position. This protection is a constructive factor because a minority viewpoint influences only when facts favor it (Maier 1950, 1952; Maier and Solem 1952).

The leader also plays a constructive role insofar as he can facilitate communications and thereby reduce misunderstandings (Maier 1952; Solem 1965). The leader has an adverse effect on the end product when he suppresses minority views by holding a contrary position and when he uses his office to promote his own views (Maier and Hoffman 1960b, 1962; Maier and Solem 1952). In many problem-solving discussions the untrained leader plays a dominant role in influencing the outcome, and when he is more resistant to changing his views than are the other participants, the quality of the outcome tends to be lowered. This negative leader-influence was demonstrated by experiments in which untrained leaders were asked to obtain a second solution to a problem after they had obtained their first one (Maier and Hoffman 1960a). It was found that the second solution tended to be superior to the first. Since the dominant individual had influenced the first solution, he had won his point and therefore ceased to dominate the subsequent discussion which led to the second solution. Acceptance of a solution also increases as the leader sees disagreement as idea-producing rather than as a source of difficulty or trouble (Maier and Hoffman 1965). Leaders who see some of their participants as troublemakers obtain fewer innovative solutions and gain less acceptance of decisions made than leaders who see disagreeing members as persons with ideas.

THE LEADER'S ROLE FOR INTEGRATED GROUPS

TWO DIFFERING TYPES OF GROUP PROCESS

In observing group problem solving under various conditions it is rather easy to distinguish between cooperative problem-solving activity and persuasion or selling approaches. Problem-solving activity includes searching, trying out ideas on one another, listening to understand rather than to refute, making relatively short speeches, and reacting to differences in opinion as stimulating. The general pattern is one of rather complete participation, involvement. Persuasion activity includes the selling of opinions already formed, defending a position held, either not listening at all or listening in order to be able to refute, talking dominated by a few members, unfavorable reactions to disagreement, and a lack of involvement of some members. During problem solving the behavior observed seems to be that of members interacting as segments of a group. The interaction pattern is not between certain individual members, but with the group as a whole. Sometimes it is difficult to determine who should be credited with an idea. "It just developed," is a response often used to describe the solution reached. In contrast, discussions involving selling or persuasive behavior seem to consist of a series of interpersonal interactions with each individual retaining his identity. Such groups do not function as integrated units but as separate individuals, each with an agenda. In one situation the solution is unknown and is sought; in the other, several solutions exist and conflict occurs because commitments have been made.

THE STARFISH ANALOGY

The analysis of these two group processes suggests an analogy with the behavior of the rays of a starfish under two conditions; one with the nerve ring intact, the other with the nerve ring sectioned (Hamilton 1922; Moore, 1924; Moore and Doudoroff 1939; Schneirla and Maier 1940). In the intact condition, locomotion and righting behavior reveal that the behavior of each ray is not merely a function of local stimulation. Locomotion and righting behavior reveal a degree of coordination and interdependence that is centrally controlled. However, when the nerve ring is sectioned, the behavior of one ray still can influence others, but internal coordination is lacking. For example, if one ray is stimulated, it may step forward, thereby exerting pressure on the sides of the other four rays. In response to these external pressures (tactile stimulation), these rays show stepping responses on the stimulated side so that locomotion successfully occurs without the aid of neural coordination. Thus integrated behavior can occur on the basis of external control. If, however, stimulation is applied to opposite rays, the specimen may be "locked" for a time, and in some species the conflicting locomotions may divide the animal, thus destroying it (Crozier 1920; Moore and Doudoroff 1939).

Each of the rays of the starfish can show stepping responses even when sectioned and removed from the animal. Thus each may be regarded as an individual. In a starfish with a sectioned nerve ring the five rays become members of a group. They can successfully work together for locomotion purposes by being controlled by the dominant ray. Thus if uniformity of action is desired, the group of five rays can sometimes be more effective than the individual ray in moving the group toward a source of stimulation. However, if "locking" or the division of the organism occurs, the group action becomes less effective than individual action. External control, through the influence of a dominant ray, therefore can lead to adaptive behavior for the starfish as a whole, but it can also result in a conflict that destroys the organism. Something more than external influence is needed.

In the animal with an intact nerve ring, the function of the rays is coordinated by the nerve ring. With this type of internal organization the group is always superior to that of the individual actions. When the rays function as a part of an organized unit, rather than as a group that is physically together, they become a higher type of organization — a single intact organism. This is accomplished by the nerve ring, which in itself does not do the behaving. Rather, it receives and processes the data which the rays relay to it. Through this central organization, the responses of the rays become part of a larger pattern so that together they constitute a single coordinated total response rather than a group of individual responses.

THE LEADER AS THE GROUP'S CENTRAL NERVOUS SYSTEM

If we now examine what goes on in a discussion group we find that members can problem-solve as individuals, they can influence others by external pushes and pulls, or they can function as a group with varying degrees of unity. In order for the latter function to be maximized, however, something must be introduced to serve the function of the nerve ring. In our conceptualization of group problem solving and group decision (Maier 1963) we see this as the function of the leader. Thus the leader does not serve as a dominant ray and produce the solution. Rather, his function is to receive information, facilitate communications between the individuals, relay messages, and integrate the incoming responses so that a single unified response occurs.

Solutions that are the product of good group discussions often come as surprises to discussion leaders. One of these is unexpected generosity. If there is a weak member, this member is given less to do, in much the same way as an organism adapts to an injured limb and alters the function of other limbs to keep the locomotion on course. Experimental evidence supports the point that group decisions award special consideration to needy members of groups (Hoffman and Maier 1959). Group decisions in industrial groups often give smaller assignments to the less gifted (Maier 1952). A leader could not effectually impose such differential treatment on group members without being charged with discriminatory practices.

Another unique aspect of group discussion is the way fairness is resolved. In a simulated problem situation involving the problem of how to introduce a new truck into a group of drivers, the typical group solution involves a trading of trucks so that several or all members stand to profit. If the leader makes the decision the number of persons who profit is often confined to one (Maier and Hoffman 1962; Maier and Zerfoss 1952). In industrial practice, supervisors assign a new truck to an individual member of a crew after careful evaluation of needs. This practice results in dissatisfaction, with the charge of *unfair* being leveled at him. Despite those repeated attempts to do justice, supervisors in the telephone industry never hit upon the notion of a general reallocation of trucks, a solution that crews invariably reach when the decision is theirs to make.

In experiments involving the introduction of change, the use of group discussion tends to lead to decisions that resolve differences (Maier 1952, 1953; Maier and Hoffman 1961, 1964a, 1964b). Such decisions tend to be different from decisions reached by individuals because of the very fact that disagreement is common in group problem solving. The process of resolving difference in a constructive setting causes the exploration of additional areas and leads to solutions that are integrative rather than compromises.

Finally, group solutions tend to be tailored to fit the interests and personalities of the participants; thus group solutions to problems involving fairness, fears, face-saving, etc., tend to vary from one group to another. An outsider cannot process these variables because they are not subject to logical treatment.

If we think of the leader as serving a function in the group different from that of its membership, we might be able to create a group that can function as an intact organism. For a leader, such functions as rejecting or promoting ideas according to his personal needs are out of bounds. He must be receptive to information contributed, accept contributions without evaluating them (posting contributions on a chalk board to keep them alive), summarize information to facilitate integration, stimulate exploratory behavior, create awareness of problems of one member by others, and detect when the group is ready to resolve differences and agree to a unified solution.

Since higher organisms have more than a nerve ring and can store information, a leader might appropriately supply information, but according to our model of a leader's role, he must clearly distinguish between supplying information and promoting a solution. If his knowledge indicates the desirability of a particular solution, sharing this knowledge might lead the group to find this solution, but the solution should be the group's discovery. A leader's contributions do not receive the same treatment as those of a member of the group. Whether he likes it or not, his position is different. According to our conception of the leader's contribution to discussion, his role not only differs in influence, but gives him an entirely different function. He is to serve much as the nerve ring in the starfish and to further refine this function so as to make it a higher type of nerve ring.

This model of a leader's role in group process has served as a guide for many of our studies in group problem solving. It is not our claim that this will lead to the best possible group function under all conditions. In sharing it we hope to indicate the nature of our guidelines in exploring group leadership as a function quite different and apart from group membership. Thus the model serves as a stimulant for research problems and as a guide for our analyses of leadership skills and principles.

CONCLUSIONS

On the basis of our analysis, it follows that the comparison of the merits of group versus individual problem solving depends on the nature of the problem, the goal to be achieved (high quality solution, highly accepted solution, effective communication and understanding of the solution, innovation, a quickly reached solution, or satisfaction), and the skill of the discussion leader. If liabilities inherent in groups are avoided, assets capitalized upon, and conditions that can serve either favorable or unfavorable outcomes are effectively used, it follows that groups have a potential which in many instances can exceed that of a superior individual functioning alone, even with respect to creativity.

This goal was nicely stated by Thibaut and Kelley (1961, p. 268) when they

> . . . wonder whether it may not be possible for a rather small, intimate group to establish a problem solving process that capitalizes upon the total pool of information and provides for great interstimulation of ideas without any loss of innovative creativity due to social restraints.

In order to accomplish this high level of achievement, however, a leader is needed who plays a role quite different from that of the members. His role is analogous to that of the nerve ring in the starfish which permits the rays to execute a unified response. If the leader can contribute the integrative requirement, group problem solving may emerge as a unique type of group function. This type of approach to group processes places the leader in a particular role in which he must cease to contribute, avoid evaluation, and refrain from thinking about solutions or group *products*. Instead he must concentrate on the group *process*, listen in order to understand rather than to appraise or refute, assume responsibility for accurate communication between members, be sensitive to unexpressed feelings, protect minority points of view, keep the discussion moving, and develop skills in summarizing.

REFERENCES

Crozier, W. J. Notes on some problems of adaptation. *Biological Bulletin,* 1920, 39, 116-129.

Duncker, K. On problem solving. *Psychological Monographs,* 1945, 58 (5, Whole No. 270).

Hamilton, W. F. Coordination in the starfish, III. The righting reaction as a phase of locomotion (righting and locomotion). *Journal of Comparative Psychology,* 1922, 2, 81-94.

Hoffman, L. R. Group problem solving. In L. Berkowitz (Ed.), *Advances in Experimental Social Psychology,* Vol. 2. New York: Academic Press, 1965, pp. 99-132.

Hoffman, L. R., Harburg, E., & Maier, N.R.F. Differences and disagreement as factors in creative group problem solving. *Journal of Abnormal and Social Psychology,* 1962, 64, 206-214.

Hoffman, L. R., & Maier, N.R.F. The use of group decision to resolve a problem of fairness. *Personnel Psychology,* 1959, 12, 545-559.

Hoffman, L. R., & Maier, N.R.F. Quality and acceptance of problem solutions by members of homogeneous and heterogeneous groups. *Journal of Abnormal and Social Psychology,* 1961, 62, 401-407.

Hoffman, L. R., & Maier, N.R.F. Valence in the adoption of solutions by problem-solving groups: II. Quality and acceptance as goals of leaders and members. Unpublished manuscript, 1967 (mimeo).

Kelley, H. H., & Thibaut, J. W. Experimental studies of group problem solving and process. In G. Lindzey (Ed.), *Handwork of Social Psychology.* Reading, Mass.: Addison-Wesley, 1954. Pp. 735-785.

Maier, N.R.F. The quality of group decisions as influenced by the discussion leader. *Human Relations,* 1950, 3, 155-174.

Maier N.R.F. The quality of group decisions as influenced by the discussion leader. *Human Relations,* 1950, 3, 155-174.

Maier, N.R.F. *Principles of Human Relations.* New York: Wiley, 1952.

Maier, N.R.F. An experimental test of the effect of training on discussion leadership. *Human Relations,* 1953, 6, 161-173.

Maier, N.R.F. *The Appraisal Interview.* New York: Wiley, 1958.

Maier, N.R.F. Screening solutions to upgrade quality: A new approach to problem solving under conditions of uncertainty. *Journal of Psychology,* 1960, 49, 217-231.

Maier, N.R.F. *Problem solving discussions and conferences: Leadership methods and skills.* New York: McGraw-Hill, 1963.

Maier, N.R.F., & Hayes, J. J. *Creative Management,* New York: Wiley, 1962.

Maier, N.R.F., & Hoffman, L. R. Using trained "developmental" discussion leaders to improve further the quality of group decisions. *Journal of Applied Psychology,* 1960, 44, 247-251. (a)

Maier N.R.F., & Hoffman, L. R. Quality of first and second solutions in group decisions. *Journal of Applied Psychology,* 1960, 44, 278-283. (b)

Maier, N.R.F., & Hoffman, L. R. Organization and creative problem solving. *Journal of Applied Psychology*, 1961, 45, 277-280.

Maier, N.R.F., & Hoffman, L.R. Group decision in England and the United States. *Personnel Psychology*, 1962, 15, 78-87.

Maier, N.R.F., & Hoffman, L. R. Financial incentives and group decision in motivation change. *Journal of Social Psychology*, 1964, 64, 369-378. (a)

Maier, N.R.F., & Hoffman, L. R. Types of problems confronting managers. *Personnel Psychology*, 1964, 17, 261-269. (b)

Maier, N.R.F., & Hoffman, L. R. Acceptance and quality of solutions as related to leaders' attitudes toward disagreement in group problem solving. *Journal of Applied Behavioral Science*, 1965, 1, 273-386.

Maier, N.R.F., & Maier, R. A. An experimental test of the effects of "developmental" vs. "free" discussions on the quality of group decisions. *Journal of Applied Psychology*, 1957, 41, 320-323.

Maier, N.R.F., & Solem, A. R. The contribution of a discussion leader to the quality of group thinking: The effective use of minority opinions. *Human Relations*, 1952, 5, 277-288.

Maier, N.R.F., & Solem, A. R. Improving solutions by turning choice situations into problems. *Personnel Psychology*, 1962, 15, 151-157.

Maier, N.R.F., & Zerfoss, I. F. MRP: A technique for training large groups of supervisors and its potential use in social research. *Human Relations*, 1952, 5, 177-186.

Moore, A. R. The nervous mechanism of coordination in the crinoid Antedon rosaceus. *Journal of Genetic Psychology*, 1924, 6, 281-288.

Moore, A. R., & Doudoroff, M. Injury, recovery and function in an aganglionic central nervous system. *Journal of Comparative Psychology*, 1939, 28, 313-328.

Osborn, A. F. *Applied imagination*. New York: Scribner's, 1953.

Schneirla, T. C., & Maier, N.R.F. Concerning the status of the starfish. *Journal of Comparative Psychology*, 1940, 30, 103-110.

Solem, A. R. Almost anything I can do, we can do better. *Personnel Administration*, 1965, 28, 6-16.

Thibaut, J. W., & Kelley, H. H. *The social psychology of groups*. New York: Wiley, 1961.

Wallach, M. A., & Kogan, N. The roles of information, discussion and consensus in group risk taking. *Journal of Experimental and Social Psychology*, 1965, 1, 1-19.

Wallach, M. A., Kogan, N., & Bem, D. J. Group influence on individual risk taking. *Journal of Abnormal and Social Psychology*, 1962, 65, 75-86.

Wertheimer, M. *Productive thinking*. New York: Harper, 1959.

2

Relevant Background Factors

THE TUBBS MODEL OF SMALL GROUP INTERACTION

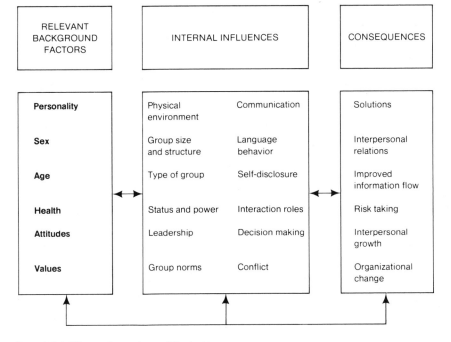

RELEVANT BACKGROUND FACTORS	INTERNAL INFLUENCES		CONSEQUENCES
Personality	Physical environment	Communication	Solutions
Sex	Group size and structure	Language behavior	Interpersonal relations
Age	Type of group	Self-disclosure	Improved information flow
Health	Status and power	Interaction roles	Risk taking
Attitudes	Leadership	Decision making	Interpersonal growth
Values	Group norms	Conflict	Organizational change

Concepts in **boldface** are the emphases of this chapter.

CASE STUDY

Don and Karen have been married five years. He is an instructor in a small liberal arts college; she is headmistress of a private school that teaches first through twelfth grades. They dated for two years before getting married and have been quite happy for most of their time together.

Don has a problem at work, in that he has not finished his Ph.D. degree as he indicated he would when he took his current job. As a result, he is in serious danger of not getting tenure at his college, and thus of being fired within the next year.

Karen's career has been very successful. She has received several promotions since coming to her school and is very happy and excited about her job. Her salary is quite a bit larger than Don's.

Their biggest problem is that Don wants to start a family, which would require that Karen take at least a temporary leave of absence from her job. Don does not want her to go back to work until the child would go to school; thus Karen would have to stay at home for the first five years of the child's life, which Don feels are crucial years for a child to have close parenting.

Although Karen had originally wanted a family when they got married, she now feels that her career means much more to her than she had ever anticipated. She now feels that having children *at all* is highly questionable, and stopping her career for five years (or even six months) is not at all what she wants to do at this time.

1. *What should this couple do?*

2. *How would you handle this situation if you were Don or Karen?*

T his case study illustrates a problem of differing values. As we shall see in this chapter, individual differences among group members sometimes create difficulties. Sometimes we refer to these as personality conflicts. But before we examine the issue of personalities, let us turn to the broader issue of motivation.

Why do people behave the way they do? This question has intrigued humans for centuries. Behaving in specific ways is usually seen as an attempt to meet the individual's needs.

For example, have you ever been in a group situation and wondered why you were there? Suppose you look out a classroom window and see a beautiful sky — it is a great day for being outside. You begin to experience competing needs: the need to go outside and have fun and the need to accomplish whatever the group's purpose is (such as studying for an upcoming exam). Whichever need is more intense will most probably determine the behavior you pursue.

Probably one of the best-known models for explaining people's needs is Maslow's (1970) hierarchy of needs (see Fig. 2.1).

Physiological needs must be met in order to survive. Some groups formed in the days of the cave dwellers to fight off saber-toothed tigers, as well as other unfriendly cave people, and to help gather food.

Security needs often motivate the formation of groups by individuals who lack sufficient power on their own. This is demonstrated by the beginning of the union movement, which resulted from the fact that there were far more workers than jobs. With ten people waiting to fill each job, workers were somewhat hesitant to make demands of their bosses. Thus unions helped workers gain power and eventually job security.

Belongingness needs are easy for most people to identify with. Think about what you felt like during your first week as a college freshman. One student member of a freshman discussion group wrote about this belonging-ness need not being fulfilled: "During our discussion, I felt like I wasn't even supposed to be in my group. The others seemed like they were all very familiar with each other and discussed almost entirely among themselves. They took over the discussion basically by looking only at each other and asking a lot of questions of each other (and cracking a lot of

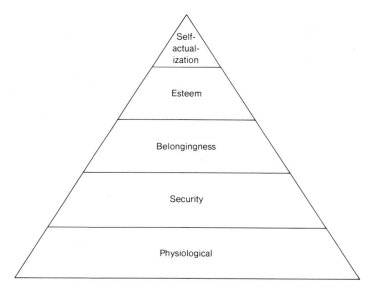

FIGURE 2.1
Maslow's need hierarchy.

really funny jokes). I tried to contribute but felt ignored. It was very uncomfortable and I became quiet after a few more attempts to contribute. I'm glad I didn't receive a grade on that discussion because I was annoyed at how little I participated." Eventually, the feelings of aloneness begin to subside as people develop their own circles of friends (social groups).

Esteem needs may also be met by groups. Often people are attracted to certain fraternities or sororities because of the prestige of membership, which adds to their feeling of self-esteem. All people need to feel that they are important, and being a part of a good group or organization is one very good way to accomplish that goal.

Self-actualization needs are the highest-level needs Maslow identified. A person may be attracted to a group because of the need for self-development. Encounter groups are one particular type of group devoted to the growth and development of members. Educational groups or work groups may also help individuals achieve a higher level of human potential.

Maslow argued that the needs lowest on the hierarchy must be satisfied before the higher-level needs are activated. For example, we worry less about self-actualization in a job when we are unemployed and the bills haven't been paid.

The needs in Maslow's hierarchy are common to all individuals. In the next section we examine personality needs, which differ greatly from one individual to another.

PERSONALITY

Notice how each of the following three college freshmen describes the same discussion based on his own unique personality.

John's View
There were five in our problem-solving group, Al, Peter, Ed, Randy, and I. We encountered a few difficulties in basic personality clashes. Randy became leader and whenever he or I would suggest anything, the others would only tear it apart. This slowed us down for a while. They could not think of much to contribute yet were very ready to reject others' ideas.

Randy's View
I would like to do a brief personality sketch on each member of the group. I am Randy — and while I am usually fairly quiet and calm, I get very involved in discussions. I have a personality that is considered very egotistical and bullheaded (especially in a group). I usually feel I'm right because I rarely say things I am not sure of. Therefore, what I say I expect others to listen to. I am not a great listener myself and I realize this, which is at least some help. I am also a spontaneous thinker (ideas pop into my head). The other members were Ed, Al, Pete, and John. Ed and Al seemed to like to examine

things closely and come to decisions slowly, also their ideas are slow to appear. Pete is quiet and seems to listen well but he doesn't comment much on what he thinks. John and I seem much alike in our process of thought.

The problems in our discussion seemed to stem from basic differences in personalities. I believe some people are spontaneous thinkers with a constant flow of ideas. Often opposing them is the type who will tear an idea apart and then discard it as not good enough. A third type watches and says nothing.

Al's View
Randy was the most boisterous of the group. . . . Of course it is only natural that a group have a spokesman to get things rolling, but in this case I think that our spokesman was too overbearing and carried on extensive communication with John only. If the rest of us spoke, we seemed to be ignored. That definitely made me quite silent most of the time. In questioning Ed and Pete I found that they felt much the same way. Consequently, our group discussion was not a total group effort but the comments of only one or two people.

Krech, Crutchfield, and Ballachey (1962) have stated that effective groups are simply made up of effective individuals. This implies that some individual characteristics are more valuable to group effort than others, and combine more constructively to lead to effective group performance.

Humans have been fascinated with personality needs for centuries. In the second century A.D., Galen, a medical philosopher, theorized that four different types of body fluids, which he called humors, caused differences in temperament (Brock 1952). In the healthy person, the humors were in balance. In the ill, one humor predominated over the other three and produced personality differences. It was believed that the four humors and their accompanying characteristics were:

□ Blood — cheery, gay, optimistic, warmhearted

□ Black bile — melancholic, gloomy, sad

□ Yellow bile — choleric, hot-tempered

□ Phlegm — phlegmatic, slow, sluggish

In his recent book, *The Right Stuff,* Tom Wolfe (1980, pp. 18-19) attempted to describe the personality required of an aspiring astronaut. He wrote:

> A young man might go into military flight training believing that he was entering some sort of technical school in which he was simply going to acquire a certain set of skills. Instead, he found himself all at once enclosed in a fraternity. And in this fraternity, even though it was military, men were not rated by their outward rank as ensigns, lieutenants, commanders, or whatever. No, herein the world was divided into those who had it and those who did not. This quality, this *it,* was never named, however, nor was it talked about in any way.

> As to just what this ineffable quality was . . . well, it obviously involved bravery. But it was not bravery in the simple sense of being willing to risk your life. The idea seemed to be that any fool could do that, if that was all that was required, just as any fool could throw away his life in the process. No, the idea here (in the all-enclosing fraternity) seemed to be that a man should have the ability to go up in a hurtling piece of machinery and put his hide on the line and then have the moxie, the reflexes, the experience, the coolness, to pull it back in the last yawning moment — and then to go up again *the next day,* and the next day, and every next day, even if the series should prove infinite — and, ultimately, in its best expression, do so in a cause that means something to thousands, to a people, a nation, to humanity, to God. Nor was there *a test* to show whether or not a pilot had this righteous quality. There was, instead, a seemingly infinite series of tests. A career in flying was like climbing one of those ancient Babylonian pyramids made up of a dizzy progression of steps and ledges, a ziggurat, a pyramid extraordinarily high and steep; and the idea was to prove at every foot of the way up that pyramid that you were one of the elected and anointed ones who had *the right stuff* and could move higher and higher and even — ultimately, God willing, one day — that you might be able to join that special few at the very top, that elite who had the capacity to bring tears to men's eyes, the very Brotherhood of the Right Stuff itself.

Modern-day theorists have come a long way in identifying personality needs, yet these needs still remain somewhat like mercury (difficult to get a grip on). Schutz (1958, 1967, 1971) has theorized that each of us joins into association with groups to meet three interpersonal needs: (1) inclusion, (2) control, and (3) affection. *Inclusion* refers to our concern for belonging, feeling a part of, and being together with others. *Control* refers to areas of power, influence, and authority. *Affection* refers to the emotional intimacy between two persons. It involves friendship and love. Schutz (1967) makes this statement:

> A difference between inclusion behavior, control behavior, and affection behavior is illustrated by the different feelings a man has in

being turned down by a fraternity, failed in a course by a professor, and rejected by his girl. . . . Inclusion is concerned with the problem of *in* or *out*, control is concerned with *top* or *bottom*, and affection with *close* or *far*. [Italics added.]

In each of these three areas we have both the need to receive these behaviors *from others* and the need to express them *toward others*. Wanted inclusion would be hoping to be asked to go to a party, while expressed inclusion would be inviting someone else to go with you to a party. A compatible need level would exist when a person's wanted and expressed needs were about the same intensity. Compatibility between individuals seems to occur when their needs are similar on the inclusion and affection dimensions and complementary on the control dimension. Compatibility on these dimensions tends to reduce conflict and increase harmony and satisfaction. For example, talkative people get along well with other talkative people, and quiet people tend to be compatible with one another.

See the article by William Schutz at the end of this chapter for more on the dimensions of inclusion, control, and affection.

A somewhat different personality conceptualization has been developed by Johnson (1972). This is sometimes referred to as the D-A-S-H model, for dominance-affiliation-submission-hostility (Fig. 2.2). Each of the four quadrants contains descriptive terms that indicate the type of behavior that would be manifested in a group.

Another highly respected method for conceptualizing as well as measuring personality grew out of the work of Murray (1938). The Edwards Personal Preference Schedule (EPPS), based on Murray's work, measures the level of 15 personality needs. These (Edwards 1953) are described as:

	High dominance	Low dominance
High affiliation	advises coordinates directs initiates leads	acquiesces agrees assists cooperates obliges
Low affiliation	analyzes criticizes disapproves judges resists	concedes evades relinquishes retreats withdraws

FIGURE 2.2
The Johnson D-A-S-H personality model. David W. Johnson, *Reaching Out: Interpersonal Effectiveness and Self-Actualization,* © 1972, pp. 6, 35. Reprinted by permission of Prentice-Hall, Inc., Englewood Cliffs, N.J.

Achievement   To do one's best, to be successful, to accomplish tasks requiring skill and effort, to be a recognized authority, to accomplish something important, to do a difficult job well

Deference   To get suggestions from others, to find out what others think, to follow instructions and do what is expected, to praise others, to accept leadership of others, to conform to custom

Order   To keep things neat and orderly, to make advance plans, to organize details of work, to have things arranged so they run smoothly without change

Exhibition   To say clever and witty things, to have others notice and comment upon one's appearance, to say things just to see the effect upon others, to talk about personal achievements

Autonomy   To be able to come and go as desired, to say what one thinks about things, to be independent of others in making decisions, to do things without regard to what others may think

Affiliation   To be loyal to friends, to participate in friendly groups, to form strong attachments, to share things with friends, to write letters to friends, to make as many friends as possible

Intraception   To analyze one's motives and feelings, to understand how others feel about problems, to judge people by why they do things rather than by what they do, to predict others' behavior

Succorance   To have others provide help when in trouble, to seek encouragement from others, to have others be kindly and sympathetic, to receive a great deal of affection from others

Dominance   To argue for one's point of view, to be a leader in groups to which one belongs, to persuade and influence others, to supervise and direct the actions of others

Abasement   To feel guilty when one does something wrong, to accept blame when things do not go right, to feel that personal pain and misery do more good than harm, to feel timid and inferior

Nurturance   To help friends when they are in trouble, to treat others with kindness and sympathy, to forgive others and do favors for them, to show affection and have others confide in one

Change	To do new and different things, to travel, to meet new people, to have novelty and change in daily routine, to try new and different jobs, to participate in new fads and fashions
Endurance	To keep at a job until it is finished, to work hard at a task, to work at a single job before taking on others, to stick at a problem even though no apparent progress is being made
Heterosexuality	To engage in social activities with the opposite sex, to be in love with someone of the opposite sex, to be regarded as physically attractive by those of the opposite sex
Aggression	To attack contrary points of view, to tell others off, to get revenge for insults, to blame others when things go wrong, to criticize others publicly, to read accounts of violence

It seems quite plausible from the descriptions that people high in one or another of these needs will be likely to exhibit such behaviors consistently from one group to another, across different tasks, times, and situations. These behaviors will elicit certain predictable responses that will in turn affect the group's outcomes. Thus we refer to these personality characteristics as *causal variables.* It is a tautology to say that personality predicts behaviors and then to use the behaviors to indicate that the personality need exists. However, personality variables do seem to influence verbal and nonverbal behaviors across different groups and different tasks. Thus their role in predicting interaction is an important one and deserves to be studied in this context. Furthermore, the basis for identification comes from paper-and-pencil tests, predicting overt behaviors in groups, and not vice versa.

Not all personality characteristics are equally important to small group behavior. Likewise, not all have been studied in this context. However, a few are quite relevant and merit closer examination.

Need for *achievement* has been studied extensively by David McClelland (1953, 1955, 1961) and his associates at Harvard. Individuals with high need for achievement (N-ach) are concerned with accomplishing things, doing things well, and doing them faster than others. They tend to be highly competitive in group discussions. One college student stated that her objective in taking the small group interaction course was to "learn enough about how a group functions to (1) be able to most persuasively present my ideas and opinions and (2) get the most productivity out of a group." She went on to add that her life's ambition was to become the first woman president of General Motors or some other major company.

Another striking example of a high achiever is Francis Otto Schmitt, a professor of neuroscience and a leading molecular biological researcher at the Massachusetts Institute of Technology. As described by *Time* magazine (1974), he is a classic example of a high need achiever:

> Schmitt studied medicine at Washington University, published two papers in *Science* before his 20th birthday, and received his doctorate in physiology . . . Schmitt has a Teutonic dedication to hard work, moves at constant flank speed and . . . has a tendency to "take every red traffic light as a personal affront."

Those with high need for achievement tend to be extremely task oriented in groups and will quite often attempt to organize the group effort by suggesting procedures and by criticizing others for "getting off the track." Need for achievement is often helpful in motivating the group toward its goal. Schneider and Delaney (1972) found that high achievers tend to be more efficient than low achievers in performing group problem-solving tasks, especially if the problems are complex and difficult to solve. They cite at least five other studies in which this result has been substantiated.

On the other hand, the opposite of need for achievement is fear of failure. Atkinson (1966) states that motivation to achieve success is one of a class of motives described as appetites or approach tendencies, the aim of which is to maximize satisfaction. Motivation to avoid failure, on the other hand, is one of a class of motives described as aversion or avoidance tendencies, the aim of which is to minimize pain. Studying both of these variables, Giffin and Gilham (1971) found that college students high in fear of failure and low in achievement motivation had very high levels of speech anxiety. Thus high achievers appear to be more confident, exhibiting significantly less speech anxiety.

A second important personality attribute might be loosely labeled *extroversion* and is related to dominance and exhibition. Extroverts would be expected to participate frequently in group discussions regardless of topic, situation, or group composition. These individuals might be described by Schutz as having a high need to control. Randy's view at the beginning of this chapter offers a good example of such a person. Extroverts frequently find themselves in leadership positions and are often popular with other members of the group. They may come in conflict with one another in attempting to compete for the group's attention. Summarizing the research on this topic, Shaw (1981) states that these individuals generally facilitate group functioning and influence group decisions more than the average member.

A third personality attribute, *social sensitivity*, relates to need for affiliation and nurturance. Affiliators subscribe to the belief that "people who need people are the luckiest people in the world." They frequently thrive on the open sharing of affection that exemplifies many encounter groups. They score high on Schutz's need to receive and express affection. They are better able to feel empathy toward others. Similarly, Rosenfeld (1966) found that high affiliators tend to sit closer, smile more, gesture

THE BORN LOSER   by Art Sansom

FOR STARTERS, MR. VEEBLEFESTER, YOU ARE POSSESSED OF AN EXTREMELY DOMINANT PERSONALITY.

Reprinted by permission. © 1975 NEA. Inc.

more, and nod their heads more than low affiliators. To put it another way, they are more encouraging or reinforcing both verbally and nonverbally than low affiliators. These people tend to facilitate social interaction, cohesiveness, and satisfaction in groups. Also, they tend to behave "in ways in which enhance their acceptance in the group and the group effectiveness" (Shaw 1981, p. 195).

A fourth personality attribute is *need for approval*. This is related to abasement, deference to authority, and what Schutz calls desire to be controlled by others. This variable has been studied extensively by Crowne and Marlowe (1964). Individuals high in need for approval tend to look to others for cues indicating the proper way to behave. They are more susceptible to social influence and show greater attitude change following a persuasive communication (Adams 1972). Further evidence has been found that during the course of a discussion high approval seekers try harder to do what they think is expected of them in a given situation than do low approval seekers. In one study, a norm was established for openness and self-disclosure. High approval group members then adapted and became more self-disclosing. The authors (McLaughlin and Hewitt 1972, p. 257) state:

> When it became obvious at the end of the first interaction period that peer evaluations would be based solely on openness and when openness had been previously equated with social desirability, people with high Need for Approval seemed to alter their normal behavior and adopt behaviors during subsequent interaction periods that resulted in increased ratings of openness from others.

McCroskey, Larson, and Knapp (1971, p. 132) summarize the work of Couch and Keniston (1960) among others when they describe this sort of individual as a "yea-sayer" as opposed to a "nay-sayer." Their description of the "yea-sayer" sounds very similar to that of the person with the high need for approval.

1. The yea-sayer's general attitude is one of stimulus acceptance, by which Couch and Keniston mean "a pervasive readiness to

respond affirmatively or yield willingly to both inner and outer forces demanding expression."

2. Yea-sayers seem to be impulsive and quick in their expression of themselves. They would be likely to accept or evaluate quickly the messages they receive, and their evaluations are likely to be based upon their own wishes or desires rather than upon "objective criteria."

3. Yea-sayers desire "novelty, movement, change, adventure." Yea-sayers appear to be attracted by items that have an enthusiastic, colloquial tone, whereas such items appear to repel nay-sayers.

4. On the other hand, nay-sayers are likely to be extremely careful and critical of messages they receive.

It would be fun to try to identify which of your acquaintances seem to fit this description. Does this fit your behavior?

DOGMATISM

Dogmatism is closely related to personality needs but is not usually included as a dimension of personality. Dogmatism refers to a person's degree of open- or closed-mindedness (the more *closed*-minded, the more dogmatic). Rokeach (1954, p. 195) defines dogmatism as

(a) a relatively closed cognitive organization of beliefs and disbeliefs about reality, (b) organized around a central set of beliefs about absolute authority which, in turn, (c) provides a framework for patterns of intolerance toward others.

Dogmatic individuals are inclined to be demanding, directive, argumentative, abusive, and controlling in their relations with those less powerful than themselves. However, when they are in subordinate positions, they are obedient, submissive, and overly dependent on the leader.

The study of dogmatism grew out of the research on fascism and authoritarianism that resulted from observing the methods employed by the Nazis in Germany during the Second World War (Adorno *et al.,* 1950). Highly dogmatic (high dog) individuals are less educated, more anxious and insecure, and more intolerant of ambiguity (conflicting information) than low dogs (Rokeach 1960). Theoretically, this results from a child's having been punished for demonstrating natural ambivalence (love-hate feelings) toward his or her parents. Personal shortcomings develop and are denied and then attributed (projected) to others (for example, "they" are all sex-crazed).

High dogmatics behave differently than low dogs in group discussions. High dogs tend to be more rigid in their thinking, which results in their taking longer to solve complex problems, and in some cases not being able to solve problems at all. Luchins's (1942) water jar problem is a task

FRANK AND ERNEST by Bob Thaves

WAS THAT YOUR MIND I HEARD CLOSING, PINKLEY?

THAVES 4-24

Reprinted by permission. © 1981 NEA. Inc.

typically given to groups to test rigidity of thinking, sometimes known as a "mental set" or *Einstellung*. Subjects are asked to determine the best way to measure various quantities of water using bottles of specific sizes. Only full bottles (that is, no gradations) are allowed. The best solution is the shortest possible one. A sample problem appears below. See if you can find the solution.

Given: Containers of capacities 31, 61, and 4 quarts.

Obtain: 22 quarts.

Solution:[1]

Luchins presents five more problems in which the same solution formula is the best method (see the solution below). This results in a "mental set" for solving the problem. However, the seventh problem has a better solution. Can you think what it might be?

Given: 49, 23, 3

Obtain: 20

Solution:[2]

Better
solution:[3]

Rokeach (1948) consistently found that highly dogmatic individuals displayed more rigidity in solving these problems. This illustrates an intolerance of ambiguity and a tendency to rely on a standard or "pat" solution rather than to attempt novel or creative problem-solving methods. Burgoon (1971a) found that individuals with low tolerance for ambiguity are less

---

Solutions to the Water Problem

1. Fill the bottle that holds 61 quarts; from it fill the 31 quart bottle; from the remainder withdraw 4 quarts twice. In short, $61 - 31 - 4 - 4 = 22$.

2. $49 - 23 - 3 - 3 = 20$.

3. $23 - 3 = 20$.

likely to even engage in group discussions that they expect will involve large amounts of conflicting information.

A very interesting finding is that, although high dogs are very confident of their ability, their perception, and their solutions to problems, they are *not* more accurate than others who have considerably less confidence in their own abilities, perceptions, and solutions (Crockett and Meidinger 1956). The implications of this are striking. Those who dominate and bulldoze the group may very well be influencing it to the wrong solution, yet be highly confident that what they are doing is best for the group.

Dogmatic individuals also tend to stereotype others and have bits of contradictory information neatly pigeonholed in their thinking. For example, they may believe in freedom and equality, yet practice racial and religious discrimination. In the Watergate scandal, several nationally prominent politicians who professed to stand for law and order broke the law and covered it up when it was convenient because at their level it was "in the national interest."

High dogs tend to exaggerate the differences they perceive between themselves and others. "All those bums want is a handout from Uncle Sam. They wouldn't know the meaning of the term *pride in your work.*"

From a communication standpoint, perhaps one of the most interesting aspects of dogmatism is the tendency to make so-called *opinionated rejection* statements that not only express an idea about the topic, but also ridicule the person who holds a contrasting idea. This may also be referred to in transactional analysis terminology as an ulterior transaction (see Chapter 5). Rokeach (1960, p. 46) offers several examples: " 'Only a simple-minded fool would think that . . .' 'A person must be pretty stupid to think that . . .' 'The idea that . . . is pure hogwash' (poppycock, rubbish, drivel, crazy, ridiculous, insane, piddling, etc.)."

In contrast to opinionated rejection, Rokeach (1960, p. 46) refers to *opinionated acceptance* as including such statements as: " 'Any intelligent person knows that . . .' 'Plain common sense tells you that . . .' " Leathers (1970, p. 184) studied the effects of five such descriptive statements in group discussions. The five statements were:

1. That's a ridiculous statement. I disagree.

2. Are you serious in taking such an absurd position?

3. You are wrong. Dead wrong!

4. I don't understand why I ever agreed with you.

5. That's downright foolish.

Leathers (1970, p. 187) found that these statements resulted in a destruction of trust within the group and (1) tension (squirming, rubbing hands together nervously), (2) inflexibility ("Oh you think so, huh . . . that is the way it is"), and (3) personal reactions ("Man, you are a strange cat"). Thus it appears that dogmatism breeds opinionated statements that result in the reduction of trust within a group.

Other negative by-products have been found to result from dogmatism. Rokeach (1960, p. 201) found that high dogmatics had a significantly harder time solving a problem (about 24 minutes) than low dogmatics (about 17 minutes). Rokeach reasoned that high dogmatics are less capable of processing the necessary information in such a way as to be able to solve the problem. He states (p. 286): "High scorers on the Dogmatism scale . . . repeatedly . . . differ from low scorers in the ability to synthesize new beliefs into a new system, but not in the ability to analyze or break down single beliefs" (i.e., the facing, direction, and movement beliefs).

In the same context, Miller and Bacon (1971, p. 152) conducted a study to test the ability of high and low dogmatics to understand the humor in a humorous visual stimulus. Subjects were shown a centerfold from a 1966 *Harvard Lampoon* parody of *Playboy* magazine. As they indicate, "the picture showed a nude woman reclining on a beach towel . . . tanned where one would normally expect her to be untanned." Miller and Bacon found that dogmatic subjects took significantly longer to recognize the humor depicted in the centerfold. They reason (p. 157) that closed-minded persons take longer to see the humor since it "stems from the introduction of information that conflicts with existing beliefs."

Other research indicates that closed-minded persons are less tolerant of unfamiliar pieces of music (Mikol 1958), are more resistant to change (Ehrlich and Lee 1969), and are more likely to conform to group norms (Nadler 1959).

On the positive side, however, is evidence that dogmatism levels can be reduced. Haiman (1963) and Larson and Gratz (1966) have found that group communication course work can bring about significantly lower dogmatism scores.

MACHIAVELLIANISM

Another factor that influences behavior in small groups is Machiavellianism. It is named after Niccolo Machiavelli, who in 1532 wrote *The Prince* and inspired the familiar point of view that "the end justifies the means." Christie and Geis (1970, p. 1) define the Machiavellian as "someone who views and manipulates others for his own purposes." Machiavellians are pragmatists. They tell people what they want to hear. They have a high need to control others regardless of any attending ethical consideration. They see people as objects to be manipulated to their own ends. They are good at lying to others while looking them right in the eye (Exline *et al.* 1970). They feel no remorse or so-called cognitive dissonance after saying or doing things that do not coincide with their own beliefs or attitudes (Widgery and Tubbs 1972). They seem to be most effective in unstructured situations where they can control and structure things. In fact, Burgoon

(1971) found that high Machs actually obtain higher grades in courses in which small group and dyadic (two-person) communication activities predominate, as compared to more highly structured courses in which public speaking assignments predominate. Burgoon, Miller, and Tubbs (1972) found that high Machs are more responsive than low Machs to a situation in which there is a high reward for manipulating others.

Machiavellians are different from authoritarians. Christie and Geis (1970, p. 38) state that the authoritarian view is, "People are no damned good, but they *ought* to be." In contrast, the Machiavellian view is, "People are no damned good. So what? Take advantage of it." For this reason Machiavellians have the so-called cool syndrome, while low Machiavellians are referred to as "the soft touch" (p. 285).

Christie and Geis (1970, p. 311) report that in small groups, high Machs tend to take over the leadership to the extent that they are allowed to. High Machs do not seem to get emotionally attached to others. After working together in task-oriented groups, high Machs

> reported less enjoyment, less liking for the group, and less interest in working with the same group in the future than lows. . . . High Machs appear to have greater ability to organize their own and others' resources to achieve task goals, but this ability is not elicited by demand or request, but only by situations which are intrinsically motivating.

Machiavellianism is a fairly good predictor of behavior in small group situations. If we are to better understand what motivates given utterances in group discussions, we also need to take into account the background factors of individuals composing the group. The model in Fig. 2.3 summarizes the tactics commonly exhibited in two types of situations by high versus low Machs.

See the article by Christie at the end of this chapter for a more detailed description of the Machiavellian.

SELF-ESTEEM

Self-esteem (sometimes called self-concept) is the level of respect or positive feeling a person has toward himself. Two extreme examples of high and low self-esteem would be Mohammad Ali ("I am the greatest") and Marilyn Monroe, who committed suicide. Self-esteem is often measured using the following scale:

Attractive ____:____:____:____:____ Unattractive

Intelligent ____:____:____:____:____ Unintelligent

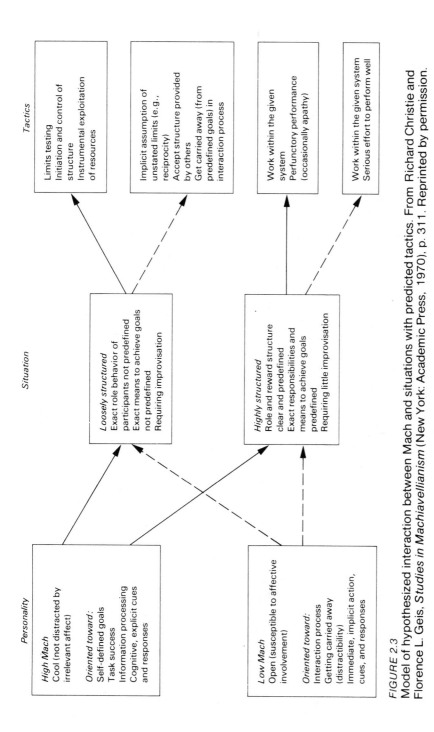

FIGURE 2.3
Model of hypothesized interaction between Mach and situations with predicted tactics. From Richard Christie and Florence L. Geis, *Studies in Machiavellianism* (New York: Academic Press, 1970), p. 311. Reprinted by permission.

First, persons are asked to rate their *ideal selves,* that is, the type of people they would like to be. Then they are asked to rate themselves on each dimension the way they think they really are (their *real selves*). These ratings are given numerical weightings, and the difference between real self and ideal self indicates a person's level of self-esteem. The smaller the difference, the higher the self-esteem.

Self-esteem has a profound effect on the success of individuals in all areas of life. Individuals with defeatist attitudes tend to make half-hearted efforts and cause themselves to fail. Conversely, group leaders who "think positively" often find themselves succeeding on the basis of their sincere efforts. This phenomenon is known as the "self-fulfilling prophecy." This simply means that individuals' attitudes often cause their experiences to fulfill their initial feelings or predictions.

Kinch (1974) has formulated three propositions indicating the mutual influence of interpersonal communication and a person's self-concept:

1. The individual's self-concept is based on his perception of the way others are responding to him.

2. The individual's self-concept functions to direct his behavior.

3. The individual's perception of the responses of others toward him reflects the actual responses toward him.

These theoretical notions are supported in real-life experiences. One student began every oral communication assignment with this apology: "This probably won't be of much interest to you, but I hope you'll put up with me. Here goes nothing. . . ." The surprising thing was that he sooner or later convinced everyone in the class that he wasn't worth listening to. This is an example of the destructiveness of the self-fulfilling prophecy. You might be on the lookout for your own behaviors. Which of the two patterns described below do you typically follow?

The following are some verbal patterns that, according to Myers and Myers (1973, pp. 109-110), may characterize low self-concept:

- frequent use of cliché phrases or a few words ("you know," "like," "young people are like that," etc.) which are used not so much to help identify something in common with others, but because the person with a low self-concept does not trust his ability to be original;

- need to talk about self in terms of criticism, weaknesses ("all thumbs"), and difficult experiences which help explain why he is not better than he is;

□ an inability to accept praise gracefully, often with a superficially worded disclaimer which invites additional proof;

□ a defensiveness about blame to the degree that the person may be more anxious about who gets credit or blame in a project than actually getting the project accomplished;

□ a cynicism about his accomplishments or his possessions; a hypercritical attitude about those of others;

□ a persistently whining or sneering tone of voice or posture as assumed in relation to his own or others' successes, as if he dismissed as luck or special privilege any accomplishments by anyone;

□ a pessimistic attitude expressed about competition. ("In the game of 'Monopoly' I always get the cheap properties and end up in jail.")

On the other hand, here are some verbal patterns that may characterize a high self-concept:

□ talks about self less frequently and may talk about others easily in terms of their accomplishments; needs less constant reassurance of his own personal worth;

□ is able to accept praise or blame gracefully. In working on projects is likely to take risks and verbalize positions other than the "correct" ones; does not spend so much time figuring out the safe way of approaching problems to avoid blame;

□ looks at his own accomplishments with a balance of credit to his ability and to circumstances, is willing to give credit to others for their part in what is done;

□ a confident tone of voice; avoids condescending tone or attitude and is capable of saying "I don't know" or "I was wrong";

□ admits to a wide range of feelings and empathy for others whether or not these are popular;

□ an optimistic attitude about competition; willingness to try new games, enter discussion about new topics with questions (risk displaying his ignorance in an effort to learn more);

□ is generally less dogmatic about beliefs; less tendency to be biased, to stereotype others, or classify events too broadly.

It is interesting to note the effect of self-esteem on one's behavior in small groups. Aronoff and Messe (1971, pp. 320, 323) found that homogeneous groups of low self-esteem subjects tended to prefer more structured social hierarchies with fewer individuals assuming more of the leadership functions (for example, giving a procedural suggestion, suggesting a solution, giving an opinion, giving orientation, drawing attention, integrating past communications, and asking opinions). However, groups composed of only high self-esteem individuals preferred more widespread democratic sharing of these task-oriented group leadership functions. The authors reason that

> the [high esteem] individuals' strong concern [is] to demonstrate . . . competence and achieve respect from others. These needs are manifested in desires for establishing confidence, mastery, dominance, reputation and/or recognition. . . . In contrast, the [low esteem] person, who is characterized by insecurity, anxiety, and dependency, feels reluctant to assume the initiative in organizing the group's activities.

In the following example, a student with low self-esteem describes his behavior in a problem-solving discussion. Note the reactions of the others.

Dan's View
I did not start in [talking] right away. Being on the timid side, I hoped one of the talkers would encourage me to try and give some of my opinions. But as the discussion continued, there was little or no encouragement. After a while it seemed like I was left out of the group. I know I should have said something, but I was completely unfamiliar with these people and therefore, I guess, I was hesitant to give my views. So I remained silent, writing down some of what was said and my thoughts too.

Paul's View
Dan never really got started and was almost in a stupor looking at the other five of us nuts. . . .

Kay's View
. . . one of the problems that our group encountered was the lack of participation of one member, Dan. He wrote down his ideas on what was being discussed, but did not share them with the group. We did not shut him out of the discussion. In fact, we would ask his opinion, but he did not seem to want to give it. I feel that some valuable information may have been lost.

Ron's View
. . . a problem we experienced, although more an annoyance than a problem, was that Dan never entered into the discussion. He just sat back and let the rest of us complete the assignment.

Carol's View
Generally, our group made progress rapidly and there was very little behavior which kept us tied back. However, Dan offered few, if any, opinions. It was not as though he had not formed any ideas about the subject because he was constantly writing down his feelings. Yet he would not share them with the rest of us. It was as though he did not

feel he needed to be in the group. Of course, every other member of the group could have accomplished the assignment by himself or herself, too. But the main idea was to work with each other. Therefore, I felt Dan's behavior stifled the group's progress to some extent.

Bruce's View
I thought that our informal and newly acquainted group handled the discussion quite nicely. Everyone was interested in the discussion. At no time did anyone get off on a tangent or disrupt our progress. From this experience I learned that even a group of total strangers can have a worthwhile and meaningful discussion.

What a diversity of viewpoints to come out of the same discussion! Dan thought it was the other members' responsibility to encourage his participation. Paul, Kay, Ron, and Carol obviously misinterpreted and resented Dan's lack of participation. And Bruce (who, it turns out, did most of the talking) thought the entire discussion was a smashing success and was oblivious both to Dan's problem and to the negative reactions of the others. Dan's comments probably explain why Ober and Jandt (1973) found that low self-esteem students enjoy group discussion courses significantly less than high self-esteem students.

Self-esteem (or lack of it) seems to play a significant role in influencing group discussion behaviors. The self-fulfilling prophecy of success or failure is quite potent. In fact, Deutsch and Solomon (1959) found in one classic study that persons with low self-esteem who got good feedback concerning their group participation derogated the person who gave them positive feedback rather than believe the positive feedback. Conversely, high self-esteem subjects rated the evaluator high when they received positive feedback and derogated the evaluator only when they received negative feedback. Deutsch and Solomon (1959, p. 110) state:

> There was a clear tendency for Ss to respond more favorably to evaluations from another which were consistent, rather than inconsistent, with their own evaluations of their performances. These results support our initial hypothesis of a "cognitive balance effect."

In the preceding example, Dan saw the group as shutting him out and rejecting him, even though several others in the group report that they made several attempts to draw him into the discussion. Although self-esteem can be improved, it seems more likely that this perceptual bias operates in such a way so that the "strong get stronger, and the weak get weaker."

A survey of over 2000 adults (Bruskin 1973) indicated that out of 14 potentially fearful items, "speaking before a group" ranked highest, with 40.6 percent of the adults indicating that this was a fear-producing situation. Two types of anxiety have traditionally been identified as (1) free floating and (2) situation specific. The first type plagues the individual who is fearful in all situations, while the second type is restricted to certain specific situations.

Speech anxiety is an even more narrow category than situation specific anxiety. Speech anxiety refers to an irrational fear of a given communication situation; it is frequently thought of in relation to public speaking but is also present in small group situations. Rosenfeld and Frandsen (1972) studied the relation of speech anxiety to interpersonal behaviors as measured by Schutz's FIRO-B. They reasoned that so-called reticent students would avoid leadership positions, and would exhibit relatively few affection and inclusion behaviors. The data supported their hypothesis. In other words, anxiety restricted the amount that these students interacted.

Shaw (1981) reviewed several studies relating anxiety to small group interaction. He concluded that the anxious individual exhibits a general feeling of inadequacy in relating to others. The anxious individual expects less from the group, conforms more, and is highly dependent on others.

Anxious persons are more likely to be defensive and resistant to changes that they perceive as threatening (which might include most any changes since most things would be threatening). Therefore groups composed of highly anxious individuals might be expected to be highly conservative in adopting new ideas, since new things usually are associated with some degree of uncertainty, risk, and also threat. We shall look more closely at resistance to change in Chapter 7.

Although personality is one of the most important background factors in small group communication, other factors are also involved. *Organismic* factors or variables are those that are part of the organism. This includes a number of characteristics, but three seem to be especially pertinent to small group interaction. They are (1) sex, (2) age, and (3) health.

SEX

Perhaps the most obvious thing about groups that include both sexes is that they are most interesting! Schutz (1971, p. 226) writes:

> Usually, if there's a girl in the group who attracts me I find more interest in the group as a whole, and must watch myself because I tend to find everything she says and does somehow much more fascinating than I do anyone else's contribution.

Women emphatically point out that the increased arousal brought about by a member of the opposite sex is every bit as much a part of the feminine response pattern as it is the masculine.

Differences in behavior between the sexes have for years been known to be a function of cultural influences and childhood learning experiences. Margaret Mead (1968) found as early as in 1935 that certain behaviors that the Western world had assumed were innately masculine or feminine were instead culturally determined. In her studies of New Guinea tribes she found certain societies in which women dominated. She writes (p. 259), "Among the Tchambuli the woman is the dominant, impersonal, managing partner, the man the less responsible and the emotionally dependent person." Mead describes the husband, on the other hand, as being catty toward other men but charming toward women. He danced in the tribal ceremonies, spent hours on his personal makeup, and gossiped about the other *men* in the village. Obviously such behaviors cannot be an inherent function of one's sex.

Terman and Miles (1936) found that women in our society are more compassionate, sympathetic, and emotional than men, while men are more aggressive, self-assertive, and less anxious than women. Berg and Bass (1961) report that men tend to be more task oriented in groups, while women are more concerned with interpersonal harmony. Scheidel (1963), in reviewing numerous such studies, concluded that women are more susceptible to persuasion than men. However, Kibler, Barker, and Cegala (1970) found that there were no differences between sexes in ability to comprehend and retain information from orally communicated messages. Furthermore, in a more recent study Rosenfeld and Christie (1974) found no significant differences in persuasibility between men and women. They cite four other studies between 1968 and 1973 that also failed to find sex differences in persuasibility, while older studies from 1935 to 1968 more often than not found that women were more persuasible. Rosenfeld and Christie (1974, p. 253) concluded that

> if earlier studies were correct concerning persuasibility . . . women are gradually growing away from the "traditional" dependence upon others and acquiring more confidence in their own judgments. It is futile to attempt to conclude that one sex is more persuasible than another based upon the present study and other available research.

It would seem that the same futility presently exists in attempting to predict *group* communication behaviors on the basis of sex alone. However, it is important to emphasize that certain stereotypes concerning male and female roles are probably outdated, and new research is needed to establish if any sex differences do exist regarding small group behaviors. For example, review the stereotypes listed below.

How to Tell a Businessman from a Businesswoman
A businessman is aggressive; a businesswoman is pushy.
A businessman is good on details; she's picky.
He loses his temper because he's so involved in his job; she's bitchy.
When he's depressed (or hungover), everyone tiptoes past his office.
She's moody so it must be her time of the month.
He follows through; she doesn't know when to quit.
He's confident; she's conceited.

He stands firm; she's impossible to deal with.
He's firm; she's hard.
His judgments are her prejudices.
He is a man of the world; she's been around.
He drinks because of excessive job pressure; she's a lush.
He isn't afraid to say what he thinks; she's mouthy.
He exercises authority; she's power mad.
He's close-mouthed; she's secretive.
He's a stern taskmaster; she's hard to work for.

It seems reasonable to predict that groups comprised of both sexes will be different from those whose members are all of the same sex. We might expect that sexually heterogeneous groups would have more socially oriented behaviors and fewer task-oriented behaviors, since members would be more interested in promoting social relationships than in homogeneous groups. South (1927) found that a one-sex committee is usually more efficient than a mixed one for this reason. However, much more research is needed to systematically establish the role of sex in group discussion. As women's role in our society changes, more modern research can help to clarify and probably disprove some long-held beliefs.

AGE

Obviously communication patterns differ from childhood through adolescence to adulthood and old age. Older group members in college-age groups (for example, married students, veterans, and so forth) tend to be more influential, based on their relatively greater number of years of experience. While this may not always hold true, it tends to be the case. There is some evidence (Bass *et al.* 1953) that older college women are held in higher esteem than younger college women. It generally takes time to develop leadership qualifications. In fact, one recent study (Quinn 1973) indicated that one reason younger people in general have lower job satisfaction is that they tend to have lower-level jobs, which are inherently less satisfying. On the other hand, as they gain in age and experience, they move into more challenging job capacities and gain in satisfaction.

Over two thousand years ago Aristotle made what today seems like a very sound observation regarding the differences in behavior that go along with age differences. As quoted by Roberts (1941, pp. 1404-1406), he wrote:

Younger men have strong passions, and tend to gratify them indiscriminately. Of the bodily desires, it is the sexual by which they are most swayed, in which they show absence of self-control. . . .
They are hot-tempered and quick-tempered, and apt to give way of their anger; bad temper often gets the better of them, for . . . they cannot bear being slighted, they are indignant if they imagine

themselves unfairly treated. While they love honor, they love victory still more; for youth is eager for superiority over others, and victory is one form of this. . . . They look at the good side rather than the bad. . . . They trust others readily. . . . They would always rather do noble deeds than useful ones. . . . All their mistakes are in the direction of doing things excessively and vehemently. . . . They think they know everything, and are always quite sure about it.

. . . the character of elderly men — men who are past their prime — . . . . is the contrary of all these. . . . They have often been taken in, and often made mistakes; and life on the whole is a bad business. . . . They "think," but they never "know"; and because of their hesitation they always add a "possibly" or a "perhaps". . . . They are cynical. . . . They are small-minded, because they have been humbled by life. . . . They are not generous. . . . They lack confidence in the future. . . . They live by memory rather than by hope.

. . . As for men in their prime . . . they have a character between that of the young and that of the old. . . . They have neither that of excess of confidence which amounts to rashness, not too much timidity, but the right amount of each. They neither trust everybody nor distrust everybody, but judge people correctly.

Finally, Shaw (1981, pp. 181-182), summarizing the literature on age and group behavior, stated that

there is good evidence that chronological age of the group member is related to several aspects of group interaction. With increasing age, the individual has an increasing . . . selectivity of contacts and greater complexity of . . . interaction. . . . Age is related to behavior in groups, it provides the time required for the individual to learn appropriate social reponses . . . in most cases it is not the mere fact that the individual has aged that is important, but rather that he has had greater experience in social situations.

It is also interesting to speculate that groups with age heterogeneity would perform differently than those with age homogeneity. A number of studies indicate that some member heterogeneity relates positively to such group outcomes as cohesion (Hare 1962). It is apparent that age, and the experiences that go along with age, will impact on group interaction and subsequent group outcomes. For the time being, the exact nature of these relationships is not clear.

HEALTH

Although health may not be a highly significant factor in the study of small groups, it does play a part. Deficiencies in both physical and mental health would seem to impede group performance. A member who fails to attend meetings or who is unable to carry his or her portion of the group work load will sooner or later reduce the total group output. Also, physical health frequently affects a person's stamina. Strength and stamina may not be important in relatively short discussions (lasting up to an hour); however, discussions and conferences frequently last for days. Labor-management negotiations may go 20 hours a day for a week or even longer. In one case, a local labor agreement was settled after a prolonged strike, and the week after the agreement was reached, the local union president died of a heart attack. Physical health and stamina can play a part in small group interaction.

Those who are spaced out on drugs or who are hung over from the night before will also harm group performance. In one case a college professor was consistently abusive and aggressive in department meetings. He later admitted that he had been so high on drugs that he didn't even remember being at the meetings. Yet his behavior caused severe setbacks in his department, since he argued vociferously against all attempts to cover the items in the group's agenda, and he seriously hurt the feelings of other group members through his verbal assaults. Physical and mental health factors, like these other external causal variables, are out of the control of other group members, yet have an ultimate effect on the group's end results.

As each of us develops through childhood and adolescence, a myriad of experiences shape our view of the world. Since we each have different experiences, we would expect our outlooks to differ also. These experiences are called developmental factors, and we will look at three that are related to small group interaction: (1) attitudes, (2) values, and (3) anxieties.

ATTITUDES

Almost fifty years ago, Allport (1935) defined an attitude as "a mental and neural state of readiness, organized through experience, exerting a directive or dynamic influence upon the individual's response to all objects and situations with which it is related." According to Triandis (1971), attitudes have three components: (1) a cognitive component, which refers to an idea or a concept, such as "Chevrolets," (2) an affective component or the emotion toward the idea (Chevrolets are good), and (3) a behavioral component, which is the readiness to act (that is, to drive or buy a Chevrolet).

McGrath and Altman (1966) indicate that group members may hold several types of attitudes that are relevant to their participation in small groups. For example, they have attitudes toward the task itself, toward the situation within which the group is operating, toward people inside and outside of the group, and toward other issues that may be related to the one under discussion. All of these attitudes will ultimately affect their behavior in the group, which in turn will affect the group's end results. How many times have you been a member of a project team or group in which either you or others in the group have found that you just can't seem to get too enthusiastic about accomplishing the task? Or perhaps you would ordinarily be interested in the task, but it comes at a time when you are preoccupied with other things, such as romantic difficulties or financial worries. These illustrations help to indicate the important role that attitudes may play in determining one's actions in the group.

Some of the most intuitive yet provocative theories concerning attitudes are the so-called cognitive consistency theories. These closely related theories are all based on the assumption that human beings have a strong psychological need for consistency. Heider (1958), the first of the consistency theorists, refers to this as a need to maintain *balance*. He reasons that if we hold an attitude X and another person holds the same value, then we are likely to feel positively toward that person. For example, if Lance likes motorcycles and Brad also likes motorcycles, Lance is likely to have positive feelings toward Brad. This can be illustrated as shown in Fig. 2.4. If on the other hand, Brad does not like motorcycles, Lance would feel some imbalance and would be motivated to resolve it in one of several ways. First, he could try to change Brad's evaluation of motorcycles. Second, he could change his feeling toward Brad. Finally, he could change his own evaluation of motorcycles. The specific alternative Lance chooses would depend on the relative strength of his attitudes toward Brad and toward motorcycles.

Heider predicts that balanced triads are rewarding, or pleasant to experience, while imbalanced triads result in pressure to restore balance. An easy rule of thumb for differentiating between balanced and imbalanced triads is that if the algebraic product of the three elements in the triad is positive, the triad is balanced. If the algebraic product is negative, the triad is imbalanced. Which of the triads in Fig. 2.5 is imbalanced, thus creating pressure to restore balance? How could balance be restored?

A related consistency theory is called *cognitive dissonance theory* (Festinger 1957). In this theory, *consonance* is the same as Heider's concept of balance, and *dissonance* is equivalent to imbalance in that it serves to motivate a change back to consonance. One of the interesting finds of research in this area is that a severe initiation for attaining group member-

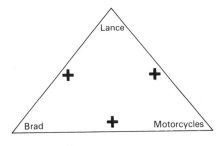

FIGURE 2.4

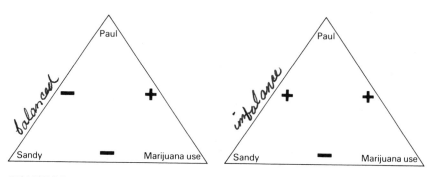

FIGURE 2.5

ship creates a high level of dissonance, which is usually resolved by the person valuing membership in the group more than if the initiation was less severe (Aronson and Mills 1959).

Fraternities and sororities have used pledgeship as a device to increase the severity of initiation into membership. The result is usually that one who endures these experiences reduces the dissonance caused by them and begins to believe they are necessary and even desirable for the new pledge class to endure. The traditional pride in being a United States Marine has also resulted largely from the severity of initiation experienced in Marine Corps boot camp.

Group interaction may also create dissonance. If you are confronted in a discussion with an opinion contrary to your own, some degree of dissonance will result. The dissonance will increase if you value the other person and if the issue over which you disagree is one of high relevance. According to Festinger and Aronson (1968) you may reduce the dissonance in these five ways (starting with the most likely and going to the least likely approach): (1) devalue the importance of the issue, (2) derogate the disagreeing person, (3) attempt to change his or her attitude, (4) seek additional social support for your view, and (5) change your attitude. Aronson (1973) posits that although people like to think of themselves as rational animals, they are more likely than not a "rationalizing animal." It is important to point out that we all use these methods of dissonance reduction and we need to have them. Although rationalizing may sound like something we should avoid, it can be a helpful tool if we are consciously aware of it.

VALUES

Although an overwhelming amount of research has been conducted on attitudes and attitude change, Rokeach (1968, 1971, 1973) has argued that people's *values* are quite important as a predictor of behavior. His ratio-

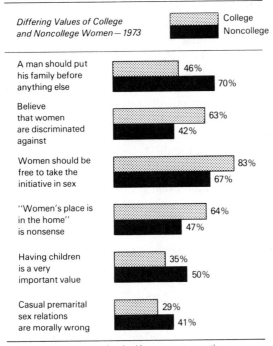

Women's movement has had its warmest reception on America's campuses. The recent Yankelovich "Study of American Youth" reports that the values of Women's Lib have created a wide schism between women in college and women who do not have a college education.

FIGURE 2.6
Bar graph from the *Flint Journal,* November 13, 1974.

nale is that while we have thousands of different attitudes, we have only several dozen values. Values, then, are seen as more fundamental than attitudes and are more stable and long lasting than attitudes. For an exercise concerning your own values and how they relate to the values of others, see Exercise 1 at the end of this chapter.

Value differences may significantly influence the course of any given group discussion. Suppose you are in a group attempting to determine a policy regarding pregnancy leaves of absence for employees of a company. Suppose also that your committee consists of six women, three who have been to college and three who have not. Based on the study data in Fig. 2.6, how likely do you think it would be that the committee might achieve consensus on this issue?

This research indicates that educational differences would generate severe value differences between the two subgroups on the committee. If one group, the noncollege women, basically valued motherhood and devalued careers for women, it would probably be difficult for them to agree with the others on a leave-of-absence policy decision. Similar difficulties arise in discussions dealing with sexual behaviors, obscenity, abortion, religion, politics, and others. Any discussion on a topic on which people have strong value differences will likely be complicated by such differences.

Earlier we discussed the influence of age on values and behaviors. As it turns out, recent research corroborates Aristotle's intuitive observations (Payne, Summers, and Stewart 1973, pp. 24-25. Subjects from three generations (college students, their parents, and their grandparents) were asked to respond on a seven-point scale (1) "not at all bad" to (7) "extremely bad" to each of 85 items. Sample items were:

- Becoming involved in unusual sex practices with persons of the opposite sex

- Being unpatriotic

- Cheating on your income tax

- Cheating on an exam and getting caught

- Going to a party in casual clothes and finding that everyone is dressed up

- Having to go on welfare to feed or clothe your children adequately

The researchers found that college students were significantly less severe in their judgments than were their parents, who were in turn less severe than the grandparents.

Although these differences exist between generations, it is also likely that major differences exist between individuals in the same age group. A question arises as to the degree of value differences that can be tolerated in a group before these differences become a major obstacle to group functioning. Fortunately, some related research exists that sheds light on this question. Rogers and Shoemaker (1971) discussed this issue with regard to homophily and heterophily of relationships. Homophily is defined as "the degree to which pairs of individuals who interact are similar in certain attributes (beliefs, values, education, social status)" (McCroskey 1971, p. 174). Rogers and Bhowmik (1971, p. 213) state that "heterophilic interaction is likely to cause message distortion, delayed transmission, restriction of communication channels, and may cause cognitive dissonance, as the receiver is exposed to messages that may be inconsistent with his existing beliefs and attitudes, an uncomfortable psychological state." In other words, two students would probably communicate more easily than would a student and a professor. While considerable research has been conducted on the effect of homophily-heterophily on the diffusion of innovations, more research is needed to determine the effects these factors have on group functioning and on group outcomes.

THE SYSTEMS PERSPECTIVE

As pointed out in Chapter 1, small group interactions are the result of influences that can be labeled inputs, throughputs, and outputs. These factors are in a constant state of simultaneous and reciprocal influence. This chapter has focused on some of the inputs, namely the relevant background factors of the group members. Through the discussion of personality we tried to illustrate the role that personality plays in shaping individual behavior. For example, high affiliators or extroverts will probably be more inclined to join groups in the first place (if we assume that membership is voluntary). They are very likely to smile more, express more feelings both verbally and nonverbally than low affiliators, give more direct eye contact to more members of the group, and agree more than low affiliators. We would expect that high affiliators would have higher satisfaction resulting from harmonious group experiences, and greater dissatisfaction with groups that experience a high degree of conflict and disagreement. The recluse or introvert would tend to avoid meetings and group memberships whenever possible and would avoid talking in the groups he or she was forced to be in. Group interaction would generally be viewed by the introvert as threatening and therefore less satisfying than engaging in the same activity alone. However, if the group were conducted by a highly supportive and nonthreatening leader, the introvert's satisfaction level would increase dramatically (Giffin and Bradley 1969).

High achievers tend to enjoy working alone on task-oriented projects, since they are more highly task oriented than most others and find that the group tends to slow down their progress. The exception, of course, would be a group composed of a lot of high achievers. In this case, high cohesion or high conflict might result, depending on the way the members decided to reward their efforts. Thus the group norms, the leadership style, and the communication patterns would all tend to influence the satisfaction level of group members. In the example at the beginning of this chapter, the freshman group including John, Randy, and Al provided an illustration of a discussion among high achievers that resulted in a low level of satisfaction. Randy was seen by the rest of the group as too domineering. Throughout the semester, Randy got into one argument after another with other members of the class. In this case, his high degree of dominance and dogmatism seemed to overshadow most of his interpersonal and small group experiences.

The three organismic factors discussed in this chapter were sex, age, and health. It was shown that a group with both sexes included tends to have more socially oriented communication patterns and fewer task-oriented comments resulting. A clever study by Rosenfeld and Fowler (1976) found that sex and personality combined to influence an individual's leadership style. For example, a *democratic female* would score low on dogmatism and four personality characteristics measured by the Edwards

Personal Preference Scale — change, achievement, aggression, and abasement. *Autocratic females* scored high on dogmatism, change, achievement, aggression, and abasement and low on nurturance. *Democratic males* scored high on achievement and intraception and low on aggression, while *autocratic males* scored low on achievement and intraception and high on aggression. The most interesting finding of this study seems to be that men and women who act similarly are perceived differently. According to Rosenfeld and Fowler (1976, p. 324):

> whereas democratic males were characterized as forceful, analytical, and as valuing the love of people . . . democratic females were characterized as open-minded and nurturing. The democratic male may appear to group members as analytical and thereby aloof, while the democratic female may appear to be warm and affectionate.

This study illustrates what is meant by the systems aspects of small group interaction. Personality, sex, style of leadership behavior, and the resulting perception of the person behaving — all of these factors are interrelated.

This chapter also dealt with age as an organismic variable. Age seems to be somewhat similar to attitudes and values in that the more similar group members are (in age, attitudes, and values), the easier it is for them to communicate in a way that leads to higher satisfaction. It stands to reason that it is more comfortable to be in groups with people like ourselves (in terms of age, attitudes, and values) than it is to be in groups in which we feel we "don't fit in" as well. However, some of the most interesting experiences occur when we meet someone of a drastically different age group who shares some of our attitudes and values. Conversely, even people of one's own age may differ so much in attitude or personality that severe hard feelings sometimes result, as seen in the case study at the beginning of this chapter.

In the readings at the end of this chapter, William Schutz shows the importance of people's need for inclusion, control, and affection in relation to several aspects of their group behavior. The second selection, by Richard Christie, examines the relationship between the Machiavellian trait and the "con artist" form of behavior that it spawns. Keep in mind the point that was made earlier in this chapter that Machiavellian behavior seems to thrive in an unstructured, face-to-face situation, and it subsides considerably in more structured situations.

Exercises

1. Employee Selection Problem

You are a member of a personnel selection committee. You need to hire two people as first-line supervisors in an industrial foundry. The supervisors would be in charge of 30-person (mostly male) work groups who do machining processes (grinding, drilling, polishing) on metal castings made from molten metal in a different part of the foundry. Examine all five information sheets, which describe the candidates who have passed the physical examination and are available for immediate employment.

1

NAME: Sally A. Peterson   AGE: 23

MARITAL STATUS: Married   NUMBER OF CHILDREN: 0

NUMBER OF DEPENDENTS OTHER THAN SELF (explain relation): 1 - husband

EDUCATION:

	Years	Degree or Diploma	Major (where applicable)
Elementary	8	Yes	
High School	4	Yes	College prep.
College	4	Yes (B.A.)	Sociology

CURRENT EDUCATIONAL OR VOCATIONAL SITUATION: Has been management trainee for four months with XYZ Aircraft Company. Began with XYZ immediately after serving two years with Peace Corps.

VOCATIONAL SKILLS OR EXPERIENCE: None other than a few elementary skills learned while in Peace Corps.

POLICE RECORD: None

ADDITIONAL COMMENTS: Currently active in volunteer community social work. Has taken over Junior Achievement group in underprivileged neighborhood.

2

NAME: Thomas Browne   AGE: 26

MARITAL STATUS: Married   NUMBER OF CHILDREN: 0

NUMBER OF DEPENDENTS OTHER THAN SELF (explain relation): 1 - wife

EDUCATION:

	Years	Degree or Diploma	Major (where applicable)
Elementary	8	Yes	
High School	4	Yes	College prep.
College	4	Yes (B.A.)	Economics
	½	(toward M.A.)	Economics

CURRENT EDUCATIONAL OR VOCATIONAL SITUATION: Is completing first year in graduate school working toward M.A. in economics which should be completed in one more semester. Is classified in top third of his graduate school class. Is currently a research assistant to leading economist in graduate school of business.

VOCATIONAL SKILLS OR EXPERIENCE: None

POLICE RECORD: Arrested with a number of other students involved in campus disturbance — released without charges being made.

ADDITIONAL COMMENTS: None

3

NAME: William Cross   AGE: 20

MARITAL STATUS: Married   NUMBER OF CHILDREN: 0
                                                          (expecting first child in 6 months)

NUMBER OF DEPENDENTS OTHER THAN SELF (explain relation): 1 - wife

EDUCATION:

	Years	Degree or Diploma	Major (where applicable)
Elementary	8	Yes	
High School	4	Yes	Vocational
College			

CURRENT EDUCATIONAL OR VOCATIONAL SITUATION: Plumber's apprentice completing second year of apprenticeship. Employed by large building contractor.

VOCATIONAL SKILLS OR EXPERIENCE: Plumbing, some automotive repair skills, welding. General construction work.

POLICE RECORD: Two arrests, no convictions.
First arrest while in high school — no details because of juvenile status. Second arrest for disorderly conduct — charges dismissed.

ADDITIONAL COMMENTS: None

4

NAME: Jane Williams   AGE: 24

MARITAL STATUS: Single   NUMBER OF CHILDREN:

NUMBER OF DEPENDENTS OTHER THAN SELF (explain relation): 0

EDUCATION:

	Years	Degree or Diploma	Major (where applicable)
Elementary	8	Yes	
High School	4	Yes	College prep.
College	4	Yes (B.A.)	Sociology
	1½	Yes (M.B.A.)	Production Management

CURRENT EDUCATIONAL OR VOCATIONAL SITUATION: Completing second year of graduate school. Has B.A. in sociology, working toward Ph.D. which should be completed in 3 to 4 semesters. Ranks in middle third of graduate class. Working one-half time as a teaching assistant. Doing volunteer work and beginning research on urban sociology project.

VOCATIONAL SKILLS OR EXPERIENCE: None

POLICE RECORD: None

ADDITIONAL COMMENTS: None

5

NAME: Robert Smith   AGE: 21

MARITAL STATUS: Single   NUMBER OF CHILDREN:

NUMBER OF DEPENDENTS OTHER THAN SELF (explain relation): 0

EDUCATION:

	Years	Degree or Diploma	Major (where applicable)
Elementary	8	Yes	
High School	4	Yes	College prep.
College	3½	B.S. expected at end of semester	Business Administration

CURRENT EDUCATIONAL OR VOCATIONAL SITUATION: College senior expecting degree at end of current (spring) semester. "A−" student.

VOCATIONAL SKILLS OR EXPERIENCE: Typing. Has also worked part time in selling, construction work, and on farms.

POLICE RECORD: None

ADDITIONAL COMMENTS: Father unemployed for medical reasons. Mother works to support family. It is known that he has worked his way through college and has incurred a small debt in the form of a student loan.

Group task   After reviewing all five information sheets, meet as a group for 30 minutes to decide which two candidates should get the jobs. Each of you in the group will be assigned to argue in favor of one of the five candidates. After each of you presents the best "case" for your candidate, you must work together collectively to determine in the best interest of everyone concerned who should be hired. Your company is an equal opportunity/affirmative action employer.

2. Self-Esteem Exercise

Rate yourself on the following list of terms. First put an *I* in the appropriate blank indicating how you would like to be *ideally*. After completing all the items, begin the list again. This time put an *R* in the appropriate blank indicating how you think you *really* are. After you have rated your ideal self and your real self, compare the two. You may want to talk to others to see how their ratings compare.

 1. Attractive   ___:___:___:___:___:___   Unattractive

 2. Intelligent   ___:___:___:___:___:___   Unintelligent

 3. Weak   ___:___:___:___:___:___   Strong

 4. Passive   ___:___:___:___:___:___   Active

 5. Fair   ___:___:___:___:___:___   Unfair

 6. Kind   ___:___:___:___:___:___   Unkind

 7. Quiet   ___:___:___:___:___:___   Loud

 8. Introverted   ___:___:___:___:___:___   Extroverted

 9. Nervous   ___:___:___:___:___:___   Relaxed

10. Liberal   ___:___:___:___:___:___   Conservative

11. Happy   ___:___:___:___:___:___   Sad

12. Boastful   ___:___:___:___:___:___   Humble

13. Controlled   ___:___:___:___:___:___   Uncontrolled

14. Vulnerable   ___:___:___:___:___:___   Invulnerable

15. Excited   ___:___:___:___:___:___   Calm

16. Sexy   ___:___:___:___:___:___   Unsexy

17. Trusting   ___:___:___:___:___:___   Untrusting

18. Powerful   ___:___:___:___:___:___   Weak

19. Conforming   ___:___:___:___:___:___   Independent

20. Sensitive   ___:___:___:___:___:___   Insensitive

3. Personal Styles Exercise

Read the descriptions of the tough battler, friendly helper, and objective thinker that follow. Then anonymously rate volunteer class members on these three dimensions by placing an *X* inside a triangle as illustrated.

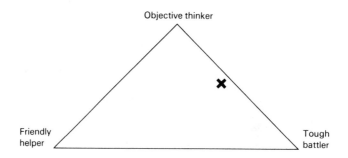

After this has been done, distribute them to the person who is rated. Class members may ask questions to get more feedback on what behaviors create these impressions on fellow students.

Listed below are three characteristic types that may be found in any group or organization.

	Tough Battler	Friendly Helper	Objective Thinker
Emotions	Accepts aggression, rejects affection	Accepts affection, rejects aggression	Rejects both affection and interpersonal aggression
Goal	Dominance	Acceptance	Correctness
Influences others by	Direction, intimidation, control of rewards	Offering understanding, praise, favors, friendship	Factual data, logical arguments
Value in organization	Initiates, demands, disciplines	Supports, harmonizes, relieves tension	Defines, clarifies, gets information, criticizes, tests
Overuses	Fighting	Kindness	Analysis
Becomes	Pugnacious	Sloppy, sentimental	Pedantic
Fears	Being "soft" or dependent	Desertion, conflict	Emotions, irrational acts
Needs	Warmth, consideration, objectivity, humility	Strength, integrity, firmness, self-assertion	Awareness of feeling, ability to love and to fight

Above are shown characteristic emotions, goals, standards of evaluation, techniques of influence of each type, and his/her service to the organization.

Each can be overdone and distorted. The *Tough Battler* would be a better manager, a better parent, a better neighbor, and a more satisfied person if he/she could learn some sensitivity, accept his/her inevitable dependence on others, and come to enjoy consideration for them. The Tough Battler would be more successful if he/she recognized that some facts will not yield to pugnacity.

The *Friendly Helper* would be a better manager, parent, citizen, and person if he/she could stand up for his/her own interests and for what is right, even against the pleas of others. This type needs firmness and strength and courage not to evade or smooth over conflicts. He/she must face facts.

The *Objective Thinker* would be a better human being and a better business leader if he/she could become more aware of his/her own feelings and the feelings of others. The Objective Thinker needs to learn that there are times when it is all right to fight and times when it is desirable to love.

---

* This material is adapted from the *Reading Book* of the NTL Institute for Applied Behavioral Science, associated with the National Education Association. The papers were originally prepared for theory sessions at the Institute's laboratories.

4. Gender Conditioning and the Stress It Produces

In groups of five or so, discuss your feelings about the following statements on the topics of sex roles and gender conditioning. The outline that follows this list may help you get started.

1. I am moving away from the idea that there is one role for men and one role for women, but I feel guilty when the man or woman in my life does something I have traditionally felt responsible for.

2. I know that society's view of a man's showing emotion, or its traditional rules of what he may eat or wear, is no measure of the man, but openly breaking these rules is just asking for people to question his sexuality and not worth the hassle.

3. Women's liberation, carried to the extreme, is responsible for the high rate of male impotency and homosexuality we find today.

4. Right or wrong, a man's sexuality is measured by his status and ability to make money. By many people's standards, all a woman needs to be successful is to find a man who will take care of her.

5. The thing a man should be most proud of is his success in his work. Mainly, he works to provide the "good life" for his wife and family. Not having a job is the worst thing that can happen to him.

6. I think I (my husband) work(s) too hard, but not maintaining our present life-style would cause more problems and be even harder to deal with than my (his) overwork.

For Men:

1. Since adulthood I have found it difficult to become close friends with another male. It really doesn't matter though, since, once I become involved with a woman, I find I really don't need any other close friends.

2. I understand that the woman in my life has a need to be liberated, but I am still doing everything that I always did and constantly she wants more from me. Her liberation is costing me mine.

For Women:

1. The man in my life finds activities he can do without me that bring him satisfaction, partly because we agree that everyone is responsible for his own happiness. I don't enjoy going out without him. Social events seem to be designed for couples and I feel out of place when I am alone or with women.

2. For the first time the man in my life feels that it is important for me to know who I am and what I want out of life. I am so accustomed to "not wanting anyting" that I can't answer those two questions. I jump from one idea to another and it is driving us both crazy.

I. Gender conditioning distorts one's "world consciousness"

   A. His vision of the world situation

   B. Her vision of the world situation

II. Gender conditioning distorts one's body consciousness

   A. View of pain: Male denies pain — e.g., drops dead at 54. Female affirms pain — e.g., lives in Palm Springs till age 90.

   B. View of dependency: Male denies dependency — e.g., won't go to doctor. Female affirms dependency — e.g., likes doctors.

   C. View of passivity: Male feels need to be aggressive. Female feels need to be dependent/passive.

D. View of diet: Male equates food with masculinity: the more food, the more masculine. Female is obsessed with diet.

E. View of touching: Male gets touched only as prelude to sex. Female desires to be touched often.

F. View of emotions: Male denies emotions. Female affirms emotions.

Summary: The process (gender conditioning) undermines the content (feelings) of a relationship.

III. What holds traditional relationships together

    A. Role: Male knows what society expects of his role and so does female

    B. Ritual: Life is programmed by events

    C. Religion: Sanctifies traditional relationship

IV. Actor/reactor: The roles created by society over the centuries

    A. Actor = Male = Mr. Macho: Is aggressive, emotionless, does not have needs, is a sexual performer and initiator and feels like a machine

    B. Reactor = Female = Earthmother: Is passive, indirect aggressor, gives up autonomy, is sexually submissive, is emotional, sees self as a child who is controlled and used

    C. Result can be withdrawing, passive men and raging women who destroy one another

---

5. A Fable

Read the following fable and rank the characters on the basis of how much you like each person. Your number-one rank will be the person you like best; number five, the person you like the least. This information will be shared.

Once upon a time, four people lived on a river. On one side of the river lived Ann and Jack. On the other side of the river, Ralph and Mike lived. None of the people could cross the river because they had no boats and there were no bridges or safe places to swim across. The river was infested with crocodiles and piranhas. It was possible to talk across the river, and over a period of time Ann and Ralph fell in love and spent a great deal of time looking at and talking to each other. They became engaged but had no way of getting together.

Ann and Jack were friends and Jack was Ann's confidant. On the other side of the river, Mike and Ralph were also friends.

One day a sailor, Sinbad, came down the river on his boat. He was hailed by Ann, who asked him to take her across the river so that she could be with Ralph, her betrothed. Sinbad agreed to do this on one condition — that she let him sleep with her.

Ann was placed in a deep conflict by this offer and she sought help from Jack, her friend and confidant. Jake spent several hours talking with Ann. He was most sympathetic to her plight, but essentially communicated that he had confidence that Ann could make up her own mind about this decision.

Ann decided to take up Sinbad's offer. She spent the night with Sinbad on his boat, and the next day Sinbad deposited her on the opposite shore. Ralph was awaiting her landing and they embraced at once.

After a while, Ralph asked her how she had managed to convince Sinbad to take her across and Ann told him the whole story.

Upon hearing the story, Ralph pushed Ann away and said he would have nothing more to do with her.

Just at this time, Mike came by. He had overheard what happened, and as soon as he saw Ralph pushing Ann away, he moved in and beat up Ralph thoroughly.

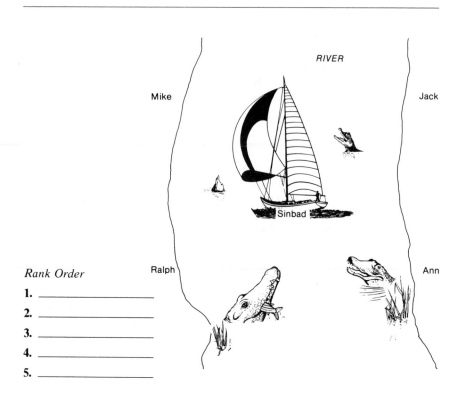

Rank Order

1. _____
2. _____
3. _____
4. _____
5. _____

OVERVIEW OF READINGS

William Schutz has been studying the influence of personality needs on interpersonal and small group interaction for over forty years. During this time he has identified the three basic needs described in this chapter of *inclusion, control,* and *affection.* In this article he elaborates on the manner in which these needs consistently influence our interaction patterns with others.

In the second article, Richard Christie elaborates on the topic of Machiavellianism discussed in this chapter. In the past ten years or so, this individual characteristic has been found to be very important in predicting interactions with others. Machiavellian behaviors are at once some of the most interesting and the most frightening to observe and to study. To learn why Christie chose to study Machiavellianism, read on.

The
Interpersonal

William Schutz

Our self-concept is largely derived from our relations with other people. In our dealings we exchange various commodities with these people and must make adjustments. In order to understand this interpersonal level I will use a framework first introduced in my book *FIRO*.

Each person has three basic interpersonal needs that are manifested in behavior and feelings toward other people. But this activity is rooted in a person's feelings about himself, his self-concept. The three basic need areas are posited to be *inclusion, control,* and *affection.*

Inclusion refers to feelings about being important or significant, of having some worth so that people will care. The aspect of the self-concept related to *control* is the feeling of competence, including intelligence, appearance, practicality, and general ability to cope with the world. The area of *affection* revolves around feelings of being lovable, of feeling that if one's personal core is revealed in its entirety it will be seen as a lovely thing.

Inclusion behavior refers to associations between people, being excluded or included, belonging, togetherness. The need to be included manifests itself as wanting to be attended to, and to attract attention and interaction. The college militant is often objecting mostly to the lack of attention paid him, the automated student. Even if he is given negative attention he is partially satisfied.

Being a distinct person — that is, having a particular identity — is an essential aspect of inclusion. An integral part of being recognized and paid attention to is that the individual be distinguishable from other people. The height of being identifiable is to be understood, since it implies that someone is interested enough to discover a person's unique characteristics.

An issue that arises frequently at the outset of group relations is that of commitment, the decision to become involved in a given relationship. Usually, in the initial testing of a relationship, individuals try to present themselves to one another partly to find out what facet of themselves others will be interested in. Frequently a member is silent at first because he is not sure that people are interested in him.

Inclusion is unlike affection in that it does not involve strong emotional attachments to individual persons. It is unlike control in that the preoccupation is with prominence, not dominance. Since inclusion involves the process of formation, it usually occurs first in the life of a group. People must decide whether they do or don't want to form a group.

A person who has too little inclusion, the undersocial, tends to be introverted and withdrawn. He consciously wants to maintain this distance between himself and others, and insists that he doesn't want to get enmeshed with people and lose his privacy. Unconsciously, however, he definitely wants others to pay attention to him. His biggest fears are that people will ignore him and would just as soon leave him behind. His unconscious attitude may be summarized by, "No one is interested in me, so I'm not going to risk being ignored. I'll stay away from people and get along by myself." He has a strong drive toward self-sufficiency as a technique for existence without others. Behind his withdrawal is the private feeling that others don't understand him. His deepest anxiety, that referring to the self-concept, is that he is worthless. He thinks that if no one ever considered him important enough to receive attention, he must be of no value whatsoever.

The oversocial person tends toward extroversion. He seeks people incessantly and wants them to seek him out. He is also afraid that they will ignore him. His unconscious feelings are the same as those of the withdrawn person, but his overt behavior is the opposite. His unconscious attitude is summarized by, "Although no one is interested in me, I'll make people pay attention to me in any way I can." His inclination is always to seek companionship, for he is the type who can't stand to be alone. All of his activities will be designed to be done in a group.

The interpersonal behavior of the oversocial type of person is designed to focus attention on himself, to make people notice him, to be prominent. The direct method is to be an intensive, exhibitive participator. By simply forcing himself on the group, he forces the group to focus attention on him. A more subtle technique is to try to acquire power (control) or to be well-liked (affection), but it is still for the primary purpose of gaining attention.

To the individual for whom inclusion was resolved in childhood, interaction with people presents no problem. He is comfortable with or without people. He can be a high or low participant in a group without anxiety. He is capable of strong commitment to and involvement with certain groups, but can also withhold commitment if he feels it is appropriate. Unconsciously, he feels that he is a worthwhile, significant person.

On the physical level, inclusion has to do with penetration of the boundaries between the self and the rest of the world, and therefore deals primarily with the periphery of the body, the skin and sense organs, the eyes, ears, nose, and mouth. Attitudes toward these organs may be related to attitudes toward being included with people. If contact with people is a fearsome thing, then the eyes keep people from intruding by not seeing others clearly, and then in order to see them clearly, it is permitted to put up a barrier — a barrier called glasses. When eyes are in the active process of seeing, and don't really want to see, they become dull and seem to retire toward the back of the head. Ears which don't want inclusion hear people who are close as if they were far away. Closeness is not accepted and people are kept at a distance. The mouth and lips become tight and impenetrable. The skin shies away from being touched; it is easily tickled, gets rashes and hives easily so that people will not come near. The muscles of the skin may also become tightened so that feeling is minimized, resulting in a leathery touch feeling.

All of these devices need not be used by one individual. There are probably special circumstances that bring about the preeminence of one over the other. The rock opera *Tommy* describes a boy who sees his mother in bed with another man and becomes blind, who hears them talking and becomes deaf, and who is told never to tell anyone what he saw and heard and becomes mute. In a dramatic form this is probably a good example for the reason for specifying which sense organ is the preferred one for avoiding inclusion.

On a recent trip that involved discussing work with a large number of people, my voice started getting hoarse, which I took to mean that I didn't want to talk any more. But then I noticed my hearing becoming erratic. Of course it was psychological; I simply didn't want to listen to all these people anymore. I began to understand how desirable and possible it would be to become deaf, at least in that situation.

If being included is important, the body may reflect it by having these peripheral organs perform in the opposite way. The eyes become vigilant, looking for people in order to see them clearly. They try to see people who are far away as actually being closer. Possible outcomes of this are especially good vision and perhaps vertical lines between the eyebrows reflecting the effort put into seeing clearly. You can try this right now by looking at some boject, preferably a person, in two ways. First look at him dully, as if your eyes were open but actually way back in your head and seeing as little as possible while appearing to give attention. Then look at the same object and feel your eyes leap out and grab him, taking in every aspect of him. The difference in the two feelings is usually very marked and gives some sense of how voluntary such a common phenomenon as looking can be.

The person with a high need for inclusion will have acute senses of smell and hearing, bringing far things near. The skin is receptive to touch and probably is open and soft. This is the pure inclusion pattern. Very quickly complications arise. The person open to inclusion can be sensitive to rejection and develop a barrier. Or he may allow touch and then be afraid.

An interesting body difference occurred in a class in Rolfing. One man who was learning to be a Rolfer, reacted to the assaults of the teacher Ida Rolf — who uses assault as a teaching method — by immediately responding with a defense, a self-justification, a counterattack, a lengthy explanation. I on the other hand responded to her attacks with utter coolness and calm, allowing her to continue unabated, sometimes agreeing with her point, possibly joking away some of her steam, while underneath, quietly knowing that I was right.

When it came to Rolfing each of us, a startling difference appeared in the way we responded at the periphery of our bodies, the skin. When my friend was physically penetrated he would scream and holler, ask for time out, complain, cry, and reassess the competence of the Rolf practitioner. I would feel most of those things, too, but be very stoic and allow the practitioner to penetrate quite far. But then he would be disconcerted by two things. When he took his hand out my skin would spring back to where it was like rubber, apparently unaffected by his push. Also, if he pushed deeply enough into the flesh, he met a barrier that felt like steel. In other words, he and I represented in our bodies almost the identical reactions we made psychologically, his immediate response, my apparent acceptance but deeper resistance.

Another possibility in exploring the physical correlates of inclusion comes from a comment about sexual intercourse, and brings up physical function to add to the structural physical considerations I have been talking about. In the sexual act, various phases can be distinguished that parallel inclusion, control, and affection. Inclusion problems refer to the initial phases of the act, the feelings about penetration. A male with problems of inclusion will probably have erection problems. His conflict over whether or not to penetrate would be reflected in the nervous enervation of the penis and its willingness or not to be ready to enter. A similar situation arises for a woman where inclusion problems are reflected in the readiness of her vagina to receive the penis, whether she's loose enough and moist enough. Also, the pelvic muscles for both that should be relaxed for maximum pleasure may be tightened if conflict still exists.

Breathing is also primarily an inclusion phenomenon. It's the way of entering or leaving any situation. If no commitment is desired the breath is cut off along with a tightening of the muscles. This cuts down virtually all vital functions. A full commitment of a person's time and energy involves full breathing, a charged-up body. The Indians and yogis have recognized the importance of breathing control, pranayama, for centuries. It is the key to someone's involvement. Routinely, when I'm giving a lecture or demonstration to a large group, I will begin by doing some activity that requires them to breathe deeply, either screaming, pounding, deep breathing, or anything that gets them pumped up. I find it makes a big difference in the audience's attention and presence.

The same holds for an encounter group. Whenever a member shows a lack of involvement, getting him into some activity requiring deep breathing almost inevitably brings him in. Breathing patterns become ingrained early in life, and a person is usually not aware of his lack of full breathing. Improving the breathing pattern is probably one of the fastest ways to change the feeling of the entire organism. In bioenergetic therapy, the "air or breath is equivalent to the spirit, the pneuma of ancient religions, a symbol of the divine power residing in God, the father figure. Breathing is an aggressive act in that inspiration is an active process. The body sucks in the air. The way one breathes manifests one's feeling about his right to get what he wants from life."

In terms of the body systems, not only are the sense organs and respiration related to inclusion, but so are the digestive and excretory systems, which focus on exchange with the environment and which deal with whether an object will be in or out of the body. These systems express the body's desire to incorporate or reject outside objects. A person with a desire to exclude will reject food and/or excrete readily and, in the extreme, develop vomiting and diarrhea. One who is anxious to include will go in the other direction, namely, overeating and constipation. A well-resolved relation in the inclusion area should result in good digestion and elimination.

If we consider the interaction between a person and his body, the inclusion problem is one of energy. A body excludes itself in the world by being energyless. The difference between living and not living is the difference between having the flows of energy, nerve impulses, blood circulation, breathing, and so on, and not having them. When a body includes itself, it is filled with energy and feeling.

Hence the problem of inclusion is in or out; the interaction centers on encounter, and the physical aspect is that of energy.

Control behavior refers to the decision-making process between people and areas of power, influence, and authority. The need for control varies along a continuum from the desire for authority over others (and therefore over one's future) to the need to be controlled and have responsibility lifted from oneself.

An argument provides the setting for distinguishing the inclusion-seeker from the control-seeker. The one seeking inclusion or prominence wants very much to be one of the participants in the argument, while the control-seeker wants to be the winner, or, if not the winner, on the same side as the winner. If forced to choose, the prominence-seeker would prefer to be the losing participant, while the dominance-seeker would prefer to be a winning nonparticipant.

Control is also manifested in behavior directed toward people who try to control. Expressions of independence and rebellion exemplify lack of willingness to be controlled, while compliance, submission, and taking orders indicate various degrees of accepting control. There is no necessary relation between an individual's behavior toward controlling others and his behavior toward being controlled. The sergeant may domineer his men, for example, and also accept orders from his lieutenant with pleasure and gratefulness, while the neighborhood bully may dominate his peers and also rebel against his parents.

Control behavior differs from inclusion behavior in that it does not require prominence. The power behind the throne is an excellent example of a role that would fill a high-control need and a low need for inclusion. The joker exemplifies a high-inclusion and low need for control. Control behavior differs from affection behavior in that it has to do with power relations rather than emotional closeness. The frequent difficulties between those who want to get down to business and those who want to get to know one another better illustrate a situation in which control behavior is more important for some and affection behavior for others.

Concern about one's competence, especially in the area of masculinity, leads to overmasculine responses. This is often seen in politics, where concern about one's assertiveness often leads to absurd overreaction to physical threats, especially when a government official has police or soldiers at his disposal.

Control problems usually follow those of inclusion in the development of a group or of an interpersonal relationship. Once the group has formed, it begins to differentiate; different people take or seek different roles, and often power struggles, competition, and influence become central issues. In terms of interaction, these issues are matters of confrontation, to use a term now in vogue.

The extreme person who is too low on control, called an abdicrat, is one who tends toward submission and abdication of power and responsibility in his interpersonal behavior. He gravitates toward a subordinate position where he will not have to take responsibility for making decisions, where someone else takes charge. He consciously wants people to relieve him of his obligations. He does not control others even when he should; for example, he would not take charge even during a fire in a children's schoolhouse in which he was the only adult. He never makes a decision if he can refer it to someone else.

For the individual who has successfully resolved his relations in the control area in childhood, power and control present no problem. He feels comfortable giving or not giving orders, taking or not taking orders, whatever is appropriate to the situation. Unlike the abdicrat and autocrat, he is not preoccupied with fears of his own helplessness, stupidity, and incompetence. He feels that other people respect his competence and will be realistic with respect to trusting him with decision-making.

Speculation on the physical concomitants of control behavior begins with control of the muscles through tightening and through intellectual or nervous system activity. The central nervous system, along with the endocrine system, is generally credited with controlling the anatomy.

Ida Rolf has a fascinating concept of the relation of the core of the body, by which she means the head and spinal column, to the envelope, which includes the two girdles, the pelvic and shoulder girdles with attached appendages, legs and arms. Her idea is that the core represents *being* and the envelope *doing*. Some people develop one and not the other, both, or neither.

For a male, a great deal of control is usually expressed in the formation of the upper arms, shoulders, and neck. Attaining masculinity is frequently related to having hulking, heavily developed shoulders and neck and back muscles. Wrestlers and football linemen typify this formation in the extreme, as the large muscle that goes from the middle of the back up into the neck, the trapezius, is so overdeveloped that it appears that they have no necks.

The feeling of being out of control, and thereby vulnerable, was brought home to me personally when a Rolfer working on my neck freed the trapezius muscle that I had held chronically tight so that my head and neck began to rise up out of my shoulders. As I stood there with my head elevated to a place where it felt both unfamiliar and wonderfully free, I felt frightened. The image that came to mind was of the boy in the circus who sticks his head through the bullseye of a target for people to throw balls at. I felt very exposed, very much in plain sight for everyone to see, with no place to hide. You may capture some of that feeling by standing up straight, putting your chin in and letting your head rise up as if it had a string through the crown, and let your shoulders relax down. When you get as high as you can, look around. When this happened to me I had a clear feeling of why my head had sunk into my shoulders. It was safer, more protected, and less vulnerable.

In general, the pattern of muscle tensions represents the defense pattern of a person. It is the way in which he controls himself so that he can cope with the world. A pattern of no chronic muscle tensions — as opposed to muscle tone — would then represent a nondefensive state, perhaps something like the egolessness of the Eastern mystics.

Intellectual control involves voluntary shaping of the body propensities. Control is exercised over the body's desires by moral codes and in line with parental upbringing so that thought is used to govern action.

In the interaction between a person and his body, the control problem is one of centering. A body undercontrolled is disorganized; a body overcontrolled is rigid. A well-controlled body functions with integration among its parts so that they flow easily and appropriately. Inappropriate movement and coordination result when the body is uncertain of what it is doing. Centering means placing everything in its appropriate place so that one is "hooked-up." Being off center makes all movement slightly disconnected.

In the sexual act, control has to do with the occasion and timing of the orgasms and the direction of movement. Withholding an orgasm is an act of personal control that often has a hostile motive, "you can't satisfy me." Sexual control problems would include difficulty of orgasm, premature ejaculation, and the lack of ability to let go.

Thus the problem of control is top or bottom; the primary interaction is confrontation, and the physical aspect is that of centering.

Affection behavior refers to close personal emotional feelings between two people, especially love and hate in their various degrees. Affection is a dyadic relation, that is, it can occur only between pairs of people at any one time, whereas both inclusion and control relations may occur either in dyads or between one person and a group of persons.

Since affection is based on building emotional ties, it is usually the last phase to emerge in the development of a human relation. In the inclusion phase, people must *encounter* each other and decide to continue their relation; control issues require them to *confront* one another and work out how they will be related. To continue the relation, affection ties must form and people must embrace each other to form a lasting bond, and also to say goodbye.

The person with too little affection, the underpersonal type, tends to avoid close ties with others. He maintains his one-to-one relations on a superficial, distant level and is most comfortable when others do the same with him. He consciously wishes to maintain this emotional distance, and frequently expresses a desire not to get emotionally involved, while unconsciously he seeks a satisfactory affectional relation. His fear is that no one loves him, and in a group situation he is afraid he won't be liked. He has great difficulty in genuinely liking people, and distrusts their feelings toward him.

His attitude could be summarized by, "I find the affection area very painful since I have been rejected, therefore I shall avoid close personal relations in the future." The direct technique of the underpersonal is to avoid emotional closeness or involvement, even to the point of being antagonistic. The subtle technique is to be superficially friendly to everyone. This behavior acts as a safeguard against having to get close to, or become personal with, any one person.

In his self-concept, the underpersonal believes that if people knew him well, they would discover traits that make him unlovable. As opposed to the inclusion anxiety that the self is worthless and empty, and the control anxiety that the self is stupid and irresponsible, the affection anxiety is that the self is nasty and unlovable.

The overpersonal type attempts to become extremely close to others. He definitely wants others to treat him in a very close way. The unconscious feeling on which he operates is, "My first experiences with affection were painful, but perhaps if I try again they will turn out to be better." Being liked is extremely important to him in his attempt to relieve his anxiety about being always rejected and unloved. The direct technique for being liked is an overt attempt to gain approval, be extremely personal, ingratiating, intimate, and confiding. The subtle technique is more manipulative and possessive, to devour friends and subtly punish any attempts by them to establish other friendships.

The basic feelings for the overpersonal are the same as those for the underpersonal. Both responses are extreme, both are motivated by a strong need for affection, both are accompanied by a strong anxiety about ever being loved and basically about being unlovable, and both have considerable hostility behind them stemming from the anticipation of rejection.

For the individual who successfully resolved his affectional relations in childhood, close emotional interaction with another person presents no problem. He is comfortable in such a personal relation as well as in a situation requiring emotional distance. It is important for him to be liked, but if not he can accept the fact that the dislike is the result of the relation between himself and one other person; in other words, the dislike does not mean that he is a totally unlovable person. And he is capable of giving genuine affection.

The primary interaction of the affection area is that of embrace, either literal or symbolic. The expression of appropriate deeper feelings is the major issue, particularly in group situations, where a paradox arises. At the beginning of the group there are many expressions as to how difficult it is to express hostility to people. It often later develops that there is only one thing more difficult — expressing warm, positive feelings.

A difference between inclusion, control, and affection behavior is illustrated by the different feelings a man has in being turned down by a fraternity, failed in a course by a professor, and rejected by his girl. The fraternity excludes him, telling him that as a group they don't have sufficient interest in him. The professor fails him and says, in effect, that he finds him incompetent in his field. His girl rejects him, implying that she doesn't find him lovable.

The affectional aspect of the sexual act is the feeling that follows its completion. This can be anything from a flood of warm, affectionate, loving feelings to a revulsion and thoughts of "what am I doing here?" It depends partly on how well the heart and genitals are connected. The circulatory (heart) and reproductive (genital) systems are most directly related to the area of affection.

In the interaction between a person and his body, the affectional problem is one of *acceptance*. The body may be charged up with energy and coordinated through centering, but the problem of body acceptance remains. An accepted body can allow feeling to flow through it without avoiding any part. Sensation is not blocked. An unaccepted body works against itself, trying to become sickly or dissociated. Thus, the ideal body feels energetic, centered, and acceptable.

With respect to an interpersonal relation, inclusion is concerned primarily with the formation of a relation, whereas control and affection are concerned with relations already formed. Within existent relations, control is the area concerned with who gives orders and makes decisions, whereas affection is concerned with how emotionally close or distant the relation becomes.

In summary, the problem of affection is close or far; the interaction is embrace, and the physical aspect is acceptance.

Why Machiavelli?

Richard Christie

Since the publication of *The Prince* in 1532, the name of its author has come to designate the use of guile, deceit, and opportunism in interpersonal relations. Traditionally, the "Machiavellian" is someone who views and manipulates others for his own purposes. But is it true that the person who agrees with Machiavelli's ideas behaves differently from one who disagrees with him? This book describes efforts to answer this question.

Historians disagree as to whether Machiavelli was a cynic who wrote political satire, a patriot, or the first modern political scientist. The present concern is not with Machiavelli as an historic figure, but as the source of ideas about those who manipulate others.

Our readings confirmed the impression that much of the speculation about the personal characteristics of those wielding power over others was in terms of lay psychology or had been largely influenced by concepts taken from psychopathology. The social visibility of leaders tends to draw attention to them. Both their virtues and their flaws are more publicized and written about than those of less outstanding members of society. This makes it possible to develop a psychiatric interpretation of Napoleon's sexual behavior, while similar behavior by foot soldiers in his armies is more apt to elicit a sociological examination. Although depth psychology has been more frequently invoked to explain the behavior of prominent figures than those of less renown, it does not necessarily follow that those who exert influence are more prone to psycho-

From Richard Christie and Florence L. Geis, *Studies in Machiavellianism* (New York: Academic Press, 1970), pp. 1-9. Reprinted by permission.

pathology. We were reluctant to accept the premise implicit in much of the literature that pathology and power are intertwined in the manipulator.

Consequently, Agger, Pinner, and I adopted the strategy of viewing the manipulator or operator in terms of an hypothetical role model. We asked ourselves what abstract characteristics must someone who is effective in controlling others have? What kind of person should he be?

The following characteristics struck us as being important:

1. *A relative lack of affect* [feelings] *in interpersonal relationships.* In general, it seemed that success in getting others to do what one wishes them to do would be enhanced by viewing them as objects to be manipulated rather than as individuals with whom one has empathy. The greater the emotional involvement with others, the greater is the likelihood of identifying with their point of view. Once empathy occurs, it becomes more difficult to use psychological leverage to influence others to do things they may not want to do.

2. *A lack of concern with conventional morality.* Conventional morality is difficult to define, but we were thinking here in terms of the findings that most people think lying, cheating, and other forms of deceit are, although common, reprehensible. Whether manipulators are amoral or immoral is a moot problem, and one which probably concerns them less than those who are manipulated. The premise here is that those who manipulate have a utilitarian rather than a moral view of their interactions with others.

3. *A lack of gross psychopathology.* The manipulator was hypothesized as taking an instrumentalist or rational view of others. Such a person would make errors in evaluating other individuals and the situation if his emotional needs seriously distorted his perceptions. Presumably, most neurotics and psychotics show deficiencies in reality testing and, by and large, fail in crucial ways in relating to others. Note that we were not suggesting that manipulators are the epitome of mental health; we were proposing that their contact with at least the more objective aspects of reality would have to be, almost by definition, within the normal range.

4. *Low ideological commitment.* The essence of successful manipulation is a focus upon getting things done rather than a focus upon long-range ideological goals. Although manipulators might be found in organizations of diverse ideologies, they should be more involved in tactics for achieving possible ends than in an inflexible striving for an ultimate idealistic goal.

3

Internal
Influences

Group Circumstances and Structure

THE TUBBS MODEL OF SMALL GROUP INTERACTION

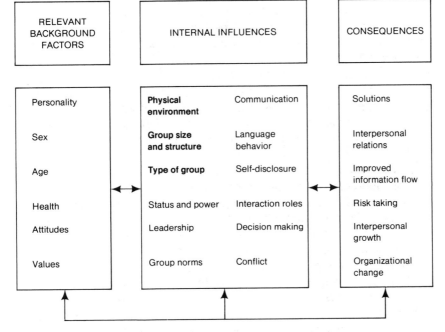

RELEVANT BACKGROUND FACTORS	INTERNAL INFLUENCES		CONSEQUENCES
Personality	**Physical environment**	Communication	Solutions
Sex	**Group size and structure**	Language behavior	Interpersonal relations
Age	**Type of group**	Self-disclosure	Improved information flow
Health	Status and power	Interaction roles	Risk taking
Attitudes	Leadership	Decision making	Interpersonal growth
Values	Group norms	Conflict	Organizational change

Concepts in **boldface** are the emphases of this chapter.

CASE STUDY

Where have I been and where am I going? These questions plague all people at times. This is the story of Scheryl Schultz, who's been around for 43 years and feels fortunate to understand where she's been, what she has been doing, and where she hopes to go.

The summer of 1977 began my search for some inner peace. My husband had a blocked coronary artery, and a change of life-style was in order. He had conferred with three top doctors in Detroit, Ann Arbor, and Cleveland, who recommended bypass surgery within two years. He had in the previous eight months altered his diet, but altering his life-style was more difficult. When you've spent your whole life as a competitive person in all your endeavors, it's difficult to assimilate the finality of the doctor's advice.

My husband became depressed, but he figured that if he could use strict discipline with his diet and cut down on the number of miles he ran a day he could buy some extra time before he would have to submit to an operation. In April he was given the diagnosis and by Labor Day his head had cleared and his outlook was brighter. He went for a casual run through the neighborhood on a very humid day and collapsed in the street.

I got a call from the neighbor, who had investigated some muffled sounds and found my husband. She had called for emergency aid and my husband was ready to leave for the hospital by the time she called me. The thoughts that flew through my head were that he would be okay and that this was exactly what the doctors in Cleveland had predicted. We had been told that he had a classic case of hereditary coronary artery disease, and that if he continued to run, within six months he'd be a statistic we'd read about in the paper.

Jerry came through the collapse all right, but the decision had to be made as to when to have the operation. The two-year option plan had run out! We opted for a December 12th date, because of complicating circumstances like one son in Colorado in school, one about to leave for New Jersey for school, and a daughter with a Bat Mitzvah at Thanksgiving. I had been looking forward to the boys going away to school so that I could take some more graduate classes or get a part-time job. The reality of the matter was that I had my hands full. My husband's self-confidence dwindled and all the talking I did on a layperson's level didn't seem to work. I felt he needed professional counseling, but he was opposed to that prospect. The only other option that I knew was to help myself by becoming stronger and more definite in my opinions. Jerry sought out friends to talk to, both business and professional, but that brought only momentary relief. His capability to work diminished. By the time we left Detroit for Cleveland I was determined to advise the doctor of his depression as soon as we got there and get him professional counseling through the Cleveland Clinic. I knew that your attitude toward yourself was either a positive or negative factor in your recovery.

During the four-hour drive to Cleveland my husband came to terms with himself and became determined to give it his best shot. It was amazing how just leaving town removed an enormous weight and helped him to regain control of his senses. The pre-op counseling for patients and family at the hospital was not as good as we had expected. The families of patients had to be at the hospital by 6:30 a.m. the day of the operation and then walk with the patients while they were being wheeled to surgery. That procedure sure didn't reassure me. The patient was sedated so how would he know who was walking and wheeling him to surgery? Then we were sent to a large waiting room where people from the whole hospital waited for surgery patients to return. All I can say is that if you didn't take up smoking or drinking or both while you waited for at least three and one-half hours with phones ringing off the hook and names being called — you would never smoke or drink. I went to the ladies' room and did light stretching exercises, and when I found it helped me I brought in a couple of other women in the same circumstances.

After the operation was over the surgeon called us in and told us it was successful. My sister-in-law and I both brought pads and pens to take notes. The first thing the doctor said was to put down our pads and pens and look and listen to him. I was impressed by his self-confidence and the enthusiasm with which he spoke of his skills. His incredible good looks, fine physique, and soothing voice certainly did help my nerves as well. He not only educated us on the spot, but made us feel positive about a total recovery.

Consequently, when I did see my husband for thirty minutes two days later, the doctor's enthusiasm was still with me and I could share it with my husband. The two days he was in intensive care were the worst for me because I had no privacy. My brother-in-law and sister-in-law felt that if we kept on the move it would be better for us all.

After they left and I had my own room and freedom to choose how to spend my time, I became my old self again. I could only see my husband for thirty minutes each evening, so that left a lot of time for self-disclosure sessions with relatives of other patients. We all stayed at the same hotel and had husbands or parents with varying degrees of heart disease. It didn't matter that we weren't the same age, sex, color, or from the same social background. In these informal sessions we rid ourselves of tension by disclosing our personal feelings. By the time we left the Cleveland Clinic we were all buddies, and so were the patients. Their disclosing themselves to one another while being hospitalized was an important ingredient in both their mental and physical recovery. My husband, during his hospitalization, became a real negotiator among the other men to help them get their spirits up to more normal standards.

After we returned to Detroit, he continued to work on getting himself back together by walking, writing, reading, and eating properly. His confidence was coming back, but it would take some time. His six-week checkup was positive, and after a two-week vacation of sun and rest he went back to work.

It was just six weeks after his return to work that our next crisis occurred. While I was out doing some "shopping therapy," as a friend calls it, and my husband was at the YWCA exercising, our younger son took the telephone call that would dramatically change all our lives. Our 28-year-old son had been in a terrible automobile accident in Nevada. His car was demolished, his friend was dying, and our son was in critical condition. Both boys were being helicoptered from Nevada to Salt Lake City, Utah, for more specialized care. By the time I got home, around four o'clock, I had one hour to make arrangements for my children and leave with my husband. Luckily our 18-year-old son was home from school on spring break and could stay with his sister. I called in an older woman to help take care of them and the house.

On the plane to Salt Lake City I was overwhelmed with what to worry about first. My first impulse was, wouldn't it be great to run away? Then I realized I was really and truly needed and would have to play it by ear and help whomever needed it the most. I knew my son's life was out of my hands. It was a matter that only God and the doctors could help. I knew he was scheduled for the second helicopter ride; his friend would go first because he was in worse condition. I knew I'd get through this mess one way or another, but I really didn't know about my husband. It might be one blow too many for him.

When we got to the hospital we were met by the neurosurgeon, Dr. Hood. He cautiously explained to us what had happened, what we could expect, and what was being done for our son. We are grateful to this day for his communication skills as well as his professional expertise.

My husband and I settled in for a long wait. I went to see our son, who was in a coma. He lay strapped to the bed with tubes coming out from seemingly everywhere, and several screens were monitoring his responses. His hands were literally skinned and so were his knees and feet. The biggest concern was a deep skull fracture. We knew his friend was worse. They lay side by side in the same room with every bodily function being monitored as hour after hour dragged by. I have seen sick and dying middle-aged people, and sick and withering old people, but there is nothing worse than watching two boys, their bodies in their prime, fighting for their lives. The doctors and nurses said the same thing.

What do you do in a situation like this? My husband talked and cried a lot. He talked to everyone — the doctors, nurses, relatives by long-distance phone, his own doctor, the other boy's parents, and me. Under extreme stress I talked only to my husband, a Catholic Sister, and myself. I sat on the carpeted floor of the intensive-care hallway, where I watched and waited. For some reason I felt secure on that floor and sat there most of the night.

When the doctors realized for sure that my son's friend was dying, they ordered the boys put in separate rooms. An additional pressure at that time was that his parents were donating his eyes and his kidneys to the University of Utah Donor Bank. Paul was kept alive artificially until the operations could be arranged. The worst pressure I felt during the whole three-week ordeal was when the head of the body parts center came to look over the donor. He also watched my son's monitoring systems. I wanted to run and beat on him when he entered my son's room. It was like he was casting an evil eye on my son and I wanted to pull him away.

When Paul died and my boy was still alive, although in a coma, I felt as a mother a tremendous guilt. The expression from the Bible about "who shall live and who shall die" floated through my head. I realized how many basic questions have no answers.

Once Paul's parents and family left Salt Lake City, we felt a great sense of relief. We could then concentrate our efforts on helping ourselves and survey our realizable possibilities for our son. Luckily you can only live a day at a time, because under those circumstances that is difficult enough.

After our son had spent five days in a drug-induced coma, the doctors decided to try to bring him out. Their timing was right and after two days of reduced drugs he regained consciousness. His girl friend was there with us when he started to wake up. The love he showed for this young girl was the most singularly beautiful emotion I have ever witnessed. He could only use his eyes to make contact because his mouth had a cork in it and he was taped and tubed everywhere else.

I wanted to document this occasion for myself as well as for the girl friend. The next morning I went off by myself to look around and be alone with my thoughts. I thought of buying a crystal paperweight for this girl because the properties it possessed came so close to what I was feeling about life and death and love. When I walked into a gift shop I was overcome with emotion and couldn't talk. I asked for a paper and pencil and wrote the saleswoman a note explaining to her what had happened, what I wanted, why I wanted it, and I asked her opinion of what I wanted to do. The salesperson started to cry and I knew I was on the right track.

1. *If you were a counselor, how would you try to offer help to this family?*

2. *Are there any issues in this case that apply to families in general? If so, what are they?*

T he case study beautifully illustrated a family group. In this chapter we will be looking at several very different types of groups ranging from the family or primary group to street gangs, encounter groups, and problem-solving groups. Although each type of group differs from the others, some common conceptual links connect all types of groups. The first factor that is relevant to all groups is the so-called ecology of the group.

The dispute over the size and shape of the negotiating table at the Paris peace talks in 1968 represents one of the most significant examples in our nation's history of ecology in group discussion. The disagreement lasted eight months and was typical of the many political implications of each issue under negotiation. McCroskey, Larson, and Knapp (1971, p. 97) explain the reasons for the dispute:

> The United States (US) and South Viet Nam (SVN) wanted a seating arrangement in which only two sides were identified. They did not want to recognize the National Liberation Front (NLF) as an "equal" party in the negotiations. North Viet Nam (NVN) and the NLF wanted "equal" status given to all parties — represented by a four-sided table. The final arrangement was such that both parties could claim victory. The round table minus the dividing lines allowed North Viet Nam and the NLF to claim all four delegations were equal. The existence of the two secretarial tables (interpreted as dividers), the lack of identifying symbols on the table, and an AA, BB speaking rotation permitted the United States and South Viet Nam to claim victory for the two-sided approach. Considering the lives lost during the eight months needed to arrive at the seating arrangement, we can certainly conclude that territorial space has extremely high priority in some interpersonal settings.

In this chapter we will look more closely at small group ecology as well as other internal influences in small group interaction.

Chapter 1 defined *internal influences* on a group as factors that are influenced by the individual characteristics of group members and that in turn influence a group's functioning and its ultimate end results. Internal influences are somewhat under the control of group members (that is, members are able to change them). In this chapter we will examine three major types of internal influence: (1) physical environment, (2) group structure, and (3) type of group.

PHYSICAL ENVIRONMENT

For many years writers have hypothesized that a room's environment influences the interaction within it. Supposedly, "warm" colors, hues of orange, red, and brown, facilitate interaction, while "cool" hues of blue and green tend to encourage reserved, formal conversation. A series of studies conducted to systematically test these assumptions (Maslow and Mintz 1956; Wong and Brown 1923; Bilodeau and Schlosberg 1959) found that people consistently associated an ugly room with monotony, fatigue, irritability, headache, discontent, and hostility. A beautiful room evoked such reactions as pleasure, enjoyment, importance, comfort, and a desire to remain in the room. The ugly room was stark, gray, and disheveled, while the beautiful room had carpeting, drapes, and warm beige walls. These studies also showed that mental functioning was better in beautiful rooms. Both memory and ability to solve problems were found to be better in the beautiful room. Along this same line, Barnlund (1968, p. 514) writes: "A colleague after attending a meeting in a conference room created by [Frank Lloyd] Wright was similarly impressed, confessing that he believed interpersonal antagonism could not be provoked in such a setting." Although it is doubtful that we could ever design a room that would eliminate all antagonism, it seems plausible that rooms can be designed that at least do not act as a source of irritation. It is also interesting to speculate that inadequate ventilation, heating, lighting, and roominess might serve to detract from the overall effectiveness of groups.

TERRITORIALITY

Edward Hall (1959) coined the term *territoriality* to describe the tendency for man and other animals to lay claim to and defend a particular area or territory. We are all familiar with this behavior among dogs, birds, and gorillas, but we may be less aware of our own attempts to defend our territories. It has been estimated that college students begin to identify a particular seat in the class as "their chair" by as early as the second class period. Although we probably would not ask a person to give up the chair, we would feel some annoyance at having to move to another one. This is reminiscent of the home-court advantage in basketball: teams traditionally play better on their home court than they do at "away" games.

In addition to identifying certain places as our territory, we also move about in a portable space bubble of about 18 inches in each direction that we let only certain people violate. This is referred to as our *personal space.* Sommer (1959, p. 248) distinguishes personal space from territory in the following way:

> The most important difference is that personal space is carried around while territory is relatively stationary. The animal or man will usually mark the boundaries of his territory so that they are visible to others, but the boundaries of his personal space are invisible. Personal space has the body at its center, while territory does not.

Kinzel (1969) conducted a study of inmates at the United States Medical Center for Federal Prisoners. He found that men who had committed violent crimes had a personal space or "body buffer zone" twice as large as that of prisoners classified as nonviolent. The violent group stated that they felt threatened when a person came close to them, as if the person were an intruder who was "looming up" or "rushing in" at them.

Hall (1959) describes the humorous situation in which people with different-sized space bubbles try to communicate. Arabs or South Americans will try to step closer, thus reducing the distance between them and their listeners. North American or German listeners will then step backwards to reestablish what they feel is a comfortable distance for conversation. And so it continues as one individual ends up backing the other all the way around the room. Rosenfeld (1965) found that personality factors influenced the size of one's personal space. Those high in need for affiliation (see Chapter 2) sat an average of 57 inches away from a target person, while those low in affiliation averaged 94 inches in distance.

Hall (1959) refers to the study of personal space and distance as *proxemics.* He has identified four zones that seem to influence interaction in North American culture. He points out, however, that these distances do not apply to other cultures that have different zones. The four types of distances are intimate, personal, social, and public.

Intimate distance extends from touching to about 18 inches. This distance encourages soft whispers about very confidential matters. It also allows us to use more of our senses in communicating (for example, touching, smelling, and even tasting). *Personal distance* ranges from 18 inches to about 4 feet. Conversation is usually soft and topics are usually personal. *Social distance* refers to the distance between 4 and 12 feet. At this distance voices are usually raised and the topics are nonpersonal public information for anyone to hear. *Public distance* refers to 12 feet and beyond. This requires a loud voice and impersonal topics. As we shall see later in this chapter, different groups may at one time or another involve the use of all of these four distances. Encounter groups frequently include physical touching, while large committees may be seated around tables more than 25 feet in diameter. Figure 3.1 gives more examples of various distances and kinds of communication.

DISTANCE	CONTENT	VOCAL SHIFTS
3-6 inches	Top secret	Soft whisper
8-12 inches	Very confidential topics	Audible whisper
12-20 inches	Confidential topics	Soft voice
20-36 inches	Personal topics	Soft voice
4½-5 feet	Nonpersonal topics	Full voice
5½-8 feet	Public information	Loud voice
8-20 feet	Public information to a group	Very loud voice
20-100 feet	Hailing and departing comments	Very loud voice

FIGURE 3.1
Source: Adapted from Hall 1959, pp. 163-164.

SEATING PATTERNS

Have you ever noticed the difference in interaction between a group sitting on the grass or the floor and one whose members are seated indoors around a rectangular table? One difference is that sitting on the floor or grass allows greater informality and tends to facilitate interaction. However, research has shown that even the seating patterns around rectangular tables have a major impact on interaction as well. Strodbeck and Hook (1961) found that in jury deliberations, members from professional and managerial classes took positions at the head of the table significantly more often than people from other classes. Paper-and-pencil tests revealed that those seated at the head position were chosen significantly more often as the leader. Hare and Bales (1963) found that those seated in positions marked A, C, and E in Fig. 3.2 were frequent talkers and frequently scored high on dominance in personality tests.

Sommer (1969) also studied several possible seating patterns (see Fig. 3.3). The corner-to-corner or face-to-face arrangements were most often

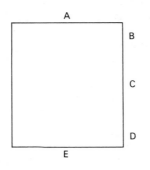

FIGURE 3.2
Seating pattern.

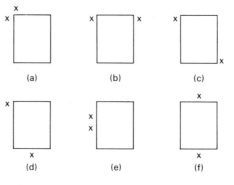

FIGURE 3.3
Seating patterns at rectangular tables:
(a) corner-to-corner, (b) face-to-face,
(c) distant-opposite, (d) corner-to-end,
(e) side-by-side, and (f) end-to-end.

preferred for casual conversation, while cooperating pairs (studying together) preferred the side-by-side arrangement. Competing pairs chose the face-to-face or the distant-opposite arrangements about equally often. Coacting pairs (those doing simultaneous but unrelated activities) preferred the distant-opposite positions, which maximized distance without the potential eye contact that might result from the end-to-end arrangement. Russo (1967) found that people seated in the more distant positions (when all positions around the rectangular table were occupied) were perceived to be less friendly, less well acquainted, and less talkative than those seated closer to the person filling out the questionnaire.

Hearn (1957) verified a phenomenon known as the "Steinzor effect" (Steinzor 1950), in which members of groups with minimal leadership directed many more comments to those facing opposite them than to those sitting on either side. However, with a dominant, assertive leader, the behaviors were reversed and significantly more conversation was directed to those sitting next to them.

Sommer (1965) also studied the seating preferences at round tables (Fig. 3.4). He found that conversing or cooperating pairs preferred to sit side by side, while competing pairs preferred to sit at distant-opposite points, and coacting pairs preferred the so-called side-to-end arrangement. These findings have been more recently corroborated by Batchelor and Goethals (1972), who found much the same information with groups who had no tables at all, but simply were allowed to move their chairs to positions they preferred.

All of this research taken collectively indicates that groups with differing personalities and tasks will exhibit predictable seating patterns. Also, dominant seating positions at the ends of rectangular tables will tend

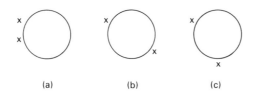

FIGURE 3.4
Seating preferences at round tables: (a) side-by-side,
(b) distant-opposite, and (c) side-to-end.

to give some members a leadership advantage and will result in some frustration and disenchantment for those in the "blind spots" on the sides of the tables.

GROUP SIZE AND STRUCTURE

The concept of group structure refers to the idea that groups are made up of people who are related to one another in a number of ways. Although group structure may include a number of interrelated topics, we will be concerned with only two: (1) communication networks and (2) group size.

COMMUNICATION NETWORKS

The research on communication networks commonly employs five different networks, which are illustrated in Fig. 3.5. Leavitt (1951) found that the central person in a network such as the wheel usually becomes the leader and enjoys the position more than those on the periphery, whose communication is much more restricted. That is, the central person can communicate to any of them, but they must direct *all* of their comments through the center. Both the chain and the Y networks have characteristics similar to the wheel. On the other hand, the circle and the all-channel patterns are much less centralized and are sometimes leaderless.

A person who dominates the discussion will sometimes create a network similar to the wheel. While this may be more centralized and efficient, it results in dependency on the leader and lower group satisfaction for everyone but the leader. The chain or the Y network allows members to communicate with one or two other persons, but not with all others in the group. This produces subgroups, decreased satisfaction, and a relatively poor amount of idea-sharing.

The all-channel network may be relatively slow, but it is superior in terms of idea-sharing and member satisfaction. Feedback is more immediate and, as a result, accuracy of communication is better. Shaw (1964) summarized the findings of 18 group network studies by concluding that

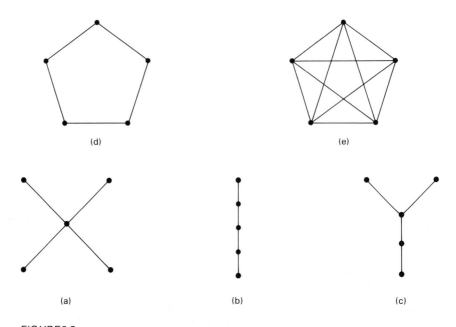

(d)   (e)

(a)   (b)   (c)

FIGURE3.5

Communication networks: (a) wheel, (b) chain, (c) Y, (d) circle, and (e) all-channel.

centralized networks such as the chain and the wheel are better for solving simple problems, such as identifying colors or picturelike symbols. However, when the problem is complex (as most real-life problems are) the *decentralized networks* such as the circle and the all-channel are faster and more accurate and result in higher member satisfaction. It seems clear that the all-channel network is the most desirable for most problem-solving situations a group would be likely to encounter.

GROUP SIZE

Perhaps one of the questions most frequently asked by students of small group interaction is, "What is the best size of group to work with?" On one hand, it seems that a relatively small group would be more efficient, while on the other hand, larger groups would have more resources from which to draw. A great deal of research has been conducted on this question and some fairly clear results emerge.

Groups of only two people may find themselves deadlocked in statements on many questions. They also suffer the disadvantage of having too few members to contribute ideas. Groups of three are still too small, and tend to result in two-against-one coalitions that leave one person out. Groups of four begin to be effective, but due to their even number of members may end up with tie votes on decisions. Bales (1954) found that the optimum group size appeared to be five. This size seems to be small enough for meaningful interaction, yet large enough to generate an adequate number of ideas for problem solving.

As groups grow larger than five, members complain that the group is too large and that they are not able to participate as often as they would like. Also, as size gets larger, there is an increasing tendency for subgroups to form, which may carry on side conversations that annoy the rest of the group and detract from the group's progress. In addition, groups of ten or more tend to spend an inordinate amount of time simply organizing themselves, so that more attention is diverted away from the task and toward simply maintaining the group's functioning.

As the group's size increases arithmetically (linearly), the potential number of interactions increases geometrically (exponentially). Bostrom (1970, p. 257) shows how rapidly these interaction patterns multiply. In a dyad (two people) only two relationships are possible, A to B and B to A, but in a triad (three people) there are nine possibilities:

A to B	B to C	A to B and C
A to C	C to B	B to A and C
B to A	C to A	C to A and B

The calculations from group sizes 2-8 are (Bostrom 1970, p. 258):

Number in Group	Interactions Possible
2	2
3	9
4	28
5	75
6	186
7	441
8	1056

Bostrom (p. 263) concludes from his study:

> The data here seem to indicate that the individual who sends more than he receives is not only more often chosen as a good discussant but is also more satisfied with the discussion than the member who receives more than he sends . . . satisfaction apparently comes from talking, not listening.

As a result of these findings it would seem obvious that it is desirable to keep the group size to about five *whenever possible,* unless some other objective such as increased widespread participation seems to be worth increasing group size. Even when increasing participation (for example, to include all members of a fraternity or sorority) is the goal, subcommittees of about five would allow the widespread participation *as well as* the efficiency and satisfaction of working in a small group. This optimal size, however, depends on the type of group. Five is the recommended size for a problem-solving group. Obviously, a work group, family group, or even some problem-solving groups may require a different number of group members, depending on the particular situation.

TYPE OF GROUP

One of the confounding problems in the study of small groups is the variety in types of groups that have been studied. It is obvious that certain critical differences will emerge when the term *group* is applied to studies of primitive tribes, street gangs, factory work groups, and artificially formed laboratory groups. Although there may be some important similarities among these various groups, we would also expect to find some real confusion resulting from attempts to compare these different groups across the board. In addition, it seems likely that differing group types will have an effect on subsequent interaction and group outcomes or end results. For example, we can be assured that social groups will interact differently from work groups, and that the outcomes of their separate group interactions will be different. In this section we will look at six commonly recognized different types of groups.

PRIMARY GROUPS

Primary groups usually include one's family and closest friends. Certainly the vast majority of attitudes and values people hold are a result of the influences of their primary groups. Primary groups influence self-concept as well as personality from childhood to adulthood. (For example, see Faris 1932, and Shils 1951.) The members of our primary groups are sometimes referred to as our "significant others," since they are probably the most important people in our lives. Although we may sometimes develop deep friendships from other associations on the job, in school, and so forth, our family members usually remain our most significant others throughout our lives.

CASUAL AND SOCIAL GROUPS

Casual and social groups include neighborhood groups, fraternities, bowling partners, golf partners, and in some cases, fellow members of street gangs. While these relationships may be relatively short-lived, their impact on behavior can be quite profound.

Whyte (1943) conducted an in-depth study of a street group — the Norton Street Gang — from a slum district in a large eastern city. The gang

FRANK AND ERNEST   by Bob Thaves

IF IT'S ALL THE SAME TO YOU, WE'D RATHER OPT FOR A LESS-STRUCTURED LIFESTYLE.

had a status hierarchy with the toughest member (Doc) at the top. The group norms dictated that each member steal and "make it" with a woman if he could, but only a "sucker" got married. Some more modern gangs require their members to commit murder as an initiation into the gang. According to one source, Los Angeles alone has nearly 200 gangs, and in 1973 New York had 27 gang-related murders, while in Philadelphia (the City of Brotherly Love) 191 youths were killed in gang wars and assassinations in a five-year period. A large percentage of gangs include mostly blacks and Chicanos. Here is a description (from *Time*, July 23, 1973, p. 32) of one black gang in Philadelphia, the Norris Avenue corner gang:

> Each Norris [gang member] is reputed to have two or three "bodies" under his belt . . . shooting someone in another gang is the surest way a younger member has of "getting a rep" and climbing in the corner hierarchy. . . . Serving a term in jail also boosts a member's reputation.

While these behaviors may seem unbelievable, they are quite real to the group members (especially the victims).

Newcomb (1943, 1963) conducted an in-depth study of the influence of college friendships on political attitudes at Bennington College. Data were collected from all of the 250 students and 50 faculty members at the school at that time. The girls had relatively conservative political views upon entering as freshmen and became progressively more liberal over the course of their four years. Newcomb found that even 30 years later these women had maintained a relatively liberal set of political attitudes. He concluded that although the college women had begun adopting liberal ideas and practices to gain acceptance with their peers, the changes remained for a lifetime. It might be interesting to stop for a moment and think about what changes you are undergoing as a result of the college experience. It is likely that these changes will differentiate you for the rest of your life from your high school friends who did not go to college.

Another systematic study of social groups was conducted by Gardner and Thompson (1956). The subjects were members of the nine fraternities at Syracuse University. Several questionnaire measures were constructed to measure the degree to which members of the fraternity reciprocally respected and liked one another. As we might expect, an individual might choose four different fraternity brothers to meet the four different psychological needs measured in the study. The four needs were (1) affiliation — simply a friendship choice; (2) playmirth — someone to go on a double date or to go have a beer with; (3) succorance — someone to tell your troubles to; and (4) achievement-recognition — someone to help you make a good impression somewhere. There was also considerable overlap in choices (that is, one friend may be chosen to meet two or more of these social needs).

Once Gardner and Thompson had conducted their measurements, they were able to determine which fraternities had the highest levels of morale or esprit de corps. In addition, independent judges (deans, housemothers, and so on) ranked the nine fraternities from best to worst based on number of honors, members, average grade point, number of trophies, and the like. On the basis of this analysis, the researchers concluded that the more a fraternity developed a high level of reciprocal liking and respect among its members, the more successful the fraternity was (that is, the higher its rank in comparison with the other fraternities). Gardner and Thompson (1956, p. 257) concluded that "cooperative group action is favored by mutually satisfying interactions between all possible pairs within the membership." In other words, compatible individual personalities tended to develop more effective groups. They also found a negative relationship between the number of other extracurricular activities of members and the success of the fraternity. It appears that a group with members who accept leadership positions in other groups suffers from that diversification of member commitment. A person who gets overextended simply doesn't have enough time for each of his or her commitments.

These studies of street gangs, college friendships, and fraternities show the profound influences that social groups have on each of us. It may very well be that we profoundly influence the social groups as well. It is worth keeping in mind that we are all creatures of experience and that these experiences help shape us for a lifetime.

EDUCATIONAL GROUPS

Educational groups may also be called learning groups or enlightenment groups. They get together for the primary purpose of study or instruction. These may include, for example, management training seminars, orientation meetings, or quarterback clubs. These groups may discuss recent books, movies, child rearing, meditation, Kung Fu, or many other topics centering around personal development. Brilhart (1974) refers to an enlightenment discussion as one in which members may attempt to solve problems without having authority to implement their decisions. Small group interaction classes frequently conduct problem-solving discussions concerning national or international issues. Unfortunately, although these groups may develop worthwhile answers to important real world problems, they are not usually in a position to implement their decisions. The experience of attempting to improve problem-solving skills, however, is a worthwhile end result even if the group's decision doesn't always actualize. It is interesting to note that even when we *do* have the authority to implement, the results are sometimes not as dramatic or satisfying as we might like. For example, one group determined an excellent solution to a campus parking problem. The solution was accepted by the university administration. However, due to a major construction program, the parking lot was torn up and replaced by a new classroom building before the new parking plan had ever been implemented.

At Harvard Business School each class may include up to one hundred people. But since group dynamics literature has shown that this number is too large for effective group discussion, the classes are broken up into smaller discussion groups of ten people each. This discussion group then becomes the school's working unit and is small enough for members to effectively relate to. Students learn from each other in discussion groups. Over the course of the term, the discussion groups often become social groups and, for some, surrogate families as well.

WORK GROUPS

Some of the most influential small group research ever to be conducted has occurred in work groups. The now-classic studies conducted by Harvard Business School in the Western Electric Hawthorne plant in Chicago are a case in point. This company is a subsidiary of AT&T and manufactures telephone equipment for the Bell System. The studies lasted from 1927 to 1932 and are described in detail by Mayo (1933) and Roethlisberger and Dickson (1939).

The studies were originally designed to determine the influence of illumination on industrial productivity. It was hypothesized that improved lighting would improve productivity. The first study showed that productivity increased whether lighting levels were increased or *decreased* to a level darker than moonlight (three footcandles). This of course puzzled the researchers.

A second study was conducted to determine the effect of periodic rest breaks on productivity. Once again it was found that productivity kept increasing whether a rest break was added or taken out of the work schedule. The researchers hypothesized that the productivity increases resulted from the workers' changed social situation, increased satisfaction, and new patterns of social interaction brought about by the creating of an experimental condition and paying of special attention to the workers. This productivity increase resulting from special attention has since been labeled the "Hawthorne effect."

In order to more carefully determine the influence of these social factors on productivity, a second set of studies was designed and labeled the Bank Wiring Observation Room experiment. Workers were observed as they wired, soldered, and inspected switchboards or "banks" of switches. Workers were on an economic incentive system that allowed them to earn more pay if they produced more. The experiment showed that workers were producing far below what they were capable of producing, due to the group's social norm enforced by the co-workers. The researchers referred to this as artificial restriction of output.

The group norm or unwritten rule was to set a relatively low level of work, which was called a fair day's work for a fair day's pay. Anyone who produced much more was branded a "rate buster" or a "speed king." Those who underproduced were called "chiselers," and those who might tell anything to a supervisor that would get them in trouble were called "squealers." In each case, the person who violated the group's norm was punched hard in the arm or shoulder, a punishment affectionately referred to as "binging." These social practices did indeed influence the workers' output more than the opportunity to earn more money for more work. The major findings of the Hawthorne studies were summarized by Etzioni (1964, pp. 34-35):

1. The level of productivity is set by social norms, not by physiological capacities.

2. Noneconomic rewards and sanctions significantly affect the behavior of the workers and largely limit the effect of economic incentive plans.

3. Often workers do not act or react as individuals but as members of groups.

See the reading by Hatvany and Pucik at the end of this chapter for an example of the effective use of work groups.

It was also found that the informally chosen group leader was the best liked, and most represented the values of the group. This leader was often more influential than the appointed leader (the supervisor). On the basis of these studies, management theorists began to stress the importance of (1) communication within the work group, (2) the importance of participation in the decision-making process, and (3) the potential values of democratic leadership. The emphasis on these three factors was later to be referred to as the human relations approach to management.

ENCOUNTER GROUPS

Encounter groups are a special type of educational group that developed partially out of the human relations approach to management. The encounter group has been defined as "an intensive group that emphasizes development and improvement in interpersonal communication" *(Psychology Today* 1970, p. 154). Encounter groups have a number of different names, such as sensitivity groups, T-groups (T for training), therapeutic groups, process groups, personal growth groups, and Gestalt groups, among others. Depending on its focus, the encounter group may be designed to improve personal growth, marital relations, group dynamics, or organizational effectiveness. The sessions may vary in length from a minilab or microlab lasting 2-3 hours to a marathon lasting 12-24 hours to a semester course lasting about 45 hours over 15 weeks. The group may have one or more leaders (often called facilitators or trainers), it may be leaderless, or it may involve the use of taped instructions for each segment of its meetings (Lomranz, Lakin, and Schiffman, 1972).

Egan (1973, pp. 8-13) has summarized the characteristics most encounter or personal growth groups have in common:

1. Learning through actual experience in the small group
2. Cultural permission, that is, the group is a microcosm of society and as such develops its own culture and norms for appropriate behavior
3. A climate of experimentation so that behaviors which might normally be frowned on outside the group are encouraged
4. A relatively small group size (8-16 members)
5. Feedback which is personal, spontaneous and constructive
6. Leadership in the form of a trainer or facilitator
7. Discussing the influences of emotion on the communication process
8. Providing psychological support for members to try new behaviors, and to help ameliorate the anxiety produced by the different way the group operates
9. Structured exercises to generate firsthand learning experiences
10. Suspension of judgment or tolerance for the unusual ways of behaving in the group until those behaviors have been given a chance

An additional goal of encounter groups is to *learn more about group dynamics.* Through the firsthand group experiences, members begin to emotionally understand such concepts as group cohesiveness. Members really learn the meaning of the term *resistance to change* (see Chapter 7) when they make a suggestion and absolutely nobody appears to hear it.

This is commonly referred to as a "plop." Also, nobody has to explain the meaning of the term *conformity pressure* (see Chapter 4) when everyone else in the group is urging you to tell more of your inner feelings and take off the mantle of secrecy. For this reason one student referred to the encounter group experience as a "psychological striptease."

Not all encounter group experiences are positive. Some people feel hurt by the feedback and leave with a worsened self-concept. However, these cases are definitely in the minority (Lieberman, Yalom, and Miles 1972).

Given the unique goals and methods of encounter groups, it is not surprising that the end results will be different from those of the other types of groups described. If you are interested in reading more on encounter groups, see Golembiewski and Blumberg (1970), Lakin (1972), and Giffin and Patton (1974).

PROBLEM-SOLVING GROUPS

Although we have looked at other types of groups, by far the greatest emphasis in group discussion textbooks has been on improving problem-solving and decision-making abilities (Barnlund and Haiman, 1959; Collins and Guetzkow 1964; Harnack and Fest 1964; Gulley 1968; Sattler and Miller 1968; Bormann 1969; Patton and Giffin 1973; Applbaum *et al.* 1974; Brilhart 1974; Gouran 1974; and Goldberg and Larson 1975).

The terms *task-oriented, problem-solving,* and *decision-making* groups have been used interchangeably to stress the emphasis on cognitive end products of group discussion. Although interpersonal relations are often discussed, they are considered secondarily important and merely a means to an end (that is, to solve a problem). As shown in the last section, this is just the reverse emphasis from encounter groups, which focus primarily on interpersonal relations. Weaver (1971, pp. 203-204) has succinctly differentiated between the problem-solving group (he refers to it as group discussion) and the encounter group. The following four characteristics seem representative:

1. Discussion often has a group goal, while the encounter group member often has an individual goal.

2. Discussion focuses . . . on problems which can be solved through logical analysis, while the encounter group relies more on emotional experiencing.

3. The basic function of discussion is often to reach solutions on problems, while the function of encounter groups is to achieve deeper self-insight.

4. Discussions generally have leaders, while encounter groups may or may not have leaders.

These differences are indeed representative; however, it is interesting to note that at least one study (Larson and Gratz 1970) found that both methods produced *improvements* in participants' (1) dogmatism level, (2) critical thinking ability, and (3) problem-solving accuracy. In fact, in the encounter group, problem-solving skills improved more than in the discussion groups. From this it is apparent that significant improvements in small group skills can occur as a result of course work in this area. Even though the methods differ, the results seem worthwhile.

Problem-solving groups must spend a great deal of time and energy in careful deliberation over their discussion question. Generally, the group will be attempting to provide some answer or answers to the discussion question. Sample discussion questions include:

1. How can we keep from eliminating the earth's ozone shield?

2. What can be done about the problem of cheating in our school?

3. How do we determine local obscenity and pornography standards?

4. What are the long-term effects of marijuana use?

5. How do we achieve equal opportunity for women and minorities?

6. How can we reduce energy consumption?

7. Should abortion or contraception be made mandatory for families that already have two children?

8. What is an acceptable level of unemployment?

9. Should marijuana be legalized?

10. Should handguns be outlawed?

11. Has the decline of civilization begun in this country?

12. How can we curb drug abuse in industry?

An effective problem-solving discussion begins with an effectively structured discussion question. First, a topic should be limited to one issue at a time. Notice that question number 7 includes both abortion and contraception in the topic. These two issues may require different answers; thus only one should be included in the discussion question. An improved version of number 7 would be, "How can we help curb population growth?"

Questions of Fact   Questions of fact deal with truth and falsity. Is it or is it not so? "What are the long-term effects of marijuana use?" is a question of fact. The Judiciary Committee of the United States House of Representatives was faced with determining a question of fact when they determined that Richard Nixon had committed impeachable offenses against the United States.

Discussions involving questions of fact require evidence and documentation to establish whether or not the phenomenon exists. For example, "Does the Bermuda Triangle really pose a major threat to ships and planes traveling in the area?" or "Does intelligent life exist in outer space?" Frequently, such questions remain somewhat unresolvable, but they are interesting to discuss anyway.

Questions of Definition   Questions of definition are fairly narrow, but are often quite difficult to answer. The problem of defining obscenity and pornography has been with us for decades. The emotionalism experienced in numerous states over textbook wording is but one of many examples of disagreement over what is obscene. Several years ago the Supreme Court ruled that no one definition could be made for all communities, so each local community had to define obscenity and pornography for itself.

In the medical arena, lawsuits are arising over differences in the medical definition of death. If accident victims become organ transplant donors, what signs do doctors use to determine if the donor is dead? Cessation of the heartbeat is certainly not a reliable sign, since numerous people walking around today have had their hearts stop temporarily. What about cessation of brain activity? The point is that the definition is important and is not as easily determined as it might first appear.

Questions of Value   Questions of value invoke an evaluation of the issues once the facts and the definitions have been determined. Whereas facts can be verified by others, values are personal and often differ drastically from one individual to another. Perhaps we can agree on a definition of affirmative action as *unequal* opportunity for women and minorities to undo the wrongs that have existed for decades. Yet can we agree that *unequal* opportunity of any kind is desirable? Some judges have ruled that this is still another form of discrimination (against white males) and is inconsistent with the ideals of the Equal Employment Opportunity Commission. Yet others feel strongly that reverse discrimination is required to tip the scales of justice to where they should have been a long time ago.

Differences in values are at the base of the controversies over abortion and contraception as well. Those who believe in the right of the unborn child see abortion and even contraception as unthinkable. Those on the other side feel that the individual woman should have the right to decide whether she wants a child and that these decisions should not be dictated by others. Here is another case in which the "right" answer will definitely vary depending on one's own personal and very individual value system.

Questions of Policy   Questions of policy involve the establishing of facts, determining of definitions, a discusson of values, and the determination of the ways and means of solving a problem. "What can be done to solve the problems of drug abuse?" "What should our state's policy be toward

GRIN AND BEAR IT   by Lichty & Wagner

"We're an ad hoc committee from our room,
and we demand to know what ad hoc means."

abortions?" "Should the United States provide more public service jobs for the unemployed?" "How can the misuse of handguns be reduced?" All of these are examples of policy questions. Discussions regarding questions of policy are often the most complicated, since they encompass some of the other three types of discussion questions (fact, definition, and value). Let us look at one topic (equal rights for women) as it might be discussed in each of the four ways.

1. *Fact:* "Do women have equal rights in this country?"

2. *Definition:* "What do we mean by the term *equal rights for women?*"

3. *Value:* "Is it desirable to change women's role in our society?"

4. *Policy:* "How can we achieve equal rights for women in this country?"

As you can see, the policy question assumes, to some extent, that (1) equal rights do not presently exist, (2) agreement on a definition of equal rights can be reached, (3) equal rights for women are desirable, and (4) something ought to be done to bring about equal rights for women. It is important to remember that policy discussions may bog down on these earlier questions if all group members do not agree on these assumptions.

In addition to trying to bring about a solution to the problem, policy questions frequently must deal with the question of how to implement the solution. Should equal rights be dictated by law? Should they evolve through generations of attitude change produced by the mass media and word of mouth? Should they be implemented at the local level as are obscenity laws or at the national level as are crimes against the government? All of these are questions dealing with the specifics of how the solution actually gets enacted.

Figure 3.6 summarizes the elements involved in various types of discussion questions.

Discussion Group Formats   Discussion questions may be approached in a variety of different small group formats. The selection of an appropriate format largely depends upon group members' own needs and circumstances. Although there are any number of possible formats available, here are five that are representative of most problem-solving discussions:

Dialogue: The dialogue is simply a discussion or conversation between two people. It may be conducted privately or in front of an audience.

Panel: The panel discussion usually involves a small number of people (up to five or six) conducting an informal discussion on a topic they have all thought about and possibly researched beforehand. One person is appointed as a moderator to help move the group along its planned agenda. Conversation is mostly spontaneous and participants may interrupt one another.

Symposium: The symposium includes several participants, each of whom gives a short formal presentation on a prepared topic usually built around a central theme. Participants do not interrupt each other during the formal presentations, but a less formal discussion usually follows.

Forum: A forum is a question-and-answer period designed to allow audience members to interact with the discussion group. A forum period often follows a panel discussion or a symposium. It is customary for the chairperson to introduce the panel or symposium members and to serve as a moderator for the forum period.

Colloquy: A colloquy may take a number of forms, but each involves the questioning of experts by the other experts on the panel, lay persons on a second panel, or lay persons in the audience. This format is very similar to the panel discussion except that experts are involved and a second panel of lay persons may also be involved.

Elements	Type of discussion			
included	Fact	Definition	Value	Policy
Facts	x	x	x	x
Definitions		x	x	x
Values			x	x
Policies				x
Implementation				x

FIGURE 3.6
Elements involved in discussion questions.

Discussion Group Techniques   In addition to the major formats discussed above, there are a number of subformats or techniques that may be employed in discussion groups. These techniques are often used for short periods of time as *part* of a discussion group format.

Phillips 66:	Phillips 66 is a specific technique developed by J. D. Phillips (1948). It simply allows all the members of an audience to form groups of about six people to discuss a specific topic for about six minutes and then report their group's conclusion through a spokesman. Realistically, this technique is more useful if longer time limits are allowed (up to an hour or so). The general term for this, when the time and group size are not limited to six, is a *buzz group* or *buzz session*. The technique offers the advantage of allowing a lot of people to participate in a fairly efficient manner. The results from all groups are compiled and used to solve the problem faced by the entire assembly.
Case discussion:	A case discussion is an educational discussion centered on a real or hypothetical event. The case problem is presented to the group and they attempt to solve it as best they can. A case problem is included at the beginning of each chapter in this book to illustrate the way in which small group theory and research *apply* to real-life problems.
Role playing:	Role playing simply allows participants to adopt a new "role" or set of behaviors other than their own. For example, quiet individuals may be assigned the role of leader, or argumentative members may be assigned the role of harmonizer or compromiser. Meek members may be asked to play the role of the "devil's advocate," who promotes a clash of ideas. In each case the individual gets

an opportunity to practice a role in an attempt to build his or her group skills. This helps develop role flexibility so that participants can adopt new and different role behaviors as the need arises. Role playing also may be used to demonstrate to the rest of the group what a given role may do to a group discussion. The chronic nonconformist role can be secretly given to one member to demonstrate how the others will react. The typical reaction is that that person gets a lot of attention from the rest of the group for a while, but will be ignored after a time if he or she continues to deviate. (See Chapter 4 for more on deviation.)

Another version of role playing is the role reversal. In this case, participants try to take the part of another person (usually one with whom they have a conflict). Biracial groups, labor-management groups, and others frequently use this technique to develop empathy for the other person's point of view. It often results in funny situations, which also help relieve some of the tension. Try some of the role-playing exercises in this book to help get a feel for what role playing is like, for example, Exercise 1 at the end of Chapter 2.

Fishbowl: The fishbowl technique has one small group attempt to solve a problem for a specified period of time (often 30 minutes), while a second group, seated around the outside of the first group, observes the group process. After the discussion, the observer group gives feedback to the first group as to what behaviors they were able to identify as helpful or harmful to the group's progress. Then the two groups reverse positions and roles: the observers become the observed, and vice versa. This technique may be aided by the use of videotape equipment to more vividly describe and analyze the group process.

Conference: A conference is a series of meetings on topics of common interest between and among people who represent different groups. For example, representatives from different colleges and universities may gather at a conference to discuss problems of finance, curriculum, community service, and others. Conferences often involve hundreds of people and may last several days. For the past several years, different countries have hosted the world food conferences in an attempt to better plan for the feeding of the world's population. Conferences may also be quite small and last a short period of time. The critical element is that different groups are represented. An example of the latter type of conference is the plant manager's weekly conference in a manufacturing plant where representatives from production, engineering, maintenance, inspection, personnel, and other departments get together to organize their efforts and to solve common problems.

THE SYSTEMS PERSPECTIVE

In this chapter we have looked at some of the elements that constitute the internal influences section of our model. In systems theory these elements would be called part of the *throughput* of small groups. Early in the chapter we examined territoriality, physical environment, and seating behavior in groups. As suggested by the Viet Nam negotiations, different cultures have drastically differing perceptions of how to position furniture or whether to have furniture at all. This illustrates the way in which relevant background factors influence such internal influences as territoriality, physical environment, and seating behavior. For example, in Western culture, we typically place furniture along the walls with open space in the middle of the room. The Japanese tend to cluster furniture in the center of the room, leaving the space along the walls open. Also, imagine conducting a group discussion while seated barefoot on the floor around very low tables. This should help you picture the importance of background factors in relation to seating behaviors.

Probably the most important internal influence in the model is the type of group. Obviously the procedures, norms, expectations, and outcomes of a work group will be radically different from those in a social group. For example, a norm of openness in both self-disclosure and candid feedback to others exists in many social groups. However, you might find that to tell your boss or friend exactly what you do *not* like about them is certainly inappropriate. The type of group has an enormous impact on the way in which that group functions.

In this chapter we also looked at the literature on communication networks. We saw that the all-channel network was best for group-member satisfaction, while the wheel produced the fastest results. As our systems perspective leads us to believe, determining the "best" network depends, among other things, on the demands of the situation.

When we discussed the issue of group size we especially began to see the connection between the type of group and the appropriate group size. All other things being equal, five seems to be the optimum size for a problem-solving group. However, the optimum size for a group discussion in a classroom may be radically different from that of a work group on an assembly line or in a large office. Even the idea of the "right" size of family group depends on each of our relevant background factors. Typically people have quite strong feelings about what is the "right" sized family. These feelings usually result from a lifetime of attitude formation influenced by parents, friends, and perhaps religious affiliation.

Group size is also related to the idea of communication networks. As the size increases, the all-channel network begins to bog down in the confusion and a more controlled network tends to be more appropriate. Group size is also related to the consequences of group interaction. Larger groups tend to produce lower levels of satisfaction and interpersonal relations among participants. Bostrom's research cited in this chapter is very revealing. It showed that most people like to talk far more than they like to listen in groups.

In the preceding section of this chapter we looked at different group formats and techniques (for example, panel, symposium, role playing, fishbowl, conference). Obviously there is a connection between the type of group and the appropriateness of these formats. Can you imagine the U.S. president's cabinet engaging in role-playing and fishbowl simulations? Certainly educational groups use these formats and techniques with a great deal of success, but work groups would be more likely to use panels, symposiums, and conferences.

The type of group format is also related to the desired group outcome. If personal growth is the goal, then role playing or fishbowls are helpful. On the other hand, if the group goal is to solve a task-oriented problem, such as how to cut energy consumption by 10 percent, the panel discussion is probably more appropriate. As usual, it all depends . . .

Exercises

1. Discussion of Case Studies

Divide into five-person groups. Each group can discuss *one* of the cases below.* Each of these cases describes real-life psychological studies involving naive human subjects. Ask yourself, "How do I feel about the use of this procedure in social research?" Then, within each group try to agree on one of the six reactions listed below.

   a) I am totally unopposed to its use.
   b) I am basically unopposed to its use.
   c) I am slightly more unopposed to its use.
   d) I am slightly more opposed than unopposed to its use.
   e) I am basically opposed to its use.
   f) I am opposed to its use under any circumstances.

---

* These cases were used in a study on ethics in social research practices conducted by Edwin A. Rugg (personal correspondence, May 20, 1975).

After you have arrived at group agreement on one of the six reactions above, each group should share its reaction and the reasoning behind it. Discuss the different reactions among the groups.

Case 1 — Homosexual attitudes   Men are recruited to participate in an experiment on sexual attitudes, although they are not told that it is actually a study of attitudes toward homosexuality. Participants are led to believe that a "psycho-galvanometer" used in the experiment is capable of detecting sexual arousal. They are also told that if the galvanometer registers when an individual looks at slides of nude males, the individual is probably a latent homosexual. The galvanometer is rigged so that all participants are led to believe they are latent homosexuals. Following the experiment, the researcher informs the participants that the galvanometer was rigged and gives detailed information about the study and its true purpose.

Case 2 — Obedience   Individuals are recruited to participate in an experiment on memory and learning, although the actual purpose of the experiment is to study obedience. Participants are given the role of "teacher" and told to administer increasingly strong electric shocks to the "learner" whenever the learner makes an error in the memory task. The learner is actually an assistant to the researcher and receives no actual shocks. He only pretends to experience pain as the shock level becomes more and more severe. The psychological dilemma for the participant involves deciding whether to obey the experimenter, who insists that the participant continue to shock the learner, or to side with the learner, who begs the participant to stop administering shocks. When the participant refuses to continue or when the highest shock level is reached, the experiment is over. At that point, the participant is told that the shocks and cries of pain were faked. The true purpose and details of the study are explained.

Case 3 — Reactions to fear and anxiety   Students, participating in a series of experiments for course credit, are told when they arrive at one of the research laboratories that they will receive an electric shock as part of the experiment. The researcher is interested in the reactions of groups under conditions of fear and anxiety. In order to facilitate anxiety arousal, the researcher describes in detail the pain and uncomfortable side effects that usually accompany the electric shock. Actually, no shocks are ever administered. Following the experiment, the researcher informs the participants that they will not be shocked after all. He then explains the actual experiment that took place and why they were purposefully misled.

Case 4 — Self-concept and achievement   Students at a teacher's college complete a series of placement tests but are not told that the tests are actually part of a psychological experiment. The experiment involves giving half of the students false test results that indicate that they are unfit for a teaching career. The researcher is interested in studying the effects of lowered self-concept on subsequent achievement. Two weeks later the study is completed, and the researcher tells the students that the test results were falsified and explains the details of the research project.

Case 5 — Reward and performance   Individuals are promised two dollars if they participate in an experiment that involves performing a simple but boring task. Some of the participants are later led to believe that they may receive up to twenty dollars for their participation, even though the researcher has no intention of paying participants more than two dollars for their time. The researcher is interested in the effects of different anticipated rewards on attitudes toward the task and the quality of task performance. At the end of the experiment, the researcher explains why he/she cannot pay participants more than the two dollars intially agreed upon and discusses the purpose and nature of the research.

OVERVIEW OF READINGS

In the first article, Sommer discusses the research on small group ecology. This article illustrates the interesting combinations between seating patterns and people's interaction.

In the second article, Hatvany and Pucik describe the important role that groups play in the Japanese method for achieving high productivity in their society. To what extent do you think these group methods could be used in the Western world?

Studies of Small Group Ecology

Robert Sommer

The study of ecology covers both the distribution and the density of organisms. Within the social sciences the major ecological studies have taken place at the societal rather than at the small group level (e.g., demography) although it has been known for a long time that the arrangement of individuals in face-to-face groups is not accidental. In American society, leaders tend to occupy the head positions at a table with their lieutenants at their sides, while opposition factions frequently are found at the other end of the table.[1] Numerous accounts of these phenomena are found in observational studies such as those by Whyte[2] and Wilmer.[3] Considering the number of studies concerned with small discussion groups, relatively few have made the arrangement of people a variable. The early studies by Steinzor[4] and Bass and Klubeck[5] were primarily concerned with other factors (e.g., leadership) and only afterwards was the physical arrangement of individuals examined for its effects upon interaction. This is also the procedure followed by Strodtbeck and Hook[6] who reanalyzed their jury trial data to learn the effects of table position on contribution to the discussion, and more recently Hare and Bales[7] who reexamined group discussion data for positional effects.

One of the oldest problems in social psychology concerns the classification of face-to-face groups.[8] A heuristic taxonomy of groups resolved some of the contradictory findings of experiments concerned with "social facilitation," some of whose results indicated a social increment while others showed a social

From Robert Sommer, "Further Studies of Small Group Ecology," *Sociometry*, Vol. 28 (1965), pp. 337-348. Copyright © 1965 by The American Sociological Association. Reprinted with permission.

TABLE 1
ARRANGEMENT OF PAIRS AT RECTANGULAR TABLES (IN PERCENT)

| | | SERIES 2 | |
| | SERIES 1 | CONVERSING | CO-ACTING |
SEATING ARRANGEMENT	(N = 50)	(N = 74)	(N = 18)
Corner	40	54	0
Across	43	36	32
Side	8	6	0
Distant	10	4	68
Total	100	100	100

decrement. It was Allport[9] who made the distinction between cooperating, competing, and co-acting groups. Since most of the small group research of the last decades has concerned itself with discussion groups, this distinction has been largely neglected. The goal of the present study is to learn how people in different types of face-to-face groups arrange themselves. . . .

OBSERVATIONAL STUDIES

THE SITUATION WHERE PEOPLE DESIRE TO INTERACT
Over a fourteen-month period, observations were made during non-eating hours in the student union cafeteria at a California university. During these hours the cafeteria is used by students for casual conversation and studying (and to a lesser extent by faculty and nonteaching staff for coffee breaks.) The observations were made irregularly and there was some bias in these times in that the writer's schedule led him to pass this way at certain times rather than others but most of the daylight non-eating hours were covered. Records were kept of the seating of pairs of people. In the first series of observations, no distinction was made whether the people were conversing, studying together, or studying separately. The only category specifically excluded from the study was a pair where one or both people were eating. This criteria contained two different table sizes: single pedestal square tables (36 inches per side) each surrounded by four chairs, one to a side; double pedestal rectangular tables (36 × 54 inches) each surrounded by six chairs, two on the long sides and one at each end.

The 50 pairs seated at the small square tables showed a preference for corner rather than opposite seating (35 pairs sat corner to corner while 15 sat across from one another).[10] The double pedestal tables permit side-by-side and distant seating as well as corner and opposite seating. During the course of the observations, 60 pairs were observed at double tables. Table 1 shows clearly that side-by-side and distant seating were infrequent. The vast majority of pairs chose to occupy the corners or sit across from one another.

It was planned to continue these observations for another six months, but in February 1965 the furniture of the cafeteria was changed. In order to accommodate more people the management moved in new tables and rearranged others. Rather than combine these new observations with the previous ones, it seemed preferable to look upon them as a new series in which additional information could be gained. In the next four months 52 additional observations were made in which the *major activity* of the people as well as their seating arrangement was recorded. A distinction was made between those pairs who were interacting (conversing, studying together) and those who were co-acting (occupying the same table but studying separately). In order to keep the data comparable to the previous observations, the present analysis focused upon the square tables (36" × 36") observed previously, as well as rectangular tables (36" × 72") which were made by pushing two of the small square tables together. The situation at the other rectangular tables (36" × 54") was confused since these tables now accommodated anywhere from four to eight people, sometimes with end chairs and sometimes without, so these are excluded from the analysis.

Of the 124 pairs seated at the small square tables, 106 were conversing or otherwise interacting while 18 were co-acting. The interacting pairs showed a definite preference for corner seating, with 70 seated corner-to-corner compared to 36 seated across from one another. However, co-acting pairs chose a very different arrangement, with only two pairs sitting corner-to-corner and 18 sitting opposite one another. These results support the previous studies in which corner seating was preferred over opposite and side-by-side seating in a variety of conditions where individuals interact. It suggests that corner seating preserves the closeness between individuals and also enables people to avoid eye contact since they do not sit face to face. The co-acting pairs use the distance across the table for books, handbags, and other belongings, and can avoid visual contact by looking down rather than across the table.

Seating at the rectangular tables is shown in the second and third columns of Table 1. The interacting groups prefer corner-to-corner seating, and to a lesser extent opposite seating, with little use made of side-by-side or distant seating. On the other hand, more than two-thirds of the co-acting groups chose a distant seating arrangement which separated the people geographically and visually.

THE SITUATION WHERE INTERACTION IS DISCOURAGED

One set of observations took place in the reading area adjacent to the reserve room of a university library. This is a large room (29' × 83') containing 33 rectangular tables (48" × 64") in the main area. Each table has a capacity of four persons, two sitting on opposite sides with the ends free. The room was generally quiet even when filled to capacity. This made it a good place to study how people arranged themselves when they did *not* want to interact. All observations took place when the room was relatively uncrowded since this provided some choice as to seating. Due to the size of the room, it was not possible to record the arrangements at all the tables in the room without appearing conspicuous. Thus the observer randomly selected some location in the room and diagrammed the seating arrangements within the visible portion of the room on a prepared chart.

A pilot study[11] had shown that the majority of people who came alone sat alone if there was an empty table. This trend was more marked for the males

(70%) than for the females (55%). The next largest group arranged themselves diagonally across from whoever already occupied the table. Only 10% of the students sat opposite or beside another student (i.e., in either of the two near positions) when there were empty seats available elsewhere.

Following this, there were 19 occasions when the seating patterns of those individuals presently in the reserve room were recorded, including people who came alone as well as those who came with friends. The sample consisted of 193 males and 304 women. Again it was found that a higher percentage of males (34%) than females (25%) sat alone. However, the major focus of the study was on those students who sat two at a table (since there is only one possible way that people can arrange themselves three or four to a table (since there is only one possible way that people can arrange themselves three or four to a table). The results showed that 30% of the pairs sat across from one another, 15% sat side-by-side, while 56% used the diagonal or distant arrangement. Although the observations were cross-sectional and spanned only several minutes each, a record was made of any conversations at the table. Conversations were observed among 8% of the pairs sitting across from one another, 3% of those pairs sitting in a diagonal or distant arrangement, and 37% of those sitting side-by-side.

A second set of observations was made independently in the Periodical Room of the same library. The same general technique was followed in that the arrangement of all pairs was diagrammed on 14 occasions over a two month period. This room, excluding the magazine and transit areas, was 36' × 74' and contained two types of rectangular tables, one (48" × 64") with two chairs on each side and the ends free, and the other (48" × 90") with three chairs on each side and the ends free. The arrangements of pairs at the two types of tables were similar; and the pooled data show that of the 74 pairs, 19% sat across from one another, 13% sat side-by-side, and 68% sat in a distant arrangement. Conversations were noted between 14% of the people sitting opposite one another, 6% of those people sitting in a distant relationship, and 60% of those pairs sitting side-by-side.

QUESTIONNAIRE STUDIES

RECTANGULAR TABLE ECOLOGY

To learn something of the way that group task influences the way people arrange themselves, a paper-and-pencil test was administered to 151 students in an introductory psychology class. Each student was asked to imagine how he and a friend of the same sex would seat themselves under four different conditions: a.To chat for a few minutes before class; b. To study together for the same exam; c. To study for different exams; and d. To compete in order to see which would be the first to solve a series of puzzles. Each time the student was asked to indicate his own seating and that of his friend on a diagram showing a table and six chairs (see Figure 1). There was one chair at the head and one at the foot and two chairs on each of the sides. In order to maximize the realism of the test, the hypothetical activity was located in the student union cafeteria during *non*-eating hours (which is, as has been noted, actively used for casual conversation, studying, etc., and has similar rectangular tables). The tasks set for the students included cooperating, co-acting, and competing activity. In addition, a distinction was made between casual interaction such as conversation and structured cooperative activity (joint studying for an exam). The different tasks were presented in random order in the test booklet.

There were no significant differences between the sexes in seating arrangements under any of the conditions. This was unexpected, since previous studies have shown that females make greater use of side-by-side seating while males prefer to sit across from other people.

Figure 1 shows the seating preferences for the total group of 151 students. If we take "near seating" to include side-by-side, corner and opposite arrangements, and let "distant seating" refer to all other patterns. Figure 1 shows that distant seating was rarely used by casual or cooperating groups. People who want to converse or work together use the near arrangements. On the other hand distant seating is the dominant pattern in co-acting groups. The most common distant pattern shows people sitting on opposite sides of the table but not directly facing one another rather than the more physically distant head-foot arrangement. This suggests that it is the visual contact between people rather than bodily presence that is the major source of distraction in co-acting groups. Distant seating is important in competing groups although the dominant arrangement here is opposite seating.

People conversing overwhelmingly chose a corner-to-corner or opposite arrangement. On the other hand, those studying together strongly prefer to sit side-by-side. In no other condition is side seating used anywhere near this frequency. There is a metaphorical quality to these arrangements with people competing sitting "in opposition," people cooperating sitting "on the same side," people conversing sitting "in a corner" and people co-acting choosing a "distant" arrangement.

The identical questionnaire was given to 26 students in a social psychology class. After the students completed the questionnaire in the usual way, each was asked to go through his responses and explain why he chose this particular arrangement.

For the *casual group,* the dominant preference was for corner seating, and the student's explanations were: "We would be sitting close to each other and yet be able to see each person." "It's nice to be close when chatting but you should face each other instead of side-by-side." "You would be closer with only a corner than across the table, you'd have to turn less than side-by-side." "The corner arrangement is the most intimate. You wouldn't have to shout *across* the table, but, sitting adjacent you could still face the person. Sitting beside the person it is hard to look at them when you're talking." Those people who chose to sit across from one another emphasized the desirability of a direct face-to-face arrangement.

In the *cooperating group,* those people who liked the corner arrangement mentioned the ease of conversing in corner chairs ("Because we could look at each other's notes with the least change of place and effort.") while those people who chose the side arrangement emphasized the ease of sharing things in this position.

For the *co-acting group,* the dominant arrangement was a distant one and those students emphasized the need to be apart yet feel together ("This would allow for sitting far enough apart so we wouldn't interfere with each other, but if we wanted to pass comments we were close enough." "Effectively divides

Percentage of Ss Choosing This Arrangement

Seating Arrangement	Condition 1 (conversing)	Condition 2 (cooperating)	Condition 3 (co-acting)	Condition 4 (competing)
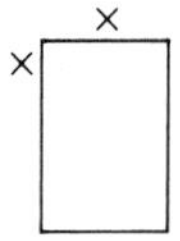	42	19	3	7
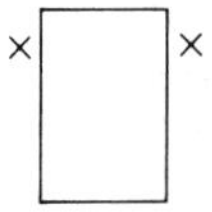	46	25	31	41
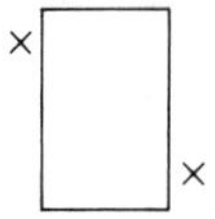	1	5	43	20
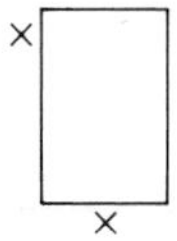	0	0	3	5
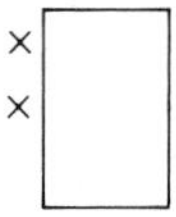	11	51	7	8
	0	0	13	18
TOTAL	100	100	100	99

FIGURE 1
Seating preferences at rectangular tables.

table into two halves yet allows brief remarks without having to raise voice. Also allows staring into space and not at neighbor's face.").

As in the previous study, opposite, distant-opposite, and distant seating were preferred by *competing groups*. The way that a face-to-face arrangement stimulates competition was frequently mentioned: e.g., "Able to see how friend is doing but there's enough room"; or, "In this situation the friend can be watched to determine his progress." The reason given most frequently by people preferring the distant-opposite arrangement was that it reduced the temptation to look at the other person's answers while the long distance aided concentration. Those people electing a distant arrangement explained that this would minimize distraction. Two of the three people preferring a side arrangement mentioned that it was easier to concentrate when not looking directly at the other person.

ROUND TABLE ECOLOGY

In order to learn how the group task would affect the arrangement of people at a round table, 116 students in another introductory psychology class were asked to fill out a questionnaire similar to that of the preceding study except that the diagram showed a *round* table surrounded by six chairs. The same four situations were described (i.e., conversing with a friend, studying for the same exam, for different exams, or competing). Since the results showed no significant difference between the 65 females and 51 males, the composite totals are presented in Figure 2. People can sit in only three possible arrangements under these conditions (see Figure 2), these three arrangements comprising a rank order of physical distance.

Figure 2 shows that casual and cooperating groups made greatest use of adjacent chairs. This trend was most marked among the cooperating groups where 83% chose adjacent chairs. Although the co-acting group makes heavy use of an arrangement where one empty chair is left between the people, the majority of co-acting groups places a gap of two seats between them (i.e., sit directly opposite one another). The trend for opposite seating is most pronounced in the competing group.

If we make certain assumptions on the basis of our previous study with rectangular tables, it is possible to formulate hypotheses as to how positions at a round table compare with those at a rectangular table. Adjacent seating at a round table seems somewhere between side and corner seating. Physically, it places people side-by-side at a lesser angle than in a corner arrangement. Sitting one seat away from another person at a round table does not seem to be as "distant" an arrangement as leaving the same gap at a rectangular table. This suggests that people at a round table are psychologically closer than at a corresponding position at a rectangular table. Opposite seating in the round table arrangement used here seems to serve some of the functions of both distant and opposite seating at a rectangular table.

The same questionnaire was given to 18 students who, after filling out the questionnaire in the usual way, explained why they arranged themselves as they did. Most of the students in the *conversing condition* selected adjacent seats: "I want to chat with my friend, not the whole cafeteria, so I sit next to her"; "More intimate, no physical barriers between each other." In the *cooperating group,* the vast majority chose to sit in adjacent chairs. Their explanations stressed the advantages of this arrangement for comparing notes and sharing materials. Most students in the co-acting condition chose to sit two seats away from one another, the greatest physical distance permitted in this diagram. Of those who chose to sit one seat away, several mentioned that this "Doesn't put us directly opposite each other . . . keep looking at each other if we look up from studying," and "Not directly across from each other because we'd have more of a tendency to talk then." In the *competing condition,* most students chose to leave two seats between them which placed them directly opposite one another. The explanations emphasized the need to keep separate in order to avoid seeing each other's material. Several mentioned that opposite seating

Percentage of Ss Choosing This Arrangement

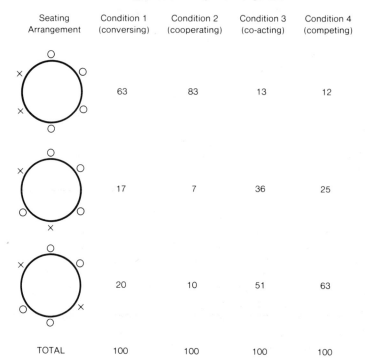

Seating Arrangement	Condition 1 (conversing)	Condition 2 (cooperating)	Condition 3 (co-acting)	Condition 4 (competing)
	63	83	13	12
	17	7	36	25
	20	10	51	63
TOTAL	100	100	100	100

FIGURE 2
Seating preferences at round tables.

permitted them to see how the other person was doing and enhanced feelings of cooperation.

DISCUSSION
These results indicate that different tasks are associated with different spatial arrangements; the ecology of interaction differs from the ecology of co-action and competition. Exactly why these particular arrangements are chosen we do not know for certain. On the basis of what our subjects report, eye contact seems an important factor in spatial arrangements. Under certain conditions direct visual contact represents a challenge to the other, a play at dominance. Among chickens and turkeys in confinement, McBride[12] has shown that the dominant bird in the flock has the most eye space. When he looks at a submissive bird, the latter looks away. When birds are crowded together, they stand at the wire of the coop facing outward to avoid the stress that would be generated by extended visual contact. We may only speculate as to the extent to which eye contact regulates spatial arrangements, though it is interesting to note that the only questionnaire condition in which opposite seating was chosen over other distant alternatives was in the competitive task where the subject indicated a desire to "keep an eye on what the other person was

doing." It is hypothesized that gestures of threat (agonistic displays) are more appropriate in competitive conditions than cooperative or strictly social tasks. On the other hand, agonistic displays are stressful to both parties, and in the animal kingdom are generally terminated by ritualized submissive behavior rather than actual combat. In a previous pilot study,[13] people were asked how they would seat themselves at a table already occupied by someone they disliked. It was found that people chose to sit at some distance from the disliked person, but *not* directly opposite him, i.e., in a distant-side position. In this way they were removed visually as well as geographically from the source of stress. The relationship between distance and aggressive behavior among chaffinches has been studied nicely by Marler.[14] placing the cages of chaffinches various distances apart, he found the point at which aggressive displays began. Female chaffinches tolerated closer presence than males, while females whose breasts were dyed to resemble males were kept at the typical male distance by other birds.

Most stressful encounters are avoided through spatial segregation. The orbits in which people travel tend to remove them from contact with those with whom they disagree or dislike. Avoidance is the first line of defense against interpersonal stress but when this is not possible or effective, an individual develops alternate methods. Limiting the range of visual contact through social conventions or actual physical barriers are other possibilities. The present studies all took place in settings whose furnishings consisted solely of tables and chairs. No attempt was made to explore the role of physical barriers such as posts, partitions, tables, etc., in regulating interaction. The ways in which people gain privacy in public areas warrants further exploration in a society in which more and more people share a finite amount of space. In settings such as libraries, study rooms, and large open offices, it is exceedingly important to develop methods whereby unwanted or stressful interpersonal contact is avoided.

Chapin,[15] in his discussion of housing factors related to mental hygiene, indicated the importance of ease of circulation as well as areas that can be closed off from the main traffic flow. Just as people moving about a house require resting places for solitude or individual concentration, people rooted to a given spot in a public area require places where their eyes can rest without stress. There is the apocryphal story of the stress produced by the newspaper strike in New York City where the seated men were unable to "retreat into" newspapers and had to look at the other occupants, particularly women standing above them. Subway officials believe that the advertisements on the wall provide safe resting places for the patron's eyes.

Since the topological similarities between different arrangements of people make it necessary to experiment with every conceivable physical arrangement, it seems most fruitful to isolate the socially and psychologically genotypic arrangements. The two most obvious ones are near and distant seating. In ordinary social intercourse, near seating is the rule. In American society it is only among strangers, co-acting individuals or schizophrenic mental patients that one finds distant seating patterns in any frequency.

One can divide seating patterns into several important subclasses. One possible category involves arrangements which maximize direct visual contact between individuals. According to Goffman,[16] Hall,[17] and Birdwhistell,[18] direct visual contact can be exceedingly uncomfortable and disconcerting under ordinary conditions, producing feelings of anxiety in the person upon whom the eyes are directly centered. There are cultural differences in the use of visual contact can be exceedingly uncomfortable and disconcerting under ordinary conditions, producing feelings of anxiety in the person upon whom also distinguish between near arrangements according to the extent to which they facilitate tactile or olfactory contact. The number of possible arrangements is still small enough to permit clear categorization and conceptualization.

REFERENCES

1. Edward T. Hall, *The Silent Language* (Garden City: Doubleday, 1959); Robert Sommer, "Leadership and Group Geography," *Sociometry,* 24 (March, 1961), pp. 99-110; Fred L. Strodtbeck and L. Harmon Hook, "The Social Dimensions of a Twelve-Man Jury Table," *Sociometry,* 24 (December, 1961), pp. 397-415.

2. William H. Whyte, *The Organization Man* (New York: Simon and Schuster, 1956).

3. Harry A. Wilmer, "Graphic Ways of Representing Some Aspects of a Therapeutic Community," *Symposium on Preventive and Social Psychiatry* (Washington: Government Printing Office, 1957).

4. Bernard Steinzor, "The Spatial Factor in Face-to-Face Discussion Groups," *Journal of Abnormal and Social Psychology,* 45 (July, 1950), pp. 552-555.

5. Bernard M. Bass and S. Klubeck, "Effects of Seating Arrangements in Leaderless Group Discussions," *Journal of Abnormal and Social Psychology,* 47 (July, 1952), pp. 724-727.

6. Strodtbeck and Hook, *op. cit.*

7. A. Paul Hare and Robert F. Bales, "Seating Position and Small Group Interaction," *Sociometry,* 26 (December, 1963), pp. 480-486.

8. F. H. Allport, *Social Psychology* (Boston: Houghton Mifflin, 1924); W. Moede, *Experimentelle Massenpsychologie* (Leipzig: S. Hirzel, 1920).

9. Floyd Allport, *Social Psychology.*

10. A similar preference for corner seating was found in subsequent study of eating pairs in a hospital cafeteria. Of the 41 pairs, 29 sat corner-to-corner while 12 pairs sat across from one another.

11. This study was carried out by David Addicott.

12. Glen McBride, *A General Theory of Social Organization and Behavior* (St. Lucia: University of Queensland Press 1964.)

13. This study was conducted by Vera Stevens and Corinne Sundberg.

14. Peter Marler, "Studies of Fighting Chaffinches: Proximity as a Cause of Aggression," *British Journal of Animal Behavior,* 4 (1956), pp. 23-30.

15. F. S. Chapin, "Some Housing Factors Related to Mental Hygiene," *Journal of Social Issues,* 7 (1951), pp. 164-171.

16. Erving Goffman, *Behavior in Public Places* (Glencoe: Free Press, 1963).

17. Edward T. Hall, "Silent Assumptions in Social Communication," in *Disorders of Communication,* 42 (1964), pp. 41-55.

18. Ray Birdwhistell, "Field Methods and Techniques," *Human Organization,* 11 (Spring, 1952), pp. 37-38.

Japanese Management Practices and Productivity

Nina Hatvany
Vladimir Pucik

The [United States] is the most technically advanced country and the most affluent one. But capital investment alone will not make the difference. In any country the quality of products and the productivity of workers depend on management. When Detroit changes its management system we'll see more powerful American competitors.
— Hideo Suguira, Executive Vice-President, Honda Motor Co.

Productivity — or output per worker — is a key measure of economic health. When it increases, the economy grows in real terms and so do standards of living. When it declines, real economic growth slows or stagnates. Productivity is the result of many factors, including investment in capital goods, technological innovation, and workers' motivation.

After a number of years of sluggish productivity growth, the United States now trails most other major industrial nations in the rise in output per worker, although it still enjoys the best overall rate. This state of affairs is increasingly bemoaned by many critics in both academic and business circles. Some reasons suggested to "explain" the U.S. decline in productivity rankings include excessive government regulation, tax policies discouraging investment, increases in energy costs, uncooperative unions, and various other factors in the business environment.

Some observers, however — among them Harvard professors Robert Hayes and William J. Abernathy — put the blame squarely on American managers. They argue that U.S. firms prefer to service existing markets rather than create new ones, imitate rather than innovate, acquire existing companies rather than develop a superior product or process technology and, perhaps most important, focus on short-run returns on investment rather than long-term growth and research and development strategy. Too many managers are setting and meeting short-term, market-driven objectives instead of adopting the appropriate time-horizon needed to plan and execute the successful product innovations needed to sustain worldwide competitiveness.

The performance of the American manufacturing sector is often contrasted with progress achieved by other industrialized countries — particularly Japan. Japan's productivity growth in manufacturing has been nearly three times the U.S. rate over the past two decades — the average annual growth rate between 1960 and 1978 was 7.8 percent. In the last five years alone, the productivity index has increased by more than 40 percent and most economists forecast similar rates for the 1980s. Such impressive results deserve careful examination.

Students of the Japanese economy generally point out that Japanese investment outlays as a proportion of gross national product are nearly twice as large as those in the United States, and this factor is backed by a high personal savings ratio and the availability of relatively cheap investment funds. Also, a massive infusion of imported technology contributed significantly to the growth of productivity in Japan. Among noneconomic factors, the Japanese political environment seems to support business needs, especially those of advanced industries. In addition, the "unique" psychological and cultural characteristics of the Japanese people is frequently cited as the key reason for Japan's success.

It is indeed a well-known fact that absenteeism in most Japanese companies is low; turnover rates are about half the U.S. figures, and employee commitment to the company is generally high. But although cultural factors are important in any context, we doubt that any pecularities of Japanese people (if they exist) have much impact on their commitment or productivity. In fact, several recent research studies indicate that Japanese and American workers show little or no difference in the personality attributes related to performance. Rather, we join Robert Hayes and William Abernathy in believing that, in this context, productivity stems from the superior management systems of many Japanese firms. But the focus of our analysis is not on such areas as corporate marketing and production strategies. Instead, we will examine management practices in Japan as they affect one key company asset: human resources.

Our analysis is guided by our experience with subsidiaries of Japanese firms in the United States. Typically, these companies are staffed by a small group of Japanese managers with varying levels of autonomy relative to the company's parent. The rest of the employees are American. Although they operate in an alien culture, many of these subsidiaries are surprisingly successful. While it is often very difficult to measure the performance of newly established operations, it is no secret that production lines in several Japanese subsidiaries operate at the same productivity rate as those in Japan (for example, the Sony plant in San Diego).

This example — as well as others — serves to demonstrate that what works in Japan can often work in the United States. The techniques used by the management of Japanese subsidiaries to motivate their American workers seem to play an important part in the effort to increase productivity. Therefore, a careful examination of management practices in Japan is useful not only for a specialist interested in cross-cultural organization development, but also for the management practitioner who is losing to foreign competition evèn on his or her homeground. What is it that the Japanese do better?

Our discussion attempts to answer this question by presenting a model of the Japanese management system that rests on a few elements that can be examined in different cultural settings. The model will be used to highlight the relationship between the management strategies and techniques observed in Japan and positive work outcomes, such as commitment and productivity. Our review is not intended to be exhaustive, but rather to suggest the feasibility of integrating findings from Japan with more general concepts and theories. We will therefore focus on relationships that may be verified by observations of behavior in non-Japanese, especially U.S., settings.

We propose that positive work outcomes emanate from a complex set of behavioral patterns that are not limited to any specific culture. The emphasis is on management practices as a system and on the integration of various strategies and techniques to achieve desired results. We hope thus to provide an alternative to statements — often cited but never empirically supported — that the high commitment and productivity of Japanese employees is primarily traceable to their cultural characteristics.

A MANAGEMENT SYSTEM FOCUSED ON HUMAN RESOURCES

Most managers will probably agree that management's key concern is the optimal utilization of a firm's various assets. These assets may vary — financial, technological, human, and so on. Tradeoffs are necessary because utilization of any one asset may result in underutilization of another. We propose that in most Japanese companies, *human assets are considered to be the firm's most important and profitable assets in the long run.* Although the phrase itself sounds familiar, even hollow, to many American managers and OD consultants, it is important to recognize that this management orientation is backed up by a well-integrated system of strategies and techniques that translate this abstract concept into reality.

First, long-term and secure employment is provided, which attracts employees of the desired quality and induces them to remain with the firm. Second, a company philosophy is articulated that shows concern for employee needs and stresses cooperation and teamwork in a unique environment. Third, close attention is given both to hiring people who will fit well with the particular company's values and to integrating employees into the company at all stages of their working life. These general strategies are expressed in specific management techniques. Emphasis is placed on continuous development of employee skills; formal promotion is of secondary importance, at least during the early career stages. Employees are evaluated on a multitude of criteria — often including group performance results — rather than on individual bottom-line contribution. The work is structured in such a way that it may be carried out by groups operating with a great deal of autonomy. Open communication is encouraged, supported, and rewarded. Information about pending decisions is circulated to all concerned before the decisions are actually made. Active

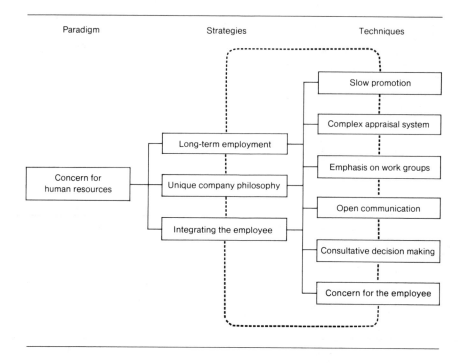

FIGURE 1
Japanese management paradigm.

observable concern for each and every employee is expressed by supervisory personnel (Figure 1). Each of these management practices, either alone or in combination with the others, is known to have a positive influence on commitment to the organization and its effectiveness.

We will discuss these practices as we have observed them in large and medium-size firms in Japan and in several of their subsidiaries in the United States. Although similar practices are often also in evidence in small Japanese companies, the long-term employment policies in these firms are more vulnerable to drops in economic activity and the system's impact is necessarily limited.

STRATEGIES

Once management adopts the view that utilizing human assets is what matters most in the organization's success, several strategies have to be pursued to secure these assets in the desired quality and quantity. These strategies involve the following:

Provide Secure Employment   Although Japanese companies typically provide stable and long-term employment, many smaller firms find it difficult to do so in times of recession. The policy calls for hiring relatively unskilled employees (often directly from high schools or universities), training them on the job, promoting from within, and recognizing seniority.

The implicit guarantee of the employee's job, under all but the most severe economic circumstances, is a marked departure from conventional managerial thinking about the need to retain flexibility in workforce size in order to respond efficiently to cyclical variations in demand. However, this employment system, at least as practiced in large corporations in Japan, is far from being inflexible. Several techniques can be applied to ride out recession with a minimum burden of labor cost while keeping a maximum number of regular workers on their jobs — a freeze on new hiring, solicitation of voluntary retirement sweetened by extra benefits, use of core employees to replace temporaries and subcontractors doing nonessential work, and so forth. Thus a labor force cut of approximately 10-15 percent in a short time period is not an unusual phenomenon. In addition, across-the-board salary and bonus cuts for all employees, including management, would follow if necessary.

Japanese managers believe that job security has a positive impact on morale and productivity, limits turnover and training costs, and increases the organization's cohesiveness. For that reason, they are willing to accept its temporary negative effect in a period of reduced demand. Long-term employment security is also characteristic of all the U.S. subsidiaries that we have visited. Layoffs and terminations occur extremely rarely. For example, the Kikkoman Company instituted across-the-board wage cuts in an attempt to preserve employment during the last recession. Murata instituted a four-day workweek, and at Matsushita's Quasar plant, a number of employees were shifted from their regular work to functions such as repairs, maintenance, and service. It should be noted that there are several well-known U.S. corporations — for example, IBM and Hewlett-Packard — that follow similar practices when the alternative would be layoff.

In Japanese companies, even poor performers are either retrained or transferred, instead of simply being dismissed. The plant manager in an electronics component factory explained how the company copes with personal failures: "We give a chance to improve even if there has been a big mistake. For example, the quality control manager didn't fit, so we transferred him to sales engineering and now he is doing fine."

Research on behavior in organizations suggests that the assumptions of Japanese managers and some of their U.S. colleagues about the positive impact of job security are, at least to some degree, justified. It has been shown that long tenure is positively associated with commitment to the organization, which in turn reduces turnover. High commitment in conjunction with a binding choice (employees of large firms in Japan have difficulty finding jobs of the same quality elsewhere, given the relatively stable labor market) also leads to high satisfaction, but whether this contributes to high productivity still remains to be proved. It is, however, necessary to view the policy of secure employment as a key condition for the implementation of other management strategies and techniques that have a more immediate impact on the organization's effectiveness.

Articulate a Unique Company Philosophy A philosophy that is both articulated and carried through presents a clear picture of the organization's objectives, norms, and values — and thus helps transform commitment into productive effort. Familiarity with organizational goals gives direction to employees' actions, sets constraints on their behavior, and enhances their motivation. The understanding of shared meanings and beliefs expressed in the company philosophy binds the individual to the organization and, at the same time, stimulates the emergence of goals shared with others, as well as the stories, myths, and symbols that form the fabric of a company philosophy. William Ouchi and Raymond Price suggest that an organizational philosophy is an elegant informational device that provides a form of control at once pervasive and effective; at the same time it provides guidance for managers by presenting a basic theory of how the firm should be managed.

An explicit management philosophy of how work should be done can be found in many successful corporations in both Japan and the United States; examples in the United States include IBM, Texas Instruments, and U.S. Homes. Nevertheless, it is fair to say that the typical Japanese firm's management philosophy has a distinct flavor. It usually puts a heavy emphasis on cooperation and teamwork within a corporate "family" that is unique and distinct from that of any other firm. In return for an employee's effort, the family's commitment to the employee is translated into company determination to avoid layoffs and to provide a whole range of supplementary welfare benefits for the employee and his or her family. Naturally, without reasonable employment security, the fostering of team spirit and cooperation would be impossible. The ideal is thus to reconcile two objectives: pursuit of profits and perpetuation of the company as a group.

In a number of cases, a particular management philosophy that originated within the parent company in Japan is also being actively disseminated in its U.S. subsidiaries. Typically, claims of uniqueness range from the extent of the company's concern for employees' worklives to the quality of service to the customer. We quote from the in-house literature issued by one of the fastest growing Japanese-owned electronics component makers in California:

Management Philosophy
Our goal is to strive toward both the material and the spiritual fulfillment of all employees in the Company, and through this successful fulfillment, serve mankind in its progress and prosperity.

Management Policy
[. . .] Our purpose is to fully satisfy the needs of our customers and in return gain a just profit for ourselves. We are a family united in common bonds and singular goals. One of these bonds is the respect and support we feel for our fellow family co-workers.

Integrate Employees into the Company   The benefits of an articulated company philosophy are lost, however, if it's not visibly supported by management's behavior. A primary function of the company's socialization effort, therefore, is to ensure that employees have understood the philosophy and seen it in action. Close attention is given to hiring people who are willing to endorse the values of the particular company and to the employees' integration into the organization at all stages of their working life. The development of cohesiveness within the firm, based on the acceptance of goals and values, is a major focus of personnel policies in many Japanese firms.

Because employees are expected to remain in the company for a major part of their careers, careful selection is necessary to ensure that they fit well into the company climate. In many U.S.-based Japanese firms also, new hires at all levels are carefully screened with this aspect in mind. As in Japan, basic criteria for hiring are moderate views and a harmonious personality, and for that reason a large proportion of new hires come from employee referrals. In general, "virgin" workforces are preferred, since they can readily be assimilated into each company's unique environment as a community.

The intensive socialization process starts with the hiring decision and the initial training program and continues in various forms thereafter. Over time, the employee internalizes the various values and objectives of the firm, becomes increasingly committed to them, and learns the formal and informal rules and procedures, particularly through job rotation. That process usually includes two related types of job transfers. First, employees are transferred to new positions to learn additional skills in on-the-job training programs. These job changes are planned well in advance for all regular employees, including blue-collar workers. Second, transfers are part of a long-range, experience-building program through which the organization develops its future managers; such programs involve movement across departmental boundaries at any stage of an employee's career.

While employees rotate semilaterally from job to job, they become increasingly socialized into the organization, immersed in the company philosophy and culture, and bound to a set of shared goals. Even in the absence of specific internal regulations that might be too constraining in a rapidly changing environment, a well-socialized manager who has held positions in various functions and locations within the firm has a feel for the organization's needs.

TECHNIQUES

The basic management orientation and strategies that we have just discussed are closely interrelated with specific management techniques used in Japanese firms and in their subsidiaries in the United States. The whole system is composed of a set of interdependent employment practices in which the presence of one technique complements as well as influences the effectiveness of others. This interdependence, rather than a simple cause-effect relationship, is the key factor that helps maintain the organization's stability and effectiveness. Additional environmental variables may determine which of the strategies or techniques will require most attention from top management, but in their impact on the organization no single technique listed below is of prime importance.

Slow Promotion, Job Rotation, and Internal Training   All Japanese subsidiaries that we have visited have seniority-based promotion systems. At one of them, a medium-size motorcycle plant, a seniority-based promotion system has been reinstituted after an experiment with a merit-based system proved highly unpopular with employees. Training is conducted, as expected, mostly on the job, and as one textile company executive noted, career paths are flexible: "You can get involved in what you want to do." Hiring from outside into upper-level positions is rare. According to another Japanese plant manager: "We want someone who understands the management system of the company. We want to keep the employees with us; we want to keep them happy."

Although promotion is slow, early informal identification of the elite is not unusual and carefully planned lateral job transfers add substantial flexibility to job assignments. Not all jobs are equally central to the workflow in an organization, so employees — even those with the same status and salary — can be rewarded or punished by providing or withholding positions in which they could acquire the skills needed for future formal promotions.

Job-rotation in U.S.-based Japanese firms seems less planned or structured than in Japan and more an ad-hoc reaction to organizational needs — but in general, the emphasis on slow promotion and job rotation creates an environment in which an employee becomes a generalist rather than a specialist in a particular functional area. For the most part, however, these general skills are unique to the organization. Several of the Japanese manufacturers that invested in the United States were forced to simplify their product technology because they were not able to recruit qualified operators versatile enough to meet their needs, and there was not enough time to train them internally.

In Japan, well-planned job rotation is the key to the success of an in-company training program that generally encompasses all the firm's employees. For some categories of highly skilled blue-collar workers training plans for a period of up to ten years are not unusual. Off-the-job training is often included, again for managers and nonmanagers alike. However, whether such an extensive training system will be transferred to U.S. subsidiaries remains to be seen.

In addition to its impact on promotion and training, job rotation also promotes the development of informal communication networks that help in coordinating work activities across functional areas and in resolving problems speedily. This aspect of job rotation is especially important for managerial personnel. Finally, timely job rotation relieves an employee who has become unresponsive to, or bored with, the demands of his or her job.

Some observers argue that deferred promotion may frustrate highly promising, ambitious employees. However, the personnel director of a major trading company has commented: "The secret of Japanese management, if there is any, is to make everybody feel as long as possible that he is slated for the top position in the firm — thereby increasing his motivation during the most productive period of his employment." The public identification of "losers," who of course far outnumber "winners" in any hierarchical organization, is postponed in the belief that the increased output of the losers, who are striving hard to do well and still hoping to beat the odds, more than compensates for any lags in the motivation of the impatient winners. By contrast, top management in many American organizations is preoccupied with identifying rising stars as soon as possible and is less concerned about the impact on the losers' morale.

Complex Appraisal System   In addition to emphasizing the long-term perspective, Japanese companies often establish a complex appraisal system that includes not only individual performance measures tied to the bottom line, but also measures of various desirable personality traits and behaviors — such as creativity, emotional maturity, and cooperation with others as well as team performance results. In most such companies, potential, personality, and behavior, rather than current output, are the key criteria, yet the difference is often merely symbolic. Output measures may easily be "translated" into such attributes as leadership skills, technical competence, relations with others, and judgment. This approach avoids making the employee feel that the bottom line, which may be beyond his or her control, in part or in whole, is the key dimension of evaluation. Occasional mistakes, particularly those made by lower-level employees, are considered part of the learning process.

At the same time, evaluations do clearly discriminate among employees because each employee is compared with other members of an appropriate group (in age and status) and ranked accordingly. The ranking within the cohort is generally not disclosed to the employees, but of course it can be partially inferred from small salary differentials and a comparison of job assignments. At least in theory, the slow promotion system should allow for careful judgments to be made even on such subjective criteria as the personality traits of honesty and seriousness. However, the authors' observations suggest that ranking within the cohort is usually established rather early in one's career and is generally not very flexible thereafter.

Employees are not formally separated according to their ability until later in their tenure; ambitious workers who seek immediate recognition must engage in activities that will get them noticed. Bottom-line performance is not an adequate criterion because, as noted, it is not the only focus of managerial evaluation. This situation encourages easily observable behavior, such as voluntary overtime, that appears to demonstrate willingness to exert substantial effort on the organization's behalf. The evaluation process becomes to a large degree self-selective.

Several other facets of this kind of appraisal system deserve our attention. Because evaluations are based on managerial observations during frequent, regular interactions with subordinates, the cost of such an evaluation system is relatively low. When behavior rather than bottom-line performance is the focus of evaluation, means as well as ends may be assessed. This very likely leads to a better match between the direction of employee efforts and company objectives, and it encourages a long-term perspective. Finally, since group performance is also a focus of evaluation, peer pressure on an employee to contribute his or her share to the group's performance becomes an important mechanism of performance control. Long tenure, friendship ties, and informal communication networks enable both superiors and peers to get a very clear sense of the employee's performance and potential relative to others.

Among the management techniques characteristic of large Japanese enterprises, the introduction of a complex appraisal system is probably the least visible in their U.S. subsidiaries. Most of their U.S.-based affiliates are relatively young; thus long-term evaluation of employees, the key point in personnel appraisal as practiced in Japan, is not yet practicable. Furthermore, the different expectations of American workers and managers about what constitutes a fair and equitable appraisal system might hinder acceptance of the parent company's evaluation system.

Emphasis on Work Groups   Acknowledging the enormous impact of groups on their members — both directly, through the enforcement of norms, and indirectly, by affecting the beliefs and values of members — Japanese organizations devote far greater attention to structural factors that enhance group motivation and cooperation than to the motivation of individual employees. Tasks are assigned to groups, not to individual employees, and group cohesion is stimulated by delegating responsibility to the group not only for getting the tasks performed, but also for designing the way in which they get performed. The group-based performance evaluation has already been discussed.

Similarly, in the U.S.-based Japanese firms that we have visited, the group rather than an individual forms the basic work unit for all practical purposes. Quality of work and speed of job execution are key concerns in group production meetings that are held at least monthly, and even daily in some companies. The design function, however, is not yet very well developed; many workers are still relative newcomers unfamiliar with all aspects of the advanced technology. Intergroup rivalry is also encouraged. In one capacitor company, a group on a shift that performs well consistently is rewarded regularly. Sometimes news of a highly productive group from another shift or even from the Japanese parent is passed around the shop floor to stimulate the competition.

In Japan, group autonomy is encouraged by avoiding any reliance on experts to solve operational problems. One widely used group-based technique for dealing with such problems is quality control (QC) circles. A QC circle's major task is to pinpoint and solve a particular workshop's problem. Outside experts are called in only to educate group members in the analytical tools for problem solving or to provide a specialized technical service. Otherwise, the team working on the problem operates autonomously, with additional emphasis on self-improvement activities that will help achieve group goals. Fostering motivation through direct employee participation in the work process design is a major consideration in the introduction of QC circles and similar activities to the factory floor.

Nevertheless, work-group autonomy in most work settings is bound by clearly defined limits, with the company carefully coordinating team activities by controlling the training and evaluation of members, the size of the team, and the scope and amount of production. Yet within these limits, teamwork is not only part of a company's articulated philosophy, it actually forms the basic fabric of the work process. Job rotation is encouraged both to develop each employee's skills and to fit the work group's needs.

From another perspective, the group can also assist in developing job-relevant knowledge by direct instruction and by serving as a model of appropriate behavior. The results of empirical studies suggest that structuring tasks around work groups not only may improve performance, but also may contribute to increased esteem and a sense of identity among group members. Furthermore, this process of translating organizational membership into membership in a small group seems, in general, to result in higher job satisfaction, lower absenteeism, lower turnover rates, and fewer labor disputes.

Open and Extensive Communication   Even in the Japanese-owned U.S. companies, plant managers typically spend at least two hours a day on the shop floor and are readily available for the rest of the day. Often, foremen are deliberately deprived of offices so they can be with their subordinates on the floor throughout the whole day, instructing and helping whenever necessary. The same policy applies to personnel specialists. The American personnel manager of a Japanese motorcycle plant, for example, spends between two and four hours a day on the shop floor discussing issues that concern employees. The large number of employees he is able to greet by their first name testifies to the amount of time he spends on the floor. "We have an open-door policy — but it's their door, not management's" was his explanation of the company's emphasis on the quality of face-to-face vertical communication.

Open communication is also inherent in the Japanese work setting. Open work spaces are crowded with individuals at different hierarchical levels. Even high-ranking office managers seldom have separate private offices. Partitions, cubicles, and small side rooms are used to set off special areas for conferences with visitors or small discussions among the staff. In one Japanese-owned TV plant on the West Coast, the top manager's office is next to the receptionist — open and visible to everybody who walks into the building, whether employee, supplier, or customer.

Open communication is not limited to vertical exchanges. Both the emphasis on team spirit in work groups and the network of friendships that employees develop during their long tenure in the organization encourage the extensive face-to-face communication so often reported in studies involving Japanese companies. Moreover, job rotation is instrumental in building informal lateral networks across departmental boundaries. Without these networks, the transfer of much job-related information would be impossible. These informal networks are not included in written work manuals, thus they are invisible to a newcomer; but their use as a legitimate tool to get things done is implicitly authorized by the formal control system. Communication skills and related behavior are often the focus of yearly evaluations. Frequently, foreign observers put too much emphasis on vertical ties and other hierarchical aspects of Japanese organizations. In fact, the ability to manage lateral communication is perhaps even more important to effective performance, particularly at the middle-management level.

Consultative Decision Making   Few Japanese management practices are so misunderstood by outsiders as is the decision-making process. The image is quite entrenched in Western literature on Japanese organizations: Scores of managers huddle together in endless discussion until consensus on every detail is reached, after which a symbolic document, "ringi," is passed around so they can affix their seals of approval on it. This image negates the considerable degree of decentralization for most types of decisions that is characteristic in most subsidiaries we have visited. In fact, when time is short, decisions are routinely made by the manager in charge.

Under the usual procedure for top-management decision making, a proposal is initiated by a middle manager (but often under the directive of top management). This middle manager engages in informal discussion and consultation with peers and supervisors. When all are familiar with the proposal, a formal request for a decision is made and, because of earlier discussions, is almost inevitably ratified — often in a ceremonial group meeting or through the "ringi" procedure. This implies not unanimous approval, but the unanimous consent to its implementation.

This kind of decision making is not participative in the Western sense of the word, which encompasses negotiation and bargaining between a manager and subordinates. In the Japanese context, negotiations are primarily lateral between the departments concerned with the decision. Within the work group, the emphasis is on including all group members in the process of decision making, not on achieving consensus on the alternatives. Opposing parties are willing to go along, with the consolation that their viewpoint may carry the day the next time around.

However, the manager will usually not implement his or her decision "until others who will be affected have had sufficient time to offer their views, feel that they have been fairly heard, and are willing to support the decision even though they may not feel that it is the best one," according to Thomas P. Rohlen. Those outside the core of the decision-making group merely express their acknowledgement of the proposed course of action. They do not participate; they do not feel ownership of the decision. On the other hand, the early communication of the proposed changes helps reduce uncertainty in the organization. In addition, prior information on upcoming decisions gives employees an opportunity to rationalize and accept the outcomes.

Japanese managers we have interviewed often expressed the opinion that it is their American partners who insist on examining every aspect and contingency of proposed alternatives, while they themselves prefer a relatively general agreement on the direction to follow, leaving the details to be solved on the run. Accordingly, the refinement of a proposal occurs during its early implementation stage.

Although the level of face-to-face communication in Japanese organizations is relatively high, it should not be confused with participation in decision making. Most communication concerns routine tasks; thus it is not surprising that research on Japanese companies indicates no relationship between the extent of face-to-face communication and employees' perceptions of how much they participate in decision making.

Moreover, consultation with lower-ranking employees does not automatically imply that the decision process is "bottom up," as suggested by Peter Drucker and others. Especially in the case of long-term planning and strategy, the initiative comes mostly from the top. Furthermore, consultative decision making does not diminish top management's responsibility for a decision's consequences. Although the ambiguities of status and centrality may make it difficult for outsiders to pinpoint responsibility, it is actually quite clear within the organization. Heads still roll to pay for mistakes, albeit in a somewhat more subtle manner than is customary in Western organizations: Departure to the second- or third-ranking subsidiary is the most common punishment.

Concern for the Employee   It is established practice for managers to spend a lot of time talking to employees about everyday matters. Thus they develop a feeling for employees' personal needs and problems, as well as for their performance. Obviously, gaining this intimate knowledge of each employee is easier when an employee has long tenure, but managers do consciously attempt to get to know their employees, and they place a premium on providing time to talk. The quality of relationships developed with subordinates is also an important factor on which a manager is evaluated.

Various company-sponsored cultural, athletic, and other recreational activities further deepen involvement in employees' lives. This heavy schedule of company social affairs is ostensibly voluntary, but virtually all employees participate. Typically, an annual calendar of office events might include two overnight trips, monthly Saturday afternoon recreation, and an average of six office parties — all at company expense. A great deal of drinking goes on at these events and much good fellowship is expressed among the employees.

Finally, in Japan the company allocates substantial financial resources to pay for benefits for all employees, such as a family allowance and various commuting and housing allowances. In addition, many firms provide a whole range of welfare services ranging from subsidized company housing for families and dormitories for unmarried employees, through company nurseries and company scholarships for employees' children, to mortgage loans, credit facilities, savings plans, and insurance. Thus employees often perceive a close relationship between their own welfare and the company's financial welfare. Accordingly, behavior for the company's benefit that may appear self-sacrificing is not at all so; rather, it is in the employee's own interest.

Managers in U.S.-based companies generally also voiced a desire to make life in the company a pleasant experience for their subordinates. As in Japan, managers at all levels show concern for employees by sponsoring various recreational activities or even taking them out to dinner to talk problems over. Again, continuous open communication gets special emphasis. However, company benefits are not as extensive as in Japan because of a feeling that American employees prefer rewards in the form of salary rather than the "golden handcuff" of benefits. Furthermore, the comprehensive government welfare system in the United States apparently renders such extensive company benefits superfluous.

In summary, what we observed in many Japanese companies is an integrated system of management strategies and techniques that reinforce one another because of systemic management orientation to the quality of human resources. In addition to this system's behavioral consequences, which we have already discussed, a number of other positive outcomes have also been reported in research studies on Japanese organizations.

For example, when the company offers desirable employment conditions designed to provide job security and reduce voluntary turnover, the company benefits not only from the increased loyalty of the workforce, but also from a reduction in hiring, training, and other costs associated with turnover and replacement. Because employees enjoy job security, they do not fear technical innovation and may, in fact, welcome it — especially if it relieves them of tedious or exhausting manual tasks. In such an atmosphere, concern for long-term growth, rather than a focus on immediate profits, is also expected to flourish.

An articulated philosophy that expresses the company's family atmosphere as well as its uniqueness enables the employee to justify loyalty to the company and stimulates healthy competition with other companies. The management goals symbolized in company philosophy can give clear guidance to the employee who's trying to make the best decision in a situation that is uncertain.

Careful attention to selection and the employee's fit into the company results in a homogeneous workforce, easily able to develop the friendship ties that form the basis of information networks. The lack of conflict among functional divisions and the ability to communicate informally across divisions allow for rapid interdivisional coordination and the rapid implementation of various company goals and policies.

The other techniques we've outlined reinforce these positive outcomes. Slow promotion reinforces a long-range perspective. High earnings in this quarter need not earn an employee an immediate promotion. Less reliance on the bottom line means that an employee's capabilities and behaviors over the long term become more important in their evaluations. Groups are another vehicle by which the company's goals, norms, and values are communicated to each employee. Open communication is the most visible vehicle for demonstrating concern for employees and willingness to benefit from their experience, regardless of rank. Open communication is thus a key technique that supports consultative decision making and affects the quality of any implementation process. Finally, caring about employees' social needs encourages identification with the firm and limits the impact of personal troubles on performance.

What we have described is a system based on the understanding that in return for the employee's contribution to company growth and well-being, the profitable firm will provide a stable and secure work environment and protect the individual employee's welfare even during a period of economic slowdown.

THE TRANSFERABILITY OF JAPANESE MANAGEMENT PRACTICES

As in Japan, a key managerial concern in all U.S.-based Japanese companies we have investigated was the quality of human resources. As one executive put it, "We adapt the organization to the people because you can't adapt people to the organization." A number of specific instances of how Japanese management techniques are being applied in the United States were previously cited. Most personnel policies we've observed were similar to those in Japan, although evaluation systems and job-rotation planning are still somewhat different, probably because of the youth of the subsidiary companies. Less institutionalized concern for employee welfare was also pointed out.

The experience of many Japanese firms that have established U.S. subsidiaries suggests that the U.S. workers are receptive to many management practices introduced by Japanese managers. During our interviews, many Japanese executives pointed out that the productivity level in their U.S. plants is on a level similar to that in Japan — and occasionally even higher. Other research data indicate that American workers in Japanese-owned plants are even more satisfied with their work conditions than are their Japanese or Japanese-American colleagues.

The relative success of U.S.-based Japanese companies in transferring their employment and management practices to cover the great majority of their U.S. workers is not surprising when we consider that a number of large U.S. corporations have created management systems that use some typical Japanese techniques. Several of these firms have an outstanding record of innovation and rapid growth. A few examples are Procter & Gamble, Hewlett-Packard, and Cummins Engine.

William Ouchi and his colleagues call these firms Theory Z organizations. Seven key characteristics of Theory Z organizations are the following:

1. Long-term employment.

2. Slow evaluation and promotion.

3. Moderately specialized careers.

4. Consensual decision making.

5. Individual responsibility.

6. Implicit, informal control (but with explicit measures).

7. Wholistic concern for the employee.

The Theory Z organization shares several features with the Japanese organization, but there are differences: In the former, responsibility is definitely individual, measures of performance are explicit, and careers are actually moderately specialized. However, Ouchi tells us little about communication patterns in these organizations, the role of the work group, and some other features important in Japanese settings.

Here's an example of a standard practice in the Theory Z organization that Ouchi studied in depth:

> [The Theory Z organization] calculated the profitability of each of its divisions, but it did not operate a strict profit center or other marketlike mechanism. Rather, decisions were frequently made by division managers who were guided by broader corporate concerns, even though their own divisional earnings may have suffered as a result.

A survey by Ouchi and Jerry Johnson showed that within the electronics industry perceived corporate prestige, managerial ability, and reported corporate earnings were all strongly positively correlated with the "Z-ness" of the organization.

It is also significant that examples of successful implementation of the Japanese system can be found even in Britain, a country notorious for labor-management conflict. In our interpretation, good labor-management relations — even the emergence of a so-called company union — is an effect, rather than a cause, of the mutually beneficial, reciprocal relationship enjoyed by the employees and the firm. Thus we see the coexistence of our management paradigm with productivity in companies in Japan, in Japanese companies in the United States and Europe, and in a number of indigenous U.S. companies. Although correlation does not imply cause, such a casual connection would be well supported by psychological theories. Douglas McGregor summarizes a great deal of research in saying: "Effective performance results when conditions are created such that the members of the organization can achieve their own goals best by directing their efforts toward the success of the enterprise."

CONCLUSION

Many cultural differences exist, of course, between people in Japan and those in Western countries. However, this should not distract our atttention from the fact that human beings in all countries also have a great deal in common. In the workplace, all people value decent treatment, security, and an opportunity for emotional fulfillment. It is to the credit of Japanese managers that they have developed organizational systems that, even though far from perfect, do respond to these needs to a great extent. Also to their credit is the fact that high motivation and productivity result at the same time.

The strategies and techniques we have reviewed constitute a remarkably well-integrated system. The management practices are highly congruent with the way in which tasks are structured, with individual members' goals, and with the organization's climate. Such a fit is expected to result in a high degree of organizational effectiveness or productivity. We believe that the management paradigm of concern for human resources blends the hopes of humanistic thinkers with the pragmatism of those who need to show a return on investment. The evidence strongly suggests that this paradigm is both desirable and feasible in Western countries and that the key elements of Japanese management practices are not unique to Japan and can be successfully transplanted to other cultures. The linkage between human needs and productivity is nothing new in Western management theory. It required the Japanese, however, to translate the idea into a successful reality.

ACKNOWLEDGMENTS

The authors would like to thank Mitsuyo Hanada, Blair McDonald, William Newman, William Ouchi, Thomas Roehl, Michael Tushman, and others for their helpful comments on earlier drafts of this paper. We are grateful to Citibank, New York, and the Japan Foundation, Tokyo, for their financial support of the work in the preparation of this paper.

SELECTED BIBLIOGRAPHY

Robert Hayes and William Abernathy brought the lack of U.S. innovation to public attention in their article, "Managing Our Way to Economic Decline" *(Harvard Business Review,* July-August 1980).

Thomas P. Rohlen's book, *For Harmony and Strength: Japanese White-Collar Organization in Anthropological Perspective* (University of California Press, 1974), is a captivating description of the Japanese management system as seen in a regional bank. Peter Drucker has written several articles on the system, including "What We Can Learn from Japanese Management" *(Harvard Business Review,* March-April 1971). His thoughts are extended to the United States by the empirical work of Richard Pascale, "Employment Practices and Employee Attitudes: A Study of Japanese and American Managed Firms in the U.S." *(Human Relations,* July 1978).

For further information on the Theory Z organization see "Type Z Organization: Stability in the Midst of Mobility" by William Ouchi and Alfred Jaeger *(Academy of Management Review,* April 1978), "Types of Organizational Control and Their Relationship to Emotional Well-Being" by William Ouchi and Jerry Johnson (*Administrative Science Quarterly,* Spring 1978), and "Hierarchies, Clans, and Theory Z: A New Perspective on Organization Development" by William Ouchi and Raymond Price (*Organizational Dynamics,* Autumn 1978).

Douglas McGregor explains the importance of a fit between employee and organizational goals in *The Human Side of Enterprise* (McGraw-Hill, 1960).

4

Internal Influences

Leadership and Social Influence Processes

THE TUBBS MODEL OF SMALL GROUP INTERACTION

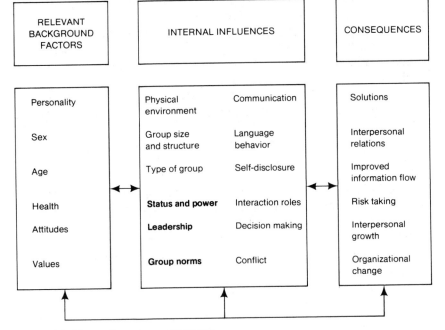

Concepts in **boldface** are the emphases of this chapter.

CASE STUDY*

Mayhall House is an independent men's dormitory on the campus of a large midwestern university. The grade average of the dorm was one of the lowest of any house on campus. This was mainly because almost all of our 65 residents were majoring in either engineering or commerce — generally acknowledged as the most difficult schools in the university. And, of course, we had our share of "goof-offs" — five or six fellows who had ability but had never been able to apply themselves to their studies. We chalked them up as immature and hoped they would "see the light" before their academic probation ran out. But as long as they didn't disturb anyone we felt we would get along with them.

As a matter of fact, there was very little "horsing around" in the house. I had visited a number of the other dorms and was surprised to see college men, or rather "boys," running up and down the halls yelling and chasing one another and playing silly pranks on one another. As I said, I had always considered our house remarkably calm and dignified — until this year. Now, you wouldn't know it. Everyone's calling it "Mayhem House."

When we started school in September, two important events (at least to me) occurred. I was elected president of Mayhall House, and a new counselor moved in. His name was John Morrison, 23, a graduate student in theology. John seemed to be very pleasant but made it clear in his first meeting with the residents of the house that he had heard our grade average was low and hoped we could raise it. He gave quite a pep talk and said if we would all pull together, we might put Mayhall near the top of the list.

I agreed with this, but I didn't see how there could be much improvement, in view of the fact that most of us were in the toughest schools.

The first evidence that John meant what he said occurred when he established his "closed-door policy." The fellows had the custom of leaving the doors of their rooms open and occasionally talking across the corridor to one another. If John happened to be passing by, he would simply close the doors without saying a word. I suppose he thought the fellows would take the hint, but they only got sore about the situation and started doing more transcorridor communicating. It got to be quite a joke. John would start at one end

---

* From William V. Haney, Communication and Interpersonal Relations, 4th ed. (Homewood, Ill.: Richard D. Irwin, Inc., 1979). Reprinted with permission.

of the corridor and close ten sets of doors as he walked to the other end. Two minutes after John was gone, all the doors would be open, and the talking would start in again — only louder and more of it. On one occasion, a student yelled, "Go to hell, John!" after John had closed his door. John opened the door again and put the student on formal warning.

Next was the radio episode. About the middle of November, John posted a notice: "In order to provide proper study conditions, no radios will be turned on after 7 p.m.; effective this date."

This seemed high-handed and unnecessary to me. Radios had never been a problem in the house before. A few students liked to study with some soft music in the background. But if anyone objected, they would turn their radios off.

The fellows seemed to accept this as a challenge. The night the notice was posted, about seven or eight men turned on their radios to get them warmed up but not loud enough for anyone to hear.

Then one radio blared up full blast for a second and was quickly snapped off. John came bolting down the corridor to find the radio. When he got near the room, another radio blared up for a moment at the opposite end of the hall. John wheeled and streaked back. At this moment two other radios opened up, and John started twirling around in circles! It was the most ridiculous thing you ever saw, and the fellows couldn't help bursting out laughing.

John was furious. "All right, children! If you can't take proper care of your toys, someone will have to take care of them for you!"

He then started moving from one room to the next, confiscating the radios. It took him about two hours, but he picked up every radio in the house, put them in a storeroom, and locked the door. Maybe the seven or eight pranksters deserved this, but he took *all* the radios — mine included!

Well, that was the sign for open warfare. What happened then was one continuous nightmare. The next night, somebody brought some firecrackers into the house, and the mayhem started! Someone tied a firecracker to a burning cigarette and laid it in front of John's door. A few minutes later, the cigarette burned down and ignited the firecracker. John threw open his door, and not a soul was to be seen. He was fit to be tied. That was a night to be remembered! All night long, about every ten minutes, a firecracker went off somewhere — outside the dorm, in the corridor, in somebody's room, or outside John's door! John didn't even come out.

The next day it snowed, and that night it was snowballs. I won't go into the gory details, but the end result was the damage of various property, including five broken windows!

This, of course, brought in the Dean of Men. I was surprised that he didn't come in before. I guess John never mentioned our situation. . . The rest is history. John has been transferred to another house, and we are on social probation for the rest of the semester.

1. *What mistakes do you think John made as a leader in this case?*

2. *What, specifically, would you have done differently if you had been John?*

3. *What would you do if you were a new counselor coming in after John?*

I n this case study we see a problem that is not unique to leaders in dormitories. The problem has to do with being able to develop effective leadership behaviors. Each of us from time to time will be called upon to act in the role of a group leader. For some, the role may seem comfortable; others will have to work hard to grow into it. In any case, leadership is a topic that seems to capture the interest of most students of small group interaction.

An indication of the times is revealed in the story that if a Martian spaceman were to land on Earth and demand, "Take me to your leader," we would not know where to take him. No subject in the small group literature has received more attention than leadership. As an achievement-oriented society, Americans are almost obsessed with the topic of leadership. We build and destroy heroes like so many clay pigeons. Charles Lindbergh was reportedly so worshipped that it was even newsworthy when one reporter caught him off guard, picking his nose. Compare this orientation to that of the Japanese, whose ancient proverbs include the saying, "A nail that protrudes is hammered down," and among whom the idea of standing out above one's peers is considered in poor taste. This chapter will examine the process of personal influence and its various ramifications. We begin with a discussion of power and status, then move to the ever-popular topic of leadership, and conclude with an analysis of the uses and abuses of social influence.

STATUS AND POWER

Most farmers who have raised poultry are familiar with the chickens' pecking at one another in an attempt to determine which animal dominates. The eventual result is that one chicken rises to the most dominant position, a second chicken dominates all others but the top chicken, the third chicken dominates all but the top two, and so on down the line. This order of dominance is generally referred to as the "pecking order," and when a new chicken is introduced to the barnyard, it must fight all the others to establish its position in the pecking order.

Pecking orders are also found in human interaction. Most often they are informal and adhered to almost unconsciously. They may also be formalized, as in an organization chart. An example of such a pecking order in the United States government is referred to as the "order of precedence"; it formally designates who precedes whom in the pecking order (or in order of importance as they might be officially introduced to a visiting dignitary or head of state). James Symington (1971, pp. 94-95) remarked that, as Chief of Protocol, "It was always a humbling reminder to read over this list" (since he was at the bottom).

Table of Precedence

The President of the United States
The Vice-President of the United States
The Speaker of the House of Representatives
The Chief Justice of the United States
Former Presidents of the United States
The Secretary of State
The Secretary-General of the United Nations
Ambassadors of Foreign Powers — individually ranked by order of
    date of presentation of credentials
Widows of former Presidents of the United States
United States Representative to the United Nations
Ministers of Foreign Powers (Chiefs of Diplomatic Missions)
Associate Justices of the Supreme Court of the United States
    and Retired Associate Justices
The Cabinet
    The Secretary of the Treasury
    The Secretary of Defense
    The Attorney General
    The Postmaster General
    The Secretary of the Interior
    The Secretary of Agriculture
    The Secretary of Commerce
    The Secretary of Labor
    The Secretary of Health, Education and Welfare
    The Secretary of Housing and Urban Development
    The Secretary of Transportation
The Senate
Governors of States (unless the function in question occurs in a
    Governor's own State, in which case he ranks after the Vice-
    President)
Former Vice-Presidents of the United States
The House of Representatives
Charges d'affaires of Foreign Powers

The Under Secretaries of the Executive Departments and the
Deputy Secretaries
Administrator, Agency for International Development
Director, United States Arms Control and Disarmament Agency
Secretaries of the Army, the Navy, and the Air Force
Director, Office of Management and Budget
Chairman, Council of Economic Advisers
Chairman, Board of Governors, Federal Reserve
Chairman, Joint Chiefs of Staff
Chiefs of Staff of the Army, the Navy, and the Air Force (ranked
according to date of appointment)
Commandant of the Marine Corps
(5-Star) Generals of the Army and Fleet Admirals
The Secretary-General, Organization of American States
Representatives to the Organization of American States
Director, Central Intelligence Agency
Administrator, General Services Administration
Director, United States Information Agency
Administrator, National Aeronautics and Space Administration
Administrator, Federal Aviation Administration
Chairman, Civil Service Commission
Chairman, the Atomic Energy Commission
Director, Defense Research and Engineering
Director, Office of Emergency Planning
Director, the Peace Corps
Director, Office of Economic Opportunity
Special Assistants to the President
Deputy Under Secretaries
Assistant Secretaries of the Executive Departments
United States Chief of Protocol

TYPES OF STATUS

Status is defined as one's position or rank relative to the others in a group.
Higher status tends to result in greater personal power or ability to influence
others. Increased power, in turn, tends to elevate an individual's status
level. Power and status tend to go hand in hand, reciprocally influencing
one another.

Think of the many ongoing groups you have joined. They often have
an established pecking order into which you must insert yourself. How
does this pecking order come about in the first place? *Ascribed status*
refers to the prestige that goes to a person by virtue of some characteristic
such as his or her family wealth, good looks, or age. One man who attended
an Ivy League school remarked that it was a bit awesome to be in classes
with the children of *the* Rockefellers, *the* Firestones, *the* Kennedys. Those
born into such families are likely to have high status even though as
individuals they have done nothing to earn it.

But what about the many occasions in which a new group forms and there is no established pecking order? How does one get established? What are the effects once it has been set up? Those who rise to positions of status based on the merits of their own individual accomplishments acquire what is called *attained status*. The United States is known as one country in which the Horatio Alger story can still occur — where the person from humble origins can still rise from one socioeconomic class to a higher one more easily than in many other countries.

What kinds of behaviors enable a person to acquire a position of attained status? Goldhamer and Shils (1939) hypothesized that power and status is a function of the ratio of the number of successful power acts to the number of attempts to influence:

$$\frac{Number\ of\ successful\ power\ acts}{Number\ of\ attempts\ made} = Power\ and\ status$$

One student stated: "The impact of this ratio dawned on me during our fraternity's officer elections. One brother tried many times, all unsuccessful, for a variety of positions. He is a good worker, so that was not his problem. His problem was that within the fraternity he did not have any status. The number of attempts made was many, but the number of successful acts was zero. His status fell further with each new failure."

Obviously the success rate and relative status of any individual will vary from group to group. Most of us find that we have a relatively higher status level in high school than we achieve when we attend college. This is usually because colleges and universities draw from a much larger population than most high schools and the competition gets tougher as the size of the total population increases.

TYPES OF POWER

Although each of us has encountered situations in which people have power over one another, we may not have been very systematic in identifying the types or sources of that power. French and Raven (1959) identified five different types of power that can be brought to bear in groups. They classify them as (1) reward power, (2) coercive power, (3) legitimate power, (4) referent power, and (5) expert power.

Reward power refers to the ability an individual has to give or withhold rewards. A company executive obviously has this type of power, which can take the form of financial rewards through raises and promotions, as well as of social rewards such as recognition and compliments or praise. *Coercive power* is the opposite of reward power in that it utilizes punishment rather than reward. A supervisor can reprimand, discipline, and even fire an employee who does not live up to certain behavioral standards. An IBM employee was once sent home when he showed up for work without a tie. Most companies reserve the right to set what they believe to be appropriate standards for employees' dress. Coercive power is sometimes used to enforce these standards.

Legitimate power is defined as the influence we allow others to have over us based on the value we place on certain of their characteristics. For example, we feel that it is legitimate for a judge to determine a sentence in a court case, or for a supervisor to determine work schedules or assignments. A person who is elected to office is felt to have a legitimate right to exercise the power of that office. Of course, this right may be abused and the official may be removed from office.

Referent power is extremely potent, since it is based on the person's identification with the source of power. If you had a teacher you really admired, you would do many things (such as studying hard, or putting off social activities) to accomplish things that would bring approval or praise from that teacher. Ringwald *et al.* (1971, p. 47) studied different types of college students and found that one type (which they called cluster four students) was especially prone to identify with the professor and to be the "model student" in the eyes of the professor. These students were described as "self-confident, interested, involved; tend to identify with [the] teacher and see him as a colleague. Older than average [mostly upperclassmen]." Although Ringwald *et al.* studied only undergraduates, this description would also apply to a large segment of graduate students.

Expert power refers to our acceptance of influence from those whose expertise we respect. We accept the advice of lawyers in legal matters, of physicians in medical matters, or of others whom we perceive as having credibility on a given topic. In a group discussion concerning the dangers of heroin addiction, the speakers who had the most expert power of persuasion were the former heroin addicts who told the tragic stories of how heroin had destroyed parts of their lives.

As we think in terms of status and power, we might want to keep in mind that these different types of power exist and usually overlap. A person may be in a position to use reward power as well as coercive power, but may prefer to rely on referent power, legitimate power, or expert power. In any event, there are different types of power that can be used (and abused).

Assuming that different group members have different levels of status and power, what effect does this fact have on the interaction in the group? Cartwright and Zander (1953, p. 415) state that if you were to observe a company board meeting, you would be able to differentiate between a lower status person (the junior executive) and the vice-president by the following differences in their behavior.

> The man whom you believe to be the junior executive addresses the majority of his remarks to the man you believe to be the vice-president. Moreover, he chooses his words with care in order that he

not seem to imply any criticism of the other man or appear inadequate. He listens carefully to what the vice-president has to say and is usually ready to see the reasonableness of the arguments made by him. He is friendly toward the boss, ready to tell a joke or talk about his family, and to copy some of the older man's mannerisms.

In contrast, the vice-president talks pretty much to the entire group. He freely offers information, advice, and even criticism to others. He seldom makes critical remarks about himself. Nor is he nearly so ready as the younger man to listen to statements made by the rest of the group. He is more likely to defend his own position than to see the value in the points made by the staff. And on the whole he is less inclined to idle talk than is the junior executive.

You may come away from the meeting feeling that the two men acted the way they did because they had quite different personalities, and you would undoubtedly be correct — in part. If, however, you were to see the junior executive in a meeting with *his* staff in which he is now the boss, you would probably be surprised to see how differently he behaves. Now it is likely that you would find the young man acting toward others in a way very similar to that shown by the vice-president in the earlier meeting.

The scene described above is one example of the *results* of differences in status or power. We also know that information directed toward high-status persons tends to be "whitewashed" in that it is more often positive than negative. One company plant manager told a friend of mine that he appreciated having a consultant who was independent enough of his operation to give him the honest truth. My friend told the manager that if he worked in that company he wouldn't tell the manager the truth either. The manager demanded so much success from his subordinates that they were afraid to tell him of the failures (he acted as if he did not want to hear about them). This was a little like the old custom of killing the messenger when he delivered bad news to a king; pretty soon all the king ever got was good news. According to a former White House official (Bird 1974), Richard Nixon used his Chief of Staff Robert Haldeman as a buffer against receiving bad news. Haldeman even kept cabinet members away from Nixon. The result was that Nixon became more and more out of touch with the reality of national problems.

Another application of power in groups is the use of the group itself by a higher authority to develop support for decisions. Pfeffer (1981, pp. 175-176) writes:

> Given that committees are established to legitimate decisions and provide outlets for the expression of various interest, the important aspect of committees in organizational politics is not their function as much as their very existence. It is the process of cooptation, the process of interest representation, and the process of meeting and

conferring which is critical in providing acceptance and legitimacy of decisions. These processual aspects may be as important as the substance of the decisions actually reached.

Thus the very process of involving groups in making decisions may increase the boss's power to have those decisions implemented.

It has also been found that comments in small groups tend to be directed more often (by direction of eye contact) to higher-status group members than to those of lower status. If you want to quickly determine who are the high-status members of any group, just notice to whom people direct their comments. Thibaut and Kelley (1950) found this phenomenon in an experimental study and hypothesized that this type of upward communication acts as a substitute for a member's own upward mobility in the group's pecking order. Thus if we can't be football stars or sorority presidents, we can at least try to become friends with them.

Finally, high status results in a group's being willing to tolerate deviation on the part of a group member. Highly successful people are notoriously idiosyncratic. It has been suggested that a person who is idiosyncratic but not successful is simply considered weird. Albert Einstein and Thomas Edison both were considered eccentric, yet their eccentricities were tolerated because of the magnitude of their contributions. Most groups will tolerate member deviations from those who are highly valued in the group. One rule of thumb is that new members are not allowed to deviate nearly as much as those who are old-timers. This is true among college faculty members, in companies, government agencies, and even in prisons. We shall further discuss deviation and conformity pressure later in this chapter.

LEADERSHIP

Note the following descriptions of four people and try to decide which you would choose as leaders based on your intuitive reaction. These descriptions are from Jennings 1950, pp. 169-197.

Ruth

Appearance   Above-average height; medium weight; good posture, rather graceful; small, delicate, pretty features; attractive coloring with curly, crisp, reddish hair; straightforward, trusting, appealing expression. Well poised. Voice resonant; speech marked by very clear, almost clipped enunciation; talks freely in interesting, effortless manner.

Personality-behavior picture   Self-confident, capable, realistic, ambitious, but "unprincipled"; easily wins rapport with and confidence of others with whom she comes into contact and then uses their attraction to and trust in her for purposes they had not intended. Shows marked lack of integrity in her relations to others.

Tries to "climb" by playing up her own achievements and playing down those of others. Gives an impression of naiveté but is actually highly circumspect and capable of considerable scheming to gain her ends quickly. Temporarily can produce discord in a group by carrying remarks confided to her. Appears to deliberately aim to produce discord out of resentment toward other individuals being looked to to direct activities; seems unable to tolerate others having a more important role than herself and contrives to disrupt their plans.

Jessie
Appearance   Chubby and small but very muscular physique; brown, wavy, thick hair kept dishevelled by habit of running fingers through it; pasty complexion but very red lips; beautifully shaped blue eyes; expression almost desperate, watching other person as if she expected some dire thing to happen; manner rough; voice very low, almost a whisper, except when angry.

Personality-behavior picture   Petulant, quarrelsome, easily upset, given to pouting and sullen defiance of reasonable requests; seldom reports what, if anything, is bothering her at the time until she first has exhibited a temper tantrum; apparently makes little effort to control temper, displaying it even on very inauspicious occasions (as during a party). Has a habit of staring that is annoying if not distressing to other girls. Seldom verbally communicative except during temper outbursts; then expresses notions that indicate she considers herself persecuted and hated by those around her. Extremely resistant to suggestion; wants to have her own way even in a group where falling in with common effort is needed. Appears to feel others are forcing her to do things their way; frequently gets attention by behaving in such a manner that she cannot be ignored. Apprehensive, aggressive, self-centered, suspicious, and ill at ease with contemporaries.

Olga
Appearance   A big, large-boned, awkward girl; wide, plain face; pleasant, interested look; stringy blond hair; blue eyes; smiling expression quick to break into laughter. Gives the impression of being irritation-proof, never "on-the-outs" with life or with those around her. A perfectly at-ease manner. Pleasant voice.

Personality-behavior picture   Completely unself-conscious. Never appears to think of what impression she is making on others or whether she is making any impression; direct and frank to the point of naiveté. Indiscriminately affectionate manner toward everybody, whether her friends or others, and whether newly met individuals or old acquaintances; very demonstrative. Solicitous for the physical well-being of others, generous to a fault. Talkative, always full of news; interested in whatever is afoot, whether work or fun events. Works rapidly at own task, then jumps in and helps those nearest at their work. Her continuous goodheartedness does not appear to be taken advantage of; is not asked to do things for others; it is she who volunteers; others won't ask her because they know she'll consent and they just "like her so much they don't."

Jean

Appearance   Athletic, well-proportioned physique, square shoulders; bounding walk; alert bright blue eyes; pert, confident, merry, look-you-through expression; a poised-to-go posture; bright gold hair very curly and tangled; complexion covered with freckles so as to appear quite dark. Gives immediate impression of adequacy, tenseness, and jovial outlook. Attractive resonant voice. Manner somewhat arrogant. Speech and gesture have a decisive quality.

Personality-behavior picture   A dynamic, strong personality, very self-aware, and apparently little aware of others as individuals; camaraderie manner, loud, cheery, and friendly towards others, chiefly as a group. Skips the verbal efforts of person-to-person rapport that other leaders make or seek to make with others. Calls out to a roomful of girls as she enters, "How's everybody?" in a manner that makes them all feel equally "near" to her. Seems to get a group response rather than a person-to-person response for the most part. Pitches into things without hesitation; epitomizes "freshness," vivacity, gaiety, and urge for endless activity. The group often appears to be interpreted in her conduct; others would like to have the "nerve" to do as she does. Never once was known to "wait on" other girls' needs or to bid them wait on her wishes; the latter is not necessary as they seek to wait on her often against her desire; they seem to want to serve her, just to be near so much "life."

If your reaction was like those of the group members that Jennings studied, the first two girls (Ruth and Jessie) were not considered leaders, while Olga and Jean were. Based on choices of peers, the girls were chosen or rejected as leaders by the number of peers indicated below.

	Chosen by	Rejected by
Ruth	1	7
Jessie	0	17
Olga	19	2
Jean	24	2

Each of us has some "gut-level" feeling about what kind of person constitutes a leader, but our intuition may be misleading. In this section we will examine leadership in a way that should help clarify what we already know about leadership through our own experiences.

Definitions of leadership are numerous and, in some cases, contradictory. For our purposes we will accept the definition of Tannenbaum, Weschler, and Massarik (1961, p. 24), who define leadership as

interpersonal influence, exercised in [a certain] situation and directed, through a communication process, toward the attainment of a specified goal or goals. Leadership always involves attempts on the part of a leader (influencer) to affect (influence) the behavior of a follower (influencee) or followers in [a certain] situation.

This straightforward definition includes three of the most important factors of leadership: (1) successful or real influence (as opposed to the attempt to influence exemplified by the military leader who charged up the hill with no soldiers willing to follow), (2) the recognition that the situation involved may make a big difference, and (3) acknowledgment that the influence occurs through communication both verbal and nonverbal (see Chapter 5). With these three factors in mind, let us examine what people have historically thought about leadership.

HISTORIC TRENDS

During the eighteenth and nineteenth centuries, philosophers argued the relative merits of two viewpoints regarding leadership. These were the trait or "great man" theory and the circumstances theory. Although we have come a long way in our study of leadership, it is still interesting to go back and examine the evolution of the different approaches to the study of leadership.

Trait Theory   Trait theory grew out of the idea that leaders are born, not made. Examples from history could include Alexander the Great, Madam Chiang Kai-shek, John F. Kennedy, and Ronald Reagan. The assumption was that certain physical traits or personality traits better enable a person to be a leader.

The physical traits associated with leadership were height, weight, and physical attractiveness and body shape. In our culture, taller people are sometimes asssociated with higher status and vice versa. In one study (Wilson 1968) a speaker named Mr. England was introduced to each of five different college classes by a different title:

☐   Class 1 — a student from Cambridge

☐   Class 2 — a demonstrator in psychology from Cambridge

☐   Class 3 — a lecturer in psychology from Cambridge

☐   Class 4 — Dr. England, senior lecturer from Cambridge

☐   Class 5 — Professor England from Cambridge

When students were asked to estimate the speaker's height, the average estimate increased from class 1 to class 5. In other words, the more prestigious England's title, the taller the students thought he was. A study at the University of Pennsylvania showed that height in inches correlated more closely with a graduate's starting salary after graduation than did any other index used (such as grade-point average, number of extracurricular activities, parents' education level). Although correlation does not prove causality, it is still interesting to see the anecdotal evidence supporting the belief that height is viewed positively. As one student aptly put it, "I would define a leader as someone I can look up to, both figuratively and literally."

What relationship might there be between weight and leadership? The heavier the better? No, actually the predicted relationship is curvilinear (see Fig. 4.1). Thus people who are too thin or too heavy would be considered either too weak and fragile or too self-indulgent and undisciplined to be good leaders. In one unpublished study conducted in a large company, employees were divided into groups, one whose members weighed within 10 percent of their "desirable" weight (based on a doctor's chart of height and weight), and one whose members deviated more than 10 percent above or below their charted body weight. The percentage of promotions was tabulated for the two groups, and it was found that the medium-weight group had more promotions.

In a study conducted by a Madison Avenue employment agency with branches in 43 American cities, it was found that overweight persons may be losing as much as $1,000 a year for every pound of fat. According to the agency's president, Robert Hall (1974), their survey showed that among executives in the $25,000-50,000 salary group only 9 percent were more than ten pounds overweight. In the $10,000-20,000 group only 39 percent were more than ten pounds overweight (according to the standards established by life insurance companies). Hall said that the overweight "are unfairly stereotyped as slow, sloppy, inefficient, and overindulgent. When important, high-paying jobs are at stake and candidates are under close scrutiny, the overweight are less likely to be hired or promoted into them." Hall also stated that companies frequently specify their preference for slim candidates, but only once in 25 years did a company request a plump executive; the company was a manufacturer of oversized clothing.

Closely related to body weight is body type. Sheldon (1940, 1942, 1954) identified three different body types or *somatotypes*. The very thin person is called an *ectomorph,* the very heavy and soft person an *endomorph,* and the medium weight, muscular type is the *mesomorph.* Intuitively we might expect the leaders to come from the mesomorphic body type. Although there are no studies to support or refute this prediction, it is a provocative theory that might someday be tested. For example, those who are successful in political campaigns and in movie careers seem to be more often than not mesomorphic. We also know from several research studies that more attractive people are perceived as having higher credibility (for example, higher expertise and better character) on the basis of their looks alone (Mills and Aronson 1965; Widgery and Webster 1969; Widgery, 1974).

In addition to physical traits, certain personality traits were thought to be associated with leadership. A list of some of these traits includes self-confidence, dominance, enthusiasm, assertiveness, responsibility, creativity, originality, dependability, critical thinking ability, intelligence, and ability

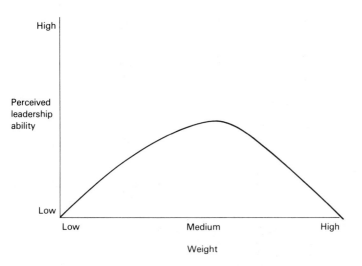

FIGURE 4.1
Hypothetical relationship between weight and leadership.

to communicate effectively. Although all of these traits have some common-sense appeal, Bird (1940) and Stogdill (1948) surveyed over 200 leadership studies and found that out of all the identified traits only 5 percent were common to four or more of the studies surveyed. In a recent update, however, Stogdill (1974, p. 93) has had somewhat greater success in securing a level of agreement among leadership trait studies. His results appear in Fig. 4.2.

In summarizing his latest thoughts on the trait theory, Stogdill (1974, p. 413) states:

> Although leaders differ from followers with respect to various aspects of personality, ability, and social skills, tests of such traits have been of limited value for selection of leaders. Traits do not act singly but in combination. . . . The leader who acquires leadership status in one group tends to emerge as leader when placed in other groups. Thus, perhaps the best prediction of future leadership is prior success to this role.

On the other side of the coin, Geier (1967) was able to identify five negative traits that consistently prevented group members from emerging as leaders. Such members were (1) uninformed about the problem being discussed, (2) nonparticipative, (3) extremely rigid in holding to their pet ideas, (4) authoritarian in bossing others around, and (5) offensive and abusive in their language style. Although the trait theory has not held as many answers as early philosophers and theorists had hoped, it has provided us with some helpful information and insight.

Factor no.	Factor name	Frequency
1	Social and interpersonal skills	16
2	Technical skills	18
3	Administrative skills	12
4	Leadership effectiveness and achievement	15
5	Social nearness, friendliness	18
6	Intellectual skills	11
7	Maintaining cohesive work group	9
8	Maintaining coodination and teamwork	7
9	Task motivation and application	17
10	General impression (halo)	12
11	Group task supportiveness	17
12	Maintaining standards of performance	5
13	Willingness to assume responsibility	10
14	Emotional balance and control	15
15	Informal group control	4
16	Nurturant behavior	4
17	Ethical conduct, personal integrity	10
18	Communication, verbality	6
19	Ascendance, dominance, decisiveness	11
20	Physical energy	6
21	Experience and activity	4
22	Mature, cultured	3
23	Courage, daring	4
24	Aloof, distant	3
25	Creative, independent	5
26	Conforming	5

FIGURE 4.2
Factors appearing in three or more studies. Reprinted
with permission of Macmillan Publishing Company from
Stodgill's Handbook of Leadership, rev. ed., by Bernard
M. Bass. Copyright © 1974, 1981 by The Free Press, a
Division of Macmillan Publishing Company.

Circumstances Theory   Ira Hayes was an American Indian who became
famous for having been one of the United States Marines who lifted the
American flag after the battle of Iwo Jima in the South Pacific during World
War II. Ira Hayes just happened to be standing nearby when the photog-
rapher solicited a group to pose for the picture that later became world
famous. Ira instantly became a national hero and was sent on cross-country
United States Savings Bond drives to raise money for the American war
effort. Ira's pride made him feel so guilty for being a "counterfeit hero" that
he began to drink. He eventually died an alcoholic.

Ira Hayes is the classic example of a person being at the right place at
the right (or wrong) time. This is sometimes called the circumstances
theory of leadership. Another facet of this theory is that a person may be
an effective leader in one circumstance, but perform poorly as a leader in a
different circumstance. Dwight David Eisenhower was a national military
hero as Commander-in-Chief of the Allied Forces during World War II.

However, he is considered to have been only a moderately successful president of the United States and perhaps even less successful as president of Columbia University. Not many of us could move into three such different types of jobs and be highly successful in all three. In many cases former successful military leaders tend to be somewhat too "militarylike" to be highly effective in business or other organizations in which subordinates can quit if they become dissatisfied (which they cannot do at many levels of the military).

Therefore some theorists would argue that the circumstances make the leader. A good example of this is the student/faculty softball, football, or basketball teams that are found on some campuses. While the professors are usually the leaders in the classroom (due to a relatively higher level of expertise in the subject), the students are usually the leaders on the athletic field, where they often know more about the game and are almost always in better physical shape than the professors.

Like trait theory, circumstances theory too seems to have some validity. However, there are many exceptions to the rule. Charles Percy was president of Bell and Howell Corporation at age 30 and has also functioned effectively as a United States senator. Robert McNamara functioned well as president of Ford Motor Company, United States Secretary of Defense, and head of the World Bank organization. Elliot Richardson and John Glenn are two more individuals who have succeeded in numerous capacities in and out of government. Circumstances theory, while somewhat valid, leaves something to be desired in explaining the complex phenomenon of leadership.

Function Theory   A theory that deviates rather dramatically from the first two is function theory. Underlying this theory is the notion that leaders are *made, not born.* That is, leadership consists of certain behaviors or *functions* that groups must have performed. These functions are identifiable behaviors that can be learned by anybody. Thus we can improve our potential as leaders by learning to perform these key functions more effectively. While trait and circumstance theories assume that there is little we can do to become leaders if we aren't a certain height, or if we never seem to be in the right place at the right time, function theory offers hope for those of us who may not have been born Kennedys or Rockefellers or who are not asked to be in nationally famous photographs.

The two important functions that have been consistently identified are referred to by a variety of terms, but are basically the same concepts. The two concepts are (1) task orientation and (2) people orientation. The terms used to describe these concepts are summarized in Fig. 4.3.

With the function theory the emphasis has shifted away from the leader as a person and toward the specific behavioral acts that facilitate group success. Leadership may be "possessed" by any group member who performs these leadership functions. The task-oriented behaviors are those

	Task orientation	People orientation
Bales 1950	Task	Social-emotional
Halpin and Winer 1957	Initiating structure	Consideration
Cartwright and Zander 1968	Goal achievement	Group achievement

FIGURE 4.3
Summary of comparable terms for leadership functions.

directed toward the group's accomplishing its goal. The people-oriented behaviors are directed toward the maintenance of the interpersonal relationships in the group. It is assumed that people-oriented activities ought to have an indirect effect on helping accomplish the group's task. An analogy would be that of a machine that manufactures parts. The machine operates to accomplish a task (producing parts). However, if the machine is not cleaned and lubricated, it will break down sooner or later, thus temporarily halting its productivity. Similarly, although task-oriented groups may require a leader who can help them accomplish their goal, they may cease functioning if they become too bogged down in personality conflicts or counterproductive interpersonal friction. Both task-oriented and people-oriented behaviors are required to enable a group to progress. Bales in Fig. 4.4 offers a summary of the 12 types of specific behavioral acts (6 task oriented, 6 people oriented) and the average percentage of the interaction in any given group discussion that would probably fall into each category. Ross summarizes the work of Bales and others in an extended model of the twelve Bales Interaction Process Analysis (IPA) categories (Fig. 4.5).

The function theory of leadership seems to hold the most promise for teaching most of us how to improve our own leadership abilities. For example, many students hesitate to participate in discussions for fear of "saying something stupid." Yet several research studies indicate that simply participating at all is one primary requirement of becoming more of a leader (Morris and Hackman 1969; Hayes and Meltzer 1972; Regula and Julian 1973). Other studies show that individuals who are able to perform both task- and people-oriented functions in groups are likely to get better results from their groups than those who are less effective in performing these two functions (Likert 1961; Stogdill 1974).

The final important implication to grow out of the function theory of leadership is that these functions need not be performed by the one person designated as group leader. In fact, the implication is the reverse. To the extent that all group members learn to perform these two functions, the overall group leadership will be improved. This is often referred to as

Category		Percentage	Estimated norms[a]
People- oriented (positive)	1. Seems friendly	3.5	2.6— 4.8
	2. Dramatizes	7.0	5.7— 7.4
	3. Agrees	18.5	8.0—13.6
Task- oriented	4. Gives suggestions	3.8	3.0— 7.0
	5. Gives opinions	24.5	15.0—22.7
	6. Gives information	8.3	20.7—31.2
	7. Asks for information	10.3	4.0— 7.2
	8. Asks for opinions	12.5	2.0— 3.9
	9. Asks for suggestions	2.3	0.6— 1.4
People- oriented (negative)	10. Disagrees	1.0	3.1— 5.3
	11. Shows tension	7.8	3.4— 6.0
	12. Seems unfriendly	0.5	2.4— 4.4
	Total:	100.0	

FIGURE 4.4
Adapted from *Personality and Interpersonal Behavior* by Robert F. Bales.
Copyright © 1970 by Holt, Rinehart and Winston, Inc. Reprinted by permission of Holt, Rinehart and Winston, CBS College Publishing.

shared leadership or democratic leadership, which we will be examining in the next section.

LEADERSHIP STYLES

A great deal of attention has been paid to the different types of available leadership styles since the early studies conducted by Kurt Lewin and his associates (Lewin, Lippitt, and White 1939; White and Lippitt 1968). The early studies identified three different leadership styles: autocratic, democratic, and laissez-faire.

The issue in these three leadership styles is the degree and location of control. The authoritarian or autocratic leader has a high need to maintain control of the group himself or herself. Some might even say that the autocratic leader has an obsession for control. When this obsession reaches the extreme, it is manifested in the following types of behaviors (Sattler and Miller 1968, pp. 250-251):

1. The authoritarian leader usually plans to get to the conference room when everyone else is assembled. He fears getting to the meeting early, for he has no interest in carrying on nontask-related conversation. This does not mean that the leader is a latecomer — he isn't; if the meeting is scheduled to start at 3:10 p.m., you will be sure that the leader will be present and the meeting will start on the proper split second.

2. Often the leader will present an extended introduction to start a meeting, in part because he wishes others to know how well informed he is.

	Major categories	Subcategories	Illustrative statements or behavior
Social emotional area	Positive reactions	1. Shows solidarity	Jokes, gives help, rewards others, is friendly
		2. Shows tension release	Laughs, shows satisfaction, is relieved
		3. Shows agreement	Passively accepts, understands, concurs, complies
Task area	Attempted answers	4. Gives suggestion	Directs, suggests, implies autonomy for others
		5. Gives opinion	Evaluates, analyzes, expresses feeling or wish
		6. Gives information	Orients, repeats, clarifies, confirms
	Questions	7. Asks for information	Requests orientation, repetition, confirmation
		8. Asks for opinion	Requests evaluation, analysis, expression of feeling
		9. Asks for suggestion	Requests direction, possible ways of action
Social emotional area	Negative reactions	10. Shows disagreement	Passively rejects, resorts to formality, withholds help
		11. Shows tension	Asks for help, withdraws, daydreams
		12. Shows antagonism	Deflates other's status, defends or asserts self, hostile

Key:
a. Problems of communication   b. Problems of evaluation   c. Problems of control
d. Problems of decision   e. Problems of tension reduction   f. Problems of reintegration

FIGURE 4.5

Interaction process analysis, categories of communicative acts. Based on Robert F. Bales, *Interaction Process Analysis*, Reading, Mass.: Addison-Wesley, 1950, p. 9; A. Paul Hare, *Handbook of Small Group Research*, New York: Free Press of Glencoe, 1962, p. 66; and Clovis R. Shepherd, *Small Groups: Some Sociological Perspectives*, San Francisco: Chandler, 1964, p. 30.

3. Sometimes the authoritarian will outline precise procedures on how the discussion is to be conducted. Thus, he might tell the group that Mr. A will comment on Item 1, B and C on Item 2, and D on Item 3. Such advice on procedure is not given in order to be helpful to others; largely, it seems, the authoritarian uses rules of order to make his own task easier.

4. Authoritarians, more than other leaders, specialize in questions directed to specific persons such as, "Jones, what are your facts . . . ?" . . . "Now I want to hear from Smith. . . ." Such leaders do not frequently use open or "overhead" questions that any person in the group may answer.

5. Authoritarians appear to be unable to withstand pauses in discussion — if such leaders cannot get rapid verbalization from others, they will themselves supply verbal noises.

6. The leader almost invariably maintains strict control over the order and sequence of topics; he appears to love placing group members in a "straitjacket" of restrictions.

7. The authoritarian leader interrupts others often, for at least three reasons: to correct errors whether major or insignificant, to keep persons talking about what he desires, and in general to show who is in command.

8. Clever authoritarians at times encourage group members to discuss irrelevant matters at considerable length. This is true, of course, only when to discuss the irrelevant is in keeping with the leader's designs.

9. When the leader clarifies contributions he is sometimes guilty of changing the intent of statements to make them more acceptable to himself. (Here, of course, we have both procedural and content control.)

The laissez-faire style of leadership goes to the opposite extreme. Not only is there no concern for control, but there is no direction, concern for task accomplishment, or concern for interpersonal relationships. The laissez-faire style is not really a style of leadership at all; it is nonleadership.

The democratic leadership style represents an attempt to find a reasonable compromise between the other two extremes. The leader does attempt to provide direction and both task and social leadership functions, but at the same time tries to avoid dominating the group with one person's views. Some would argue that no matter how hard an individual tries, some domination cannot be avoided, as evidenced in the accompanying cartoon.

Which leadership style is best? In order to answer this question we must determine the criteria for judging effectiveness. Some criteria would include (1) the quality of the group output, (2) the time taken to accomplish the task, (3) the satisfaction of the group members, (4) the absenteeism of

"*Now, the round table symbolizes our equality while my fancy chair and golden crown signify that I, perhaps, am just a smack more equal.*"

group members, and (5) the independence developed in group members. White and Lippitt (1968) reported (1) that the quality of group output in their study was better under democratic leadership, (2) that democratic leadership took more time than autocratic, (3) that member satisfaction was higher under democratic leadership (in fact, hostility was 30 times as great in the autocratic groups, and 19 out of 20 preferred the democratic group to the autocratic), (4) the democratic group had the lowest absenteeism, and (5) the democratic group fostered more independence, while the autocratic style bred dependence and submissiveness among group members. Thus the democratic style got better results in each case except in time taken to accomplish the task. However, subsequent studies (Likert 1967) have shown that the autocratic leader gets fast results in the short run, but that these results may be of poor quality or may be resisted by others. The net effect is that the solution may not be enacted and the problem will have to be dealt with again on future occasions. Since this amounts to less efficiency, the democratic may even prove to be less time-consuming in the long run. (See Chapter 7 for more on this.) In addition, the hostility bred by autocratic leadership produces counterproductive results. For example, in industrial groups, absenteeism, grievances, work stoppages, and sabotage are all ways in which employees attempt to "get back" at what they consider to be harsh leadership. "Goldbricking" in the military is another typical example. An autocratic leadership style fosters group norms that say, "Do as little as possible to get by and look busy when the boss is around. However, when the cat's away . . ."

Group-centered leadership or nondirective leadership is a method that has grown out of the desire to develop more effective forms of democratic leadership. Haiman (1951, p. 40) wrote:

> Probably the most important single concept that has emerged in the last twenty years from the ever growing wealth of psycho-therapeutic experience is the realization that the most effective way to direct the behavior of human beings is simply to help them direct themselves.

Thirty years later we can see that, if anything, Haiman's conclusion is even more relevant today than it was when written.

Gordon (1955) outlined the philosophy of group-centered leadership in further detail. He criticized the long-held assumption that leadership involves functions that should be carried out by one person. We have already encountered this fallacy in the earlier section on the functional theory. In addition, we have seen that the autocratic leadership style breeds dependency and submissiveness. The group-centered approach would be to allow each member to grow and develop whatever leadership skills he or she possesses.

The group-centered or nondirective approach lends itself more to the social group or the unstructured encounter group than the work group or the task-oriented discussion group (see Chapter 3). However, certain aspects of the group-centered approach may be applied to any group situation. Figure 4.6 gives a detailed description of the group-centered approach and the more traditional leader-guided (or leader-centered) approach.

The group-centered leadership philosophy is well summarized in the famous words of Lao-tzu:

> A leader is best
> When people barely know that he exists,
> Not so good when people obey and acclaim him,
> Worse when they despise him.
> "Fail to honor people,
> They fail to honor you";
> But of a good leader who talks little,
> When his work is done, his aim fulfilled,
> They will say, "We did it ourselves."

FOLLOWERSHIP

While leadership is written about more than most topics relating to small group interaction, followership is much less frequently discussed. Since leadership is defined as successful attempts to influence, followers are required to make leaders. In fact, leadership and followership go hand in

Group-centered	Leader-guided

Principal behaviors

1. Allows group to diagnose its needs. Tries to facilitate communication in group during this process.
2. Allows group to plan its own experiences. Tries to facilitate communication during this process.
3. Avoids making decisions for group, except those which facilitate bringing members together initially.
4. Preparation involves doing things that will improve his own contributions to group.
5. Tries to lose his special status position so that he can participate in decision making without having his contributions given special consideration by group.
6. Leaves responsibility with each member for participating. Tries to facilitate group's developing a permissive and accepting atmosphere by being as permissive and accepting as he can.
7. Sets limits in terms of his own ability to be accepting of group action.
8. Wants to contribute resources just like any other member of group. Tries to avoid being used by group as *only* or *chief* resource person.
9. Tries to understand members' expressed wishes for him to behave in some particular role, but does not always feel compelled to do so.
10. Tries not to influence others to play some particular role.
11. Tries not to think beyond the level of expressed understanding of group members, feeling that only meaningful insights will be those arrived at by members themselves.
12. Tries not to be perceived as "the leader," believing that, as long as he is so perceived, group members will not be completely free to be themselves and often will react to his contributions either submissively and un-critically or with hostility and resistance.
13. Takes no special responsibility for seeing that group evaluates its achievement or its progress.
14. Tries to lose his "official role" in order to be free to resist group's needs for dependence and to reduce his own anxiety about the outcome of group action.
15. Takes no special responsibility to reduce anxiety, to resolve tension, etc. Feels such elements are inevitable consequence of group interaction.

1. Finds out as much as possible about group's needs, in order to provide group with situation where it can get what it needs.
2. Plans specific learning situations and/or group experiences from which group may draw insights.
3. Makes decisions for group when group seems too immature to make correct decisions
4. Preparation involves doing things that will improve his own contribution and things that he feels group needs.
5. Uses influence of his special status position in group to bring about decisions or to guide group in certain directions.
6. Facilitates participation by subtle or direct methods of involving each member in group activities.
7. Sets limits more in terms of what will be best for group.
8. Wants group members to use him as the special resource person, and generally lets himself be used by group in this way.
9. Usually accedes to members' wishes that he play some particular role or else tries to convince them that another role is best.
10. Often influences or directly manipulates members to play some particular role.
11. Often interprets group's behavior in order to give members understandings they might not acquire themselves.
12. Tries to be perceived as "the leader," believing that he will thus be better able to control the situation to meet group's needs.
13. Takes special responsibility to ensure that evaluative function is carried out in group.
14. Tries to reinforce his "official role" in order to have more influence on the group action.
15. Takes special responsibility to reduce anxiety and to resolve tension. Feels such elements hinder group purposes and should be avoided.

hand. Earlier we saw that one style of leadership (democratic) in many cases seems to be best. What style of followership is best? Let us first look at three alternative followership styles.

Meerloo (1956, pp. 33-34) describes the Korean situation in which guards in prisoner-of-war camps "encouraged" American prisoners to collaborate with the Communists in denouncing the American aggression in Korea. This so-called brainwashing also occurred during the Viet Nam conflict. The following is a description of the techniques used:

> If a prisoner accepted Communist doctrines, his life became easier according to the men's stories. But if a prisoner resisted Communist doctrines, the Chinese considered him a criminal and reactionary deserving of any brutalities. . . . ["Reactionary"] prisoners were marched barefooted to the frozen Yalu River, water was poured over their feet and they were kept for hours with their feet frozen to the ice to "reflect" on their "crimes."

Accounts of situations such as this one, the Nazi treatment of the Jews, and others make one wonder, what kind of people could do these things to other human beings? Milgram (1974) summarizes almost 15 years of research on this topic in his book *Obedience to Authority*. In Milgram's experiments, subjects were told to administer electric shocks to other subjects as a part of an experiment in learning associations between word pairs. The victim was strapped in a chair and was unable to escape the shocks. The control panel on the shock generator indicated voltage up to 450 volts, which level was labeled, "Danger: Severe Shock." As the voltage was increased, the victim screamed, "Get me out of here; I can't stand the pain: please, I have a heart condition." These protests were continued for any and all shocks administered above 150 volts. (No actual shocks were given, but the subjects really thought they were shocking the victims.) A group of psychiatrists was asked to predict how much shock the subject would administer to the victim. They predicted that almost every subject would refuse to obey the experimenter, that those who administered any shocks at all would stop at 150 volts, and that only about one in a thousand would go all the way to 450 volts (the end of the control panel). Out of Milgram's original 40 subjects, however, 26 (65 percent) obeyed the experimenter's orders and administered the shocks right up to the 450-volt limit. However, Milgram found that as situations were changed (for example, if the victim was brought into the same room with the subject), the subject was less willing to shock the victim.

FIGURE 4.6
Two contrasting approaches to leadership in small groups. Based on Thomas Gordon, *Group-Centered Leadership* (Boston: Houghton Mifflin, 1955), pp. 197-200.

The style of behavior found in Milgram's experiments illustrates what might be termed a *dependent* style of followership. In Chapter 3 we saw that individuals with high levels of dogmatism tended to behave in this manner — that is, they were abusive to peers and subordinates but meeker than average (more obedient) in their interactions with superiors. Two other situations involving *dependent* followership were the My Lai massacre and the Watergate scandal. Accounts of the My Lai incident included the following description by one participant as he was interviewed on CBS by Mike Wallace.

> **A.** . . . Lieutenant Calley told me, he said, "Soldier we got another job to do." And so he walked over to the people, and he started pushing them off and started shooting. . . .
>
> **Q.** Again — men, women, and children?
>
> **A.** Men, women, and children.
>
> **Q.** And babies?
>
> **A.** And babies. And so we started shooting them and somebody told us to switch off to single shot so that we could save ammo. . . .
>
> **Q.** Why did you do it?
>
> **A.** Why did I do it? Because I felt like I was ordered to do it, and it seemed like that, at the time I felt I was doing the right thing, because like I said, I lost buddies. I lost a damn good buddy, Bobby Wilson, and it was on my conscience. So after I done it, I felt good, but later on that day, it was getting to me.

Obviously, more than personality factors are operating in situations such as the one described above. The situation (during a war) and the role (being in the military) also have a great deal to do with producing this type of behavior. Large organizations such as the military, organized religions, and government and industrial organizations frequently produce a higher level of dependence in people. James McCord, one of the convicted Watergate burglars, was described by Woodward and Bernstein (1974, p. 22) as ". . . deeply religious, . . . ex-FBI agent, . . . military reservist, . . . [and] as the consummate 'government man' — reluctant to act on his own initiative, respectful of the chain of command, unquestioning in following orders." As we saw earlier, autocratic leadership produces a higher level of dependent followership. As the cartoon indicates, most of us are caught up to some degree in the obedience syndrome, but with much less harmful or dramatic results.

A second type of follower is the *counterdependent* person. Counterdependence is a type of behavior that is rebellious and antiauthoritarian. While the dependent personality is thought to result from overly punitive parents, the counterdependent personality is thought to result from overly

permissive parents. People who are used to doing things more or less their own way resent a leader or any authority figure who intervenes. One study of campus protestors from the 1960s showed that this type of person was considered "alienated." The alienated protestor is described by Keniston (1967, pp. 112-113) in the following way:

> The culturally alienated student is far too pessimistic and too firmly opposed to "the System" to wish to demonstrate his disapproval in any organized public way. His demonstrations of dissent are private through nonconformity of behavior, ideology, and dress, through personal experimentation, and above all through efforts to intensify his own subjective experience, he shows his distaste and disinterest in politics and society. . . . On the rare occasions when they become involved in demonstrations, they usually prefer peripheral roles, avoid responsibilities, and are considered a nuisance by serious activists. . . . The alienated are especially attracted to the hallucinogenic drugs like marijuana, mescalin, and LSD, precisely because these agents combine withdrawal from ordinary social life with the promise of greatly intensified subjectivity and perception.

This type of person would be dissatisfied with almost any style of leadership encountered. It may not be too much of an exaggeration to say that this group consists of misfits who are pretty much chronic problems. In the industrial work force they create major problems for leaders wherever they go. Steinmetz (1969, pp. 10-11) quoted Edward Cole, former president of General Motors, as stating:

> A research study found that a relatively few employees — 28% — filed 100% of the grievances and accounted for 37% of the occupational hospital visits; 38% of the insurance claims, 40% of the sick leaves, 52% of the garnishments, and 38% of the absenteeism experienced at a certain factory. Thus not only are there a comparatively small proportion of people who are absentee-oriented, but these same people tend also to be the ones who create a significant number of all the other problems generated within the organization.

This type of follower would be hard for any leader to lead. We saw earlier that a democratic leadership style tends to produce higher levels of member satisfaction. However, Runyon (1973) found in an industrial chemical plant that some hourly employees (primarily young workers) did not have high job satisfaction regardless of the type of supervisory style. Even a participative (democratic) style did not produce a high level of satisfaction. Perhaps it is fair to say that some people are simply difficult to lead, and that in dealing with them one leadership style would be about as good (or bad) as any other. The problem then would be to try to bring the followers to a point where they could accept legitimate leadership from others.

The third followership style is *independence*. The independent is one who can either take over and lead when the situation demands, or follow the lead of others when that role is more appropriate. Benjamin Franklin once said, "He that cannot obey cannot command." This implies the role flexibility required of both an effective leader and an effective follower. Note for example these comments at the beginning of one college group discussion. Randy was the group's appointed leader and John was one of the group participants.

Randy: Today our discussion topic is, "What can be done to improve the grading system at GMI?" Let's begin with a look at some facets of the causes, I mean criteria for solutions, I mean . . . *Help!*

John: You mean facets of the problem.

Randy: Yes — thanks.

Although Randy was the appointed leader and John the follower, John helped Randy assume the leadership role in getting the discussion started. Anyone who has ever had a case of "nerves" when speaking in front of a class can understand how Randy could get so tongue-tied and confused.

Keniston (1967, p. 117) found that student political protest leaders (as opposed to the alienated students)

> are generally outstanding students; the higher the student's grade average, the more outstanding his academic achievements, the more likely it is he will become involved in any given political demonstration. Similarly, student activists come from families with liberal political values; a disproportionate number report that their parents hold views essentially similar to their own, and accept or support their activities.

Similarly, Bay (1967, p. 85) found that student activists in the Free Speech Movement (FSM) at Berkeley

> were far more likely to have parents with advanced academic degrees, compared to the cross-section sample: approximately 26%

of the fathers and 16% of the mothers of the FSM sample possessed either a Ph.D. or M.A. degree compared to 11% and 4% respectively in the cross section.

Interestingly enough, in a totally different context, Milgram (1974) found that when he asked subjects to shock the victims in his studies, psychiatrists (professional group) predicted that they would disobey rather quickly, while middle-class adults (nonprofessional group) predicted that they would obey somewhat longer and give more intense shocks. It appears that to some extent education and perhaps the subsequent self-confidence tends to correlate with independence of followership and decision making.

To illustrate the contingency aspects of leadership, one student wrote:

> As a second grade instructional aide, I led dependent followers. For these students, who were highly motivated, "gifted" children, I found that a group-centered approach was best, because it forced the students to make decisions which affected them. This improved their academics and matured their thinking processes. As a resident adviser, I led counterdependent followers. The beginning of the year was handled democratically but after about six weeks the autocratic method proved more effective. Those students who became dissatisfied changed their followership style, so that they would be treated more democratically; those students who did not change at least accomplished the basic tasks — to establish a community conducive to study and to obey the rules of the school and the laws of Michigan and the U.S., which they were not doing under a demo-cratic style of leadership. Finally, as the vice-president of a fraternity, I found a democratic style to be most effective. This provides for personal development and satisfaction, while still accomplishing the tasks which are outlined. However, becoming too group-centered can be a detriment because of the physical size of the membership, and the nature of the tasks which are accomplished.

This is an excellent example of the systems aspect of small group interaction. In each of the situations described above, several factors were acting in combination to influence and determine the most effective leadership style.

In this section we have looked at three styles of followership. We have labeled them the dependent, the counterdependent, and the independent types. They have also been referred to as the slave, the rebel, and the responsible individual (Zaleznik and Moment 1964, pp. 278-279), and, in a different context, the nonassertive person, the aggressive person, and the assertive person, respectively (Jakubowski-Spector 1973, pp. 1-6). Based on this discussion, which followership style seems to describe your predominant style? How does your style change in response to different leaders and different situations? Note the trends shown in Fig. 4.7.

LEADERSHIP STYLES	FOLLOWERSHIP STYLES		
Autocratic	Dependent	Slave	Nonassertive
Democratic	Independent	Responsible individual	Assertive
Laissez faire	Counterdependent	Rebel	Aggressive

FIGURE 4.7
Leadership and followership styles.

CONTINGENCY THEORY

Building on the previous theories, two approaches have been offered that are highly consistent with the systems approach taken in this book. Fiedler (1967) has developed a situational or contingency theory of leadership. Hersey and Blanchard (1982) have developed a somewhat different theory. Although these models are both referred to as situational theories, the term *contingency theories* also seems appropriate, since the leader's effectiveness is contingent or dependent upon the combination of his or her behaviors and the situation.

Fiedler and Chemers (1974) argue that a combination of three separate factors determine a leader's effectiveness. These are (1) leader-member relations, (2) task structure, and (3) position power. For example, leader-member relations are roughly equivalent to what we have come to know as a person's interpersonal skills or people orientation. If a leader is people oriented, the leader-member relations are likely to be good. If, on the other hand, his or her orientation is that people are a necessary evil in getting something done, then the leader-member relations are likely to be poor.

Task structure is the second variable in Fiedler's theory. If a group's task is highly structured and the leader has a manual of procedures to be followed, it would be harder for group members to challenge the leader's approach. On the other hand, if the task is highly ambiguous, such as trying to determine policy by predicting future events, then the group members might have quite a bit of legitimate input that could be as good or better than the leader's idea alone.

The third variable is position power. This can be either strong or weak. If the leader heading up a work group has the power to hire and fire, to promote or not, and to determine raises or punishment, then the leader has strong position power. If, on the other hand, the group is comprised of volunteers working for a church committee or a student organization, the leader has weak position power to get people to do the task. In the model shown in Fig. 4.8, we see the results of Fiedler's research. This model clearly shows that these three variables have a strong influence on the

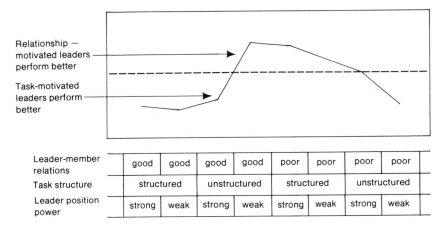

Leader-member relations	good	good	good	good	poor	poor	poor	poor
Task structure	structured		unstructured		structured		unstructured	
Leader position power	strong	weak	strong	weak	strong	weak	strong	weak

FIGURE 4.8
Fiedler's contingency leadership model. From Fiedler and Chemers, *Leadership and Effective Management* (Glenview, Ill.: Scott, Foresman, 1974), p. 80. Copyright 1974 Scott, Foresman & Co. Reprinted by permission of the author.

leader's effectiveness; in other words, leadership effectiveness is congruent upon these three variables. If we take the example described above in which a leader is working with a group of volunteers for a student organization and the task is fairly unstructured (without clear guidelines on how to proceed), then the person who is not people oriented will be very ineffective. In fact, the group members will simply not come back to the next meeting. This theory is fascinating in its implications for leadership, since the same leader acting in the same way would likely be very successful in leading a military group where the operations manual supported "going by the book," and where followers who didn't obey would end up in the guardhouse.

Over two decades ago Barnlund (1962, p. 52) wrote, "Leadership [effectiveness] is dependent upon situational variables at least two of which seem to be changes in group task and membership." More recently, Hersey and Blanchard's 1982 model very clearly pointed out the role of these variables on leadership effectiveness.

Building on the ideas we saw earlier in the functions theory, these authors also stress the two leadership functions of (1) task-oriented behavior, and (2) people-oriented or relationship behavior. To these they add a third important variable, (3) the maturity of the followers. Maturity level could be defined in various ways, but Hersey and Blanchard define it in terms of three components. The first is the ability of the group members. If their ability is quite low, the leader has to be more directive than if the group members have high ability. Second, if the followers have high levels of motivation to achieve (see Chapter 2) they need less direction than followers who are not "self-starters." In fact, one professor gave a motivation test to a

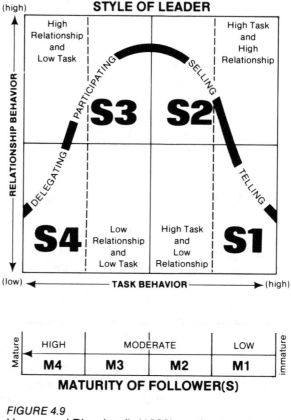

FIGURE 4.9
Hersey and Blanchard's (1982) contingency model
of leadership.

group who were so low in motivation that they would not even fill out the
test! They simply didn't care about it.

The third component of follower maturity is the level of education or
experience with that particular task. If a follower is totally inexperienced
with fixing a malfunctioning car engine, a high level of ability and motivation
may not be enough.

---

*For more on determining the maturity level of the followers, see the
article by Hersey and Blanchard at the end of this chapter.*

As we see in Fig. 4.9, when the maturity of followers is lowest (M1), the
leadership style most likely to be effective is S1, or *telling*. With an M2
level, the S2 style, *selling,* is best. *Participating* goes best with a higher level

of follower maturity, and *delegating* is the recommended supervisory style for the highest level of follower maturity.

While it is important to develop some flexibility in our approaches to leadership in different situations, it is also important to realize that we all have limitations. As one colleague remarked, "We can't be a chameleon changing drastically for each situation." Hersey and Blanchard recognize that each of us tends to prefer one or two of these leadership patterns (that is, telling, selling, participating, and delegating). In most situations we gravitate toward whichever of these patterns has worked well for us in the past. The difficulty comes when the leadership that is *required* is different from the one we feel comfortable choosing. For example, George Steinbrenner, the owner of the New York Yankees, uses a *telling* leadership pattern. However, since he has had severely unhappy players and managers, maybe a different pattern (for example, delegating to his manager) would be more appropriate. Yet it is probably quite hard for Mr. Steinbrenner to move to this other style because of his strong personality. Another factor to keep in mind is that if he were not the owner of the team and a millionaire, his behavior pattern would probably be even less tolerated by others in the organization.

In spite of their limitations, contingency models of leadership seem to offer the most promising theories to help guide us in determining the most effective leadership behaviors. They also fit well into the systems approach taken in this book.

GROUP NORMS: SOCIAL INFLUENCE AND CONFORMITY

This entire chapter deals with the process of social influence. In the earlier sections we have seen that some people tend more to be the influencers and others the influencees. In this section we will explore some of the results of social influence, namely, conformity pressure.

Every one of us has undoubtedly felt the pressure to conform at one time or another. We notice pressure from the childhood challenges where we are "chicken" if we don't go along with the group, to the high school or college scene where we are labeled a "brown-nose" if we appear to be spending more time in the teacher's office than our classmates think is normal. Note the following letter (Courtesy Ann Landers, Field Newspaper Syndicate).

Four Words That Can Ruin Teenagers
June 14, 1975

Dear Ann . . . I just read some remarks made by Dr. Chester Ewing, a physician in Chester County, Pa. He identified the four most terrible words in the English language. Please print this letter. Many a teenager's life might be changed by it.

The most terrible words are: 1. "Chicken." 2. "Square." 3. "Yellow." 4. "Brown-nosing."

Ewing said he knew of three instances where kids had been hounded by the word "yellow" until they tried dope.

He listed some conversations he had had with young people — in hospitals. They admitted the reason they were drag-racing (which leads to accidents) was because they were called "chicken."

Being called "square" has made young people ashamed of dressing decently, being courteous to adults, and showing respect for authority. All young people want to be considered with it. A "square" is out of it. That name encourages kids to prove they are gutty and up front.

"Brown-nosing" is a slang term for trying to curry favor. It is especially applied to teacher-student relationships. Students who raise their hands in class to ask questions are called "brown-nosers" because they give the teacher the impression they are interested. This stands the students in good stead with the teacher — but not with their peers.

I hope the teens who read your column will pay attention to this letter. It could change their entire outlook and lengthen their lives.

Pa. Reader

Dear Reader: Amen.

Actually the term *norms* refers to the written or unwritten laws or codes that identify acceptable behavior. Obviously norms will vary drastically from one group to another. Chronic problems surface when one travels to a place where the norms are different. Reportedly, Japanese travelers in Italy shock their Italian traveling companions by stripping to their underwear on the long train ride from Rome to Milan. So many such problems have arisen that the Japanese tourist agencies have issued a booklet for travelers telling them of the different norms and customs to be followed while traveling in Europe. According to *Time* magazine (1971, p. 39):

The Japanese male's habit of relieving himself in public is sternly condemned: "Never pass water, even in the little side street or in the corner of a bridge, or it will be a police case." Even bathing tips are included [in the booklet]: "Fill the tub to two-thirds capacity and wash yourself *in* the tub, not on the outside like in Japan."

On the other hand, the Japanese norms for group productivity have been widely admired and written about in our country. Perhaps the most fascinating spin-off is where Japanese companies have started firms in the United States and have brought their norms here. Hatvany and Pucik (1981, p. 14), in their comprehensive analysis of successful Japanese management policies, write:

Acknowledging the enormous impact of groups on their members — both directly, through the enforcement of norms, and indirectly, by affecting the beliefs and values of members — Japanese organizations devote far greater attention to structural factors that enhance group motivation and cooperation than to the motivation of individual employees. Tasks are assigned to groups, not to individual employees, and group cohesion is stimulated by delegating responsibility to the group not only for getting the tasks performed, but also for designing the way in which they get performed. The group-based performance evaluation has already been discussed.

In the Marlon Brando movie version of *Mutiny on the Bounty*, Mr. Christian is ordered by Captain Bligh to have sexual intercourse with the Tahitian king's daughter in order to *please* the king. How's that for a switch in norms?

In our society it is customary for people to engage in some degree of "one-upmanship," in which they drop names and in many ways try to impress each other with their accomplishments. (For example, What? You haven't been to Paris?). In one commune a concerted effort was made to reduce this type of social game playing. Some of the norms for this commune included the following (Kinkade, 1973):

□ We don't use titles. All members are "Equal" in the sense that all are entitled to the same privileges, advantages, and respect.

□ We don't discuss the personal affairs of other members, nor speak negatively of other members when they are not present, or in the presence of a third party.

□ Seniority is not discussed among us. This is because we wish to avoid prestige groups of any kind.

□ We try to exercise consideration and tolerance of each other's individual habits.

□ We don't boast of individual accomplishments. We are trying to create a society without heroes. We are all expected to do our best, so making a big fuss over some accomplishment is out of place.

This commune, called "Twin Oaks," was described more extensively by Kinkade (1973).

By now you may have asked yourself, "Why do we even need to have norms?" Actually, norms often serve to reduce ambiguity and to help us feel more at ease. We often feel uncomfortable when we don't know what behaviors are acceptable in a given situation — for example, in moving from elementary school to junior high or middle school; or going from junior high to high school; then graduating from high school and going to college. Remember the uneasiness you felt during your first day in each of these new situations. Only after we have learned some of the common

Reprinted by permission. © 1977 NEA. Inc.

practices or norms can we begin to relax and "be ourselves." One student who went to Harvard a few years ago learned that the norm was to buy expensive sweaters and then take scissors to fray the elbows so that the sweaters didn't look like new. A reverse attitude is prevalent today toward designer jeans. Nobody would be caught dead in what looked like old baggy jeans.

The norms in our society regarding clothing are quite strong. It is interesting to note that even going without clothes involves certain norms. On a nude beach, wearing clothes or even a bathing suit is frowned upon. Jones (1981) writes that at Black's Beach in San Diego forty to fifty thousand nude bathers gather on a given day. He describes the norms there as follows:

> Nude beaches usually are pretty remote. Gawkers aren't interested in walking very far. . . .
>
> If someone is obnoxious, if some guy keeps his clothes on and stares at the women, it's a matter of peer pressure telling him, hey buddy, what's your problem? Why don't you move on now? This isn't a peep show.

Thirty years ago, a psychologist named Leon Festinger hypothesized a theory of social comparison (1954). This theory pointed out the need each of us has to check out our own ideas with those of others. The more ambiguous the situation, the greater is this need. In addition, when we find ourselves at odds with others, we feel pressure to reduce the discrepancies one way or another. The more we are attracted to the group, the more pressure we will feel to change toward the group norms.

On the hunch that this theory might have some relevance in predicting attitude influence on pot smoking, one student (Unger 1974) conducted a modest study in which he asked, "What has been the most significant source of influence on your views toward pot smoking?" The largest source of influence (43 percent) was from peers; the second largest (37 percent) was from authoritative written documents; the next (8 percent) was from lectures; and 12 percent said from other sources. These data would seem to confirm Festinger's thesis that we are inclined to look to others to help us determine the guidelines for our own opinions and behaviors. It is also significant to note that, as we saw from the study at Bennington College discussed in Chapter 3, the value changes that we undergo in college are likely to last for a lifetime. (Newcomb 1943).

CONFORMITY: RESEARCH AND APPLICATIONS

One of the earliest conformity studies was conducted by Muzafer Sherif (1936) in the late 1930s. He showed subjects a pinpoint of light projected onto a wall in a completely darkened room. The light appeared to move even when the subjects knew that it was stationary. This optical illusion is called the *autokinetic effect*. Subjects were tested alone and in groups. Subjects were told to report when the light appeared to move and to judge about how far it moved. When tested individually, subjects estimated the light's range of movement at 3.6 inches. After they had discussed their experiences in groups of two and three the average range of estimated movement had reduced to 0.4 inches. Clearly, the group discussion provided an influence on each person's judgment of the amount of the light's movement. In Festinger's words, the subjects had a need to compare their judgment with that of others in the group. Where the judgments were discrepant, there was a felt pressure to reduce the discrepancy. This resulted in the reduced range of estimates of the light's movement. This clearly fits Kiesler and Kiesler's (1969, p. 2) definition of conformity as "a change in behavior or belief . . . as a result of real or imagined group pressure."

See the article by Ladd Wheeler, at the end of this chapter, which describes Sherif's experiments.

Solomon Asch (1952) conducted a classic series of conformity studies during the early 1950s. View the two cards with vertical lines drawn on them, shown in Fig. 4.10. Which line on card B is the same length as that on card A? If you had been in Asch's study you and the other seven subjects would announce your decisions in order as you are seated in the room. You are the seventh to answer out of eight. For the first two go-arounds there is unanimous agreement. However, on the third trial, everyone in the group agrees that line 1 is equal in length to line X. You think it is line 2 instead. What do you do? This goes on through 18 experimental trials. In 12 of the trials you are the only one disagreeing with the others. Actually, the others in the group were Asch's paid "stooges" or confederates. The

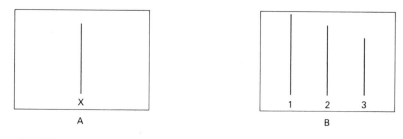

FIGURE 4.10

experiment was designed to create pressure on you to conform or yield to the others.

Asch (1955) found that, out of 123 naive subjects, 37 percent conformed to the majority opinion, while control subjects judging independent of group pressure made virtually no errors.

Another technique for constructing a conformity-inducing situation was developed by Crutchfield (Kretch, Crutchfield, and Ballachey, 1962, pp. 504-511). With this method five naive subjects at a time were seated at booths that were partitioned from each other. The front of each booth had panels of signal lights and switches. The lights supposedly indicated the responses the others made to the stimuli presented to them (these also indicated that the subject's judgment would be different from the four others). Actually, none of the panels was connected to any other panel. Rather, the investigator rigged the signal lights so that the subject would always be a minority of one. In several studies a total of more than six hundred people participated as naive subjects. Some of the results are summarized below.

1. Group pressure does indeed produce conformity.

2. Yielding can be induced even on attitudes having personal relevance to them.

3. Yielding is greater on difficult decisions than on easy ones.

4. There are large differences in amounts of yielding for different individuals.

5. When subjects are tested again without the group pressure a major part of the original yielding disappears.

Some situational factors that were found to be pertinent to the conformity process include group size, perceived competence of the group members, group unanimity, extremity of group opinion, and group cohesiveness. The size of the group affects conformity in that group pressure increases to a maximum with four people comprising the opposing majority. Numbers larger than 4, even up to 15, produce only slightly more yielding.

Higher perceived group competence produced more conformity pressure. For example, Crutchfield (1959) found that some high-level mathematicians conformed to group pressure (from other mathematics experts) on the answers to simple arithmetic problems, giving answers that were wrong and that would very likely not have been given under normal circumstances. Group unanimity appears to have a highly significant effect on conformity. Asch (1956) found that when at least one other member of the group reinforced the one-member minority, the resistance to group pressure was significantly increased. With regard to extremity of majority opinion, Tuddenham (1961) found that when the majority opinion lies well outside the range of acceptable judgments, yielding occurs among fewer individuals and to a lesser degree. Group cohesiveness caused an increase in conformity, and the second highest status group member conformed the most of anyone in the group (Harvey and Consalvi 1960).

Individual personal factors have also been studied in relation to conformity (see also Chapter 2 on personality). Some of the results of the conformity research include the following (Tuddenham 1961):

1. Conformists are less intelligent.

2. Conformists are lower in "ego-strength" and in their ability to work in stress situations.

3. Conformists tend toward feelings of personal inferiority and inadequacy.

4. Conformists show an intense preoccupation with other people, as opposed to more self-contained, autonomous attitudes of the independent person.

5. Conformists express attitudes and values of a more conventional (conservative) nature than nonyielders.

The pressure to conform is eloquently described by Walker and Heynes (1967, p. 98) in the following way:

> If one wishes to produce Conformity for good or evil, the formula is clear. Manage to arouse a need or needs that are important to the individual or the group. Offer a goal which is appropriate to the need or needs. Make sure that Conformity is instrumental to the achievement of the goal and that the goal is as large and as certain as possible. Apply the goal or reward at every opportunity. Try to prevent the object of your efforts from obtaining an uncontrolled education. Choose a setting that is ambiguous. Do everything possible to see that the individual has little or no confidence in his own position. Do everything possible to make the norm which you set appear highly valued and attractive. Set it at a level not too far initially from the starting point of the individual or group and move it gradually toward the behavior you wish to produce. Be absolutely certain you know what you want and that you are willing to pay an

enormous price in human quality, for whether the individual or the group is aware of it or not, the result will be *Conformity*.

Have you ever noticed what happens to the person who does try to deviate from the group? By definition this person is a *nonconformist*. The gets many times more comments directed toward him as these variables increase (that is, group cohesion and relevance of topic, as well as the acting in a noticeably different way). Think of Alice Cooper, Edgar Winter, and others of the "freak rock" genre as examples.

In a quantitative study of the group's reaction to a deviant, Schachter (1951) predicted that the deviant would be talked to the most (frequency of communication) and that the reaction to the deviant would depend upon (1) relevance of the discussion topic, (2) degree of group cohesiveness, and (3) degree to which the person deviated. These predictions are summarized in the chart in Fig. 4.11, which is included since the actual data supported virtually all of the predictions.

In other words, we are more likely to get hot under the collar when a person deviates from a neighborhood group discussing cross-district busing of our children (high cohesion, high relevance), than if a person deviates from a group of strangers deciding on what color to paint the walls in the school gymnasium (low cohesion, low relevance). Notice that the deviant gets many times more comments directed toward him as these variables increase (that is, group cohesion and relevance of topic, as well as the degree of deviation on the topic). Notice also that in the most extreme case (the solid curved line at the top) the frequency of communication tends to diminish after about two-thirds of the 45-minute discussion (30 minutes). This leads us to believe that a certain amount of rejection or ostracism results if the deviant doesn't come around.

While this study represents a quantitative analysis of a group discussion, Leavitt (1964) offers a qualitative analysis of the four stages of conformity pressure. The first stage might be called *reason*. We do not like hearing our ideas disconfirmed, but we are interested in logically convincing the deviant that he or she is wrong. Even at this stage, it is clear that we expect the deviant to change to conform to the group and not vice versa. The second stage is *seduction*. During this stage we attempt to appeal to the deviant's social needs. The comments begin to take on the tone of, "Aw, come on, be a sport, we know you don't want to put the whole group on the spot just for the sake of this little issue." It isn't long before the group enters stage three, which is *coercion*. During this stage the group members lose their smiles and good nature. The comments begin to take on the air of threat, something like, "Now look, this has gone far enough. If you won't play ball, then we are going to have to clip your wings but good the next time you want help from us." The fourth and final stage is *isolation*. At this point the group gives up on and ignores the deviant. This tactic may finally bring conformity if the ostracism is prolonged.

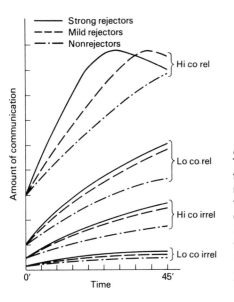

FIGURE 4.11
Theoretical curves of communications from strong rejectors, mild rejectors, and four nonrejectors to the deviant in the four experimental conditions. From Schacter 1951, Deviation, rejection, and communication. *Journal of Abnormal and Social Psychology* **46**: 202. American Psychological Association, © 1951.

Leavitt (1964, pp. 273-274) summarizes the four stages when he writes:

It's as though the members of the group were saying "Let's reason with him; if that doesn't work, let's try to tease him by emotional seduction; and if even that doesn't work, let's beat him over the head until he has to give up. Failing that, then we'll excommunicate him; we'll amputate him from the group; we'll disown him."

One student wrote of her experience with this conformity influence:

As a high school band member I experienced all four of these stages when we were to march in the Apple Blossom Parade.

The band master told everyone to wear saddle shoes. When I explained to him that I had none, he said, "Get some, since everybody needs to be dressed the same" (step 1). I told him I had no money. "Then borrow some," another band member suggested. "Come on, we need you" (step 2). I told them I couldn't borrow any because of an unusual foot size. "Then if you don't get them, you can't march in the parade," said someone else (step 3).

I didn't; I hid when the band came down the street. I never returned to the band again. I felt alone, isolated, and ostracized (step 4), and that ended my musical career. Although it was over twenty years ago, it still hurts when I think about it.

A different case in point was that of a Michigan state senator who began to criticize his fellow senators for overspending tax dollars for refurbishing their senate offices in Lansing. He reported to the news media that he experienced exactly these four stages as his colleagues tried to stop him from revealing their indulgences. He did not conform, however, because of the overwhelming support from his constituents who believed that he was right.

Janis (1971, 1972, p. 9) has conducted a thorough investigation of the problems that conformity pressure brought to some major American historical events. He refers to the results of conformity pressure as "groupthink," which he defines as

> a quick and easy way to refer to a mode of thinking that people engage in when they are deeply involved in a cohesive in-group, when the members' strivings for unanimity override their motivation to realistically appraise alternative courses of action.

Janis cites several major political decisions that were characterized by groupthink, including the escalation of the Viet Nam war and the 1961 American invasion of Cuba referred to as the Bay of Pigs invasion. Although he did not include it in his book, the Watergate scandal was another example that fits his definition.

Groupthink tends to occur when several factors are operating at once. These are called the symptoms of groupthink, and can occur in any group. The eight symptoms (Janis 1972, pp. 198-199) are summarized below.

- An illusion of invulnerability, shared by most or all the members, which creates excessive optimism and encourages taking extreme risks;

- Collective efforts to rationalize in order to discount warnings which might lead the members to reconsider their assumptions before they recommit themselves to their past policy decisions;

- An unquestioned belief in the group's inherent morality, inclining the members to ignore the ethical or moral consequences of their decisions;

- Stereotyped views of enemy leaders as too evil to warrant genuine attempts to negotiate, or as too weak and stupid to counter whatever risky attempts are made to defeat their purposes;

- Direct pressure on any member who expresses strong arguments against any of the group's stereotypes, illusions, or commitments, making clear that this type of dissent is contrary to what is expected of all loyal members;

- Self-censorship of deviations from the apparent group consensus, reflecting each member's inclination to minimize to himself the importance of his doubts and counterarguments.

- A shared illusion of unanimity concerning judgments conforming to the majority view (partly resulting from self-censorship of

"I'm awfully sorry, Dick, but we've all just had a little meeting, and we've agreed that perhaps it's best that you leave the commune."

Drawing by Weber: © 1973 The New Yorker Magazine, Inc.

deviations, augmented by the false assumption that silence means consent);

□ The emergence of self-appointed mindguards — members who protect the group from adverse information that might shatter their shared complacency about the effectiveness and morality of their decisions.

Certain groups are particularly vulnerable to groupthink. Those with members who are high in need for affiliation (see Chapter 2); those that are very cohesive (see Chapter 7); or those that have an autocratic leadership style (see this chapter) are likely candidates. However, there are some procedures that can be employed to minimize the possibilities of groupthink (Janis 1972, pp. 209-218). Some of these precautions are:

□ Assign one member to be the "devil's advocate" or critical evaluator to allow disagreements and criticism of the leader.

□ Leaders should not reveal their preferences to the group at the beginning of the discussion.

□ Several groups with different leaders can work independently on common problems to offer different perspectives.

□ Group members should discuss the group's processes with trusted friends and report their reactions to the group.

◻ Outside experts should be called in periodically as resource persons. They should be encouraged to disagree with the group's assumptions.

◻ Whenever issues involve relations with rival groups (e.g., labor and management) time should be spent discussing all warning signals from the rivals and hypothesizing alternative "scenarios of the rivals' intentions."

◻ After preliminary decisions have been reached, the group should adjourn and hold a "second chance" meeting at a later date to let their ideas "incubate."

Although these suggestions may not always be applicable (even if they are, they may not always work), they do offer a constructive alternative set of procedures to reduce the dangers of groupthink.

GROUP DEVELOPMENT

A number of writers have been interested in the social influence process as it is manifested in different stages or phases of group development. Group development seems to be partly the result of individual psychological needs and partly the result of the social influences manifested in the group. The various theories on group phases are somewhat incompatible, in that some writers identify three phases and others identify four. Also, some writers identify the phases that occur during the course of one group discussion (Tuckman 1965; Fisher 1970), while others identify the phases that occur over the course of the life of a group, including several meetings (Bennis and Shepard 1956; Thelen and Dickerman 1949). Still another viewpoint is that the phases occur in each meeting and continue to occur throughout the group's life history (Schutz 1958; Bales and Strodbeck 1951). This last viewpoint seems the most likely and the most profound in providing insight into the phenomenon of group development.

With these differing frames of reference in mind, let us look at the four group phases that seem representative of the literature. *Phase one* (forming) seems to be a period in which group members simply try to break the ice and begin to find out enough about one another to have some common basis for functioning. It is variously referred to as a period of orientation, inclusion, or group formation. In this phase people ask questions about one another, tell where they are from, what they like and dislike, and generally make small talk. An excerpt from a student paper reveals this:

Even though we had a task to accomplish for the class, we began by talking about ourselves (one guy and girl found they both liked moto-cross racing, and two others found that they had both been to Daytona Beach last spring vacation). After we had a chance to "break the ice" we were more willing to throw out ideas on how to go ahead with the group project without being afraid of having our ideas shot down in flames.

Phase one seems to be characterized by the establishing of some minimal social relationship before group members feel comfortable getting down to work. However, some executives who have experienced many years of decision-making meetings may begin work with little or no social orientation, and only the barest minimum of group orientation. With these exceptions, the vast majority of us feel better having some period to build relationships prior to launching into the group's work.

Phase two (storming) is frequently characterized by conflict of some kind or another. After the orientation phase passes, the pressure to accomplish something sooner or later intensifies whatever differences may exist. This student's description illustrates the transition from phase one to phase two:

> We talked about personal interests until some common ground was established, then we found we could talk about the assignment more freely. But after talking about nonsubject things, it was hard to keep the line of talk on the problems at hand. Some wanted to get the assignment accomplished while two guys in the group continually swayed the conversation to things that were easier to talk about, but had nothing to do with the subject (Howard has a big thing for John Deere farm machinery). At first we were constantly trying not to hurt anyone's feelings, so we let the conversation drift. We didn't question or reject each other's ideas, and I feel we often settled for less than we should have. The longer we were in the group together, the more we got to know each other and the more times we voiced our real opinions. That's when the tempers started to flare!

Typically in phase two the group begins to thrash out decisions for procedures as well as for determining the solution to the group's task. Conflict over procedures may be one way in which group members fight for influence or control in the group.

After a period of small talk in one middle-aged encounter group, one member suggested that they go around the group and introduce themselves in some detail, telling what their jobs were, what part of the country they were from, and so on. Just as they were about to begin, another member suggested that they *not* tell these things, to avoid the stereotyping that would inevitably result. A heated argument resulted. Eventually they decided to assume their fantasized identities — that is, they adopted nicknames and behaviors and job titles that represented the type of persons they wished they could be. Much later in the group they decided that the new procedure had been much better in helping them to try out new behaviors that they normally would have been too inhibited to attempt. For example, one female psychiatrist assumed the identity of "Bubbles," a cocktail waitress, since she had always wondered what it would be like to be a sex object and get outside her role as a professional person. The conflict regarding procedures turned out to be very productive for the group in the long run.

Phase three (norming) involves a resolution of the conflict experienced in phase two. Group cohesiveness begins to emerge and the group settles in to working more comfortably as a unit. This phase is described by three different sources in the following ways.

Perhaps the major pitfall to be avoided at this point is that of glossing over significant differences for the sake of harmony . . . behavior is essentially a kind of polite behavior which avoids upsetting the group. (Thelen and Dickerman 1949)

Resistance is overcome in the third stage in which ingroup feeling and cohesiveness develop, new standards evolve, and new roles are adopted. In the task realm, intimate, personal opinions are expressed. (Tuckman 1965)

Social conflict and dissent dissipate during the third phase. Members express fewer unfavorable opinions toward decision proposals. The coalition of individuals who had opposed those proposals which eventually achieve consensus also weakens in the third phase. (Fisher 1974)

Phase four (performing) is the phase of maximum productivity and consensus. Dissent has just about disappeared and the rule of the moment is to pat each other on the back for having done such a good job. Group members joke and laugh and generally reinforce each other for having contributed to the group's success. Student reactions to a group project in this phase include the following typical comments: "At first I thought this assignment would be a waste of time, but now I think it was the most worthwhile thing we have done in the course so far." "Everybody I have talked to feels like the group exercise was really good. We are looking forward to doing more of these."

Psychologically, we all need to feel that what we do is somehow justified or worthwhile (this is referred to in Chapter 3 as rationalizing or reducing cognitive dissonance). Thus, even if we have had bad experiences with a group, we tend to repress those and remember the good things that we have experienced. The various group development theories are summarized in the chart in Fig. 4.12 and in the following quotation from the earliest of the group development theorists (Thelen and Dickerman 1949, p. 316):

Beginning with individual needs for finding security and activity in a social environment, we proceed first to emotional involvement of the individuals with each other, and second to the development of a group as a rather limited universe of interaction among individuals and as the source of individual security. We then find that security of position in the group loses its significance except that as the group attempts to solve problems it structures its activities in such a way that each individual can play a role which may be described as successful or not in terms of whether the group successfully solved the problem it had set itself.

	Phase 1	Phase 2	Phase 3	Phase 4
Thelen and Dickerman (1949)	Forming	Conflict	Harmony	Productivity
Bennis and Shepard (1956, 1961)	Dependence	Interdependence	Focused work	Productivity
Tuckman (1965)	Forming	Storming	Norming	Performance
Fisher (1970, 1974)	Orientation	Conflict	Emergence	Reinforcement
Bales and Strodbeck (1951)	Orientation		Evaluation	Control
Schutz (1958)	Inclusion		Control	Affection

FIGURE 4.12
Summary of literature on group phases.

THE SYSTEMS PERSPECTIVE

In this chapter we examined the complicated and fascinating questions of who influences whom and why. In the discussion of status and power we saw that the two go hand in hand; that is, high-status individuals tend to have more power. An obvious extension of this is the notion that due to differing group norms, different characteristics bring about status in different groups. On a football team, the best athlete has the most status. Among college professors, the smartest person usually has the most status. In street gangs, the toughest member typically has the highest status. And so it goes from one group to another.

A major portion of this chapter dealt with the issues of leadership and followership. Although these two are not always discussed together, they are highly interrelated. Here the systems principle of *equifinality* applies. In other words, the leadership style that would be appropriate in one situation with one set of followers may not be the most appropriate in a different situation with a different set of followers. A great deal of study has led to the belief that the democratic leadership style is the most likely to get the best results in a great many cases. However, our systems perspective reminds us that some situations point to the authoritarian style as the most appropriate. In situations involving life-or-death decisions, or in times of crisis requiring rapid decisions, the democratic approach may be too slow or simply impractical. As we saw earlier, two popular theoretical syntheses regarding leadership styles are offered by Fiedler (1967, 1974) and Hersey and Blanchard (1982). They each suggest a "contingency theory" of leadership. In other words, the best leadership style is one flexible enough to adapt to the situation. If asked which leadership style is best, they would answer, "It depends."

This chapter also dealt with the topics of social influence and conformity. Systems theory concepts are beautifully illustrated in this literature. Conformity pressure differs depending on the type of group (for example, military vs. the commune), the style of leadership (say, authoritarian vs. democratic), the personalities of the group members (dominant vs. acquiescent), and a number of other factors. We know from the research literature that conformity is more likely (1) in a group in which membership is highly valued by its participants; (2) among members with dependent, obedient, and acquiescent personalities; (3) when the leader is more authoritarian; (4) when the group is unanimously against the deviant member; and (5) to produce public compliance than actual private acceptance. Conformity is clearly dependent on an entire constellation of other variables.

One study analyzed conformity in a systems way (although the authors did not identify their analysis as a systems analysis). Rarick, Soldow, and Geizer (1976) looked at conformity as a result of the combination of the person's personality and the situation in which he or she is placed. The personality variable was self-confidence (they call it self-monitoring) and the situational variable was group size (dyad or three- to six-person group). They found that less confident people conform more in three- to six-person groups than highly confident people. This confirms numerous previous findings. However, they also found that in a dyad, confident people did not conform any more or less than those lacking in confidence. This study very nicely illustrates the systems perspective that all these variables (and others) simultaneously influence one another.

The last section of this chapter dealt with group development. We know that groups go through some fairly common phases, depending on the type of group. As we saw earlier, some writers assume that all the phases occur during the course of one group discussion. Other writers believe that these phases evolve slowly over the group's entire lifetime. However, the systems theory approach would agree with writers such as Schutz (1958) and Bales and Strodbeck (1951) that these phases are simply parts of a recurring *cycle* of events that probably occur during a single meeting and tend to be repeated throughout the group's lifetime as well. This point of view seems to be the most theoretically valid and is supported by other authors who apply the systems approach to the analysis of small group interaction. (See, for example, Fisher and Hawes 1971.)

Exercises

1. Leadership Case Studies

Break into small groups and discuss one of the following leadership case studies. Attempt to reach agreement on one of the five comments on the case. Have each group report its choice to the class and the reasons for the choice. What issues in leadership from Chapter 4 are illustrated in these cases?

Case A   In the men's sportswear department of the Arcade department store two men and four women are employed regularly as sales personnel. In addition to salary they receive a bonus determined by the amount by which the individual's daily volume of sales exceeds a quota. Mr. Stone, the buyer, is head of the department, but during his frequent absences his assistant buyer, Mr. Jones, is in charge. In addition to the six regulars, the department also employs during the summer several extra salespersons. These are college students on vacation who have been given some training by the store's personnel department. They are eager beavers and often outsell the regulars. They also work for a salary plus a bonus.

During Mr. Stone's absence on a buying trip the regulars complained to Mr. Jones that the extras were making it difficult for them to make their quotas, that they mixed up the stock and generally were a nuisance. Mr. Jones, a close personal friend of one of the regulars, ordered the extras to take care of the stock and to sell only when customers were waiting. On his return, Mr. Stone countermanded this order; he told the extras to get in there and sell or look for other jobs. A competitive spirit, he said, was good for the department. The regulars are now more resentful than ever; customers are beginning to notice the bad feeling, and some of them have taken their trade elsewhere.

Which one of the following comments on this situation seems to you most sound?

1. Mr. Stone should return to the position taken earlier by his assistant: that is, instruct the extras to work on stock and handle customers only when no regular is free to do so.
2. In addition to telling the extras to sell to the top of their capacity, Mr. Stone should call the regulars in, take a firm stand with them, and advise them to increase their sales or look elsewhere for work.
3. Mr. Stone is right; a competitive spirit is good for the department. Beyond making this point clear, he should continue to have a hands-off policy and let the situation work itself out.
4. Mr. Stone should put the extras on a straight hourly basis of compensation.
5. Mr. Stone should investigate the activities of the extras and the sales methods and compensation plan of all employees.

Case B   Mr. Welty, publisher of a newspaper, employs a total staff of about 200. He prides himself on the high morale among his employees and on their loyalty to him and to the paper. "You my call my kind of management paternalism," he once said, "but I know all of my employees personally and don't have to buy their friendship and loyalty." Though unaware that he had any personnel problem, Mr. Welty had a personnel consultant make a survey and evaluation of the organization.

To his astonishment, Mr. Welty learned that in the pressroom morale was very low, that nearly all of the 38 employees there had bitter feelings against the foreman, Harry Fitzpatrick. They considered him arbitrary, vindictive, and indifferent to their welfare. As evidence of his indifference, they pointed to the deplorable condition of the locker room. Six of the apprentices, former servicemen, were especially sour on Fitzpatrick. He was down on all exservicemen, they said, and constantly abused and insulted them.

Shocked by these disclosures, Mr. Welty toured the pressroom and locker room with Fitzpatrick, putting questions to some of the workmen. He then ordered the locker room repaired and cleaned up, and in a long talk with Fitzpatrick reprimanded him sharply. After 23 years with the firm and 13 as foreman, he insisted, Fitzpatrick should know better than to treat employees in that way.

A few months later, on again checking the situation in the pressroom, Mr. Welty found no improvement in employee morale and no improvement in Fitzpatrick's relationship with the workmen. Obviously something more drastic than a verbal reprimand was necessary. Reluctant to dismiss Fitzpatrick, Mr. Welty appointed an acting foreman for the pressroom and for a one-year period assigned Fitzpatrick to supervise the installation of new presses in another part of the plant. "This may be a cowardly decision," he admitted to himself, "but a lot can happen in a year and I'll cross that bridge when I come to it a year from now."

How should Mr. Welty have handled this situation?

1. Exactly as he did. In the course of a year something may well happen to solve the problem.
2. He should have transferred Fitzpatrick for one year to the new job of installing presses but with the understanding that he would not again be foreman of the pressroom.
3. He should have transferred him to the new job for a year, trying in the meantime to help him improve as a foreman, but leaving open the question of what to do with him at the end of the year.
4. He should have fired Fitzpatrick immediately on making the second checkup.
5. He should have kept Fitzpatrick as a journeyman printer, if he cared to stay, but should have relieved him of the foremanship.

2. Interaction Analysis Exercise

Observe a group discussion and try to use the Bales Interaction Process Analysis scoring sheet (Fig. 4.13) to make you observations more systematic. Start by observing and recording only one person in the group. Simply place a hash mark in the appropriate row when a person says something in the group. As you gain more experience, record two or three group members. You may also want to try having several people observe the same person to check the reliability of your observations.

3. Group-Development Exercise

Observe a real-life problem-solving group. Listen carefully for statements that indicate the four phases of group development. You might take notes to record exact statements that illustrate the four phases. Notice also if the group does *not* seem to go through these four phases. Compare your observations with others who have observed different groups. Do most of the observations correspond to the research findings?

Scoring of Interaction (Bales)	Person 1	Person 2	Person 3	Row totals
1. *Seems friendly*, raises other's status, gives help, reward				
2. *Dramatizes*, jokes, laughs, shows satisfaction				
3. *Agrees*, shows passive acceptance, understand, concurs, complies				
4. *Gives suggestions*, direction, implying autonomy for other				
5. *Gives opinion*, evaluation, analysis, expresses feeling, wish				
6. *Gives information*, repeats, clarifies, confirms				
7. *Asks for information*, repetition, confirmation				
8. *Asks for opinion*, evaluation analysis, express feeling				
9. *Asks for suggestion*, direction, possible ways of action				
10. *Disagrees*, shows passive rejection, formality, withholds help				
11. *Shows tension*, asks for help, withdraws "out of field"				
12. *Seems unfriendly*, deflates other's status, defends or asserts self				
Column totals				

FIGURE 4.13
Bales Interaction Process Analysis scoring sheet.

OVERVIEW OF READINGS

In the first article, Hersey and Blanchard offer further elaboration on how to identify the maturity of group members, which influences the choice of an appropriate leadership style.

The second article, by Ladd Wheeler, describes the classic social influence studies of Sherif. The description of the studies regarding the "autokinetic effect" provide a bit more depth in the way in which social phenomena are studied.

Situational
Leadership

Paul Hersey
Kenneth H. Blanchard

The need for a significant Situational Model in the leadership area has been recognized in the literature for some time.

A. K. Korman, in his extensive review of studies examining the Ohio State concepts of Initiating Structure and Consideration, concluded that:

> What is needed . . . in future concurrent (and predictive) studies is not just recognition of this factor of "situational determinants" but, rather, a systematic conceptualization of situational variance as it might relate to leadership behavior [Initiating Structure and Consideration].

In discussing this conclusion, Korman suggests the possibility of a curvilinear relationship rather than a simple linear relationship between Initiating Structure (task behavior) and Consideration (relationship behavior) and other variables. Situational Leadership, which is an outgrowth of our Tri-Dimensional Leader Effectiveness Model, has identified such a curvilinear relationship.

Situational Leadership is based on an interplay among (1) the amount of guidance and direction (task behavior) a leader gives; (2) the amount of socioemotional support (relationship behavior) a leader provides; and (3) the readiness ("maturity") level that followers exhibit in performing a specific task, function or objective. This concept was developed to help people attempting leadership, regardless of their role, to be more effective in their daily interactions with others. It provides leaders with some understanding of the relationship between an effective style of leadership and the level of maturity of their followers.

Thus, while all the situational variables (leader, follower(s), superior(s), associates, organization, job demands, and time) are important, the emphasis in Situational Leadership will be on the behavior of a leader in relation to followers. As Fillmore H. Sanford has indicated, there is some justification for regarding the followers "as the most crucial factor in any leadership event." Followers in any situation are vital, not only because as a group they actually determine whatever personal power the leader may have. . . .

When discussing leader/follower relationships, we are not necessarily talking about a hierarchical relationship, that is, superior/subordinate. The same caution will hold during our discussion of Situational Leadership. *Thus, any reference to leader(s) or follower(s) in this theory should imply potential leader and potential follower.* As a result, although our examples may suggest a hierarchical relationship, the concepts presented in Situational Leadership should have application no matter whether you are attempting to influence the behavior of a subordinate, your boss, an associate, a friend, or a relative.

MATURITY OF THE FOLLOWERS OR GROUP

Maturity is defined in Situational Leadership as the ability and willingness of people to take responsibility for directing their own behavior. *These variables of maturity should be considered only in relation to a specific task to be performed.* That is to say, an individual or a group is not mature or immature in any *total* sense. All persons tend to be more or less mature in relation to a specific task, function, or objective that a leader is attempting to accomplish through their efforts. Thus, a saleswoman may be very responsible in securing new sales but very casual about completing the paperwork necessary to close on a sale. As a result, it is appropriate for her manager to leave her alone in terms of closing on sales but to supervise her closely in terms of her paperwork until she can start to do well in that area too.

In addition to assessing the level of maturity of individuals within a group, a leader may have to assess the maturity level of the group as a group, particularly if the group interacts frequently together in the same work area, as happens with students in the classroom. Thus, a teacher may find that a class as a group may be at one level of maturity in a particular area, but a student within that group may be at a different level. When the teacher is one-to-one with that student, he or she may have to behave very differently than when working with the class as a group. In reality, the teacher may find a number of students at various maturity levels. For example, the teacher may have one student who is not doing his work regularly; when he turns work in, it is poorly organized and not very academic. With that student, the teacher may have to initiate some structure and supervise closely. Another student, however, may be doing good work but is insecure and shy. With that student, the teacher may not have to engage in much task behavior in terms of schoolwork but may need to be supportive, to engage in two-way communication, and help facilitate the student's interaction with others in the class. Still another student may be psychologically mature as well as competent in her schoolwork, and thus can be left on her own. So leaders have to understand that they may have to behave

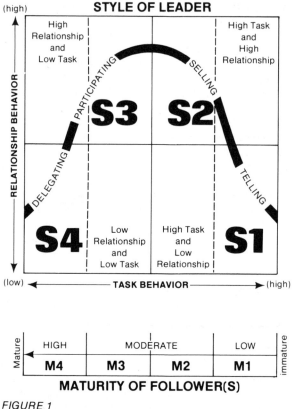

FIGURE 1
Situational leadership

differently one-on-one with members of their group from the way they do with the group as a whole.

BASIC CONCEPT OF SITUATIONAL LEADERSHIP
According to Situational Leadership, there is no one best way to influence people. Which leadership style a person should use with individuals or groups depends on the maturity level of the people the leader is attempting to influence, as illustrated in Figure 1.

STYLE OF LEADER VERSUS MATURITY OF FOLLOWER(S)
The attempt in Figure 1 is to portray the relationship between task-relevant maturity and the appropriate leadership styles to be used as followers move from immaturity to maturity. As indicated, the reader should keep in mind that the figure represents two different phenomena. The appropriate leadership style (*style of leader*) for given levels of follower maturity is portrayed by the prescriptive curve going through the four leadership quadrants. This bell-shaped curve is called a *prescriptive curve* because it shows the appropriate leadership style directly above the corresponding level of maturity.

Each of the four leadership styles — "telling," "selling," "participating," and "delegating" — identified in Figure 1, is a combination of task and relationship behavior. As discussed in Chapter 4, task behavior is the extent to which a leader provides direction for people: telling them what to do, when to do it, where to do it, and how to do it. It means setting goals for them and defining their roles.

Relationship behavior is the extent to which a leader engages in two-way communication with people: providing support, encouragement, "psychological strokes," and facilitating behaviors. It means actively listening to people and supporting their efforts.

The maturity of followers is a question of degree. As can be seen in Figure 1, some bench marks of maturity are provided for determining appropriate leadership style by dividing the maturity continuum below the leadership model into four levels: low (M1), low to moderate (M2), moderate to high (M3), and high (M4).

The appropriate leadership style for each of the four maturity levels includes the right combination of task behavior (direction) and relationship behavior (support).

"Telling" Is for Low Maturity   People who are both *unable and unwilling* (M1) to take responsibility to do something are not competent or confident. In many cases, their unwillingness is a result of their *insecurity* regarding the necessary task. Thus, a directive "telling" style (S1) that provides clear, specific directions and supervision has the highest probability of being effective with individuals at this maturity level. This style is called "telling" because it is characterized by the leader's defining roles and telling people what, how, when, and where to do various tasks. It emphasizes directive behavior. Too much supportive behavior with people at this maturity level may be seen as permissive, easy and, most importantly, as rewarding of poor performance. This style involves high task behavior and low relationship behavior.

"Selling" Is for Low to Moderate Maturity   People who are *unable but willing* (M2) to take responsibility are confident but lack skills at this time. Thus, a "selling" style (S2) that provides directive behavior, because of their lack of ability, but also supportive behavior to reinforce their willingness and enthusiasm appears to be most appropriate with individuals at this maturity level. This style is called "selling" because most of the direction is still provided by the leader. Yet, through two-way communication and explanation, the leader tries to get the followers psychologically to "buy into" desired behaviors. Followers at this maturity level will usually go along with a decision if they understand the reason for the decision and if their leader also offers some help and direction. This style involves high task behavior and high relationship behavior.

"Participating" Is for Moderate to High Maturity   People at this maturity level are *able* but *unwilling* (M3) to do what the leader wants. Their unwillingness is often a function of their lack of confidence or *insecurity*. If, however, they are competent but unwilling, their reluctance to perform is more of a motivational problem than a security problem. In either case, the leader needs to open the door (two-way communication and active listening) to support the follower's efforts to use the ability he already has. Thus, a supportive, nondirective,

"participating" style (S3) has the highest probability of being effective with individuals at this maturity level. This style is called "participating" because the leader and follower share in decision making, with the main role of the leader being facilitating and communicating. This style involves high relationship behavior and low task behavior.

"Delegating" Is for High Maturity   People at this maturity level are both *able and willing, or confident,* to take responsibility. Thus, a low-profile "delegating" style (S4), which provides little direction or support, has the highest probability of being effective with individuals at this maturity level. Even though the leader may still identify the problem, the resonsibility for carrying out plans is given to these mature followers. They are permitted to run the show and decide on the how, when, and where. At the same time, they are psychologically mature and therefore do not need above average amounts of two-way communication or supportive behavior. This style involves low relationship behavior and low task behavior.

It should be clear that the appropriate leadership style for all four of the maturity designations — low maturity (M1), low to moderate maturity (M2), moderate to high maturity (M3), and high maturity (M4) — correspond to the following leadership style designations: *telling* (S1), *selling* (S2), *participating* (S3), and *delegating* (S4). That is, low maturity needs a *telling* style, low to moderate needs a *selling* style, and so on. These combinations are shown in Table 1.

In using the shorthand designations (S1, S2, S3, S4) and labels ("telling," "selling," "participating," and "delegating") for leadership styles that are identified in Figure 1 and Table 1, one must keep in mind that they should only be used when referring to behaviors represented by the effective face of the Tri-Dimensional Leader Effectiveness Model. However, when discussing basic or ineffective styles, we shall refer to them only by quadrant number: Q1, Q2, Q3, or Q4. For example, when a low relationship/low task style is used appropriately with the corresponding maturity level M4, it will be referred to as S4 or "delegating." But when that same style is used inappropriately with any of the other three maturity levels, it will only be called Q4 and might be better described as abdication or withdrawal rather than "delegating."

Situational Leadership not only suggests the high probability leadership style for various maturity levels, but it also indicates the probability of success of the other style configurations if a leader is unable to use the desired style. The probability of success of each style for the four maturity levels, depending on how far the style is from the high probability style along the prescriptive curve in the style of leader portion of the model, is as follows:

M1   S1 high, S2 2nd, Q3 3rd, Q4 low probability
M2   S2 high, S1 2nd, S3 2nd, Q4 low probability
M3   S3 high, S2 2nd, S4 2nd, Q1 low probability
M4   S4 high, S3 2nd, Q2 3rd, Q1 low probability

In indicating the probability of success of each style above, in some cases the "S" designation was used for a style, and in other cases the "Q" designation was used. As discussed, the shorthand designations (S1, S2, S3, S4) and labels ("telling," "selling," "participating," and "delegating") should only be used when

TABLE 1
LEADERSHIP STYLES APPROPRIATE FOR VARIOUS MATURITY LEVELS

MATURITY LEVEL	APPROPRIATE STYLE
M1 *Low Maturity* Unable and unwilling or insecure	S1 *Telling* High task and low relationship behavior
M2 *Low to* *Moderate Maturity* Unable but willing or confident	S2 *Selling* High task and high relationship behavior
M3 *Moderate to* *High Maturity* Able but unwilling or insecure	S3 *Participating* High relationship and low task behavior
M4 *High Maturity* Able/competent and willing/confident	S4 *Delegating* Low relationship and low task behavior

referring to behaviors represented by the effective face of the Tri-Dimensional Leader Effectiveness Model. Thus, the high probability style and the 2nd (secondary) styles were indicated by an "S" designation, while the 3rd and low probability styles were indicated by a "Q" designation. In most cases, there are at least two leadership styles in the effective range. At the same time, there are usually one or two leadership styles that are clearly in the less effective range.

The Psychology of Social Norms

Ladd Wheeler

Sherif published this important book [*The Psychology of Social Norms*] at the age of 30, one year after he had received his Ph.D. Having been reared in Turkey, he was very much aware of cultural differences and had studied cultural anthropology and sociology. On two grounds he disagreed with those who had espoused a social psychology of the individual, particularly with F. H. Allport.

The first disagreement concerned Allport's explanation of the greater energy released in a group situation. He had attributed social facilitation to the sight and sound of others doing the same thing. Sherif argued that individuals raised in a noncompetitive society might react quite differently to the sights and sounds of others doing the same thing.

For individuals raised in the highly competitive American society, the sight of someone else doing the same thing is a conditioned stimulus for speeding up — lest one lose the race and die poor and unknown. In a different culture, however, the sight of someone else doing the same thing might be a stimulus for ceasing the activity altogether — competition being unmanly and ungodly. Sherif believed that Allport had stopped at a level of explanation where psychology should actually begin.

Sherif's second disagreement with Allport concerned the latter's position in his debate with McDougall on the group mind question. Allport had argued that a group is merely a collection of individuals and that no new and supra-

From Ladd Wheeler, *Interpersonal Influence* (Boston: Allyn and Bacon, 1970), pp. 8-12. Reprinted with permission.

individual qualities arise when individuals come together and form a group. Sherif agreed that "if you throw all the individuals of a nation into the ocean, there will be no nation" (Sherif 1963, p. 83), but he also said that "the pattern of the social situation creates a psychological atmosphere that is not inherent in its discrete parts" (p. xv).

Sherif believed that when people interact, norms develop. Norms are expected modes of behavior and belief established by a group. They facilitate interaction by specifying what is expected and acceptable behavior in a particular situation. Following the sociologist Durkheim, Sherif believed norms to have the properties of exteriority and constraint. They are to some extent outside of or exterior to any one individual, and they constrain the individual to behave in certain ways.

Sherif's argument may be stated as follows: New norms arise when people interact in fluid and ambiguous situations which contain a number of behavioral alternatives. Further, the norms persist and guide the behavior of individuals even when the individuals are no longer a part of the group in which the norm was formed.

Sherif believed he could win his point by experimentally demonstrating the formation of group norms which would then influence individual behavior outside of the group. In order to do this, he needed a situation sufficiently ambiguous that individuals could influence one another toward a common norm.

The autokinetic effect appeared to be a useful phenomenon. It is produced when one views a pinpoint of light in a completely dark room. The light cannot be localized definitely because there is nothing in reference to which you can locate it. Thus the light appears to move even if one knows perfectly well that it is not moving. It appears to move in different directions and for different distances.

In one set of conditions, the subjects were first tested alone. The subject sat at a small table on which there was a telegraph key. The following instructions (Sherif 1963, p. 95) were given:

> When the room is completely dark I shall give you a signal "ready" and then show you a point of light. After a short time the light will start to move. As soon as you see it move, press the key. A few seconds later the light will disappear. Then tell me the distance it moved. Try to make your estimates as accurate as possible.

In all cases the light was left on for two seconds after the subject indicated the beginning of movement. Judgments were expressed in inches and fractions of inches, and one hundred judgments were obtained from each subject.

Under these conditions, subjects gradually established a stable range of estimated movement. The first three judgments might be 1 inch, 3 inches and 12 inches, showing great variability. But over time, variability decreased and subjects gave judgments lying between, say, 13 and 15 inches. The ranges that were established varied. A second subject might establish a range of, say, 2 inches to 5 inches. In other words, the subjects eventually established some order in a completely chaotic situation. Written introspective reports obtained from subjects after the experiment indicated that subjects compared each movement of the light with the previous movement.

Subjects who had established their own personal range of movement were then placed together in groups of two or three. Subjects were left free as to the order in which they would give their judgments, being told to give their judgment in random order as they pleased.

The results were clear-cut. Subjects tended to converge to a common norm of movement. When tested individually, groups-to-be had an average range of estimated movement of 3.6 inches. After three sessions as groups, the average range was 0.4 inches. This movement toward a common norm was gradual and mutual. It did not occur because one person remained rigid and the other subjects moved toward his judgments. Rather, all subjects tended to gradually change their estimate to be more similar to those of the other subjects.

In another set of conditions subjects experienced the autokinetic effect for the first time in groups of two and three. They had not established their own individual norms. Under these conditions the convergence toward a common norm was even faster and more complete than in the conditions just described. By the third session as a group, subjects had reduced the average estimated range of movement to less than 0.1 inches. These subjects were then tested alone to determine if the established group norm would influence individual judgments. Again the results were in the predicted direction. The average range of estimated movement was 0.6 inches, indicating some, but very little, movement away from the previously established group norm.

Sherif carried this research further by pairing a naive subject and an experimental confederate, or what we frequently in social psychology call a "stooge." The confederate had been instructed to make all of his judgments within a predetermined range. The aim of the experiment was to find out how much the judgments of the confederate would influence the judgments of the naive subject.

Again the results are clear-cut. The naive subject quickly adopted the range of judgments used by the confederate.

On the day following this session between the naive subject and the experimental confederate the subject was placed in the autokinetic situation alone. Would the subject continue to make his judgments within the range he had adopted working with the confederate? Or would he, now free of the confederate's influence, establish his own range of movement?

The results were quite consistent with those from the other experimental conditions. Subjects did indeed, within a very close degree, maintain the range of movement which the confederate had caused them to adopt in the first place.

From these several experimental conditions involving the autokinetic effect, Sherif (1963, p. 111) wished to derive a very general conclusion about society, applicable to any group in any part of the world at any time in history.

In short, when a group of individuals faces a new, unstable situation and has no previously established interest or opinions regarding the situation, the result is not chaos; a common norm arises and the situation is structured in relation to the common norm. Once the common norm is established, later the separate individuals keep on perceiving it in terms of the frame of reference which was once the norm of the group.

Sherif has shown us that individuals in groups do indeed form norms and that these norms are binding upon the individuals even in the absence of the group. We are left with two important questions. First, why are norms formed? And second, once a norm is formed, how does it get unformed or changed?

Sherif said that norms are formed in order to reduce uncertainty and confusion. Suppose that a small isolated tribe had experienced several years of drought, with consequent crop failure and starvation. Suddenly a rainstorm begins and in the midst of it a young virgin is struck by lightning. What is the meaning of this? Members of the tribe must come to a common understanding of the event. They may decide that the rain god wants the yearly sacrifice of a virgin. Or they may decide to build a temple at the spot and worship the girl. Or they may decide that this particular girl was the evil influence causing the drought, never allowing her name to be used again in the tribe. Whatever they decide will reduce the confusion in the situation and may lead to a lasting belief and mode of behavior which will be adopted by subsequent generations.

The second question mentioned above was "how do norms get changed?" Sherif argued that situations change, so that a norm that was useful or at least harmless at one point in time creates hardship and friction at another point in time. The people for whom the norm creates the greatest hardship revolt against it, refusing to continue to behave in a way that is clearly harmful to themselves. If the norm produces clear benefits for some members of society and hardships for others, there may be strife and bloodshed. The results may be complete destruction of the norm and the consequent change of society, or it may be destruction of those who revolt and the strengthening of the norm.

Norms develop because they are needed — to increase clarity, to promote interaction, to free individuals from having to make a decision about every aspect of behavior. They last until they produce unclarity, interfere with interaction, or create burdens for the majority of the group or society. They are maintained through social sanctions, punishment for those who disregard them and reward for those who obey them.

Entering a new group and adopting its norms is sometimes a tough procedure, because these norms may be in conflict with what one has known in the past. For a group to dissolve a norm may be extremely difficult. A few people may be pinched by the norm, but the majority of citizens accept it as a normal facet of living. The few may have to resort to extreme measures to overcome the inertia of the many.

REFERENCE
Sherif, Muzafer, 1963. *The psychology of social norms.* New York: Harper & Row.

5

Internal Influences

Communication Processes

THE TUBBS MODEL OF SMALL GROUP INTERACTION

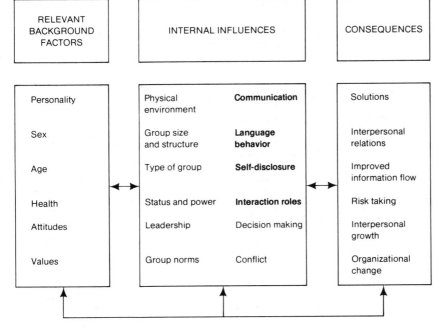

Concepts in **boldface** are the emphases of this chapter.

CASE STUDY

A committee of university faculty members were deciding whom to have vote on an important new policy statement. They had worked for several months to develop and refine this policy statement and they wanted to send a copy to all people in the university who would be affected by this policy. The committee had not anticipated any difficulty deciding whom to send the memo to. Then this problem occurred.

Prof. Brown	Now that we have all agreed on the final policy to be communicated, let's decide which method should be used to convey the policy.
Prof. Smith	Let's use an interorganization memo. (The group all agreed.) Let's send a ballot to each person through the faculty mail. (Again, general agreement.)
Prof. Brown	OK, the subject of the memo is adoption of the new faculty senate operating procedures, right? (General agreement.) All right, let's address this to all members of the faculty.
Prof. Jones	Whom are you including in the faculty?
Prof. Brown	That's obvious.
Prof. Jones	No, I don't think so. Are department chairmen included as faculty or are they administrators?
Prof. Brown	Well, they teach, don't they?
Prof. Jones	Yes, but they also serve as administrators.
Prof. Brown	What does it matter what category they go by?
Prof. Jones	OK, let me put it this way. Do the deans and the president qualify as faculty or administrators?
Prof. Thomas	Well, they are listed in the catalog as faculty.
Prof. Jones	OK; however, this policy is the first major step in allowing greater *faculty* governance at this school. How can we get greater faculty governance if we include members of administration in our definition of faculty?
Prof. James	Yeh. What if it's a close vote and all the administrators vote as a block to defeat our new policy?
Prof. Brown	I still think we are making a mountain out of a molehill.

Prof. Jones	(Getting irritated.) We work for almost a year getting a faculty senate organized and now you think it's a trivial matter whether or not the proposal gets defeated?
Prof. Brown	I didn't say anything of the kind. I only meant that I think it is unlikely that the administration has enough votes to make much difference no matter how we define the term *faculty*.
Prof. Jones	Well, I strongly disagree. I think this is a *crucial* point. Are we, the faculty, going to have a hand in running this place once and for all, or are we going to let this little bit of progress be eroded by allowing administrators to vote on *our faculty senate?*
Prof. Smith	I'm afraid our time is running out for today's meeting. Since many of us have classes to go to I think we should table this discussion until our next meeting. In the meantime let's all try to rethink our positions on this.
Prof. Jones	I don't have to do any rethinking! If we are going to go back to being dictated to by the administration, I don't want any further part of this committee. I volunteered to be on this committee because I thought we had a chance to improve things around here. I can see now I have wasted my time.
Chairperson	Do I have a motion for adjournment?
Prof. Thomas	So moved.
Chairperson	Is there a second?
Prof. Smith	Second.
Chairperson	Meeting adjourned until next week.

1. *What is the major problem for this group?*

2. *How could they have avoided this outcome?*

3. *If you could role play this discussion, what would you say to help resolve this situation?*

T

——— his group discussion, which actually occurred, illustrates one type of problem that groups may encounter: language-related problems and the relationship between language, thought, and behaviors. The committee members could not agree on how to interpret the word *faculty*. This disagreement led to emotional reactions and eventually to one member's resignation from the committee. This problem is just one type of difficulty related to problems of communication. But before we go any further, let us stop and define *our* terms so we don't run into the same problem this committee did.

COMMUNICATION ✓

COMMUNICATION DEFINED

Communication within the small group is both similar to and different from communication in other settings. Group communication involves the process of creating meanings in the minds of others. These meanings may or may not correspond to the meanings we intend to create. Group communication involves the sending and receiving of messages between and among the participants. Group communication includes both verbal and nonverbal message stimuli. In all these ways, group communication is similar to communication that occurs in other contexts, such as interpersonal communication (informal communication between two or more people); public communication (between a speaker and an audience); organizational communication (or communication in an organizational setting); or mass communication (in which a source attempts to communicate with large numbers of people, usually through some electronic or written medium). This chapter will focus on communication principles as they relate to the small group context.

INTENTIONAL-UNINTENTIONAL

Most of the time we communicate for a purpose. It may be to get our point across, to persuade another, to prompt action, or simply to have fun. These types of messages are known as *intentional;* that is, we intend to communicate in order to achieve our purpose. However, we may also transmit messages that are unintentional. The slip of the tongue, or Freudian slip, is one well-known example. Before Spiro Agnew actually resigned from the vice-presidency, Texan John Connally said in one speech that he hoped Agnew would be found guilty. Later he corrected himself and said that of course he had meant *not guilty*. Since Agnew and Connally had been political rivals for some time, it is interesting to speculate as to which he *actually meant*. It is obvious, however, that he had suffered a slip of the tongue.

According to Freud, our id or pleasure center leads us to reveal what we really feel, while our ego, the rational data processing part of our personality, tends to limit or censor what we utter. When the id forces win out over the rational ego forces, the Freudian slip results. Ruch (1972) explains that Freudian slips may occur in the form of malapropisms and spoonerisms. A malapropism is an inappropriate use of a word that sounds similar to the correct word, for example, "I illiterate him from memory" for "eliminate"; "a progeny of learning" for "prodigy"; and "the cat sautées across the floor" for "saunters." Comedian Norm Crosby has made an art of using malapropisms as the basis for his humor.

It is also possible for a Freudian slip to occur in the form of a spoonerism. A spoonerism is the interchanging of sounds in two or more words. Some examples include "blushing crow" for "crushing blow" and "it is kistomary to cuss the bride," as stated by the groom's former girl friend. Freud (Ruch, 1972, p. 102) stated that such unintentional verbal messages more than likely result when we are "distracted, confused, embarrassed, or simply not psychically engaged [or] when the thought is insufficiently worked out or the problem particularly complicated."

Unintentional messages may be transmitted by action as well as by words. The person who crosses his arms in front of him while rearing back in his chair may be unknowingly communicating his disapproval of events occurring in a group discussion. Frequently, group members will direct their remarks (through eye contact) to those members that they prefer, or that they feel have influence in the group. This is often done unconsciously and unintentionally.

The best-selling book *The Making of a Psychiatrist* (Viscott 1972) includes the description of a patient characterized by unintentional, compulsive gestures. Viscott (p. 50-54) describes him in the following manner:

> "Mr. Parker, I'm going to be taking over from Dr. Meredith and I will try to be as helpful to you as I can. . . ." "Good, good," he said, reaching over and touching me on the knee with his hand, tapping me twice. . . .

> In order to control his inner world, Harold Parker had developed an intricate system of rituals which he repeated to ward off bad luck . . . he would touch something solid twice.

> "What do you think is going to happen with your company, Mr. Parker?" I asked.

> "I think things will turn out well, as they always do. It's a sound company." He tapped my desk twice again and smiled an artificial smile. . . .

> "I'm running it," said Harold Parker, tapping his right foot once. Once? Where's the second tap? I was pretty sure there would be another tap coming. There's *supposed* to be another tap coming. The

first tap supposedly symbolizes a bad wish and the second supposedly erases it. Where was it? Maybe he didn't tap his foot magically at all. Maybe he just liked to tap his foot. Maybe I was reading a lot into all of this. Maybe this was all bullshit. Paying attention to so many details of a patient's behavior was trying.

"You're running the company from here?"

"I'm on the phone a couple of times a day to Edgar. He's my manager. That's how I'm running it." Mr. Parker tapped my desk twice.

This brief account illustrates one way in which actions can communicate without our even knowing it. This example also illustrates the potential pitfalls in trying to overinterpret or read too much into a person's verbal or nonverbal slips.

As already mentioned in Chapter 3, encounter groups are one context in which we get feedback on behaviors that helps us eliminate unintentional cues. The gap between what we intend to communicate and what is actually received is called the arc of distortion (Bennis 1961). The larger the gap, the less effective we are in our relations with others. We can reduce the gap if we are receptive to feedback from others, and if others are willing to share their impressions with us. In order for the arc to be reduced, the feedback must be of high quality. Miles (1967) suggests that effective feedback must "(1) be clear and undistorted, (2) come from a trusted nonthreatening source, and (3) follow as closely as possible the behavior to which it is a reaction."

VERBAL-NONVERBAL

As indicated above, we communicate not only with words (verbal messages), but by nonverbal means as well. In Chapter 3 we discussed the importance of environmental influences on small group interaction. Later in this chapter we will discuss verbal cues under the heading "Language Behavior." In addition, visual and vocal nonverbal cues will vary as a part of the process of discussion, and will influence the eventual results of the discussion.

Visual Cues   Visual cues are highly influential in interpersonal communication. *Facial expression* and *eye contact* are probably the two most important types of visual cues. Those who avoid looking at us communicate disapproval or disinterest. Those who look at us may still indicate a negative reaction, based on their facial expression. Probably the most rewarding cue is a smiling face and a head nod in combination with direct eye contact. From these and other cues we infer support, confirmation, and agreement. Knapp (1972, p. 119) emphasizes the importance of the face:

The face is rich in communicative potential. It is the primary site for communication of emotional states; it reflects interpersonal attitudes;

it provides nonverbal feedback on the comments of others; and some say it is the primary source of information next to human speech.

Barnlund (1968, p. 521) echoes this feeling:

> Of all the features that identify a man, none is as differentiating as his face; of all the parts of the body, none is as richly expressive.

Although facial expression is usually a critical factor in nonverbal communication, there are some rare occasions in which other factors may take precedence. Note the following news item:

> Los Angeles (AP) The braless robber has struck for the second time in two days. . . . Police said the robber, wearing a sheer blue blouse without a bra, robbed a South Pasadena branch of the Bank of America of about $400 Tuesday. . . . On Monday, a person believed to be the same woman held up a Los Angeles savings and loan office and escaped with $2,600. Police said a red-faced teller was unable to describe the robber's face, noting only that she was braless under a light-colored blouse.

One study confirmed the finding that the general tendency to look into a person's eyes can be preempted by other factors. Wahlers and Barker (1973) conducted an interview study and found that braless women got significantly less eye contact from males than their bra-wearing counterparts.

Eye contact, however, is a powerful type of nonverbal cue. Argyle (1967) estimates that in group communication we spend between 30 and 60 percent of the time exchanging mutual glances with others. Many of these may last less than a second. He summarizes (pp. 115-116) several unstated rules about visual interaction:

a. A looker may invite interaction by staring at another person who is on the other side of a room. The target's studied return of the gaze is generally interpreted as acceptance of the invitation, while averting the eyes is a rejection of the looker's request.

b. There is more mutual eye contact between friends than others, and a looker's frank gaze is widely interpreted as positive regard.

c. Persons who seek eye contact while speaking are regarded not only as exceptionally well-disposed by their target, but also as more believable and earnest.

d. If the usual short, intermittent gazes during conversation are replaced by gazes of longer duration, the target interprets this as meaning that the task is less important than the personal relation between the two persons.

Several other principles have been borne out by experimental studies as well as by systematic observation of ongoing behaviors. For example, females consistently give more eye contact than males (Mehrabian 1969).

Also, we are able to assert dominance over others almost exclusively with eye contact in a matter of seconds when we first encounter one another (Strongman and Champness 1968). We tend to direct our comments toward those from whom we expect or would like feedback (Kendon 1967). Conversely, avoiding eye contact is a way of protecting oneself from the contact of others. Argyle and Dean (1965) summarize the functions of eye contact by stating that it signals information seeking, openness to communication, concealment or exhibitionism, recognition of social relationships, and conflicts in motivation.

Hand gestures are another type of visual cue. Barnlund (1968) states, "Next to the face, the hands are probably the most expressive part of the human body." Entire books have been devoted to the study of the hands in oral communication. It was once thought that hand gestures could be taught as a means of developing greater expressiveness. For example, the outstretched hands with the palms up indicated a request for help, while the clenched fist indicated a threat. The study of gestures today is more descriptive, and leans less in the direction of trying to prescribe which gestures should be used in certain situations.

Physical appearance includes facial attractiveness as well as body shape and size and styles of dress. In one study of physically attractive vs. unattractive people, Widgery (1974) found that on the basis of faces alone, more attractive people are consistently assumed to have higher credibility than their homely counterparts. Walster *et al.* (1966) found that among 752 college students at a freshman dance, physical attractiveness was by far the most important factor in determining the extent to which a date would be liked by his or her partner. Perhaps some homely soul rationalized this by creating the old saying:

> Beauty is only skin deep,
> But ugly's to the bone.
> Beauty soon will fade away,
> But ugly holds its own.

B. F. Skinner has argued that beauty is a form of reinforcer, since it encourages us to look once again. Certainly most fashion models of both sexes are reinforcing to look at!

As we saw in Chapter 4, body shape has been described in three basic categories by Sheldon (1954). The mesomorph is muscular and athletic looking and would be considered the most attractive. The ectomorph is tall, thin, and fragile looking. The endomorph is soft, round, and fat. Three representative examples of the respective body types would be Burt Reynolds, Don Knotts, and Buddy Hackett. Our body shapes are usually some mixture of these three types. Jack Lalanne, the famous physical fitness personality, once said on a television show that if you raid the refrigerator every night, even if you are alone, your body itself communicates to everybody every day that you eat too much. So you're not fooling anybody.

Styles of dress also communicate about us. We are often judged as "straight" or "freaks" based on our clothing choices. Lefkowitz, Blake, and Mouton (1955) conducted an interesting study of the influence of a person's dress on jaywalking behavior. They collected data on jaywalking on three different days for three different one-hour periods. They wanted to determine if pedestrians (these happened to be in Austin, Texas) would violate the "wait" signal more if they saw someone else violate it than if there were no violator. They were also interested in any differential effects that would result from differences in the violator's dress. The experimenters made use of a confederate who jaywalked while dressed one of two ways. First, he dressed in a high-status manner with a freshly pressed suit, shined shoes, white shirt, tie, and straw hat (Mr. Clean). The low-status dress consisted of an unpressed blue denim shirt, soiled and patched pants, well-worn shoes, and no hat (Mr. Dirty). Observations were made on 2103 pedestrians who crossed the intersection during the hours of the experiment.

The study revealed several interesting results. Ninety-nine percent of the pedestrians obeyed the "wait" signal when no confederate was present, or when the confederate also obeyed. When "Mr. Dirty" jaywalked, 4 percent of the other pedestrians also violated the signal. When "Mr. Clean" jaywalked, 14 percent of the other pedestrians also disobeyed. Although this study is now quite dated, some students replicated it in 1973 and found quite similar results. To summarize, our appearance through facial attractiveness, body shape, and choice of clothing will determine to some extent our influence on others.

Body movements are also an influential type of nonverbal cue. Each of us can probably remember having someone say, "You seem kind of down today," as a reaction to our slumped shoulders and slightly bowed head. Probably one of Peter Falk's most memorable roles is his slouchy interpretation of the character Columbo. Although there are a wealth of other cues (gestures, raincoat, cigar), body movements stand out very vividly, as did John Wayne's swagger or Bo Derek's walk.

Body orientation is an important factor in small group interaction. Knapp (1972, p. 97) defines body orientation as "the degree to which a communicator's shoulders and legs are turned in the direction of, rather than away from, the addressee." Mehrabian (1969) found that a seated communicator who leaned forward was perceived as having a more positive attitude than one who leaned backward and away from the person judging. Goffman (1961) noted that higher-status persons were more relaxed in staff meetings in a psychiatric hospital than lower-status individuals, who sat straighter in their chairs. Body position may also add to our perceiving a person as being "uptight." Schutz (1971, p. 212) describes this in the context of an encounter group.

If a person is holding himself tight, I would either move on to someone else and count on the group interaction to loosen him up so that he can work better later, or perhaps choose to try to help him break through that defense. . . . A first step is to ask the person to relax by unlocking his arms and legs if he has them crossed, perhaps to stand up and shake himself loose, jiggle and breathe very deeply for several minutes.

Inclusiveness is another important aspect of body orientation. In a small group discussion, subgroups frequently form that are usually annoying to at least some in the group. Subgroups may be the result of one person directing comments to only one or two others. This term *directing comments* refers to body orientation and the direction of eye contact. Those who feel excluded from the discussion will sooner or later begin to withdraw their participation from the group, and the benefit of their contributions will be lost. Thus body orientation can be quite a potent factor in determining the discussion's oucome.

Vocal Cues   In addition to the verbal message and the visual cues, vocal cues affect small group interaction. There is usually some confusion between the terms *vocal cues* and *verbal cues.* Perhaps it would be helpful to remember that vocal cues are lost when a verbal (word) message is written down. Vocal cues include regional dialects, methods of pronunciation, and the five major factors of (1) volume, (2) rate and fluency, (3) pitch, (4) quality, and (5) inflection.

Try to imagine the sound of your voice saying, "Now that we are all here, we can get the meeting started." Now think of how it would sound as stated by John Wayne, Sammy Davis, Jr., Truman Capoie, Humphrey Bogart, W. C. Fields, Elizabeth Taylor, Mae West, Mary Tyler Moore, Valerie Harper, or by some of your own friends. Each person's voice is unique; sometimes voice prints are used like fingerprints for identification. This individuality results from the complex combination of vocal cues mentioned above. Speaking with adequate *volume* or loudness is the first responsibility of any communicator. Conversely, the first responsibility of listeners is to let speakers know that they can't be heard. Speakers should be asked to speak more loudly and to repeat the part that was missed (Tubbs and Moss 1983). This requires some tact, however. The intent should be to communicate, "I want to know what you're saying," rather than, "Listen, dummy, I'm important and you're not taking my listening convenience into sufficient account."

Groups tend to have more problems with adequate volume than, say, people involved in personal conversations would have. As the size of the group increases, the hearing difficulties may also increase, since there are more potential sources of interfering noise and the distance from the speaker to any given member in the group tends to be greater.

A second critical vocal cue is *rate and fluency.* Rate refers to words uttered per minute (WPM), and fluency refers to the lack of interruptions (which may influence the rate). We have all suffered the unpleasantness of listening to a person who injects long pauses in the middle of sentences, or who frequently throws in such distracting verbal fillers as "ah," "um," "er," "why I," "and-uh," "like," among others. An average speaking rate is between 125 and 175 words per minute. If the person is able to articulate well, that is, to speak distinctly, a faster rate seems to be more interesting to listen to. Studies in listener comprehension indicate that we can understand rates two and three times the normal speed with little difficulty. In group discussion, the fluent speaker is usually more pleasant to listen to.

Vocal *pitch* refers to the frequency in cycles per second (CPS) of the vocal tones. Mary Tyler Moore and Truman Capote have high-pitched (or high-frequency) voices, while John Wayne and Mae West had lower-pitched voices. There is probably no such thing as the perfectly pitched voice; however, most successful professional announcers seem to have lower-pitched voices.

Vocal *quality* refers to the resonance of the voice. Different examples would include breathiness (Connie Stevens), harshness (Nelson Rockefeller), nasality (Barbra Streisand), and huskiness (Vicki Carr). Vocal quality may determine the extent to which people may want to listen to us for any length of time. Johnny Carson's laugh was once described as being "like the sound of cracking plastic." The voice of comedian Don Adams was once compared to "the sound of scratching your fingernail across a blackboard." On the other hand, some people who try to make their voices sound more deep and resonant come across as phony and artificial.

Inflection refers to the relative emphasis, pitch changes, and duration in uttering different word parts of words in a sentence. The American southerner's accent is characterized by a drawn-out vowel sound: for example, Atlanta (northern pronunciation) versus Atlaaanta (southern pronunciation). Inflections also include the rise in vocal pitch at the end of an interrogative sentence:

Are you coming?

Probably the most critical thing to remember about vocal inflections is that they may indicate a lot of the emotional tone of a statement. The statement "Oh, great" can be said with true enthusiasm or great disgust. We can use our voices to indicate sarcasm, ridicule, and superiority, and they may be counterproductive to the group's progress.

Leathers (1976) reports that several emotions can be very reliably detected in most speakers. He has groups of students rate ten different vocal messages according to the emotions they convey. The rating instructions are as shown in Fig. 5.1. While Leathers's technique is for the purpose of research, the practical aspect is that our vocal cues do accurately convey our emotions. As we become more aware and in control of our nonverbal cues, we may improve our effectiveness in groups. For example, several students complained about a professor who was being quite abusive

FIGURE 5.1
THE VOCALIC MEANING SENSITIVITY TEST

The communicator you are listening to — either live or on tape recording — is attempting to communicate ten different classes or kinds of meaning to you. Each attempt to communicate a class of meaning will begin with the words "This is vocal message number _____." You are to listen very carefully and place the number of the vocal message in the blank across from a word, such as disgust or happiness, which comes closest to representing the meaning which has just been communicated to you vocally. Follow the same procedure for each of the ten vocal messages.

CLASS OF VOCALIC MEANING	NUMBER OF VOCAL MESSAGE
Disgust	_____
Happiness	_____
Interest	_____
Sadness	_____
Bewilderment	_____
Contempt	_____
Surprise	_____
Anger	_____
Determination	_____
Fear	_____

Source: Reprinted with permission of the author from Dale Leathers, *Nonverbal Communication Systems* (Boston: Allyn and Bacon, 1976).

in his tone of voice to them. They were considering quitting his class because of this. When he was told of this he was shocked. He had been unaware of the negative consequences his vocal tone had had on his teaching effectiveness.

Tessa Warschaw (1980) has developed a questionnaire designed to help us become more aware of our own nonverbal cues. She recommends monitoring your own behaviors in each of three settings: at home, at work (or at school if you are not working), and in social settings. Her guidelines are as shown in Fig. 5.2.

Clearly, not all of the cues in Fig. 5.2 are exhibited in the small group setting. However, as we become more aware of our nonverbal behavior overall, we can begin to change some of these cues in situations that appear to need improvement. We can also begin to develop our sensitivities to the nonverbal behaviors of others. For example, if a meeting has been going on for a long time, you can detect tiredness and low level of energy through bored facial expressions, yawns, or unenthusiastic vocal tones. These cues may indicate that the group needs to take a break in order to continue at peak efficiency. But the person not sensitive to these cues may try to keep pushing a tired group, only to accomplish less and less.

FIGURE 5.2
YOUR SYMBOL-AND-SIGN INVENTORY

Our bodies give off different clues at different times. The signals we flash vary depending on whether the environment we're in is formal or informal. Whether we're at home or in the office, whether we're on public display or in a one-to-one encounter, whether the people we're with are known to us or strangers. To understand the effect we produce on others, we must first be aware of how we appear and react in different settings.

Following are lists of fifteen different aspects of ourselves through which we broadcast signals. Check the words that best describe your attitudes, manner, or physical response in each of three different settings — home, work, and social gatherings. Think about your answers. Take your time. Be objective.

BODY				OVERALL APPEARANCE			
Home	Work	Social Setting		Home	Work	Social Setting	
___	___	___	tense	___	___	___	calm
___	___	___	relaxed	___	___	___	flamboyant
___	___	___	drooping	___	___	___	casual
___	___	___	mobile	___	___	___	conservative
___	___	___	athletic	___	___	___	femme fatale
___	___	___	stiff	___	___	___	macho male
___	___	___	graceful	___	___	___	negligent

EYES				EYE CONTACT			
Home	Work	Social Setting		Home	Work	Social Setting	
___	___	___	downcast	___	___	___	direct
___	___	___	squinting	___	___	___	indirect
___	___	___	roving	___	___	___	avoiding
___	___	___	darting	___	___	___	confrontive
___	___	___	expressive	___	___	___	seductive
___	___	___	staring	___	___	___	scrutinizing
___	___	___	blinking	___	___	___	glancing

HAND MOVEMENT				HANDSHAKE			
Home	Work	Social Setting		Home	Work	Social Setting	
___	___	___	constant hand movement on body or shaping the air	___	___	___	cordial
___	___	___	appropriate gestures	___	___	___	firm and responsive
___	___	___	rubbing together	___	___	___	quick and wet
___	___	___	covering mouth	___	___	___	brotherhood/ sisterhood grip
___	___	___	pounding table or backs	___	___	___	overgrip
___	___	___	finger pointing	___	___	___	barely brushing
___	___	___	no movement	___	___	___	limp and cold

Source: From Tessa Warschaw, *Winning by Negotiation* (New York: McGraw-Hill, 1980), pp. 88-92. Reprinted by permission of McGraw-Hill Book Company.

FIGURE 5.2 (cont.)

STANCE				WALK			
Home	Work	Social Setting		Home	Work	Social Setting	
___	___	___	stooped and burdened	___	___	___	fast
___	___	___	elastic	___	___	___	slow
___	___	___	erect	___	___	___	youthful
___	___	___	relaxed and grounded	___	___	___	heavy
___	___	___	hands on hip	___	___	___	light
___	___	___	arms crossed	___	___	___	fatigued
___	___	___	feet apart	___	___	___	shuffling

VOICE — MESSAGE				VOICE — TONE AND QUALITY			
Home	Work	Social Setting		Home	Work	Social Setting	
___	___	___	hesitant	___	___	___	tranquilizing
___	___	___	understanding	___	___	___	piercing
___	___	___	threatening	___	___	___	monotone
___	___	___	confusing	___	___	___	whining
___	___	___	confident	___	___	___	loud
___	___	___	unfeeling	___	___	___	modulated
___	___	___	encouraging	___	___	___	strained

HEAD				FACE			
Home	Work	Social Setting		Home	Work	Social Setting	
___	___	___	shaking	___	___	___	grimacing
___	___	___	nodding	___	___	___	frowning
___	___	___	rigid	___	___	___	smooth-lined
___	___	___	responsive	___	___	___	laugh-lined
___	___	___	swaying	___	___	___	stress-lined
___	___	___	drooped	___	___	___	twitching
___	___	___	tilted	___	___	___	clenched

SMILE				SIT			
Home	Work	Social Setting		Home	Work	Social Setting	
___	___	___	intense	___	___	___	slump
___	___	___	broad	___	___	___	rigid and straight
___	___	___	quick	___	___	___	legs crossed
___	___	___	constant	___	___	___	legs apart
___	___	___	twitch	___	___	___	chair straddled
___	___	___	frozen	___	___	___	informal curl
___	___	___	tight-lipped	___	___	___	comfortable

FIGURE 5.2 (cont.)

			TOUCHING

Home	Work	Social Setting	
_____	_____	_____	avoids physical contact
_____	_____	_____	hesitant
_____	_____	_____	loving
_____	_____	_____	patronizing
_____	_____	_____	conciliatory
_____	_____	_____	pat and peck
_____	_____	_____	invading

In summarizing this section on verbal and nonverbal cues, it should be pointed out that all these cues are perceived as a whole. We do not dissect them in reality as we have done in this analysis. For example, it has been found that when we say one thing, but nonverbally indicate something else (for example, "I really appreciate that" spoken sarcastically), the *nonverbal* message is more likely to be believed (Keltner 1970). In this same context, subjects in one study who were told to lie showed several nonverbal changes. There were more errors in their speech, they had less direct eye contact, and talked for shorter durations than they had when they were telling the truth (Mehrabian 1971). Obviously, nonverbal communication plays a significant role in small groups. As one source puts it, whether you talk or not, "You can't *not* communicate" (Watzlawick, Beavin, and Jackson 1967). Let us keep in mind the importance of both verbal and nonverbal messages. Although this discussion has mainly dealt with nonverbal messages, the importance of verbal messages will be dealt with later in this chapter.

DEFENSIVE-SUPPORTIVE

For several years it has been an established fact that when someone threatens you psychologically, you react by throwing up a barrier against that threat. That barrier is referred to as a defense mechanism. Once that defensive barrier has been erected, effective communication is reduced. Thus it is valuable to learn how we can avoid arousing others' protective psychological shields. Gibb (1961) described six differences between what he called defensive and supportive communication climates. These six differences are:

Supportive climates	Defensive climates
Description	Evaluation
Problem orientation	Control

Spontaneity	Strategy
Empathy	Neutrality
Equality	Superiority
Provisionalism	Certainty

When we feel that we are being evaluated, especially when someone is criticizing us, we are likely to rise to our own defense. However, when we feel that a person is objectively describing us without adding an evaluation, we are not as likely to become defensive. When someone tries to control or coerce us, we become more uncomfortable than when a person seeks to solve a problem without forcing us to go along with the solution. Then, too, a person who has a preset plan usually turns us off, as opposed to one who spontaneously reacts to situations. Strategy often implies a gimmick or some deception. Similarly, when a person is neutral toward us, as opposed to empathic or sympathetic, it usually makes us more defensive. When a person acts in a superior manner instead of treating us as an equal, we say that person is on an ego trip. Such superior behavior is deflating to our self-esteem and arouses our defenses. Finally, when someone acts as a "know-it-all," this attitude of certainty or dogmatism is less pleasant than when the person is willing to have an open mind and act with a degree of provisionalism. Gibb found that groups with defensive climates got more bogged down in worthless ego-protecting discussion and accomplished less than those groups with more supportive climates.

See the article by Gibb at the end of this chapter for a more complete description.

Another related point of view was advanced by Adler (1964, p. 42). He referred to the supportive style of relating as an index of a person's *social interest* or *lebensform* (form of life), which was "to see with the eyes of another, to feel with the heart of another. . . . This gift coincides with identification or empathy." Adler predicted that a supportive form of relationship established through communication would be instrumental in promoting effective interpersonal relations. Conversely, he also identified and described some dysfunctional patterns of interaction.

Adler's (1956) description of the striving for superiority led him to discover what he called the "depreciation tendency" characteristic of the neurotic. This tendency was characterized (pp. 268-269) by the "readiness intended to injure other persons, such as sadism, hatred, always wanting to have the last word, intolerance, and envy. . . . In brief, the neurotic may enhance his self-esteem by disparaging the other person." We will see the specific application of these concepts to small group interaction later in this section, in the discussion of self-centered roles in small group behavior.

See the article by Carl Rogers at the end of this chapter for a good explanation of the rationale behind the supportive style of communicating.

CONTENT AND PROCESS

One rather difficult distinction to make about group discussion is the difference between the content of the discussion and the process. Suppose a group is discussing the topic, "How can political corruption in the United States be reduced?" When the discussion is over, the professor asks others in the class to comment on the discussion. Comments concernng the *content* of the discussion might include the following:

☐   I think political corruption will always be with us.

☐   I think politics are not more dirty now than in the past.

☐   The political system has shown its strength by catching its own offenders.

These comments are typical of an untrained observer. They all deal with the topic of the discussion, and the observer frequently gets into the heat of the discussion topic himself.

   Comments regarding the *process* of the same discussion are quite different, as illustrated by the following:

☐   Joe dominated the group, while the others couldn't get a word in edgewise.

☐   Most of your comments were based on opinions. Few actual facts were brought out.

☐   I think you got bogged down in defining the problem and never really got to any conclusion as to how to solve the problem.

These comments deal with the process or manner in which the discussion was conducted. This type of observation usually requires more insight into group interaction. Also, this type of comment allows both participants and observers to learn from one sample discussion some principles of group interaction that can be generalized to other discussions. Thus it is important to be able to distinguish discussion content from the discussion process.

   Notice the difference in the following two students' descriptions of a group discussion. They were asked to describe the group processes in their small group. (The topic was the ethics of cloning humans — exercise 3 in Chapter 1.)

Student 1
I feel a certain resentment towards the idea of *producing* life, which I consider cloning to be. I especially feel a resentment toward

producing beings to act as slaves or to be used by us in any way. My group discussed the idea of controlling the traits of cloned human beings for specialized purposes. I do not feel that God appreciates his children tampering with the miracle of life.

Student 2
The group started with the usual "I guess we're supposed to's" and after only a minimal amount of paper shuffling, got down to the subject at hand.

Of the five-person group, only four participated. It was interesting to note who assumed the leadership role, for how long, for what reasons, how effectively, etc. I feel that the member who occupied this role initially usually does not do so in other groups — that members who seemed to know something about this subject successfully opened the discussion and maintained it by asking others questions. What I looked for but did *not* see was direct eye contact, an authoritative tone of voice (I didn't say authoritarian), and backbone enough to justify occupying the leader's role. I think she was assuming this behavior to get a good grade.

Notice how student 1 discusses only the *topic* of the discussion content. Student 2, however, really discusses the group's *process* or behavior, and therefore did a much better job of fulfilling the assignment.

THERAPEUTIC-PATHOLOGICAL

We are more and more coming to realize that some communication patterns are psychologically more healthy or unhealthy than others. One popular way of determining the difference is called transactional analysis. This method is described in the best-selling book *I'm OK — You're OK,* by Thomas Harris (1967). A transaction is defined as when "I do something to you and you do something back" (pp. 11-12). Transactions can be analyzed in terms of three types of brain functions (called ego states), namely the Parent, Adult, and Child (P-A-C). For example, the child-child transaction is shown in Fig. 5.3.

According to the theory, transactions that occur between the two participants' adult ego states are more likely to produce an I'm OK — You're OK, or a psychologically healthy outcome. The adult ego state represents the rational data-processing state of the brain. It is comparable to the *descriptive, provisional, problem-oriented,* and *equal* type of comment described by Gibb. The parent ego state is more like Gibb's *evaluative* comment and often implies *control, certainty,* and *superiority.* An example of a parent comment in a small group would be a participant's saying while waving a pointed finger at the group, "You two are always goofing around; I want you to shape up!" This type of comment is likely to produce a response from the child ego state of those on the receiving end, which might be something like, "Oh yeah, well who's gonna make me?" "What do I need with you and this dumb group anyway?"

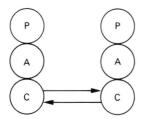

FIGURE 5.3
Child-child transaction.

The child ego state is defined as the location of feelings such as anger, happiness, fear, or love. Harris describes the four possible life conditions as: (1) I'm OK — You're OK, which is the desirable situation, basically a psychology of live and let live; (2) I'm Not OK — You're OK, the situation in which a person lacks self-esteem and considers others to be superior; (3) I'm OK — You're Not OK, wherein the person has feelings of superiority; and (4) I'm Not OK — You're Not OK, in which the person takes a pathological kill-or-be-killed position of defensiveness based on insecurity.

The objective of transactional analysis is to teach us the difference among these different types of transactions so that we can improve our communication effectiveness by keeping more of our transactions in the adult ego state. This, however, is often easier said than done. In one discussion a group member asked, "What's important here?" This question is usually generated from the adult ego state and is supposed to help group members focus their attention on the main issues before the group. However, in this case it was stated with an exasperated tone of voice and an angry facial expression. The comment did not help the group, but made other group members feel "Not OK," actually diverting attention from the significant issue under discussion. Incidentally, transactional analysts would probably argue that the comment was an ulterior transaction (Fig. 5.4) that on the surface was on the adult-adult level, but that was really motivated by the critical parent to punish the child in the group who was holding up the group's progress. (See also Tubbs and Carter 1977.)

Literally thousands of discussions begin with an adult level of problem analysis and degenerate to something less productive. Let us look at a

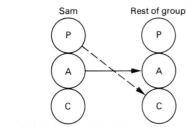

Sam: "What's important here?"

FIGURE 5.4
An ulterior transaction.

series of statements in two actual discussions. The first exemplifies a deterioration of exchanges between the participants' parent ego states to the point where they are playing the game, "Ain't it awful?" (Berne 1964). The second series represents comments on the same topic that are reality-based and were generated from the participants' adult ego states. In both cases, the discussion topic was, "What can be done to create better job equality among the races?"

Discussion I (Parent Level: "Ain't It Awful?")

A: All I know is, racism is racism. A white male today is discriminated against in finding a job.

B: I know what you mean. I've heard of cases where entrance exam results are fudged so that minorities can get in.

C: It's always the way. You work your guts out trying to get ahead and what good does it do you?

D: You're right. There's no justice!

Discussion 2 (Adult Level: Rational Thinking)

A: Earlier in our discussion we defined job equality as an equal opportunity to obtain a job assuming equal qualifications.

B: What about affirmative action programs designed to increase minority employment to a certain percentage of a work force within a certain time period, say, a year?

C: Does anybody have a thought on that?

D: Well, on one hand it does not meet our definition of equality in the short run, because some lesser qualified person may be given an unfair advantage. But in the long run, it eradicates the effects of several years of discrimination in the other direction.

A: In other words, we need short-term inequality to bring about long-term equality?

C: I guess it's a little like procrastination in studying. If you ignore your homework for several weeks, you have to study extra hard to catch up and then maintain some moderate study effort from then on.

D: In other words, once the percentage of the work force in any given job reaches the percentage of that group in the general population, then "true equality" can be realized.

A: I think that makes sense.

B: It will be uncomfortable in the meantime, but it seems to be a desirable goal.

As you can see, the second discussion focuses on the issues and avoids generalizations or such platitudes as, "It's always the way. You work your guts out trying to get ahead and what good does it do you?" The second type of discussion leads to an action plan, while the first type often ends with nothing much accomplished and with final comments such as, "Well, it's a crazy world, but what can you do about it?"

LANGUAGE BEHAVIOR

The study of the interaction between verbal symbols and the thought patterns associated with them is referred to as general semantics. If you have ever become bogged down in a group discussion due to a difficulty in defining terms or dealing with any problems with language, as in the case study at the beginning of this chapter, you will immediately see the relevance of this topic to the study of small group interaction. In fact, some discussions may even have as their task the problem of choosing the appropriate verbal symbol to represent a concept. New products frequently have several proposed names that may be market-tested for consumer response. The intermediate-sized Ford Granada had several other potential names that apparently were not popular. According to Smith (1974):

> Ford tested Eagle, Fairmont, Stallion, Lucerne, Gibralter, Scandia, and many other monikers before selecting [the name] Granada for its new compact luxury car. Chrysler Corporation's design studios have flirted with special models carrying such names as Boca Raton, Gatsby, Gandy Dancer, Easy Rider and Magnum.

Committees spend numerous hours brainstorming possible names and then determining procedures for testing market reaction to the main contenders.

Although few of us will ever make decisions concerning product names, each of us will undoubtedly be involved with language problems of one sort or another in group discussions. Our discussion will focus on four specific language-related problems that frequently plague groups: (1) by-passing, (2) inference making, (3) polarizing, and (4) signal reactions.

BYPASSING

A husband and wife invited to a party were told the dress was to be "casual." They both wore comfortable slacks and sweaters. When they arrived, they could see through the window that the men at the party were dressed in sport coats and dress slacks while the women all had floor-length skirts or long dresses. The couple felt so underdressed that they went home and changed before going in to the party.

Two students met on a college campus. One was from a foreign country. As they finished their conversation, the American student departed, saying, "I'll see you later." The foreign student came back to that spot later in the day and waited for some time for the other person, who never appeared.

A group of housewives got together for their monthly gourmet cooking club meeting. One woman gave instructions for baking peanut butter cookies with chocolate kisses on top. She said, "Just put the chocolate candy right into the peanut butter when you make them." Several in the group misinterpreted her instructions and put the candy on top before rather than after baking. The results were very disappointing.

Each of these cases illustrates a situation in which a misunderstanding occurred due to a language problem. This sort of misunderstanding is referred to as *bypassing*. It is defined as "the miscommunication pattern which occurs when the *sender* (speaker, writer, and so on) and the *receiver* (listener, reader, and so forth) *miss each other with their meaning*" (Haney 1973). In group discussions, the entire focus of the discussion may be diverted by a difference in interpretation of a given word. Note the incredible problems arising in the group as seen by one participant.

> At the start of our meeting I introduced a definition of communication (communication is an expression of ideas). While the basics were appreciated, Ed and Al requested a revision as the statement was too simple. They decided to drop the words *an expression of ideas.* I didn't believe this was a very good revision and said so. A slight altercation developed lasting about five minutes. It was resolved that other ideas would be considered.

> After sufficient waiting (about 30 seconds) I realized no great ideas were forthcoming, so I subtly suggested that my idea be reconsidered and this time Pete and John were on my side. Still my full idea could not survive Al and Ed so it was given new form. . . . In the process of getting a communication definition they had to satisfy me that their changes were justified, while I was attempting to show my original as the best. "Well, you haven't done any better," was surprisingly effective. While I had been using sword points, the best they could muster was a safety pin.

> After the mutilation of my last idea, I decided I would not volunteer any more material and thus "watch them squirm."

It seems hard to believe that such intense reactions could result from a difference of opinion over the definition of the term *communication*. However, this reaction is more typical than atypical.

Ogden and Richards (1946) inspired the diagram in Fig. 5.5, which helps us understand the relation between an object (or referent) and a symbol used to represent that object. As shown in the diagram in Fig. 5.6, the symbol may vary, but the object remains the same. The object has a word chosen to represent it, but that word and the object have no necessary inherent relationship. It is a little like selecting a name for a newborn baby. At first the choice seems arbitrary, but after a few years it seems impossible to think of that person having a different name. The relationship is indirect between symbol and referent; it exists only in the mind. Since each of us

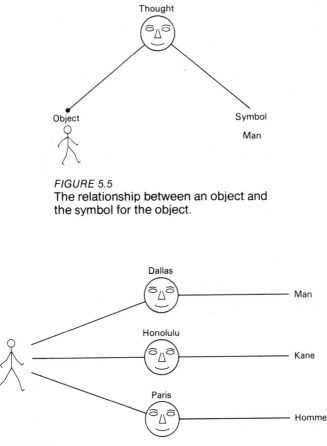

FIGURE 5.5
The relationship between an object and
the symbol for the object.

FIGURE 5.6
The same object may be represented by more than one
symbol.

has a different brain and nervous system, the relationship between any given referent and any given word will vary to some extent from person to person.

Part of the bypassing problem is that we frequently assume that words contain meaning. A different view is that words are symbols arbitrarily designated to represent concepts or referents. Over time, we begin to associate so strongly the word with its referent that they become inseparable. It is easy enough to say that the word is not the thing and that we should be able to separate the symbol from the referent, but it is difficult in practice not to respond emotionally when another person refers to us as a fascist pig, a nigger, a stupid hillbilly, or a honky.

Two problems related to bypassing occur when we use the same word to mean different things (dress "casually"), and the opposite, when different words are used to express essentially the same idea. For example, we may argue that company employees are not performing properly due to a "communication problem" as opposed to a "lack of motivation." It may be that we are really talking about related problems (that is, employees would be better motivated to perform [motivation problem] if they could suggest some new job procedures to their supervisors [communication problem]), but the issue may be clouded by arguments over the labels used to describe the problem.

Haney (1979) suggests that two outcomes can result from bypassing. On one hand, we may have apparent agreement when in fact we are calling different things by the same name (dressing casually). On the other hand, we may have actual agreement but apparent disagreement, as in the employee problem described above. Given these possible outcomes, these are some guidelines (slightly modified) that Haney (1979) suggests to remedy the potential difficulties.

- Be person-minded, not word-minded.

- Question and paraphrase.

- Be receptive to feedback.

- Be sensitive to contexts.

In a nutshell, these guidelines focus on the idea that not all of us use words precisely the same way, and that all words have the potential for multiple usage and interpretation. When you suspect that there may be a difference in word usage, ask questions, and be willing to try to restate or paraphrase the person's message. Remember to use different words in your restatement to see if the basic intent is understood. Also, be receptive to feedback. If we are too impervious or insensitive to allow for the possibility that we may not have stated something perfectly clearly, then we are unlikely to get much feedback to that effect. However, if we are willing to admit to fallibility, we invite feedback and can benefit from that information. Finally, we can often guess the intended meaning of a given statement based upon its use in a given context. For example, one supervisor frequently bade goodbye to his employees with the common phrase, "Well, take it easy now." It was quite obvious from the context that he meant this only as a casual expression. He did *not* intend for his employees to work any less hard. By employing the four techniques mentioned above, we can reduce the frequency of bypassing.

INFERENCE MAKING

Each of us makes numerous inferences every day. For example, we infer (1) that the sun will rise tomorrow; (2) that a chair won't collapse when we sit down; (3) that the sun is shining on the other side of town, since it is

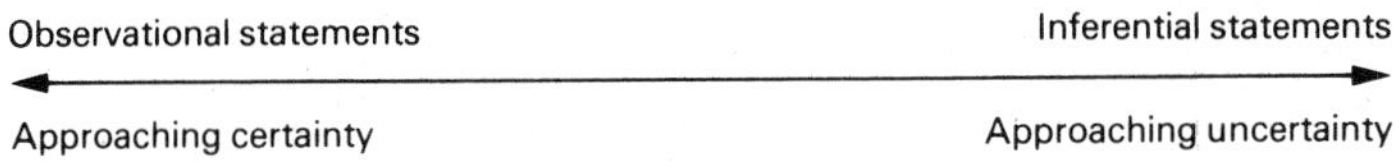

Observational statements   Inferential statements

◄───►

Approaching certainty   Approaching uncertainty

FIGURE 5.7

shining at our location; (4) that a car coming at us from a side street will stop at the stop sign and not run into the side of our car; (5) that a person who consistently fails to show up for a group discussion is not committed to our group task. In each of these five cases, there is some probability that our inference will be borne out by the actual events. However, these five examples illustrate quite a range from most probable (number 1) to least probable (number 5).

Statements of inference go beyond what we know through observations. They represent only some degree of probability of coming true. This idea is illustrated in the diagram in Fig. 5.7.

One of the major problems in groups is being able to recognize our own inference making. You can test your own ability on the following sample story. True (T) means that the inference drawn is definitely true, based upon the information in the story. False (F) means that the inference is definitely wrong based upon the information in the story. A question mark (?) means that you cannot be certain of the inference, based upon the story.

Sample Story
A customer handed the pharmacist a prescription for birth control pills. "Please fill this quickly. I have someone waiting in the car."

The pharmacist hurried to fill the order.

Statements about the Story
1. A woman was having a prescription filled
   for birth control pills.   T F ?
2. She did not want to become pregnant.   T F ?
3. She was in a hurry to have the order filled.   T F ?
4. The pharmacist did his best to speed up the order.   T F ?

If you answered T to any of the statements, you probably assumed or inferred that the customer and the pharmacist were female and male, respectively. Yet there is no statement in the story to support that assumption. Actually, a man is ordering birth control pills for his dog. The pharmacist, a female, cannot do "his" best to fill the order.

Another way of describing inference making is to say that it involves certain assumptions or conclusion drawing (sometimes jumping to the wrong conclusion). This becomes a problem in groups when we react to each other on the assumption that a person is behaving a certain way for the reason that seems obvious or apparent. However, the person may be acting that way for reasons other than the obvious. For example, a person may aggress against another by saying, "I'm sick and tired of your holding us back in our work." On the surface, this appears to be a comment intended to help the group get more accomplished. Beneath the surface, however, it may be part of an effort to undermine the other person's status in the group, and may be a part of the struggle between the two for leadership in the group. These levels can be diagramed as shown in Fig. 5.8 and Fig. 5.9. While it is helpful to recognize that all behaviors are motivated, and that they may be motivated by multiple causes, it is also dangerous to attempt to "psych out" or infer too much. Even if we make such an inference, we must recognize the possiblity of error.

On the other hand, it is often difficult to analyze the group process without making some inferences. For example, one encounter group was having its last meeting and the discussion somehow got around to the subject of death. After a somewhat extended discussion on this subject, the group leader intervened by saying, "I wonder if this discussion of death is motivated by the reluctance that we are all feeling tonight about saying good-bye for the last time." Although this comment was initially rejected by the group, it turned out that a lot of people were reluctant to end the friendships that had grown out of this group, and the topic of the discussion shifted to directly expressing and resolving those feelings.

Some inference making may be useful to the group, while at other times it may be harmful. We should in any case be conscious of inference making.

A person who tries to read too much into behaviors may become a "psychopest" (Luft 1969). For example, a person crossing arms across the chest may do this for no reason but increased comfort. An overinterpretation might be that the person is becoming defensive and is trying to put up a barrier between self and others. In attempting to analyze behaviors, it is wise to recognize that analyses often involve inferences that go beyond what we have observed and involve some probability for error.

POLARIZING

Perhaps one of the most common problems in groups is polarization. It is difficult to exchange differences in viewpoint without tending to overstate or exaggerate to make our point. When this happens, it encourages the others to exaggerate a bit more in the opposite direction to make their point. Before long the sides are so far apart that constructive discussion of the issues is often discontinued for the time being. Consider the following example:

Kyle: I can't see why women should get a job just to avoid the bore-
           dom of housework, when a man who needs to support his family
           goes without a job.

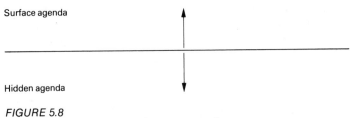

FIGURE 5.8
Surface and hidden agendas compared.

Levels of Discussion Analysis

Surface agenda

* Perceptive observation

* Shallow observation

Hidden agenda

* Superficial interpretation of motives

* Perceptive interpretation of motives

FIGURE 5.9

Sue: Just because your masculinity is threatened is no reason to keep women out of work!

Kyle: My masculinity? You women's libbers are always hung up on trying to be the dominant sex!

Sue: You men are all alike. You can't stand being bettered by anyone, especially a woman. You want us to tell you how brilliant you are because you know what day of the week it is.

This exchange actually occurred in a student discussion. The topic was, "How can greater job equality be achieved in this country?" The discussion had been progressing well until this polarization occurred. Polarization has three distinct characteristics. First, the statements get more emotionally intense. Second, they go from being specific to being more general ("You men are all alike!"). Third, they tend to move away from the topic at hand (job equality) to other issues ("You can't stand being bettered by anyone").

A simple method has been found that usually nips polarization in the bud. It is described by Rogers and Roethlisberger (1952) in the following way:

The next time you get into an argument with . . . a small group of friends, just stop the discussion for a moment and, for an experiment, institute this rule. "Each person can speak up for himself only *after* he has repeated the ideas and feelings of the speaker accurately and to that speaker's satisfaction." You see what this would mean. It would simply mean that before presenting your own point of view, it would be necessary for you to achieve the other speaker's frame of reference — to understand his thoughts and feelings so well that you could summarize them for him. Sounds simple doesn't it? But if you try it, you will discover that it is one of the most difficult things you have ever tried to do.

After you have tried this restating exercise, notice the effects. First, the tendency for statements to gain emotional intensity is significantly reduced. The calmness is quite dramatic when compared with the interchange between Kyle and Sue mentioned above. Second, the discussion tends to stay with manageable specifics, rather than moving to gross generalities that are quite frequently based on stereotypes with numerous individual exceptions (men are not all alike any more than women are all alike). Third, the discussion is more likely to remain focused on the group's discussion topic than to go off on a tangent that may be much less relevant to the group's task. This simple restatement technique can actually be quite potent in reducing the problem of polarization.

SIGNAL REACTIONS

Signal reactions are learned responses to certain stimuli. Perhaps the best-known example of a signal reaction is the salivation of Pavlov's dogs. Ivan Pavlov was a Nobel-prize-winning Russian physiologist. He accidentally stumbled on a very important concept of learning known as classical conditioning. He noticed that the carefully calibrated measurements of his test animals' salivation started to break down because his experienced dogs began to salivate in anticipation of the food when he opened the door to the room before he fed them. His coming in the door was the *conditioned stimulus* or signal that triggered the salivation response. Eventually, he brought the salivation response under stimulus control by associating a bell with food so that the dogs learned to salivate at the sound of the bell even when the food was *not* present.

It is interesting that the founder of general semantics, Alfred Korzybski, wrote that the signal response was an animallike response. He wrote (1948, p. 249):

In Pavlov's experiments a dog is shown food and a bell rung simultaneously. At the sight of food, saliva and gastric juice flow. Associations soon *relate* the ringing of a bell and the food, and, later, simply the ringing of the bell will produce the flow. In another animal some other signal, a whistle, for instance, would produce similar effects. In different people, through experience, associations, relations, meanings, and s.r. [stimulus response] patterns are built around some symbol. Obviously in grown-up humans the identification of the symbol with the thing must be pathological.

Actually, Korzybski was a little extreme in saying that we are pathological to allow such strong connections between signal and response. One study showed that the repetitive sound of a gong produced marked emotional responses in former sailors (as measured by their perspiration levels), but very little emotional reaction among former soldiers. Edwards and Acker (1962) write:

> This signal was used as a call to battle stations aboard U.S. Navy ships during the war, and it continued to elicit a strong autonomic response from the Navy veterans. Even though more than fifteen years had elapsed since this stimulus had signaled danger. . . .

Although this study did not involve reactions to verbal symbols, it does demonstrate the natural, not pathological, tendency toward strong signal reactions.

A study that directly tested emotional reactions to verbal symbols also proved that strong physiological reactions to symbols are typical rather than pathological. Subjects were exposed to various words on a screen and their perspiration was measured as an index of their reactions. There were no significant differences between reactions to positive words such as *beauty, love,* and *kiss,* and negative words such as *cancer, hate,* and *death.* However, some words did cause significant responses. These were referred to as "personal" words and included the person's first and last names, father's and mother's first names, major in school, year in school, and school name. Subjects were significantly aroused by these "personal" words (Crane, Dicker, and Brown 1970). Certainly nobody would argue that these college students were pathological or that they "confused" their own name with themselves as physical beings. Yet these studies collectively indicate that all of us learn to react to certain verbal and nonverbal stimuli in some strong and predictable ways. When the response becomes habitual, it is like a reflex action. At this point, the so-called signal, or automatic response, may create problems.

In group discussions, certain phrases may produce signal reactions that are counterproductive. Such phrases have been referred to as "idea killers" (Bittel 1956) or communication stoppers. They include, among others:

□ "That's ridiculous."

□ "We tried that before."

□ "That will never work."

□ "That's crazy."

□ "It's too radical a change."

- □ "We're too small for it."
- □ "It's not practical."
- □ "Let's get back to reality."
- □ "You can't teach an old dog new tricks."
- □ "We'll be the laughingstock."
- □ "You're absolutely wrong."
- □ "You don't know what you're talking about."
- □ "It's impossible."
- □ "There's no way it can be done."

On the other hand, "igniter phrases" that seem to promote group productivity would include some of the following:

- □ "I agree."
- □ "That's good!"
- □ "I made a mistake. I'm sorry."
- □ "That's a great idea."
- □ "I'm glad you brought that up."
- □ "You're on the right track."
- □ "I know it will work."
- □ "We're going to try something different today."
- □ "I never thought of that."
- □ "We can do a lot with that idea."
- □ "Real good, anyone else?"
- □ "I like that!"
- □ "That would be worth a try."
- □ "Why don't we assume it would work and go from there."

Other specific terms that are likely to produce signal reactions are such words as *weirdo, queer, honky, racist, male chauvinist pig,* and many swear words. In fact, even swear words have different levels of offensiveness that vary from culture to culture. Profane words have been classified as (1) religious, (2) excretory, and (3) sexual (Bostrom and Rossiter 1969). In our culture the sexual words are usually the most offensive, but in Italy, where the Roman Catholic church is very strong, religious words are considered much more offensive, and in Germany excretory swear words are considered

	(*SNOW* INDEX)	
0 external	0 bureaucratic	0 acceptance
1 authoritarian	1 group	1 solutions
2 Machiavellian	2 functional	2 consensus
3 energetic	3 logistical	3 relations
4 situational	4 interpersonal	4 commitment
5 socialized	5 instrumental	5 responsibility
6 systematic	6 managerial	6 development
7 dynamic	7 organizational	7 coordination
8 stagnated	8 executive	8 power
9 transparent	9 homogeneous	9 transactions

FIGURE 5.10
Systematic New Order (of) Words

to be the most offensive. Several studies indicate that those who swear may reduce their credibility in the eyes of others (Bauduin 1971). It also seems advisable to avoid communication stoppers and idea killers whenever possible.

Since we know that words do have a great deal of potential for influencing thought and subsequent action, note the set of terms in Fig. 5.10. Just pick any three-digit numer at random and pick the corresponding three words from the lists. These terms all have some relevance to small group interaction and, if all else fails, they can be used for fun. For example, 2, 6, 9 would be Machiavellian managerial transactions. Number 8, 4, 3 would be stagnated interpersonal relations. So if you want to impress your friends with how much you have learned by reading this book, try the *SNOW* index (Fig. 5.10).

SELF-DISCLOSURE

Perhaps one of the greatest dilemmas facing a group member is the choice between openly expressing his or her thoughts and feelings versus concealing or distorting inner feelings, thoughts, and perceptions. In a discussion on racial equality, we may not openly reveal our true feelings for fear of sounding like a racist or bigot. Nobody wants to be labeled an Archie Bunker if it can be avoided! On the other hand, if every person in the group conceals his or her thoughts, there will be little said and therefore little accomplished. The question therefore is not whether to reveal or conceal, but *how much* to reveal or conceal. Self-disclosure has been defined by Tubbs and Baird (1980) as

> a process, whereby an individual voluntarily shares information in a personal way, about his or her "self" that cannot be discovered through other sources.

You may wonder why a person should bother to let himself or herself be known to others. Jourard (1964) studied mentally disturbed individuals and concluded that a great deal of human energy is consumed in attempts to keep from being known by others. That energy could be used for other purposes, but neurotic individuals are so "wrapped up in themselves" that they are seldom able to devote sufficient energy to other problems (such as a group problem-solving discussion). All of us are periodically faced with such situations. When we get bad news from home or from a friend, it is much harder to concentrate on such mundane problems as how to budget our study time for tomorrow's exam. However, the mentally unhealthy person is habitually in this state of mind.

Part of returning to mental health involves sharing oneself with others. Jourard (1964, p. 24) states:

> Self-disclosure, or should I say "real" self-disclosure, is both a symptom of personality health . . . and at the same time a means of ultimately achieving healthy personality. . . . I have known people who would rather die than become known. . . . When I say that self-disclosure is a symptom of personality health, what I mean really is that a person who displays many of the other characteristics that betoken healthy personality . . . *will also display the ability to make himself fully known to at least one other significant human being.*

Perhaps a less self-centered motive for self-disclosure is the desire to improve the quality of communication within a group. Keltner (1970, p. 54) states:

> We probably do not reveal enough of ourselves in speech-communication to enable our co-communicators to understand us better. The complexities of the world we live in demand better communication than we have known. *To communicate better, we must understand each other better. To understand each other better, we must reveal more of ourselves through speech and speech-communication events.*

Countless students in group discussion feel that they don't know what to contribute to a discussion. They often feel that they have no good or new ideas to add to what has already been said. Yet, as we will see in the last section of this chapter, numerous roles may be adopted by group members, several of which involve some degree of self-disclosure. For example, if an idea is initiated by another, you may make a substantial contribution by offering your *reaction* to the idea (opinion giving) — by encouraging or showing agreement or disagreement. Counterproductive role behaviors may also involve self-disclosure (for example, aggressing, reporting a personal achievement, confessing a personal ideology that is irrelevant to the discussion topic, or seeking sympathy from the group).

Self-disclosure is not always desirable. An optimum amount of self-disclosure seems a desirable goal to achieve. Some of us are too closed (concealers); others of us "wear our hearts on our sleeves" (revealers). Culbert (1968, p. 19) describes the problem of overdisclosing rather vividly:

> The revealer is likely to react by immediately disclosing any self-information to which he has access. The revealer, too, is attempting to master the problem, but for him mastery seems to be attained by explicitly acknowledging and labeling all the relevant elements comprising the situation. While a concealer runs the risk of having insufficient external feedback, a revealer runs the risk of overlabeling the limited number of objective elements present or of labeling them so early that their usefulness in the relationship is nullified.

Encounter groups usually proceed under the assumption that people have learned to be too closed too often. Thus participants are encouraged to share their feelings and perceptions as openly and honestly as they can. Much of the self-disclosure involves giving feedback to others concerning the ways in which they "come across." This feedback is often useful in reducing the size of the arc of distortion discussed earlier in this chapter.

THE JOHARI WINDOW

Perhaps the most useful model for illustrating self-disclosure in groups is the Johari window (named after its originators, Joe Luft and Harry Ingham) (Luft 1970). See Fig. 5.11 for this model.

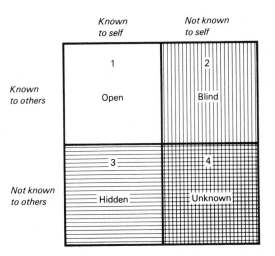

FIGURE 5.11
The Johari window. From *Group Processes: An Introduction to Group Dynamics,* by Joseph Luft, by permission of Mayfield Publishing Company. Copyright © 1963, 1970 by Joseph Luft.

This window classifies an individual's relating to others according to four quadrants (or windowpanes). The size of each quadrant represents the person's level of self-awareness. Quadrant one, the open quadrant, represents our willingness to share with others our views on such things as current national or world events, current movies, sports, and what is generally referred to as "cocktail party" conversation.

The second quadrant is referred to as the blind quadrant or the "bad breath" area. This area represents the things that others may know about us, but that we do unintentionally and unknowingly. We may continually dominate meetings, or bore people with long-winded accounts of how good our high school was. Conversely, we may annoy people by our silence, since they may feel that they have opened themselves up to the group, while we have "played our cards pretty close to the chest" by revealing little. Group members seem to resent both those who talk too much and those who talk too little.

The third quadrant is the hidden area that is most likely to be changed (reduced) by self-disclosure. It represents the feelings about ourselves that we know but are unwilling to reveal to others. It may represent our greatest fears, some past experiences we would like to forget, or our secret sexual fantasies, among other things.

The fourth quadrant is called the area of the unknown. It represents all the areas of potential growth or self-actualization. This includes almost anything outside our experience, such as the sport we've never played, the places we have never seen, the hobby we haven't taken the time to try, the organization we have never joined, the style of behaving we have never been willing to risk, and others.

Luft advocates changing the shape of the window so that quadrant one enlarges while all the others become smaller. I once participated in an encounter group in which we tried to grow interpersonally along the lines suggested by this model. One participant introduced herself as "Mickey" and told us what city she was from, and so on. She was dressed in slacks and a sweater. Only after 15 weeks did we find out that she was a nun. She had been trying to develop herself as a person without having the rest of us react to her role rather than to her. Thus her unknown quadrant was diminished by her efforts to try new, less inhibited behaviors. She also reduced her blind quadrant by asking for interpersonal feedback. We might have been more inhibited in our feedback had we known she was a nun. She also destroyed the stereotypes most of us had toward nuns.

Luft (1970) illustrates the Johari window as it applies to groups in Fig. 5.12. Each window represents a person.

APPROPRIATENESS

Within this framework, the question still arises as to when and how much self-disclosure there should be. Luft (1969, pp. 132-133) answers this question

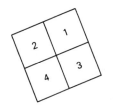

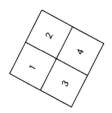

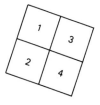

FIGURE 5.12
One way of looking at a group.

when he proposes the following guidelines designating situations in which self-disclosure is appropriate:

1. *When it is a function of the ongoing relationship.* What one shares with another belongs in the particular relationship; it is not a random or isolated act.

2. *When it occurs reciprocally.* This implies that there is some degree of interdependency and mutuality involved.

3. *When it is timed to fit what is happening.* The self-disclosure grows out of the experience that is going on between or among the persons involved. The timing and sequence are important.

4. *When it concerns what is going on within and between persons in the present.* Some account is taken of the behavior and feelings of the participants individually and of the persons collectively. There is a recognition of the relationship as an emergent phenomenon in addition to the individual selves.

5. *When it moves by relatively small increments.* What is revealed does not drastically change or restructure the relationship. The

implication is that a relationship is built gradually except in rare and special cases.

6. *When it is confirmable by the other person.* Some system is worked out between the persons to validate reception of that which has been disclosed.

7. *When account is taken of the effect disclosure has on the other person(s).* The disclosure has not only been received; there is evidence of its effect on the receiver.

8. *When it creates a reasonable risk.* If the feeling or behavior were really unknown to the other, it may have been withheld for a reason bearing on differences which have yet to be faced by the participants.

9. *When it is speeded up in a crisis.* A serious conflict jeopardizing the structure of the relationship may require that more quadrant 3 material be quickly revealed to heal the breach or help in the reshaping of the relationship.

10. *When the context is mutually shared.* The assumptions underlying the social context suggest that there is enough in common to sustain the disclosure.

Probably the most difficult problem for members of encounter groups to resolve when they go "back home" is knowing how to apply what they have learned without overdoing it. One encounter group graduate said, "How do I use this openness with my boss when he hasn't read the book?" His concern was well warranted. It may be quite difficult to put into practice any new behaviors when the others "back home" haven't changed and are still as closed and perhaps as devious as ever.

The most logical advice would be to try to use what you can, when you can. Not all of our learnings will be usable all the time. But certainly some new behaviors (such as increased openness and sensitivity) will be appropriate some, if not most, of the time. Experiences in groups frequently teach us lessons we can't possibly unlearn. Once we have experienced a greater level of personal intimacy with others, day-to-day superficiality may compare rather badly. Schutz (1971, p. 284) puts it this way:

> Relating to people more honestly is certainly possible. Find someone you have withheld something from and tell it to him. See what happens. Next time you feel like touching someone, do it. Next time you are hurt or frightened, express it. When you catch yourself trying to project an image, stop, and see if you can be real instead. If you're embarrassed to pay someone a compliment, do it anyway. If you want to know how people respond to you, ask them.

Another way to put it is that the competent communicator has a higher level of rhetorical sensitivity. That is, he or she learns when and with whom to disclose, and when and with whom to refrain from disclosure (Hart and

Burks 1972; Hart, Eadie, and Carlson 1975). Total disclosure at all times with all people would not seem to be desirable.

INTERACTION ROLES

Each of us is required to enact multiple roles in our everyday living. Usually we are able to function effectively in these different roles, which require or expect certain behaviors. We are at different times student, son or daughter, friend, counselor, leader, follower, and some are spouses, parents, and employees as well. It is important to realize that roles are simply sets of identifiable behaviors. When we say that a person is assuming a role, this does not imply that he or she is faking it or acting in a way that is not within that person's true character. In fact, some writings (Hart and Burks 1972) indicate that the more interpersonally sensitive person is one who is able to develop a considerable degree of role flexibility. It is desirable to learn to widen our repertoire of roles and to discover those roles we most enjoy.

A student relatively new to the small group field indicated an awareness of a few interaction roles:

> This group discussion was a real experience for me. I have never been mixed in with a complete group of strangers and have things work out so smoothly. In most groups you get a few quiet shy ones, who don't say anything, and opposed to them, there's usually one big mouth, normally found in a group, who says everything and has all of the ideas without giving anyone else a chance to give their opinion. It was good to work in a group that was well balanced and one in which everyone participated.

As we mentioned in the discussion of leadership, there are differing functions that can be performed by any group member. This is another way of saying that individuals assume different roles in helping the group move toward its goal. We discussed the task roles and socioemotional functions or roles in Chapter 3. Benne and Sheats (1948) proposed a classification of roles into three broad categories: (1) task roles, (2) group building and maintenance roles, and (3) individual roles. Although other sets of categories have been developed for research purposes (McCroskey and Wright 1971; Leathers 1969), this time-tested approach is still one of the most useful for learning to identify roles and to develop role flexibility.

GROUP TASK ROLES

These behaviors are directed toward accomplishing the group's objective through the facilitation of problem solving.

☐ *Initiating-contributing:* proposing new ideas or a changed way of regarding the group goal. This may include a new goal or a new definition of the problem. It may involve suggesting a solution or some way of handling a difficulty the group has encountered. It may also include a new procedure for the group to better organize its efforts.

☐ *Information seeking:* asking for clarification, for authoritative information and facts relevant to the problem under discussion.

☐ *Opinion seeking:* seeking information related not so much to factual data as to the values underlying the suggestions being considered.

☐ *Information giving:* offering facts or generalizations based on experience or authoritative sources.

☐ *Opinion giving:* stating beliefs or opinions relevant to a suggestion made. The emphasis is on the proposal of what ought to become the group's values rather than on factors or information.

☐ *Elaborating:* expanding on suggestions with examples or restatements, offering a rationale for previously made suggestions, and trying to determine the results if a suggestion were adopted by the group.

☐ *Coordinating:* indicating the relationships among various ideas and suggestions, attempting to combine ideas and suggestions or trying to coordinate the activities of group members.

☐ *Orienting:* indicating the position of the group by summarizing progress made, deviations from agreed-upon directions or goals, or by raising questions about the direction the group is taking.

☐ *Evaluating:* comparing the group's accomplishments to some criterion or standard of group functioning. This may include questioning the practicality, the logic, or the procedure of a suggestion.

☐ *Energizing:* stimulating the group to action or decision, attempting to increase the level or quality of activity.

☐ *Assisting on procedure:* helping or facilitating group movement by doing things for the group, such as performing routine tasks like distributing materials, rearranging the seating, or running a tape recorder.

☐ *Recording:* writing down suggestions, recording group decisions, or recording the outcomes of the discussion. This provides tangible results of the group's effort.

GROUP BUILDING AND MAINTENANCE ROLES

The roles in this category help the interpersonal functioning of the group. They help alter the way of working, to strengthen, regulate, and perpetuate

FRANK AND ERNEST   by Bob Thaves

CITY PLANNING COMMISSION

SO FAR, THEN, WE HAVE TWO SUGGESTIONS FOR RAISING CITY REVENUE: A WORLD'S FAIR OR A SPEED TRAP.

THAVES 4-1

Reprinted by permission. © 1976 NEA, Inc.

the group. This is analogous to preventive maintenance done to keep a mechanical device such as a car in better working order.

☐ *Encouraging:* praising, showing interest in, agreeing with, and accepting the contributions of others; showing warmth toward other group members, listening attentively and seriously to the ideas of others, showing tolerance for ideas different from one's own, conveying the feeling that one feels the contributions of others are important.

☐ *Harmonizing:* mediating the differences between the other members, attempting to reconcile disagreements, relieving tension in moments of conflict through the use of humor.

☐ *Compromising:* operating from within a conflict situation, one may offer a compromise by yielding status, admitting a mistake, by disciplining oneself for the sake of group harmony, or by coming halfway toward another position.

☐ *Gatekeeping and expediting:* attempting to keep communication channels open by encouraging the participation of some or by curbing the participation of others.

☐ *Setting standards or ideals:* expressing standards for the group and/or evaluating the quality of group processes (as opposed to evaluating the content of discussion).

☐ *Observing:* keeping a record of various aspects of group process and feeding this information, along with interpretations, into the group's evaluation of its procedures. This contribution is best received when the person has been requested by the group to perform this function. The observer should avoid expressing judgments of approval or disapproval in reporting observations.

☐ *Following:* going along with the group, passively accepting the ideas of others, serving as an audience in group discussion.

INDIVIDUAL ROLES

These behaviors are more designed to satisfy an individual's needs than to contribute to the needs of the group. These are sometimes referred to as self-centered roles (Brilhart 1974).

☐ *Aggressing:* may be accomplished by deflating the status of others, disapproving of the ideas or values of others, attacking the group or the problem it is attempting to solve, joking maliciously, resenting the contributions of others and/or trying to take credit for them.

☐ *Blocking:* resisting, disagreeing, and opposing beyond reason, bringing up dead issues after they have been rejected or bypassed by the group.

☐ *Recognition seeking:* calling attention to oneself through boasting, reporting on personal achievements, acting in inappropriate ways, fighting to keep from being placed in an inferior position.

☐ *Self-confessing:* using the group as an opportunity to express personal, nongroup-related feelings, insights, ideologies.

☐ *Acting the playboy:* showing a lack of involvement in the group's task. Displaying nonchalance, cynicism, horseplay, and other kinds of "goofing-off" behaviors.

☐ *Dominating:* Trying to assert authority or superiority by manipulating others in the group. This may take the form of flattery, of asserting a superior status or right to attention, giving directions authoritatively, and/or interrupting others.

☐ *Help seeking:* attempting to get sympathy from other group members through expressions of insecurity, personal inadequacy, or self-criticism beyond reason.

☐ *Special interest pleading:* speaking on behalf of some group such as "the oppressed," "labor," "business," usually cloaking one's own prejudices or biases in the stereotype that best fits one's momentary need. (Adapted from Benne and Sheats 1948.)

It is generally desirable to learn to perform the task roles as well as the group building and maintenance roles, while avoiding the individual roles. However, even the first and second sets of roles may be misused and abused. For example, there is a fine line between initiating and dominating, between encouraging and flattering, and between opinion giving and recognition seeking. The way in which the role is enacted can make a crucial difference in whether the behavior is viewed as constructive or self-serving. One student attempted to be a gatekeeper by asking silent members if they had any ideas that they would like to contribute. After his attempts were rebuked, he wrote the following analysis of his behavior.

On one occasion, I tried to involve another group member in the discussion against his will. The conflict was resolved in a later discussion, but my bad feelings during the intervening period made me realize that this was an area for attention. . . .

This "expansiveness" and disregard for another person's feelings is an amazing trait to find in myself, because it is something I dislike in other people. It has caused me to resolve that (1) I will not be "overbearing" with quiet people, (2) I will listen more, (3) I will attempt to be more aware of the feelings of others.

Even behaviors motivated by the best intentions may go astray in producing a desired contribution to the group effort.

THE SYSTEMS PERSPECTIVE

In this chapter we examined some issues close to the hearts of many modern communication scholars. The chapter began with an analysis of five critical issues in the study of communication. We looked at the differences between intentional-unintentional, verbal-nonverbal, defensive-supportive, content-process, and therapeutic-pathological communication. While these issues apply to all communication contexts, our examples and specific applications were focused on the small group context. These issues have considerable overlap with topics discussed in other chapters in this book. For example, how does one express leadership behavior, or establish a group norm, or manifest one's personality, or express one's values? All of these are manifested through behaviors that communicate to others in the group.

The systems perspective fits very well with the new emphasis in communication theory on the transactional model of communication. Recent writings of Sereno and Bodaken (1975), Wilmot (1975), and Tubbs (1976) stress that the participants in any communication event are highly dependent upon one another. They are simultaneously influencing one another and are both senders and receivers at all times. Wilmot (1975) goes so far as to state that "the process of your creating a message may affect you *more* than it does the person receiving it." The transactional point of view can be summarized by stating that a person's communication can be defined only *in relation* to some other or others.

In this chapter we discussed the verbal-nonverbal distinction in communication. The systems nature of this relationship is stressed by Barnlund (1968, p. 535):

In particular, Birdwhistell has emphasized that no physical motion is meaningless, but that its significance derives from the *interactional context* in which it is evoked. Persons are engaged in physical conversation even when verbally silent, modifying their positions continually in response to perceptible movements in others [emphasis added].

Knapp (1972, pp. 8-9) adds further support for this viewpoint:

We are constantly being warned against presenting material out of context. . . . There is a danger that the reader may forget that nonverbal communication cannot be studied in isolation from the total communication process. Verbal and nonverbal communication should be treated as a total and inseparable unit.

We might add that each of the communication factors discussed in this chapter is similarly related to all the others.

In the second section of this chapter we looked at four issues related to language behavior — bypassing, inference-making, polarizing, and signal reactions. Each of these factors is related to both the background factors of the individuals and the eventual consequences of group discussion. We saw that background factors were related to signal reactions in the study showing that former sailors experienced a physiological reaction to an alarm bell they had not heard for 15 years. We also saw that similar reactions can be elicited by such verbal stimuli as our own names, or our parents' names. The influence of language on group consequences was shown by the use of "idea killers" such as "It's imposible," "That's crazy," or "That will never work." The net effect of these types of statements is to reduce the potential group productivity in terms of both idea production and interpersonal relations, as we saw in the case study at the beginning of this chapter.

The third section of this chapter dealt with the question "How much should I reveal and how much should I conceal in a group?" The Johari window was offered as a helpful model for understanding one's relationship to others. Guidelines for appropriate self-disclosure were included. Obviously, appropriate self-disclosure will vary considerably from group to group. Probably high self-disclosure is appropriate in an encounter group with a highly supportive atmosphere and a norm of openness and trust. However, social groups, educational groups, work groups, and especially problem-solving groups are hardly the place for a high degree of very personal self-disclosure. Personality also interacts with self-disclosure. If we open up to persons who are highly Machiavellian, they will turn around and use those revelations to benefit themselves and possibly to harm us. Appropriate self-disclosure, then, is very much contingent on a number of relevant variables. For this reason, Tubbs and Baird (1980) have developed a contingency model of self-disclosure that suggests how much to disclose and under what circumstances.

The final section discussed the issue of which roles members may adopt in groups. Task roles and group maintenance roles were indicated as useful roles to learn and to use. Individual or self-centered roles were identified to help indicate those communication behaviors that are typically not useful to the group. These roles undoubtedly interact with people's personality traits. For example, the person who is dominant and achievement oriented will probably adopt the task roles quite comfortably. The affiliators will naturally gravitate toward the group maintenance roles. Finally, the hostile or acquiescent personality types will be tempted to adopt the self-centered roles of aggressing and blocking or help seeking and special interest pleading, respectively. One of the reasons for studying different types of roles is to increase our ability to adopt different roles in accordance with the demands of the situation. Barnlund (1968, p. 170) summarizes a great deal of literature on role taking:

> A number of studies show that role insight is associated with social maturity and a high level of general adjustment. Commenting on the close connection between role sensitivity and interpersonal effectiveness, Cameron has written, "To the extent that an individual, in the course of personality development, learns to take social roles skillfully and realistically, acquires an adequate repertory of them, and becomes adroit in shifting from one role to another when he is in difficulty, he should grow into a flexible, adaptive social adult with minimum susceptibility to behavior disorders."

The readings for this chapter deal with improving communication skills and with defensive communication.

Exercises

1. Nonverbal Communication

a) Eyelogue   Group members form two lines facing each other. Without talking, express your feelings for a few seconds to the person facing you. Then move one line so that each person is facing someone different. Repeat until you have expressed a feeling toward every person in the group.

b) Group grope   Have group members mill around the room encountering each other nonverbally while blindfolded. Afterward discuss and have group members share their impressions.

c) Nonverbal sociogram   Have group members move around and stand near others to whom they feel psychologically close. One person may want to diagram the standing positions on the board for discussion.

d) Hand-holding go-around   Stand in a circle with all group members holding hands with eyes closed. Have the instructor (or a volunteer) go around the outside of the circle putting his or her hands on each pair of clasped hands, one pair at a time. After the person has gone all the way around, discuss the impressions experienced.

2. Transactional Analysis Exercise
Observe any discussion in the class and attempt to identify the ego states that seem to motivate various comments. Write down several representative comments for each of the three ego states (Fig. 5.13).

3. Self-Disclosure Exercise
Pair off with someone you feel close to. Begin to talk about the topics listed

Ego states   Sample comments

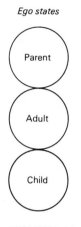

FIGURE 5.13

below. Feel free to stop if you feel the topics are too close for comfort. Discuss the following by taking turns before moving to the next topic.

    a) Your hobbies and interests
    b) Your attitude toward your body — likes and dislikes
    c) Your family's financial status
    d) Attitudes toward your parents and others in your family
    e) Attitudes toward religion
    f) Your love life, past and present
    g) Personal problems that really concern you
    h) How you react to your partner on the basis of this exercise*

4. Member Roles Exercise

Have a group discussion using the fishbowl format (a group of observers surrounding a group of discussants). Try to identify the roles that each member plays by placing a check mark in the appropriate box in the chart shown in Fig. 5.14. These observations should be fed back to the group members and discussed in a supportive way. For a variation of this, some group members can be briefed in advance to act out certain of these roles to test the observers' abilities to recognize the behavior.

OVERVIEW OF READINGS

Much has been written about the importance of developing a supportive style of personal communication in and outside of small groups. However, no one has written more eloquently or persuasively than Carl Rogers, who

---

* The topics are similar to those developed by Sidney Jourard (1971) and published in *Self-Disclosure: An Experimental Analysis of the Transparent Self* (New York: Wiley), pp. 177-178.

Roles	Members	A	B	C	D	E	F	G	H
Group Task Roles									
1. Initiator-contributor									
2. Information seeker									
3. Information giver									
4. Coordinator									
5. Orientor									
6. Evaluator									
7. Energizer									
8. Opinion giver									
Group Building Roles									
9. Encourager									
10. Harmonizer									
11. Compromiser									
12. Gatekeeper and exploiter									
13. Standard setter									
14. Follower									
Self-centered Roles									
15. Aggressor									
16. Blocker									
17. Recognition-seeker									
18. Playboy (playgirl)									
19. Dominator									
20. Help-seeker									

FIGURE 5.14
Member roles exercise chart.

was one of the earliest to promote the idea. In the first article Rogers shares in his very personal way some of his insights, which apply to any setting, not just the patient-therapist setting.

Jack Gibb offers valuable insights in the second article, "Defensive Communication." Many discussions have gone astray because of this problem. Both of these articles go further into the topics that are discussed in this chapter.

The Characteristics of a Helping Relationship

Carl R. Rogers

HOW CAN I CREATE A HELPING RELATIONSHIP?
I believe each of us working in the field of human relationships has a similar problem in knowing how to use such research knowledge. We cannot slavishly follow such findings in a mechanical way or we destroy the personal qualities which these very studies show to be valuable. It seems to me that we have to use these studies, testing them against our own experience and forming new and further personal hypotheses to use and test in our own further personal relationships.

So rather than try to tell you how you should use the findings I have presented, I should like to tell you the kind of questions which these studies and my own clinical experience raise for me, and some of the tentative and changing hypotheses which guide my behavior as I enter into what I hope may be helping relationships, whether with students, staff, family, or clients. Let me list a number of these questions and considerations.

1. Can I *be* in some way which will be perceived by the other person as trustworthy, as dependable or consistent in some deep sense? Both research and experience indicate that this is very important, and over the years I have found what I believe are deeper and better ways of answering this question. I used to feel that if I fulfilled all the outer conditions of trustworthiness — keeping appointments, respecting the confidential nature of the interviews, etc. — and if I acted consistently the same during the interviews, then this

---

Excerpts from Carl R. Rogers, *On Becoming a Person* (Boston: Houghton Mifflin, 1961), pp. 39-58. Reprinted with permission.

condition would be fulfilled. But experience drove home the fact that to act consistently acceptant, for example, if in fact I was feeling annoyed or skeptical or some other nonacceptant feeling, was certain in the long run to be perceived as inconsistent or untrustworthy. I have come to recognize that being trustworthy does not demand that I be rigidly consistent but that I be dependably real. The term "congruent" is one I have used to describe the way I would like to be. By this I mean that whatever feeling or attitude I am experiencing would be matched by my awareness of that attitude. When this is true, then I am a unified or integrated person in that moment, and hence I can *be* whatever I deeply *am*. This is a reality which I find others experience as dependable.

2. A very closely related question is this: Can I be expressive enough as a person that what I am will be communicated unambiguously? I believe that most of my failures to achieve a helping relationship can be traced to unsatisfactory answers to these two questions. When I am experiencing an attitude of annoyance toward another person but am unaware of it, then my communication contains contradictory messages. My words are giving one message, but I am also in subtle ways communicating the annoyance I feel and this confuses the other person and makes him distrustful, though he too may be unaware of what is causing the difficulty. When as a parent or a therapist or a teacher or an administrator I fail to listen to what is going on in me, fail because of my own defensiveness to sense my own feelings, then this kind of failure seems to result. It has made it seem to me that the most basic learning for anyone who hopes to establish any kind of helping relationship is that it is safe to be transparently real. If in a given relationship I am reasonably congruent, if no feelings relevant to the relationship are hidden either to me or the other person, then I can be almost sure that the relationship will be a helpful one.

One way of putting this which may seem strange to you is that if I can form a helping relationship to myself — if I can be sensitively aware of and acceptant toward my own feelings — then the likelihood is great that I can form a helping relationship toward another.

Now, acceptantly to be what I am, in this sense, and to permit this to show through to the other person, is the most difficult task I know and one I never fully achieve. But to realize that this *is* my task has been most rewarding because it has helped me to find what has gone wrong with interpersonal relationships which have become snarled and to put them on a constructive track again. It has meant that if I am to facilitate the personal growth of others in relation to me, then I must grow, and while this is often painful it is also enriching.

3. A third question is: Can I let myself experience positive attitudes toward this other person — attitudes of warmth, caring, liking, interest, respect? It is not easy. I find in myself, and feel that I often see in others, a certain amount of fear of these feelings. We are afraid that if we let ourselves freely experience these positive feelings toward another we may be trapped by them. They may lead to demands on us or we may be disappointed in our trust, and these outcomes we fear. So as a reaction we tend to build up distance between ourselves and others — aloofness, a "professional" attitude, an impersonal relationship.

I feel quite strongly that one of the important reasons for the profession-alization of every field is that it helps to keep this distance. In the clinical areas we develop elaborate diagnostic formulations, seeing the person as an object. In teaching and in administration we develop all kinds of evaluative procedures, so that again the person is perceived as an object. In these ways, I believe, we can keep ourselves from experiencing the caring which would exist if we recognized the relationship as one between two persons. It is a real achievement when we can learn, even in certain relationships or at certain times in those relationships, that it is safe to care, that it is safe to relate to the other as a person for whom we have positive feelings.

4. Another question the importance of which I have learned in my own experience is: Can I be strong enough as a person to be separate from the other? Can I be a sturdy respecter of my own feelings, my own needs, as well as his? Can I own and, if need be, express my own feelings as something belonging to me and separate from his feelings? Am I strong enough in my own separateness that I will not be downcast by his depression, frightened by his fear, nor engulfed by his dependency? Is my inner self hardy enough to realize that I am not destroyed by his anger, taken over by his need for dependence, nor enslaved by his love, but that I exist separate from him with feelings and rights of my own? When I can freely feel this strength of being a separate person, then I find that I can let myself go much more deeply in understanding and accepting him because I am not fearful of losing myself.

5. The next question is closely related. Am I secure enough within myself to permit him his separateness? Can I permit him to be what he is — honest or deceitful, infantile or adult, despairing or over-confident? Can I give him the freedom to be? Or do I feel that he should follow my advice, or remain somewhat dependent on me, or mold himself after me? In this connection I think of the interesting small study by Farson[1] which found that the less well adjusted and less competent counselor tends to induce conformity to himself, to have clients who model themselves after him. On the other hand, the better adjusted and more competent counselor can interact with a client through many interviews without interfering with the freedom of the client to develop a personality quite separate from that of his therapist. I should prefer to be in this latter class, whether as parent or supervisor or counselor.

6. Another question I ask myself is: Can I let myself enter fully into the world of his feelings and personal meanings and see these as he does? Can I step into his private world so completely that I lose all desire to evaluate or judge it? Can I enter it so sensitively that I can move about in it freely, without trampling on meanings which are precious to him? Can I sense it so accurately that I can catch not only the meanings of his experience which are obvious to him, but those meanings which are only implicit, which he sees only dimly or as confusion? Can I extend this understanding without limit? I think of the client who said, "Whenever I find someone who understands a *part* of me at the time, then it never fails that a point is reached where I know they're *not* understanding me again. . . . What I've looked for so hard is for someone to understand."

For myself I find it easier to feel this kind of understanding, and to communicate it, to individual clients than to students in a class of staff members in a group in which I am involved. There is a strong temptation to set students "straight," or to point out to a staff member the errors in his thinking. Yet when I can permit myself to understand in these situations, it is mutually rewarding. And with clients in therapy, I am often impressed with the fact that even a minimal amount of empathic understanding — a bumbling and faulty attempt to catch the confused complexity of the client's meaning — is helpful, though there is no doubt that it is most helpful when I can see and formulate clearly the meanings in his experiencing which for him have been unclear and tangled.

7. Still another issue is whether I can be acceptant of each facet of this other person which he presents to me. Can I receive him as he is? Can I communicate this attitude? Or can I only receive him conditionally, acceptant of some aspects of his feelings and silently or openly disapproving of other aspects? It has been my experience that when my attitude is conditional, then he cannot change or grow in those respects in which I cannot fully receive him. And when — afterward and sometimes too late — I try to discover why I have been unable to accept him in every respect, I usually discover that it is because I have been frightened or threatened in myself by some aspect of his feeling. If I am to be more helpful, then I must myself grow and accept myself in these respects..

8. A very practical issue is raised by the question: Can I act with sufficient sensitivity in the relationship that my behavior will not be perceived as a threat? The work we are beginning to do in studying the physiological concomitants of psychotherapy confirms the research by Dittes in indicating how easily individuals are threatened at a physiological level. The psycho-galvanic reflex — the measure of skin conductance — takes a sharp dip when the therapist responds with some word which is just a little stronger than the client's feeling. And to a phrase such as, "My, you *do* look upset," the needle swings almost off the paper. My desire to avoid even such minor threats is not due to a hypersensitivity about my client. It is simply due to the conviction based on experience that if I can free him as completely as possible from external threat, then he can begin to experience and to deal with the internal feelings and conflicts which he finds threatening within himself.

9. A specific aspect of the preceding question but an important one is: Can I free him from the threat of external evaluation? In almost every phase of our lives — at home, at school, at work — we find ourselves under the rewards and punishments of external judgments. "That's good"; "that's naughty." "That's worth an A"; "that's a failure." "That's good counseling"; "that's poor counseling." Such judgments are a part of our lives from infancy to old age. I believe they have a certain social usefulness to institutions and organizations such as schools and professions. Like everyone else I find myself all too often making such evaluations. But, in my experience, they do not make for personal growth and hence I do not believe that they are a part of a helping relationship. Curiously enough a positive evaluation is as threatening in the long run as a negative one, since to inform someone that he is good implies that you also have the right to tell him he is bad. So I have come to feel that the more I can keep a relationship free of judgment and evaluation, the more this will permit the other person to reach the point where he recognizes that the locus of evaluation, the center of responsibility, lies within himself. The meaning and value of his experience is in the last analysis something which is up to him, and no amount of external judgment can alter this. So I should like to work toward a relationship in which I am not, even in my own feelings, evaluating him. This I believe can set him free to be a self-responsible person.

10. One last question: Can I meet this other individual as a person who is in process of *becoming*, or will I be bound by his past and by my past? If, in my encounter with him, I am dealing with him as an immature child, an ignorant student, a neurotic personality, or a psychopath, each of these concepts of mine limits what he can be in the relationship. Martin Buber, the existentialist philosopher of the University of Jerusalem, has a phrase, "confirming means . . . accepting the whole potentiality of the other. . . . I can recognize in him, know in him, the person he has been . . . *created* to become. . . . I confirm him in myself, and then in him, a relation to this potentiality that . . . can now be developed, can evolve."[2] If I accept the other person as something fixed, already diagnosed and classified, already shaped by his past, then I am doing my part to confirm this limited hypothesis. If I accept him as a process of becoming, then I am doing what I can to confirm or make real his potentialities.

It is at this point that I see Verplanck, Lindsley, and Skinner, working in operant conditioning, coming together with Buber, the philosopher or mystic. At least they come together in principle, in an odd way. If I see a relationship as only an opportunity to reinforce certain types of words or opinions in the other, then I tend to confirm him as an object — a basically mechanical, manipulable object. And if I see this as his potentiality, he tends to act in ways which support this hypothesis. If, on the other hand, I see a relationship as an opportunity to "reinforce" *all* that he is, the person that he is with all his existent potentialities, then he tends to act in ways which support *this* hypothesis. I have then — to use Buber's term — confirmed him as a living person, capable of creative inner development. Personally I prefer this second type of hypothesis.

CONCLUSION

In the early portion of this paper I reviewed some of the contributions which research is making to our knowledge *about* relationships. Endeavoring to keep that knowledge in mind I then took up the kind of questions which arise from an inner and subjective point of view as I enter, as a person, into relationships. If I could, in myself, answer all the questions I have raised in the affirmative, then I believe that any relationships in which I was involved would be helping relationships, would involve growth. But I cannot give a positive answer to most of these questions. I can only work in the direction of the positive answer.

This has raised in my mind the strong suspicion that the optimal helping relationship is the kind of relationship created by a person who is psychologically mature. Or to put it in another way, the degree to which I can create relationships which facilitate the growth of others as separate persons is a measure of the growth I have achieved in myself. In some respects this is a disturbing thought, but it is also a promising or challenging one. It would indicate that if I am interested in creating helping relationships I have a fascinating lifetime job ahead of me, stretching and developing my potentialities in the direction of growth.

NOTES

1. R. E. Farson, "Introjection in the Psychotherapeutic Relationship," unpublished doctoral dissertation, University of Chicago, 1955.
2. M. Buber and C. Rogers, "Transcription of Dialogue Held April 18, 1957, Ann Arbor, Mich.," unpublished manuscript.

Defensive Communication

Jack R. Gibb

One way to understand communication is to view it as a people process rather than as a language process. If one is to make fundamental improvement in communication, he must make changes in interpersonal relationships. One possible type of alteration — and the one with which this paper is concerned — is that of reducing the degree of defensiveness.

DEFINITION AND SIGNIFICANCE
Defensive behavior is defined as that behavior which occurs when an individual perceives threat or anticipates threat in the group. The person who behaves defensively, even though he also gives some attention to the common task, devotes an appreciable portion of his energy to defending himself. Besides talking about the topic, he thinks about how he appears to others, how he may be seen more favorably, how he may win, dominate, impress, or escape punishment, and/or how he may avoid or mitigate a perceived or an anticipated attack.

Such inner feelings and outward acts tend to create similarly defensive postures in others; and, if unchecked, the ensuing circular response becomes increasingly destructive. Defensive behavior, in short, engenders defensive listening, and this in turn produces postural, facial, and verbal cues which raise the defense level of the original communicator.

Reproduced from The Journal of Communication, Vol. 11, No. 3, Copyright, September, 1961, 141-148. Reprinted by permission of the International Communication Association.

Defense arousal prevents the listener from concentrating upon the message. Not only do defensive communicators send off multiple value, motive, and affect cues, but also defensive recipients distort what they receive. As a person becomes more and more defensive, he becomes less and less able to perceive accurately the motives, the values, and the emotions of the sender. The writer's analyses of tape-recorded discussions revealed that increases in defensive behavior were correlated positively with losses in efficiency in communication.[1] Specifically, distortions became greater when defensive states existed in the groups.

The converse, moreover, also is true. The more "supportive" or defense reductive the climate, the less the receiver reads into the communication distorted loadings which arise from projections of his own anxieties, motives, and concerns. As defenses are reduced, the receivers become better able to concentrate upon the structure, the content, and the cognitive meanings of the message.

CATEGORIES OF DEFENSIVE AND SUPPORTIVE COMMUNICATION

In working over an eight-year period with recordings of discussions occurring in varied settings, the writer developed the six pairs of defensive and support- ive categories presented in Table 1. Behavior which a listener perceives as possessing any of the characteristics listed in the left-hand column arouses defensiveness, whereas that which he interprets as having any of the qualities designated as supportive reduces defensive feelings. The degree to which these reactions occur depends upon the personal level of defensiveness and upon the general climate in the group at the time.[2]

EVALUATION AND DESCRIPTION

Speech or other behavior which appears evaluative increases defensiveness. If by expression, manner of speech, tone of voice, or verbal content the sender seems to be evaluating or judging the listener, then the receiver goes on guard. Of course, other factors may inhibit the reaction. If the listener thought that the speaker regarded him as an equal and was being open and sponta- neous, for example, the evaluativeness in a message would be neutralized and perhaps not even perceived. This same principle applies equally to the other five categories of potentially defense-producing climates. The six sets are interactive.

Because our attitudes toward other persons are frequently, and often necessarily, evaluative expressions which the defensive person will regard as nonjudgmental are hard to frame. Even the simplest question usually conveys the answer that the sender wishes or implies the response that would fit into his value system. A mother, for example, immediately following an earth tremor that shook the house, sought for her small son with the question: "Bobby, where are you?" The timid and plaintive "Mommy, I didn't do it" indicated how Bobby's chronic mild defensiveness predisposed him to react with a projection of his own guilt and in the context of his chronic assumption that questions are full of accusation.

Anyone who has attempted to train professionals to use information- seeking speech with neutral affect appreciates how difficult it is to teach a person to say even the simple "who did that?" without being seen as accusing.

TABLE 1
CATEGORIES OF BEHAVIOR CHARACTERISTICS OF SUPPORTIVE
AND DEFENSIVE CLIMATES IN SMALL GROUPS

DEFENSIVE CLIMATES	SUPPORTIVE CLIMATES
1. Evaluation	1. Description
2. Control	2. Problem orientation
3. Strategy	3. Spontaneity
4. Neutrality	4. Empathy
5. Superiority	5. Equality
6. Certainty	6. Provisionalism

Speech is so frequently judgmental that there is a reality base for the defensive interpretations which are so common.

When insecure, group members are particularly likely to place blame, to see others as fitting into categories of good or bad, to make moral judgments of their colleagues, and to question the value, motive, and affect loadings of the speech which they hear. Since value loadings imply a judgment of others, a belief that the standards of the speaker differ from his own causes the listener to become defensive.

Descriptive speech, in contrast to that which is evaluative, tends to arouse a minimum of uneasiness. Speech acts which the listener perceives as genuine requests for information or as material with neutral loadings is descriptive. Specifically, presentations of feelings, events, perceptions, or processes which do not ask or imply that the receiver change behavior or attitude are minimally defense producing. The difficulty in avoiding overtone is illustrated by the problems of news reporters in writing stories about unions, communists, Negroes, and religious activities without tipping off the "party" line of the newspaper. One can often tell from the opening words in a news article which side the newspaper's editorial policy favors.

CONTROL AND PROBLEM ORIENTATION

Speech which is used to control the listener evokes resistance. In most of our social intercourse someone is trying to do something to someone else — to change an attitude, to influence behavior, or to restrict the field of activity. The degree to which attempts to control produce defensiveness depends upon the openness of the effort, for a suspicion that hidden motives exist heightens resistance. For this reason, attempts of nondirective therapists and progressive educators to refrain from imposing a set of values, a point of view, or a problem solution upon the receivers meet with many barriers. Since the norm is control, noncontrollers must earn the perceptions that their efforts have no hidden motives. A bombardment of persuasive "messages" in the fields of politics, education, special causes, advertising, religion, medicine, industrial relations, and guidance has bred cynical and paranoidal responses in listeners.

Implicit in all attempts to alter another person is the assumption by the change agent that the person to be altered is inadequate. That the speaker secretly views the listener as ignorant, unable to make his own decisions, uninformed, immature, unwise, or possessed of wrong or inadequate attitudes is a subconscious perception which gives the latter a valid base for defensive reactions.

Methods of control are many and varied. Legalistic insistence on detail, restrictive regulations and policies, conformity norms, and all laws are among the methods. Gestures, facial expressions, other forms of nonverbal communication, and even such simple acts as holding a door open in a particular manner are means of imposing one's will upon another and hence are potential sources of resistance.

Problem orientation, on the other hand, is the antithesis of persuasion. When the sender communicates a desire to collaborate in defining a mutual problem and in seeking its solution, he tends to create the same problem orientation in the listener; and, of greater importance, he implies that he has no predetermined solution, attitude, or method to impose. Such behavior is permissive in that it allows the receiver to set his own goals, make his own decisions, and evaluate his own progress or to share with the sender in doing so. The exact methods of attaining permissiveness are not known, but they must involve a constellation of cues and they certainly go beyond mere verbal assurances that the communicator has no hidden desires to exercise control.

STRATEGY AND SPONTANEITY

When the sender is perceived as engaged in a stratagem involving ambiguous and multiple motivators, the receiver becomes defensive. No one wishes to be a guinea pig, a role player, or an impressed actor, and no one likes to be the victim of some hidden motivation. That which is concealed, also, may appear larger than it really is with the degree of defensiveness of the listener determining the perceived size of the suppressed element. The intense reaction of the reading audience to the material in the Hidden Persuaders indicates the prevalence of defensive reactions to multiple motivations behind strategy. Group members who are seen as "taking a role," as feigning emotion, as toying with their colleagues, as withholding information, or as having special sources of data are especially resented. One participant once complained that another was "using a listening technique" on him!

A large part of the adverse reaction to much of the so-called human relations training is a feeling against what are perceived as gimmicks and tricks to fool or to "involve" people, to make a person think he is making his own decision, or to make the listener feel that the sender is genuinely interested in him as a person. Particularly violent reactions occur when it appears that someone is trying to make a stratagem appear spontaneous. One person has reported a boss who incurred resentment by habitually using the gimmick of "spontaneously" looking at his watch and saying, "My gosh, look at the time — I must run to an appointment." The belief was that the boss would create less irritation by honestly asking to be excused.

Similarly, the deliberate assumption of guilelessness and natural simplicity is especially resented. Monitoring the tapes of feedback and evaluation sessions in training groups indicates the surprising extent to which members perceive the strategies of their colleagues. This perceptual clarity may be quite shocking to the strategist, who usually feels that he has cleverly hidden the motivational aura around the "gimmick."

This aversion to deceit may account for one's resistance to politicians who are suspected of behind-the-scenes planning to get his vote, to psychologists whose listening apparently is motivated by more than the manifest or content-level interest in his behavior, or to the sophisticated, smooth, or clever person whose "oneupmanship" is marked with guile. In training groups the role-flexible person frequently is resented because his changes in behavior are perceived as strategic maneuvers.

In contrast, behavior which appears to be spontaneous and free of deception is defense reductive. If the communicator is seen as having a clean id, as having uncomplicated motivations, as being straightforward and honest, and as behaving spontaneously in response to the situation, he is likely to arouse minimal defense.

NEUTRALITY AND EMPATHY

When neutrality in speech appears to the listener to indicate a lack of concern for his welfare, he becomes defensive. Group members usually desire to be perceived as valued persons, as individuals of speech worth, and as objects of concern and affection. The clinical, detached, person-is-an-object-of-study attitude on the part of many psychologist-trainers is resented by group members. Speech with low affect that communicates little warmth or caring is in such contrast with the affect laden speech in social situations that it sometimes communicates rejection.

Communication that conveys empathy for the feelings and respect for the worth of the listener, however, is particularly supportive and defense reductive. Reassurance results when a message indicates that the speaker identifies himself with the listener's problems, shares his feelings, and accepts his emotional reactions at face value. Abortive efforts to deny the legitimacy of the receiver's emotions by assuring the receiver that he need not feel bad, that he should not feel rejected or that he is overly anxious, though often intended as support giving, may impress the listener as lack of acceptance. The combination of understanding and empathizing with other person's emotions with no accompanying effort to change him apparently is supportive at a high level.

The importance of gestural behavior cues in communicating empathy should be mentioned. Apparently spontaneous facial and bodily evidences of concern are often interpreted as especially valid evidence of deep-level acceptance.

SUPERIORITY AND EQUALITY

When a person communicates to another that he feels superior in position, power, wealth, intellectual ability, physical characteristics, or other ways, he arouses defensiveness. Here, as with the other sources of disturbance, whatever arouses feelings of inadequacy causes the listener to center upon the affect loading of the statement rather than upon the cognitive elements. The receiver then reacts by not hearing the message, by forgetting it, by competing with the sender, or by becoming jealous of him.

The person who is perceived as feeling superior communicates that he is not willing to enter into a shared problem-solving relationship, that he probably does not desire feedback, that he does not require help, and/or that he will be likely to try to reduce the power, the status, or the worth of the receiver.

Many ways exist for creating the atmosphere that the sender feels himself equal to the listener. Defenses are reduced when one perceives the sender as being willing to enter into participative planning with mutual trust and respect. Differences in talent, ability, worth, appearance, status, and power often exist, but the low defense communicator seems to attach little importance to these distinctions.

CERTAINTY AND PROVISIONALISM

The effects of dogmatism in producing defensiveness are well known. Those who seem to know the answers, to require no additional data, and to regard themselves as teachers rather than as co-workers tend to put others on guard. Moreover, in the writer's experiment, listeners often perceived manifest expressions of certainty as connoting inward feelings of inferiority. They saw the dogmatic individual as needing to be right, as wanting to win an argument rather than solve a problem, and as seeing his ideas as truths to be defended. This kind of behavior often was associated with acts which others regarded as attempts to exercise control. People who were right seemed to have low tolerance for members who were "wrong" — i.e., who did not agree with the sender.

One reduces the defensiveness of the listener when he communicates that he is willing to experiment with his own behavior, attitudes, and ideas. The person who appears to be taking provisional attitudes, to be investigating issues rather than taking sides on them, to be problem solving rather than debating, and to be willing to experiment and explore tends to communicate that the listener may have some control over the shared quest or the investigation of the ideas. If a person is genuinely searching for information and data, he does not resent help or company along the way.

CONCLUSION

The implications of the above material for the parent, the teacher, the manager, the administrator, or the therapist are fairly obvious. Arousing defensiveness interferes with communication and thus makes it difficult — and sometimes impossible — for anyone to convey ideas clearly and to move effectively toward the solution of therapeutic, educational, or managerial problems.

NOTES

1. J. R. Gibb, "Defense Level and Influence Potential in Small Groups," in L. Petrullo and B. M. Bass (eds.), *Leadership and Interpersonal Behavior* (New York: Holt, Rinehart and Winston, Inc., 1961), pp. 66-81.

2. J. R. Gibb, "Sociopsychological Processes of Group Instruction," in N. B. Henry (ed.), *The Dynamics of Instructional Groups* (fifty-ninth yearbook of the National Society for the Study of Education, Part II, 1960), pp. 115-135.

6

Internal
Influences

Conflict Resolution and Decision-Making Processes

THE TUBBS MODEL OF SMALL GROUP INTERACTION

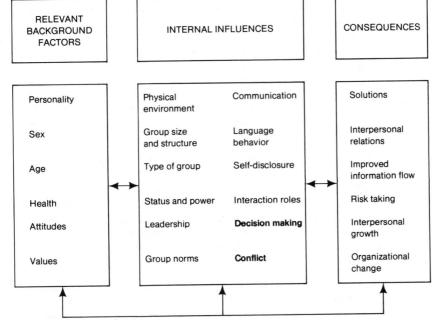

RELEVANT BACKGROUND FACTORS	INTERNAL INFLUENCES		CONSEQUENCES
Personality	Physical environment	Communication	Solutions
Sex	Group size and structure	Language behavior	Interpersonal relations
Age	Type of group	Self-disclosure	Improved information flow
Health	Status and power	Interaction roles	Risk taking
Attitudes	Leadership	**Decision making**	Interpersonal growth
Values	Group norms	**Conflict**	Organizational change

Concepts in **boldface** are the emphases of this chapter.

CASE STUDY

The situation reported in this case occurred in a classroom of a large state university. Herb Hamilton was a 48-year-old high school biology teacher taking an evening graduate-level psychology course in stress management. Dr. Martin, the professor, was 37 years old, had been teaching for 15 years, and was an adjunct professor of psychology at the university (where he taught one night a week) and a full professor at a nearby engineering college. The class had 19 people in it ranging in age from 25 to 48. (Herb was the oldest member of the class.) This is Dr. Martin's account.

Our first class met on January 12. After covering the basic description of the course, assignments, etc., I began a lecture offering a brief overview of the major sources of stress. I mentioned job, family, and community. As I proceeded to discuss divorce statistics, Herb became very upset and said the following, as best I can recall. "It's easy for you to be smug. You have a job, you are married, and you don't know the first thing about what stress feels like. You can only talk about it in an intellectual vacuum!"

After finishing the class, I talked with Herb for about fifteen minutes. He revealed to me that he was under psychiatric care; had been through a very messy divorce during which his wife broke a milk bottle across his face; was currently on a disability leave from his teaching job after having suffered an emotional breakdown; and was the father of four children who "never bothered to call him unless they wanted some money." I tried to calm him down since he was shaking noticeably. I told him that the course was designed to help each of us cope more effectively with the stresses in our lives.

He continued to be disruptive, abusive, and insulting through the next several weeks of class. Several students complained privately that they couldn't believe how antisocial his behavior was, and that he was violating their right to learn by his behavior.

Then, on the evening of March 2, Herb came to class smelling of alcohol. I was seated directly behind him. Two students were presenting a report on alcoholism. They began with a 35-item test of knowledge about alcoholism. Herb began criticizing the test by stating that he couldn't answer these items because they were statements, not questions. They explained that it was a true-false test and the items were intended to be statements of fact, which could be indicated as true or false.

As one person began to read off the correct answers, Herb debated and criticized virtually every item's answer. After the first item, I asked Herb to let the students go on with the report and then we could discuss the entire report as a class. Herb continued to argue every point. Four or five times, other class members asked Herb to be quiet and quit interrupting the presentation. By the time we got to item 21 on the test, the entire class was getting upset.

The 21st item on the test stated that alcohol is a stimulant. The speaker said that this statement was false, that it was a depressant. This particularly upset Herb, who argued that it was a stimulant in small quantities and a depressant only in large quantities. I corroborated the speaker, explaining that alcohol depressed the inhibitory mechanisms in the central nervous system, which made it *appear* that the drinker was acting like he or she had been stimulated. Herb turned around to the rest of the class and said, "People, can we tolerate this? This is absolutely wrong. We aren't even getting the accurate facts in this class. We are getting garbage," or words very similar to those.

1. *What should Dr. Martin do?*

2. *How could this conflict have been dealt with? In what ways could it have been avoided?*

P_____ erhaps one of the most frequent criticisms of committees is that they are a waste of time. By this people usually mean that groups often require a lot of effort without achieving any tangible results. Therefore it is important to note that several techniques have been developed that can help us get better results from the time we spend in problem-solving groups or committees.

DECISION-MAKING PROCESSES

As you no doubt have experienced, decision making is hard work. Often the decision-making models in textbooks are extremely simplified compared to the actual cases that confront us in real life. Some fascinating material has recently been published that reveals that even within our own brains we use two different models or methods for decision making. The left hemisphere of the brain is more prone to logical, factual, sequential, and systematic thinking and decision making. The right hemisphere tends to function more in a holistic, intuitive, emotional manner. For example, one recent advertisement for a new sports car stated that the left side of our brains would like its craftsmanship, good economy, and high resale value, and the right side of our brains would like the fact that it goes like a "bat out of hell."

The right side of the brain would enjoy the pictures and the cartoons in this book, while the left side would like the conceptual models and charts that organize the concepts. The chart in Fig. 6.1 compares the right and left brain functioning methods.

As you look at several decision-making models in this chapter, you will notice that implied in each approach is a bias toward the left brain hemisphere or the right. It is probably good to remember that both sides of the brain should be used in concert, since their functions complement each other.

Finally, some of the following models are prescriptive — that is, they prescribe a desired way to solve problems. Other models are more descriptive and describe how we tend to solve problems rather than tell us how we should do it. Each problem-solving model has some research evidence suggesting that it is helpful in improving the decisions that people make. However, our ability to solve problems will probably be helped most if we become familiar with several of these approaches and gain what we can from each, instead of picking only one.

THE REFLECTIVE THINKING PROCESS

Undoubtedly, the best-known pattern for small group problem-solving is the reflective thinking sequence first proposed by John Dewey (1910). It emphasizes the left brain functions. Although the method has several variations, the basic components are: (1) what is the problem? (2) what are its causes and limits? (3) what are the criteria for an acceptable solution? (4) what are the available solutions? (5) what is the best solution? (6) how can it be implemented? A more detailed outline includes the following:

I. Problem Phase

    a. *Identification of problem area, including such questions as:*

        1. What is the situation in which the problem is occurring?
        2. What, in general, is the difficulty?
        3. How did this difficulty arise?
        4. What is the importance of the difficulty?
        5. What limitations, if any, are there on the area of our concern?
        6. What is the meaning of any terms that need clarifying?

    b. *Analysis of the difficulty*

        1. What, specifically, are the facts of the situation?
        2. What, specifically, are the difficulties?

    c. *Analysis of causes*

        1. What is causing the difficulties?
        2. What is causing the causes?

	LEFT	RIGHT	
1	Logical, more like a computer analyzing component bits of information in a systematic manner and sequence, then drawing a conclusion from the premises.	Intuitive, more like an artist looking for an *overall* image, concept, or Gestalt. The conclusions are often reached in a flash of insight, rather than in a systematic method.	1
2	Either/or thinking, one correct answer (such as in mathematics).	Many alternatives, numerous shades of gray, subtle gradations or nuances of meaning.	2
3	Precise, literal meaning, such as in legal documents.	Nonliteral comparisons, such as in metaphors and analogies. (For example, comparing a group's leader to a ship's rudder.	3
4	Verbally oriented.	Nonverbally oriented, uses graphic or pictoral descriptions.	4
5	Explicit, carefully defined, and fully explained.	Implicit, impressionistic, like a sketch rather than a photograph.	5
6	Controlled, disciplined.	Emotional, sensual, like reacting to music or to fragrances or colors.	6
7	Pragmatic, very practical real-world orientation.	Imaginative, nontraditional, innovative, uses fantasy.	7
8	Dominant.	Passive.	8
9	Intellectual, cerebral.	Sensually oriented, prefers experiencing to intellectualizing.	9
10	Careful with time and the use of time.	Casual with time and the use of time.	10
11	Scientific.	Artistic.	11
12	Preprogrammed, organized.	Ambiguous, nebulous.	12
13	Objective, verifiable.	Subjective, personal, unique.	13
14	Skeptical, preferring evidence and factual proof	Accepting, preferring intuition and gut-level impressions.	14
15	Comparison against standards of performance.	Comparison against internal private standards.	15

FIGURE 6.1
Left and right brain functions.

II. Criteria Phase

    a. What are the principal requirements of the solution?

    b. What limitations must be placed on the solution?

    c. What is the relative importance of the criteria?

III. Solution Phase

    a. *What are the possible solutions?*

        1. What is the exact nature of each solution?

        2. How would it remedy the difficulty? by eliminating the cause? by offsetting the effect? by a combination of both?

    b. *How good is each solution?*

        1. How well would it remedy the difficulty?

        2. How well would it satisfy the criteria? Are there any that it would not satisfy?

        3. Would there be any unfavorable consequences? any extra benefits?

    c. *What solution appears to be best?*

        1. How would you rank the solution?

        2. Would some combination of solutions be best?

IV. Implementation Phase

    What steps would be taken to put the solution into effect?

While this sequence is well known and widely taught, other approaches have also been proposed that are of value.

THE KEPNER-TREGOE APPROACH

A variation of the reflective thinking sequence has been proposed by two business consultants (Kepner and Tregoe 1965). The overall format is similar to the reflective thinking sequence; however, the most important contribution seems to be the way in which a group works through the *criteria phase.* Suppose that the group is trying to solve the problem of how to get 1000 signatures on a petition that they are circulating to get an issue on the ballot for a local election. In selecting a best solution, several criteria must first be considered. There are usually certain *required* elements and other *desired* elements of any solution they might select. Kepner and Tregoe call these *musts* and *wants.* For example:

Musts	*Wants*
All signatures must be of registered voters.	To spread the work over several members, not just a few.

The deadline is November 15 (one month away).	To spread the work over several weeks, not just one or two.
One thousand signatures are the minimum required.	To get more than 1000 signatures in case some signers are not registered voters.

Using the method described above, we can assign a numerical value to each of the criteria for an acceptable solution and rank them in order of their importance. Then we can construct a grid on which to evaluate different alternatives against the relevant criteria. This method enables the group to systematically weigh one solution against another. One college management department was trying to select a new chairperson. In a series of meetings, the three most important criteria or areas of skill were identified as follows:

The critical criteria for the chairperson of the department have been structured into three areas of competence: administrative, professional, and personal.

I. Administrative Skills

a. Leads (motivates and inspires faculty).

b. Employs participative style of management (whenever possible, consults with faculty prior to making decisions that affect them).

c. Demonstrates commitment to development of faculty (allows faculty considerable personal freedom, encourages them to share leadership responsibilities and to take on projects).

d. Recognizes faculty performance and makes recommendations to administration for promotions and merit increases.

e. Leads department in keeping curriculum abreast of educational needs.

f. Is well known in the professional field, particularly to administrators in other educational institutions who can assist in recruitment and development of faculty.

g. Is committed to equal development of disciplines represented in the department.

II. Professional Skills

a. Demonstrates commitment to excellence in teaching and research.

b. Is well known and respected through publications and other professional contributions. Is a recognized scholar in his or her field.

c. Possesses a doctorate.

	CRITERIA (RANKED IN ORDER OF IMPORTANCE)		
CANDIDATES	ADMINISTRATIVE SKILLS (1)	PROFESSIONAL SKILLS (2)	PERSONAL SKILLS (3)
Tom	Good	Excellent	Excellent
Dick	Excellent	Excellent	Good
Harry	Good	Good	Good

FIGURE 6.2

III. Personal Skills

a. Possesses a high degree of integrity and maturity.

b. Is willing to listen and respond to the ideas and opinions of others.

c. Is willing to express personal and departmental convictions to faculty and administration.

d. Evokes the acceptance and trust of associates.

Over a period of some time, several potential candidates for the position were selected. Let us call them Tom, Dick, and Harry. Once the criteria had been established, and the potential candidates selected, a chart or grid shows the way in which the candidates were compared to the criteria (see Fig. 6.2). On the basis of the data in the chart, which candidate would you have chosen?

THE SINGLE QUESTION FORM

In addition to the problem-solving sequences described above, Larson (1969, p. 453) has found that another, rather brief method is about as good as the methods already described. Larson studied the differences between high- and low-success individual problem solvers and derived a technique that could be used by groups. This method involves using the following format:

What is the single question, the answer to which is all the group needs to know to accomplish its purpose?

What subquestions must be answered before we can answer the single question we have formulated?

Do we have sufficient information to answer confidently the subquestions?

What are the most reasonable answers to the subquestions?

High success	Low success
1. Starting the attack on the problem	
Able to select some phrase or concept as a point of departure. Able to state a specific objective toward which to work.	Tried to change the problem to one which they could solve more easily. Tendency to disagree with the problem, for example, "This is a stupid problem."
2. Approach to basic ideas within the problem	
Used analogies and examples to help themselves understand the concepts within the problems. Considered more implications of the ideas which they came up with, such as, "What would result from . . ." "What causes . . ."	Did not attempt to arrive at an understanding of the problem, for example, "We haven't studied that yet." Used more unconnected series of thoughts.
3. General approach to problems	
Set up hypotheses about what the correct answer would do. If unfamiliar terms were used in the problem, made an assumption about the meaning and proceeded.	Selected answers on the basis of feeling and impressions (especially in social problems). Devoted little time to considering the nature of the problem.
4. Attitudes toward solving problems	
"You can figure it out if you try."	"You either know it or you don't." Easily discouraged. Avoided complex problems. Little confidence in their own reasoning abilities.

FIGURE 6.3
Some differences between high- and low-success problem solvers. Used with permission of F. E. X. Dance, *Speech Communication: Concepts and Behavior* (New York: Holt, Rinehart and Winston, 1972), p. 128.

Assuming that our answers to the subquestions are correct, what is the best solution to the problem?

This technique evolved out of an analysis of the basic differences in communication behaviors between successful and unsuccessful problem solvers studied by Bloom and Broder (1961). It seems that the successful problem solvers were more willing and interested in getting at solutions and avoided getting bogged down with the trivial detail of the discussion. Their attitudes seemed to be characterized as, "Let's assume for the moment a few things," rather than, "How can we be expected to solve this when those guys who gave us the problem can't solve their own problems?" In other words, there is an eagerness to make progress rather than to alibi out of making progress. Dance and Larson (1972, p. 128) summarize these two different sets of behaviors in Fig. 6.3. Notice that this is a descriptive summary that has prescriptive implications.

Each of the problem-solving methods described thus far (that is, reflective thinking, the Kepner-Tregoe approach, or the single question form) will probably offer you and your group a way to get better results than if you used no systematic method at all. Try using each of these methods in solving some of the problem exercises contained in this book.

FRANK AND ERNEST   **by Bob Thaves**

THEY OFFERED ME A JOB AS A TOP LEVEL DECISION-MAKER, BUT I CAN'T MAKE UP MY MIND WHETHER OR NOT TO TAKE IT.

Reprinted by permission. © 1976 NEA. Inc.

Don't give up — most problems can be solved if we work at them long enough.

BRAINSTORMING

Another popular technique that can be applied to problem-solving is brainstorming (Osborn 1953). This technique is primarily used to generate ideas and can be applied as *part* of the problem-solving process. It emphasizes the right brain activity. For example, groups frequently dwell on one or two proposed solutions to a problem, when many more solutions may be available. Brainstorming would be one way to help generate more alternative solutions for the group to consider.

Brainstorming can be applied to any of the phases of the reflective thinking sequence discussed earlier. The problem identification phase includes the need to determine the factors causing the problem; the criteria phase requires identification of the requirements for an appropriate solution; the solution phase requires some alternatives from which to choose; and the implementation phase requires creative application of the chosen solution. The guidelines (adapted from Osborn 1953) for using the brainstorming technique are listed below.

Rules for Brainstorming

1. *Put judgment and evaluation temporarily aside*
   a. Acquire a "try anything" attitude.
   b. No faultfinding is allowed. It stifles ideas, halts association.
   c. Today's criticism may kill future ideas.
   d. All ideas are at least thought starters.

2. *Turn imagination loose and start offering the results*
   a. The wilder the ideas, the better.
   b. Ideas are easier to tame down than to think up.
   c. Free wheeling is encouraged; ideas can be brought down to earth later.

  d. A wild idea may be the only way to bring out another really good one.

3. *Think of as many ideas as you can*

  a. Quantity breeds quality.

  b. The more ideas to choose from, the more chance of a good one.

  c. There is always more than one good solution to any problem.

  d. Try many different approaches.

4. *Seek combination and improvement*

  a. Your ideas don't all have to be original.

  b. Improve on the ideas of others.

  c. Combine previously mentioned ideas.

  d. Brainstorming is a group activity. Take advantage of group association.

5. *Record all ideas in full view*

6. *Evaluate at a later session*

  a. Approach each idea with a positive attitude.

  b. Give each idea a fair trial.

  c. Apply judgment gradually.

  Osborn offers a few additional tips to further stimulate the creation of ideas (ideation). After ideas are generated, think of adding, subtracting, multiplying, and dividing as ways of modifying the ideas you already have. Effective toothpaste was improved by adding fluorides. Portable radios were made portable by subtracting size through the use of printed circuits. The common razor-blade market was revamped by the creation of a double-edged razor (multiplying). Finally, General Motors decided to divide up the production of the Oldsmobile Cutlass to several assembly plants, since the single plant at Lansing, Michigan, could not expand fast enough to keep up with demand.

  One aspect of brainstorming that may be less obvious is the incubation of ideas, allowing ideas to develop during a period of relative relaxation. Sometimes allowing ideas to incubate or "set" creates a new insight into a problem. Many company executives as well as important politicians prefer to be alone before making important decisions. This period of solitude may help you to let all the facts sink in before committing yourself to a decision.

  The brainstorming process has a success record that is hard to ignore. Several reactions to brainstorming training have been noted (Osborn 1957, p. ix):

General Electric — Graduates from our new Creative Engineering Program continue to develop new processes and patentable ideas at an average rate of almost three times that of nongraduates.

National Cash Register — As a result of 12 seminars our students showed an average improvement of 79% in fluency of ideas.

An important note about brainstorming is that a critical thinking session is often a useful follow-up to brainstorming. During this time, evaluation and sorting of the ideas is conducted. Without this critical thinking session the quantity of ideas may be great, but the overall quality may suffer.

STRUCTURING A UNIT OF PROOF

Within each step of the rational problem-solving sequence there is the assumption that ideas will be built upon one another through the use of reasoning. Although most reasoning that occurs in discussions is quite informal in nature, it still plays an important part in the process of building solutions from the bricks and mortar of individual ideas. In one discussion on curbing population growth, a college student stated, "I live in Michigan's Upper Peninsula and we have land galore. What's all this garbage about overpopulation got to do with me?" In this section we shall examine the problem of the logic behind this person's statement.

Toulmin (1958) has proposed a way of analyzing the reasoning process by diagraming the units of proof involved. He identifies six basic elements in a unit of proof: (1) data, (2) warrant, (3) claim, (4) backing, (5) rebuttal, and (6) qualifier. The word *data* refers to facts, evidence, quotes, statistics, opinions, or other kinds of information that can be stated in support of an assertion. The *warrant* is the bridge between the data on one hand and the claim or conclusion on the other. It is the mechanism by which the mental leap is made between one's data and the conclusions one draws from these data. The *claim* is the specific conclusion one draws from combining the data and the warrant. The relationship among these three elements is diagramed in Fig. 6.4.

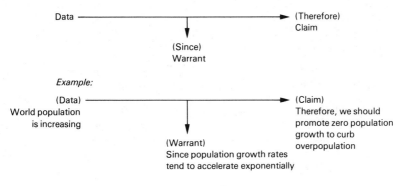

FIGURE 6.4
Toulmin's unit of proof.

It is fairly easy to analyze any unit of proof using the model illustrated in Fig. 6.4. Other elements of the unit of proof include the *backing,* which is further support for the warrant; the *rebuttal,* which is any reservation or exception that may have to be taken into consideration; and the *qualifier,* which is a method of modifying the degree to which a claim may be asserted (from possibly to probably). The relationships among these six elements are illustrated in Fig. 6.5.

The method described here looks complicated but is easy to use and should help improve the quality of reasoning that is used in group as well as in other problem-solving situations.

All of us have been in meetings that are not conducted well. Often, emotions and personal idiosyncracies prevail. Parkinson's Laws are familiar to all of us, such as, "Work expands to fill the time available." For example, a five-minute problem will take an hour to solve, if an hour was scheduled for the meeting.

In his early book, Parkinson (1957) jokes about what he calls "Parkinson's Law of Triviality," in which it is shown that major expenditures of millions of dollars pass through committees with little trouble, since most of us can't really relate to that much money. But small amounts, such as an allocation for a bicycle shed, pass through the most careful scrutiny. He writes this fictitious description (pp. 29-30):

Chairman. Item Ten. Bicycle shed for the use of the clerical staff. An estimate has been received from Messrs. Bodger and Woodworm, who undertake to complete the work for the sum of $2,350. Plans and specification are before you, gentlemen.

Mr. Softleigh. Surely, Mr. Chairman, this sum is excessive. I note that the roof is to be of aluminum. Would not asbestos be cheaper?

Mr. Holdfast. I agree with Mr. Softleigh about the cost, but the roof should, in my opinion, be of galvanized iron. I incline to think that the shed could be built for $2,000, or even less.

Mr. Daring. I would go further, Mr. Chairman. I question whether this shed is really necessary. We do too much for our staff as it is. They are never satisfied, that is the trouble. They will be wanting garages next.

Mr. Holdfast. No, I can't support Mr. Daring on this question. I think that the shed is needed. It is a question of material and cost. . . .

The debate is fairly launched. A sum of $2,350 is well within everybody's comprehension. Everyone can visualize a bicycle shed. Discussion goes on, therefore, for forty-five minutes, with the possible result of saving some $300. Members at length sit back with a feeling of achievement.

Chairman. Item Eleven. Refreshments supplied at meetings of the Joint Welfare Committee. Monthly, $4.75.

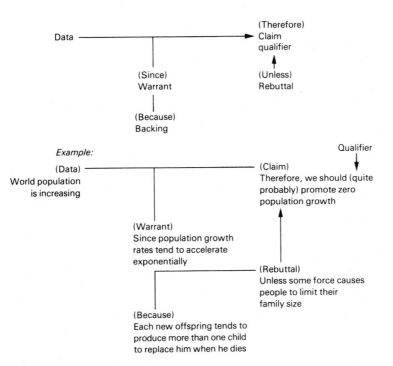

FIGURE 6.5
The relationship among six elements.

Mr. Softleigh. What type of refreshment is supplied on these occasions?

Chairman. Coffee; I understand.

Mr. Holdfast. And this means an annual charge of — let me see — $75?

Chairman. That is so.

Mr. Daring. Well, really, Mr. Chairman. I question whether this is justified. How long do these meetings last?

Now begins an even more acrimonious debate . . .

Suffice it to say that decision-making methods are not always successful.

Incrementalism   Braybrooke and Lindblom (1963) have pointed out that many economists, social scientists, political analysts, and other decision makers generally resort to a style of decision making that is far from the rational models described earlier in this chapter. They argue that numerous decisions concerning governmental policies such as welfare and social security, are arrived at partially as a result of adapting to political pressure and expediency, rather than as a result of sheer rational analysis of the available alternatives. Since environmental obstacles frequently prevent groups from choosing a "best" alternative, other alternatives may result by default. A department chairperson vacancy at a university may be filled by a "compromise candidate," one who is clearly not the most outstanding contender, but who is the only one upon whom the group can agree. This is an example of a nonrational decision.

The term *incrementalism* refers to the process of making decisions that result in change. Some decisions result in vast amounts of change, while other decisions progress toward change by small bits or *increments*. A second variable is the amount and quality of knowledge or understanding underlying a decision. When these two factors are taken in combination, the model in Fig. 6.6 results.

Braybrooke and Lindblom's analysis is primarily centered on political decisions resulting in societal change. With respect to quadrant 1 in the diagram in Fig. 6.6, the researchers contend that few decisions resulting in major social changes can be made with a high level of intellectual understanding of a problem. Numerous "think tanks" are devoted to analyzing what we should be doing to prepare ourselves for the year 2000 and beyond. Yet even the best estimates are "guesstimates" that must be continually revised based on new data. The decision to enact forced busing of school children to achieve a racial balance in public schools was an attempt to bring about a major social change. Yet the magnitude of resistance to this move was severely underestimated. In another context, the decision to have year-round daylight saving time was implemented in an attempt to save fuel. However, because of the threat of children being run down by cars in the dark early-morning hours, more parents drove their children to school, thus using more energy than daylight saving time was saving. These decisions illustrate the point that attempts to make major changes are not always accompanied by a full realization of the consequences. Thus the majority of decisions resulting in large changes would be depicted in Fig. 6.6 as falling in quadrant 4.

Quadrant 2 refers to the daily decisions of most groups that result in relatively small changes. Decisions to change the prime lending rate of a bank, to increase social security benefits, to add a few employees to a payroll, are all examples of such decisions. Obviously, defining "small" changes is a matter of judgment. These types of decisions frequently result from the careful study of experts in costing, economics, and management. Thus the chances are increased that the decision will be made with a high level of understanding of the problem. However, this may not always be the case. If the decisions result in unwanted or unanticipated problems such as inflation or unionization, the decision is defined as falling into quadrant 3. Braybrooke and Lindblom (1963, p. 73) offer the following explanation for the tendency toward incremental change:

> For a democracy like the United States, the commitment to
> incremental change is not surprising. Nonincremental alternatives

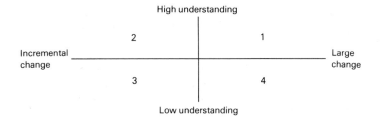

High understanding

2   1

Incremental
change ─────────────────────────────── Large
change

3   4

Low understanding

FIGURE 6.6
Model of decision making. Reprinted with permission of
Macmillan Publishing Company from *A Strategy of Decision* by
David Braybrooke and Charles C. Lindblom. Copyright © 1963
by The Free Press of Glencoe.

usually do not lie within the range of choice possible in the society or
body politic. Societies, it goes without saying, are complex structures
that can avoid dissolution or intolerable dislocation only by meeting
certain preconditions, among them that certain kinds of change are
admissible only if they occur slowly. Political democracy is often
greatly endangered by nonincremental change, which it can
accommodate only in certain limited circumstances.

Their point of view is that we make group decisions on the basis of
relatively limited information and understanding of the consequences of
those decisions. By implication, it would seem that this calls for problem-
solving strategies that are flexible and subject to change based on feedback
indicating that change is desirable. For example, the United States auto
makers at one time committed large amounts of money to the development
of a rotary engine as a possible alternative to the piston engine. However,
when the demand for more energy-efficient engines became more severe,
the work on the rotary engine was permanently halted. This type of bit-by-
bit planning is representative of the type of exploratory decision making
sometimes required in a continually changing environment.

Mixed Scanning   Etzioni (1968) offers a decision-making strategy that he
asserts is "neither rationalism nor incrementalism." Actually it is a combination of the two approaches. Rather than examining a problem compre-
hensively (rational approach), or part by part (incremental approach), we
can combine elements of both of these approaches into a so-called mixed-
scanning strategy. Etzioni offers the following example (1968, p. 284) in
support of this contention:

> Infantrymen taking positions in a new field in hostile territory scan it
> for hidden enemy troops. They are trained to scan a field. A
> rationalistic strategy is likely to be avoided because it would entail
> examining the whole field bit-by-bit, exhaustively, which would be

dangerous and fatiguing and is likely not to be completed. Incrementalists would examine places in which enemy troops have been known to hide and some others near them or similar to them. Unlike the whole field, these places can be prodded by fire. Soldiers who are tired of marching and combat will sometimes follow this procedure. But armies known for their effectiveness train their soldiers in a different procedure. A major consideration in this regard is that accuracy of aim declines with distance. The infantrymen are taught first to scan the whole field in a rough, nondiscriminating way for some obvious sign of danger (a movement, an unnatural shadow, and so on). — If none is visible, they proceed with a bit-by-bit examination from the left to the right, beginning with subfields closest to them and moving outward to more distant ones. The assumption is that scanning is going to become more superficial the longer it is carried out, which is made to coincide with the scanning of the more remote, less dangerous subfields.

The basic idea is to combine an analysis of the "big picture" with an appropriate amount of attention to detail. In an employment decision, several candidates may be assessed according to specific ratings on several criteria relevant to the job. This would be an example of paying attention to detail. It may be that one person meets all of the criteria very well, and he or she would be a strong replacement for the employee who is to be replaced. However, at the same time, perhaps a completely different level of scanning is needed to anticipate the type of employee that might be best several years from now. In one such case, a decision to replace a college debate coach resulted in hiring a professor in interpersonal and small group communication, since the debate program was getting smaller while the interpersonal and small group curriculum was increasing in size and scope.

A similar example of such a mixed-scanning model applies to the technique of efficient reading. The so-called SQ3R method of reading involves these five steps (Robinson 1961):

1. *Survey.* Glance at (or scan) the chapter outline and leaf through the pages to get a general idea of how much material is allotted to each topic in the outine.

2. *Question.* Begin to look more closely at the chapter and ask yourself questions about what the topics might be about.

3. *Read.* Read the chapter straight through once.

4. *Recite.* See how much of the material you can recite or explain to someone (or write down on a blank paper).

5. *Review.* Review the points you were able to recite and check the ones you were not.

This widely recommended study method contains elements of Etzioni's mixed-scanning model. It involves a general overview as well as an appropriate amount of attention to the necessary details. Etzioni urges that this alternating between levels of analysis enables us to "see the forest for the trees." Many groups seem to have trouble either getting down from the clouds of ambiguities and abstractions or getting up out of the quagmire of trivia long enough to see the overview. This ability to maintain a balance between attention to the general versus the specific appears to be a major factor in successful problem solving.

Tacit Bargaining   Still a third strategy for decision making that is considered an alternative to the rational-thinking approach is advanced by Schelling (1960). This strategy is referred to (p. 53) as "tacit bargaining," or "bargaining in which communication is incomplete or impossible." Examples of such situations (Schelling 1960, pp. 56-57) include the following:

1. Name heads or tails. If you and your partner name the same, you both win a prize.

2. Circle one of the numbers listed in the line below. You win if you all succeed in circling the same number.
   7   100   13   261   99   555

3. You are to divide $100 into two piles, labeled A and B. Your partner is to divide another $100 into two piles labeled A and B. If you allot the same amounts to A and B, respectively, that your partner does, each of you gets $100; if your amounts differ from his, neither of you gets anything.

In his research Schelling found that in the first problem 36 participants chose heads and only 6 chose tails. In problem 2, the first 3 numbers got 37 out of 41 votes (7 got the most, then 100, then 13). In problem 3, 36 out of 41 split the money into two equal piles of $50 each. The data suggest that people can cooperate fairly successfully in some problem-solving situations if it is to their advantage to do so. However, numerous situations exist in which the participants have divergent interests. For example, several fraternity representatives meet together on an interfraternity council; each member is interested in promoting the entire Greek system, but his primary loyalty is to his own fraternity. This divided loyalty creates an arena of "politicking" such that most members will choose *not* to communicate in a completely open and honest way. This is often referred to as a "mixed-motive" situation, in which there is simultaneous pressure to cooperate and to compete. Thus many proposed solutions are likely not to be prompted by the most honorable intentions, but to be motivated by the interests of a single person. Similar situations exist in congressional committees, which often split according to partisan (Republican and Democrat) affiliations. In these situations, decisions are frequently based on compromises and a philosophy of, "I'll support you on this issue, but you owe me support on the next issue." Rational and objective choices are less likely to prevail under these circumstances.

These bargaining situations imply communication procedures that are distinctly different from those in other kinds of problem-solving situations.

Negotiations between union and management are often characterized by each side's making highly publicized statements of extreme positions in order to strengthen its respective bargaining position. Thus the union president will call for a minimum wage increase of 10 percent and the company's representative will state flatly that 3 percent is all it can afford to give. In reality, both parties exaggerate their public position and privately acknowledge that a 6 or 7 percent agreement is what they are really trying to achieve. Keltner (1970) has graphically depicted this form of information exchange in Fig. 6.7.

Assuming that in these bargaining situations it would be naive to advise participants to simply "give in," still some reasonable suggestions can be made to increase the effectiveness of communication as well as the quality of decisions made. A good negotiator should learn to master the following abilities (adapted from Keltner, pp. 241-242):

□   He should be willing to face the issues directly and precisely.

□   He should be convinced of the position he represents.

□   He must have considerable self-confidence.

□   He must be reasonably skeptical.

□   He must inspire trust in his counterparts at the bargaining table.

□   He desires respect rather than popularity.

In concluding this section on problem solving, we should point out that, to some extent, the situation will affect the strategy of decision making chosen. In some situations one of the rational-thinking approaches will be most appropriate; in other more tentative situations, the incremental approach may be preferable. The mixed-scanning strategy seems to have application in most situations, and the tacit-bargaining strategy will be most likely in situations allowing little or no free communication among participants. In using any strategy you should know which one you are using, and understand the underlying assumptions and requirements of each. You should also expect some problems with each and realize the communication requirements inherent in each. Also, as you attempt to make decisions, you will undoubtedly encounter many and varied types of conflict, which is the subject of the next section.

CONFLICT AND CONFLICT RESOLUTION

It has been said that conflict is an inevitable part of people's relating to one another. As Johnson (1973, p. 145) puts it, "A conflict-free relationship is probably a sign that you really have no relationship at all, not that you have

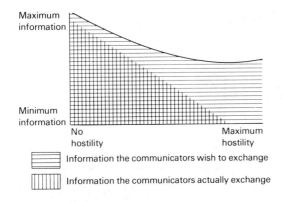

Maximum information

Minimum information

No hostility

Maximum hostility

Information the communicators wish to exchange

Information the communicators actually exchange

FIGURE 6.7
Difference between the desired and actual amount of information communicated during a conflict situation. The difference widens as the hostility increases and information decreases out of fear of reprisal. From *Interpersonal Speech-Communication, Elements and Structures* by John W. Keltner. © 1970 by Wadsworth Publishing Company, Inc. Reprinted by permission of Wadsworth Publishing Company, Belmont, California 94002.

a good relationship." It has also been said that where there is movement there is friction, and where there is friction, heat is produced. Certainly many small groups involve movement, especially if their task is to solve and act on problems. It appears obvious that in such cases the heat referred to above is the emotional heat that results from conflicts.

In our society, conflict is usually considered to be bad, that thing that results in wars, divorces, worker strikes, and bloody noses. However, several authors agree that conflict within and among groups has some *desirable* effects. Both the desirable and undesirable aspects of conflict will be discussed in this section. However, we shall first look at the sources out of which conflicts arise.

SOURCES OF CONFLICT

According to Deutsch (1969), conflict exists whenever incompatible activities occur. An incompatible action prevents, obstructs, interferes with, injures, or in some way reduces the effectiveness of the other action. Incompatible actions may occur within a single person (intrapersonal), a single group (intragroup), between two or more people (interpersonal), or between two or more groups (intergroup). Conflicts may originate from a number of

different sources, including: (1) differences in information, beliefs, values, interests, or desires, (2) a scarcity of some resource such as money, power, time, space, or position, and (3) rivalries in which one person or group competes with one another (Deutsch 1969). To these sources could be added the difficulty of the task, the pressure to avoid failure, the relative importance of a group's or individual's decision, and differences in skill levels that may cause more skilled individuals to become irritated at the less skilled; this often leads to a reciprocal irritation. In an earlier chapter we discussed personality differences. These differences lead to incompatibilities among certain members of a group. Members may be incompatible because of their differences — or they may be incompatible because of their similarities, such as in the need to achieve or dominate others. All of these factors tend to instigate conflict.

See also the article by David W. Johnson at the end of this chapter for more on the constructive use of conflict.

DESIRABILITY OF CONFLICT

As mentioned above, numerous writers believe that conflict in a group is desirable. For example, in Chapter 4 we discussed the very real problem of "groupthink," which can occur in any group. Conflict helps eliminate or reduce the likelihood of groupthink. Furthermore, Deutsch (1971, pp. 42-55) cites Simmel (1955) in his argument that conflict has other desirable functions such as preventing stagnation; stimulating interest and curiosity; providing a medium through which problems can be aired and solutions arrived at; causing personal and social change; being part of the process of testing and assessing oneself and, as such, being highly enjoyable as one experiences the pleasure of full and active use of one's capacities; demarcating groups from one another and thus helping to establish group and personal identities; fostering internal cohesion in groups involved in external conflicts; resolving tension among individuals and thus stabilizing and integrating relationships; eliminating sources of dissatisfaction in social systems by permitting immediate and direct resolution of rival claims; revitalizing existing group norms or helping the emergence of new norms in order to adjust adequately to new conditions; and ascertaining the relative strengths of antagonistic interests within a social system, thereby constituting a mechanism for the maintenance or continual readjustment of the balance of power.

Alfred Sloan was one of the early executives who helped make General Motors successful. He recognized the importance of idea conflict in decision making. Once, Sloan was chairing a meeting of the GM board of directors in which someone presented an idea for potentially buying up a small company. After the presentation Sloan asked each member around the table for an opinion. Not one gave an objection to the proposal. They all agreed the company should buy at the earliest possible moment. Finally, Sloan looked at the other board members and said: "Gentlemen, I don't see any reason not to adopt the idea either. Therefore, I suggest we postpone this decision for thirty days while we do some more thinking." Thirty days later the board decided against the plan — after finding out many negatives they had not known earlier. (See Goldhaber et al., 1979, p. 28).

Conflict clearly plays an important role in small group interaction. However, it is a double-edged sword that cuts both ways, as we shall see.

TYPES OF CONFLICT

Many people fail to differentiate between two very different types of conflict, namely, conflict of ideas versus conflict of feelings (often called personality conflict). As we saw in the example above, Alfred Sloan recognized the importance of idea conflict in making a decision. If there is too little conflict of ideas, groupthink can occur, as we saw in Chapter 4. Idea conflict, however, can very easily turn into conflict of feelings. We can call this personal conflict. Notice the difference between the conflicts in these two conversations in a group discussion.

Conversation 1

Judy: Why don't we have our next meeting at my sorority house?

Dave: I think the campus center meeting room might have fewer interruptions. I know how hard it is to have meetings at my fraternity house.

Conversation 2

Judy: Why don't we have our next meeting at my sorority house?

Dave: And have people interrupting us all the time? No, thanks, I'd rather meet in the campus center.

In the first situation there was a conflict of ideas. In the second, the conflict could have escalated to the personal level, depending on Judy's reaction. The personal animosity that may have been created by Dave is the kind that tends to get in the way of group success. As shown in Fig. 6.8, our goal in using conflict successfully is to avoid turning idea opponents into personal opponents.

UNDESIRABILITY OF CONFLICT

Our society frequently considers conflict to be undesirable. Millions of dollars are lost each year due to work stoppages and strikes. Thousands of divorces result from unchecked marital conflicts. And every once in a while a disaster like that at Kent State occurs as a result of conflict that has gotten out of control. Even in meetings, discussions, and conferences, conflict may cause reactions similar to that of one student who said, "I don't even want to go to publication council meetings anymore. Every week it is just one hassle after another. Nothing ever gets accomplished because every time we end up arguing."

Conflicts are often hard to keep under control once they have begun. There is a definite trend toward escalation and polarization. Once conflict escalates to a point at which it is no longer under control, it almost always yields negative results. In this same vein, one conflict tends to lay the groundwork for further conflicts at a later time. Part of this is because of defensive reactions. Defensiveness leads us to distort our perceptions so that ambiguous acts are more frequently misconstrued as threatening when they may in fact not be intended that way. Watzlawik, Beavin, and Jackson (1967, pp. 103-104) cite the following example of developing trust in a risky situation:

> We have established a very interesting communication pattern for the establishment of trust between humans and bottle-nosed porpoises. While this may be a ritual developed "privately" by only two of the animals, it still provides an excellent example for the analogic communication of "not." The animals had obviously concluded that the hand is one of the most important and vulnerable parts of the human body. Each would seek to establish contact with a stranger by taking the human's hand into his mouth and gently squeezing it

OPPOSITION AND SUPPORT

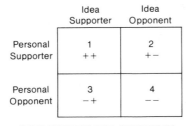

AVOID TURNING IDEA OPPONENTS
INTO PERSONAL OPPONENTS

FIGURE 6.8
Opposition and support.

between his jaws, which have sharp teeth and are powerful enough to bite the hand off cleanly. If the human would submit to this, the dolphin seemed to accept it as a message of complete trust. His next move was to reciprocate by placing the forward ventral portion of his body (*his* most vulnerable part, roughly equivalent to the human throat) upon the human's hand, leg, or foot, thereby signaling his trust in the friendly intention of the human. This procedure is, however, obviously fraught with possible misinterpretation at every step.

Nye (1973) identifies three conditions that both cause and result from conflicts. First is *competition*. In many instances there is a win-lose arrangement so that both competitors cannot possibly win. Any athletic contest illustrates that fact. Similarly, several people may seek a promotion, while only one can actually be promoted. In politics one candidate must lose, and this often produces bitter feelings, as illustrated by Nixon's famous remark after the 1962 California gubernatorial election, "You won't have Dick Nixon to kick around anymore."

Second, *domination* is related to conflict. Zimbardo (1972) conducted an experiment in which about two dozen normal, well-adjusted college students acted as either guards or prisoners (half in each group) in a simulated prison. After only four days, three of the "prisoners" had to be released because they suffered such extreme depression and anxiety. At the end of six days, extreme hostility had developed between the prisoners and guards. Zimbardo (1972, p. 8) described the situation in the following way:

> We were horrified because we saw some boys ("guards") treat others as if they were despicable animals, taking pleasure in cruelty, while other boys ("prisoners") became servile, dehumanized robots who thought only of escape, of their own individual survival, and of their mounting hatred of the guards.

The third factor is *provocation,* which Nye (1973, p. 8) defines as "intentional or unintentional harm to other persons or groups." This specific factor is most likely to promote further future conflicts. Harmful acts produce grudges that may last for years before conflict has a chance to resume. In any case, the three factors described above illustrate the negative side of conflict. The logical question that arises is, "How do we reduce conflict and keep it at a manageable level?"

TOWARD CONFLICT RESOLUTION

A number of systems have been proposed for improving our abilities to resolve conflict. Two famous psychologists (Blake and Mouton 1970) have proposed a scheme whereby we can try to avoid win-lose situations and, when it is possible, apply a win-win approach. This can best be illustrated with their model, called the Conflict Grid® (Fig. 6.9).

See the article by Robert Blake and Jane Mouton at the end of this chapter for a further elaboration of the use of this model in conflict resolution.

The Conflict Grid clearly illustrates the possibility of having *both* concern for results and concern for people at the same time. Intuitively, it would seem difficult to "have your cake and eat it too" when it comes to conflict resolution. Alternative strategies of dealing with conflict are also depicted on the Grid. Try to identify where your style would fit.

The 1,1 style is the "hands-off" approach. Neutrality is maintained with an attitude of, "the less said about it the better." The 1,9 position is excessively person oriented. Its goal is to maintain the *appearance* of harmony at all cost. In reality deep conflicts exist but are never dealt with. An uneasy state of tension exists, which is frequently characterized by lots of smiling and nervous laughter (but members avoid looking at each other). The 5,5 position represents the willingness to compromise. While compromise may be a viable alternative in some cases, it should not be a chronic way of copping out of deeper levels of conflict resolution. The bull-headed approach is depicted by the 9,1 position. This style is even worse than the compromise. Since absolute stalemates often occur, a group full of these types may get nowhere fast.

The optimum style for reducing conflict is the 9,9 approach. Here the individuals attempt to be both person and results-oriented. Conflicts are not ignored, but individuals don't go around with a chip on their shoulder either. Differences are discussed with such comments as, "I don't agree with the position that . . ." At the same time, personally insulting state-

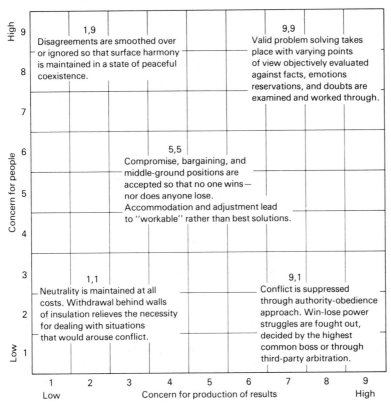

FIGURE 6.9
Blake and Mouton's Conflict Grid.® Reproduced with permission from
"The Fifth Achievement," Robert R. Blake and Jane Srygley Mouton,
Scientific Methods, Vol. 6, Chapter 4, p. 418. Copyright 1970 NTL.

ments such as "Anybody who believes that is nuts," are avoided. Tubbs and
Moss (1983, p. 223) offer four guidelines for implementing the 9,9 style:

☐   Make sure you agree on the use of your terms or definitions.

☐   Build on areas of mutual agreement.

☐   Determine the specific changes necessary for a satisfactory
resolution of the issues.

☐   Avoid personal attacks and stick to the issues.

Charles Osgood (1969) has proposed a theory based on gradual behavior modification, which he calls the GRIT theory. GRIT not only describes
a quality necessary to carry out the program, but also stands for "Graduated
Reciprocation in Tension-Reduction." If both sides in a dispute want to
reduce a conflict, they can do so by setting up a series of gradual steps

toward de-escalation. Two groups of diplomats representing the United States and Russia might decide to take the following actions over a period of months: (1) the release of medical data from space programs, (2) the removal of certain trade and travel restrictions, and (3) the deactivation of an overseas military base. The technique may be applied to any conflict situation and seems practical in that parties would be likely to de-escalate on small issues first to build trust before moving on to more risky issues. This technique seems to have been a part of Dr. Henry Kissinger's famous "shuttle diplomacy" in the early 1970s.

Tannenbaum and Schmidt (1972) proposed that one frequent source of conflict is the leadership struggle between superior and subordinate in decision making. They argue that the leader has to be flexible enough to modify his or her decision-making style to fit the "followership" of the group. Their discussion focuses primarily on the business setting, but the implications are valid for any small group setting in which conflict arises from a leadership struggle. They propose a continuum of decision-making styles that can serve as a model for the leader (in conjunction with the group) so that the group can choose the style that is most appropriate for their situation and that would reduce unnecessary conflict. This model (Fig. 6.10) has also been described as including four styles of decision making: (1) tells, (2) sells, (3) consults, and (4) joins.

A related system of conflict prevention through better decision making includes four other styles: (1) railroading, (2) teaming up, (3) majority vote, and (4) consensus. *Railroading* occurs when one or more group members force their will on the group. This technique is very likely to produce resentment and result in unnecessary conflict. *Teaming up* refers to a situation in which various minority members within a group form a coalition to help each other achieve mutually advantageous goals. This pattern is frequently used in Congress when politicians make trades through which they agree to support each other's bills. This may have short-term success, but may also result in further conflict once the scheme is discovered. *Majority vote* represents the wishes of at least 51 percent of a group's members. However, the remaining minority may be bitterly opposed to the outcome of the decision. This bitterness often results in conflict at a later time. *Consensus* denotes agreement among all members of a group concerning a given decision. Consensus is generally considered to yield the best resolution of conflict in a group decision. Few groups are as concerned as they should be about trying to reach consensus on decisions. Juries represent one of the few types of groups that are required to reach consensus. Those that don't — hung juries — are dismissed. Pfeiffer and Jones offer four relatively simple rules to help group members achieve consensus:

□   Avoid *arguing* for your own individual judgments. Approach the task on the basis of logic.

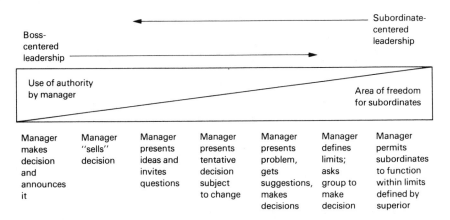

FIGURE 6.10
Continuum of leadership behavior. Reprinted by permission of the Harvard Business Review. An exhibit from "How to Choose a Leadership Pattern" by Robert Tannenbaum and Warren H. Schmidt (March/April 1958). Copyright © 1958 by the President and Fellows of Harvard College; all rights reserved.

□ Avoid changing your mind *only* in order to reach agreement and avoid conflict. Support only solutions with which you are able to agree somewhat, at least.

□ Avoid "conflict-reducing" techniques such as majority vote, averaging, or trading, in reaching your decision.

□ View differences of opinion as helpful rather than as a hindrance in decision making.

Gouran (1969) found that groups that were able to reach consensus better had a greater proportion of "orientation statements" explicitly directing the group toward the achievement of its goal or helping to resolve conflicts. A follow-up study by Kline (1970) reported that orientation statements contained fewer self-referent words and phrases — "I," "me," "my," "I think," and so on — and that highly opinionated statements, which were characteristic of groups that had difficulty reaching consensus, contained more self-referent words.

Conflict resolution seems to improve as we engage in certain types of behaviors. These can be summarized as follows:

1. Focus on the problem, not on personalities.

2. Build on areas of agreement. Most groups have at least some positions or goals that are not mutually exclusive.

3. Attempt to achieve consensus. Try consensus testing by taking a nonbinding straw vote. Then discuss why the minority might be objecting to the decision.

4. Avoid provoking further conflict. Avoid "hitting below the beltline," as one book puts it (Bach and Wyden 1968, p. 80).

5. Don't overreact to the comments of others. Extreme statements on either side tend to destroy consensus and produce a "boomerang effect" (Sherif, Sherif, and Nebergall 1965).

6. Consider compromise. This is often the best way to go from a win-lose to a win-win situation.

While these are not hard-and-fast rules, and they may not work in all cases, they should improve a group's chances of keeping conflict at a manageable level so that the group can move forward toward its goal.

THE SYSTEMS PERSPECTIVE

In this chapter we have examined the very difficult task of improving our ability to make decisions. Most untrained groups do not follow a disciplined path toward a decision. Instead, we frequently find ourselves either off the track or bogged down in conflicts that keep us from accomplishing a task. The focus in this chapter has been biased toward problem-solving groups. However, other types of groups also have to make decisions and deal with conflicts. Certainly these issues arise for families, learning groups (as we saw in the Hamilton case at the beginning of this chapter), social groups planning events, and work groups solving organizational problems. Conflict, too, is present in each of these types of groups.

It is probably apparent by now that the decision-making process in most groups can be improved. In this chapter we examined seven alternative problem-solving strategies: (1) the reflective thinking process; (2) the Kepner-Tregoe approach; (3) the single question form; (4) brainstorming; (5) incrementalism; (6) mixed scanning; and (7) tacit bargaining. You might want to become familiar enough with all of these methods so that you would be able to use whichever one seems most appropriate for a given problem and a given group. Again, this illustrates the systems principle of *equifinality* in that several alternative methods may be used to reach the same desired end result, namely, the solution to the group's problem.

By now you may have wondered how one *does* decide which of the seven problem-solving strategies to use. Should you use a rational strategy like the reflective thinking process or brainstorming, or should you use incrementalism or tacit bargaining? The systems perspective suggests that the appropriateness of any method will depend on the demands of the specific situation. Therefore we need to be familiar with all the alternatives in order to increase our tool kit of behavioral science "tools."

The rational problem-solving methods work well in most cases, but seem particularly suited to an autonomous group trying to satisfy its own needs while being allowed to do so by a democratic leader. By comparison, governmental groups are not autonomous and must answer to the taxpayers. Thus incrementalism may be appropriate, since major changes may be demanded without the luxury of enough time to gather exhaustive amounts of data on the problem. It's a little like the old story that when you are up to your hips in a swamp full of alligators, you don't want a systematic estimate of the probability of danger, you want somebody to throw you a rope!

Tacit bargaining seems to be primarily appropriate in the mixed-motive situations we described earlier. Notice the assumptions and viewpoints expressed in the following quotations. Karrass (1970, p. 4), in his book on negotiating, writes, "In a successful negotiation both parties gain, but more often than not one party wins more than the other." In a similar vein, Korda (1975, p. 4) writes, "No matter who you are, the basic truth is that your interests are nobody else's concern, your gain is inevitably someone else's loss, your failure someone else's victory." The viewpoint expressed in these two quotations indicates some of the attitudes and values relevant to the mixed-motive situation. These statements also describe the outcomes or consequences of bargaining types of problem-solving situations. Obviously, these types of competitive situations suggest very different communication behaviors and skills than would the encounter group, which stresses trust, mutual self-disclosure and risk taking. (Recall the Rogers article at the end of Chapter 5.) Thus the demands of the situation will play a great part in suggesting which problem-solving strategy we will want to employ.

The second part of this chapter dealt with conflict and conflict resolution. It should be emphasized that conflict may have some desirable consequences for the group. However, conflict that gets out of control may be destructive. Also, conflict between different ideas is usually more productive than conflict between personalities.

In terms of personality and its relation to conflict, we would expect more conflict-producing behaviors from those high in aggression, dominance, and need for autonomy. Conversely, we would expect less conflict and more conflict-resolving attempts from those high in need for affiliation and nurturance. Other background factors that would probably relate to conflict include the degree of differences or heterogeneity in group members' ages, sex, values, attitudes, and beliefs. Consistency theories would lead us to believe that the greater and more numerous these differences, the greater the group conflict and the lower the satisfaction level resulting from the discussions.

Perhaps one of the most important factors related to conflict is the style of leadership and the resulting group norms regarding conflict. In this chapter we examined Blake and Mouton's (1970) Conflict Grid and Tannenbaum and Schmidt's (1972) tells, sells, consults, and joins model. Both of these models seem to suggest practical methods for developing some leadership expertise in resolving conflicts.

The readings for this chapter both deal with conflict and conflict resolution, since this seems to be such a difficult issue for most groups to deal with.

Exercises

1. Problem-Solving Discussion Assignment

Each group should decide on a topic and should formulate a discussion question that cannot be answered yes or no. A sample question would be: "What can be done about the problem of current marijuana laws?" This form of discussion question is preferable, since it poses a problem to be answered by the group. A less desirable discussion question would be: "Should marijuana be decriminalized?" Notice that this question can be answered yes or no and is less open-ended and therefore less helpful in prompting discussion.

Each group may want to gather some preliminary information on the topic. (This is optional.) Select a moderator and work up an agenda for your discussion, including the following:

  a) Define the nature and limits of the problem. *Analyze* causes and important aspects of the problem.
  b) Determine the criteria by which to judge an acceptable solution to the problem.
  c) Identify several alternative solutions to the problem.
  d) Decide which is the best solution (based on the criteria you have identified).
  e) How might this solution be implemented?

The discussion will be approximately 30 minutes long. Moderators will be responsible for introducing and concluding the discussion as well as for moving the group along their agenda.

As a guide, you may want to review the following questions, which show in greater detail the various issues to be encountered at each phase of the agenda. Application of this pattern depends upon such factors as:

  a) Whether the discussion is one of fact, value, or policy
  b) The general scope of the problem
  c) The amount of time available
  d) The knowledge of the participants

I. Problem Phase

  a) *Identification of problem area, including questions:*
  1. What is the situation in which the problem is occurring?
  2. What in general is the difficulty?
  3. How did this difficulty arise?
  4. What is the importance of the difficulty?
  5. What limitations, if any, are there on the area of our concern?
  6. What is the meaning of any terms that need clarifying?

b) *Analysis of the difficulty:*
1. What, specifically, are the facts of the situation?
2. What, specifically, are the difficulties?

c) *Analysis of causes:*
1. What is causing the difficulties?
2. What is causing the causes?

II. Criteria Phase
a) What are the principal requirements of the solution?
b) What limitations must be placed on the solution?
c) What is the relative importance of the criteria?

III. Solution Phase
a) *What are the possible solutions?*
1. What is the exact nature of each solution?
2. How would it remedy the difficulty? by eliminating the cause? by off-setting the effect? by a combination of both?

b) *How good is each solution?*
1. How well would it remedy the difficulty?
2. How well would it satisfy the criteria? Are there any that it would not satisfy?
3. Would there by any unfavorable consequences? any extra benefits?

c) *Which solution appears to be best?*
1. How would you rank the solution?
2. Would some combination of solutions be best?

IV. Implementation Phase
What steps would be taken to put the solution into effect?

2. Adjunct of Exercise 1
In conjunction with Exercise 1, some members of the class may want to fill out the evaluation forms (Figs. 6.11 and 6.12) on the discussion group. These forms can serve as the basis of a postdiscussion feedback session by which the group can analyze its own strengths and weaknesses in conducting their assignment.

3. Brainstorming Exercise
Utilizing the rules for brainstorming given in Chapter 6, try to answer the following question: How can we limit growth in population, industrial productivity, pollution, and use of natural resources in such a way as to ensure the preservation of the human race?

For further practice, try brainstorming other topics for further brainstorming practice discussions.

4. Conflict Resolution Exercise: "Win as Much as You Can"

Directions   For ten successive rounds you and your partner will choose either an *X* or a *Y*. The "payoff" for each round is dependent upon the pattern of choices made in your cluster.

Strategy   You are to confer with your partner on each round and make a joint decision. Before rounds 5, 8, and 10 you confer with the other dyads in your cluster.

Judge's Evaluation Report on the Leader

Name of leader _____

Evaluator _____

Assign for each criterion one of the following ratings:

5—Superior
4—Excellent
3—Average
2—Below average
1—Poor

Criteria	Rating
1. *Attitude.* Impartiality, fairness; ability to help group maintain discussion attitude.	_____
2. *Knowledge.* Understanding of the problem. Knowledge of discussion method.	_____
3. *Thinking.* Ability to think quickly, to see relationships.	_____
4. *Introducing.* Skill in getting the discussion off to a good start.	_____
5. *Speaking.* Ability to express ideas clearly, rephrase unclear contributions.	_____
6. *Guiding.* Ability to keep discussion "on the track"; maintain progress; make internal summaries.	_____
7. *Regulating.* Ensuring evenness of contribution, maintaining equanimity.	_____
8. *Ending.* Summarizing group effect.	_____

General comments

FIGURE 6.11
Judge's evaluation report on the *leader.*

Instructions for participants

1. This is a learning exercise. In it, there are ten rounds and there are other teams with which you are playing.
2. The purpose of the exercise is to win as much as you can.
3. When the timekeeper says, "Begin round 1," your team will decide on its vote for the first round. Your vote may be either X or Y, and should be reported secretly on a small piece of paper. The payoff for each round will be determined by how your team's vote is related to the votes of all the other teams. The payoff possibilities are shown at the top of the tally sheet (Fig. 6.13).
4. When all votes are collected, the timekeeper will announce the total vote but *will not* disclose how each individual team voted.

Judge's Evaluation Report on the Participants

Name of participant _____

Evaluator _____

Assign the participant for each criterion one of the following ratings:

5 — Superior
4 — Excellent
3 — Average
2 — Below average
1 — Poor

Criteria	*Rating*
1. *Attitude.* Objectivity, open-mindedness; willingness to modify views in light of new evidence.	_____
2. *Knowledge.* Information on the problem.	_____
3. *Thinking.* Analysis, ability to reason about the problem.	_____
4. *Listening.* Ability to understand and interpret view of others.	_____
5. *Speaking.* Ability to communicate ideas clearly and effectively; adaptation to the speaking situation.	_____
6. *Consideration for others.* Tact, courtesy, cooperation, evenness of contribution.	_____

General comments

FIGURE 6.12
Judge's evaluation report on *participants.*

5. As shown on the tally sheet, you will have two minutes to cast your vote for the first round. For all the other rounds, you will have one minute to cast your vote except for Rounds 5, 7, and 10, which are bonus rounds.
6. During each bonus round your team will select as many representatives as it wishes to send to a meeting of the teams. The representatives from all teams will then meet separately for three minutes to discuss their strategy.
7. After the representatives have met, your team will then have one minute to make its final decision about your vote. At the end of each round, when all the votes are in, you will be told the total outcome of the vote (2 *X*'s, 2 *Y*'s, or 4 *Y*'s, and so on).
8. There are three key rules to keep in mind.
   a) You are not to talk to the other teams or signal them in any way. You may communicate with them but only during Rounds 5, 7, and 10 through your representatives.

	Strategy						
Round	Time allowed	Confer with	Choice	$ Won	$ Lost	$ Balance	
1	2 min.	partner					
2	1 min.	partner					
3	1 min.	partner					
4	1 min.	partner					
5	3 min. + 1 min.	cluster partner					Bonus round: pay is multiplied by 3
6	1 min.	partner					
7	1 min.	partner					
8	3 min. + 1 min.	cluster partner					Bonus round: pay is multiplied by 5
9	1 min.	partner					
10	3 min. + 1 min.	cluster partner					Bonus round: pay is multiplied by 10

FIGURE 6.13
"Win as Much as You Can" tally sheet.

b) All members of your team should agree on your team's vote or at least be willing to go along with it.

c) Your team's vote must be reported on a small slip of paper when it is called for at the end of each round.

4 X's:	Lose	$1.00 each
3 X's:	Win	$1.00 each
1 Y:	Lose	$3.00
2 X's:	Win	$2.00 each
2 Y's:	Lose	$2.00 each
1 X:	Win	$3.00
3 Y's:	Lose:	$1.00 each
4 Y's:	Win	$1.00 each

5. Conflict Resolution Exercise: "The Babysitter Case"

Mr. and Mrs. Todd have been using Paula Moore (age 17) as their regular baby-sitter ever since their son Brad was born two years ago. Paula has always been competent and responsible while in the Todd's home. The Todds have a policy that Paula is not to have any visitors while she is babysitting. This is consistent with the policies of other families in the neighborhood where Paula lives and babysits.

Paula babysat for the Todds on Saturday night and everything seemed routine. However, the next morning Mr. Todd's neighbor from across the street told him that two young men and Paula's 16-year-old sister had arrived in a customized van the night before, and the three young people hand gone into the Todd's house. The neighbor couldn't say how long the three had been in the house, since he had left shortly after they arrived.

Mr. Todd checked with another neighbor and had the story confirmed. The second neighbor said that the three people had been in the Todds' house. He also added, "We don't use the Moore girls anymore for our kids. They are too boy crazy."

The Todds became quite upset, since this appeared to be a clear violation of their no-visitor policy for their babysitters.

The situation is further complicated by the fact that Paula lives only a few houses down the street from the Todds and Mr. Moore (Paula's father) works in the same office with Mr. Todd. Thus the Todd and Moore families are in the same neighborhood group and Mr. Todd and Mr. Moore are in the same work group. What should the Todds do?

OVERVIEW OF READINGS

Probably one of the most troublesome issues in small group interaction is how to resolve conflicts. In the first article David W. Johnson elaborates on the same point discussed in Chapter 6 — that conflict isn't all bad. However, trying to change conflict from a destructive to a constructive force in group activities takes some doing.

While Johnson introduces the subject, the second article offers a method for improving conflict-reduction skills. Robert R. Blake and Jane S. Mouton have applied their idea of a two-dimensional grid to a number of significant problems in the behavioral sciences. In the second article, they show how conflict can be managed using the grid approach. Both articles provide a useful extension of the ideas presented in Chapter 6.

The Constructive Use of Conflict

David W. Johnson

INTRODUCTION

There can be no doubt that the area of conflict management and resolution is one of the most important areas in social psychology. Many of the difficulties individuals have in working and living together center around their destructive management of interpersonal conflicts. Within our society there are serious problems which may lead to a major armed conflict among ethnic groups and create difficulties between men and women, the older generation and the youth of our society, and advocates of the developing counterculture and protectors of the status quo. War between countries is still an ever-present reality.

In this century wars have grown more and more disastrous. World War I killed 12 million in battle. World War II cost 21 million lives in battle and 15 million more in air raids. One B-52 bomber now carries in a normal payload more explosive power than all the shells and bombs of World War II. A Third World War might kill all life over large areas and conceivably make the whole planet uninhabitable. Even during nominal peace, tests and experiments with nuclear weapons have already distributed in the atmosphere, in plants, and in the bodies of animals radioactive iodine, strontium 90, and plutonium, imperiling present and future generations. President John F. Kennedy warned:

> Today every inhabitant of this planet must contemplate the day when this planet may no longer be habitable. Every man, woman, and child lives

---

under a nuclear sword of Damocles, hanging by the slenderest of threads, capable of being cut at any moment by accident, or miscalculation, or madness.

In his Inaugural Address Kennedy spoke of two powerful groups of nations, "both racing to alter that uncertain balance of terror that stays the hand of mankind's final war." A similar theme was expressed by a Harvard psychologist, Henry A. Murray (1960, p. 12):

> A war that no one wants, an utterly disgraceful end to man's long experiment on earth is a possibility we are facing every day. Events are hanging by a thread, depending on an accident, or some finger on a trigger, on a game of wits and tricks, or pride and saving faces.

As a species, man is standing in a maze of conflicts between nations, religions, ethnic groups, and generations, any one of which could start World War III. For the last twenty years or so man has had the technology and raw materials literally to destroy every living thing upon the earth. This technological capacity has made war and other forms of violence obsolete as a means of resolving conflicts. Yet the basic answer to conflict situations seems to be "kill" or "repress by force." If man as a species is to survive, he must learn how to handle conflicts constructively. Perhaps the most important question facing the world today is whether or not man can do so.

Imagine yourself to be a visitor from another planet, engaged in a field study of man. You are to make a prediction about how successful man will be in handling future conflicts. You survey his technological capacities for self-destruction, his stockpiles of weapons; you look at his past and present behavior in conflict situations; then you make a prediction about his survival. What would your prediction be? Lorenz (1963, p. 49) says the following:

> An unprejudiced observer from another planet, looking upon man as he is today, in his hand the atom bomb, the product of his intelligence, in his heart the aggressive drive inherited from his anthropoid ancestors, which this same intelligence cannot control, would not prophesy long life for the species.

> We approach a crossroad at which we either educate ourselves, allies and enemies alike, in the nature of human behavior, using this knowledge to promote future behavior, or we continue along a road leading to the extinction of our species. And this, in the evolutionary view, will be about as significant as the extinction of the ichthyosaur.

THE NATURE OF CONFLICT

To understand the nature of conflicts it is necessary to define what a conflict is, to specify its source, and to evaluate its potential functional and dysfunctional consequences. A conflict exists whenever incompatible activities occur (Deutsch 1969); an action which is incompatible with another action prevents, obstructs, interferes with, injures, or in some way makes that action less likely or less effective. The incompatible actions may originate in one person (intra-personal), one group (intragroup), two or more persons (interpersonal), or two or more groups (intergroup). A conflict may arise from several different sources, some of which are (1) differences in information, beliefs, values, interests, or desires, (2) a scarcity of some resource such as money, power, time, space, or position, and (3) rivalries in which one person or group competes with another (Deutsch 1969).

EFFECTIVENESS OF CURRENT CONFLICT MANAGEMENT PROCEDURES

Most of the time, a person's attention is directed towards the failures to manage conflict constructively, not the successes. A strike makes the newspapers, while a peaceful settlement does not. A marriage that ends in divorce is often more attention-attracting than one which continues. Yet with all the apparent failures of constructive conflict management it should not be forgotten that many of our present procedures of conflict management are quite effective. Well over ten thousand labor-management agreements are made each year in the private sector of our economy with only a small percentage resulting in work stoppages. This remarkable success ratio is often lost in the headlines of a major labor dispute and its resulting strike. Most interpersonal conflicts are managed successfully, and most international conflicts are settled without violence. The successful use of bargaining and negotiation as mechanisms of conflict management in our society is widespread. A variety of legal procedures, joint problem-solving efforts, and the creation of third-party roles such as mediator, arbitrator, and ombudsman exist to effectively manage conflict. Yet there are failures. Without taking the obviously simpleminded position that it is not now possible to handle conflict constructively, we want to examine critically the current technology for conflict management.

CONSTRUCTIVE AND DESTRUCTIVE CONFLICT

It is inevitable that you will become involved in conflicts whenever you have a relationship with another person; this may be a personal relationship or a relationship required by a social system of which you are a part (such as a school or a job). A conflict-free relationship is probably a sign that you really have no relationship at all, not that you have a good relationship. The number of conflicts you and the other person have will vary from relationship to relationship, but even the most friendly relationships have times when conflicts appear.

Despite the inevitability of conflicts, there seems to be a general feeling in our society that conflicts are bad and should be avoided and that a good relationship is one in which there are no conflicts. Many discussions of conflict cast it in the role of causing divorces, separations, psychological distress, violence, social disorder, and even war. There is a growing recognition, however, that it is the failure of individuals to handle their conflicts in constructive ways which leads to the destruction of relationships, not the mere presence of conflict. It is through the resolution of conflicts that most construct problem solving is initiated; when conflict is handled constructively, it can lead to increased closeness and a higher quality of relationship. Many individuals seek out conflicts through such activities as competitive sports and games, movies, plays, books, and teasing. Conflicts are often of personal value, leading to personal change, growth, creativeness and curiosity. Learning how to manage your conflicts constructively may lead to increased self-confidence, greater willingness to take risks in increasing the quality of your relationships, and greater ability to handle stress and difficulty.

A superficial reading of many social psychological theories which emphasize tension reduction, dissonance reduction, good balance, and good form would seem to imply that the psychological utopia would be a conflict-free existence (Deutsch 1969). There are many social psychologists, however, who insist that conflict is basically constructive. Howell and Smith (1956) state that any good discussion among individuals is born in conflict and thrives on conflict, but it must be conflict of ideas rather than personalities. Ewbank and Auer (1946) maintain that there is a need for differences of opinion in any effective problem-solving. Harnack and Fest (1964) state that cooperation does not mean absence of conflict; it does mean absence of conflict to block individuals and the vigorous presence of conflict intended to explore ideas. Cooley (1918) states that the more one thinks of it, the more he will see that conflict and cooperation are not separable things, but phases of one process which always involves something of both. Edward Ross (1920) stated that the good side of opposition is that it stimulates. Simmel (1955) notes several positive functions of conflict: (1) it tends to create order within the group by promoting structure, that is, some form of organized hierarchy, (2) it acts as a cohesive agent upon the group, (3) it may establish communication where before there was none, and (4) it may be an indication of group stability since the more intimate and secure the group, the more intense the conflict and the greater its frequency. Pettelle (1964) states that the proper function of conflict in a discussion is to encourage inquiry, to promote objectivity, and to sharpen analysis. It also stimulates interest and concern and is a sign that interest and concern exist in the relationship. Deutsch (1971) states that his major assumption is that conflict is potentially of personal and social value.

The point of balance is very delicate between conflict that is managed so that it produces growth and conflict that is managed so that it produces disruption and incapacitation. Conflict in a social system which is handled destructively can lead to the destruction of the system; the absence of conflict in a social system can lead to stagnation. Humanistic social psychologists believe that conflict is a natural and desirable part of any relationship. If one is involved with another person and concerned about the growth of the relationship, conflicts are probably inevitable. Conflict is an inherent element in almost all social interactions. Simmell (1957, p. 195) for example, stated:

> An absolutely . . . harmonious group . . . not only is empirically unreal, it could show no real life process. The society of saints which Dante sees in the Rose of Paradise may be like such a group, but it is without any change and development; whereas the holy assembly of Church Fathers in Raphael's Disputa shows, if not actual conflict, at least a considerable differentiation of moods and direction of thought, whence flow all the vitality and the really organic structure of that group.

Conflict is a natural part of being alive and functioning in an environment which consists of other individuals. Being involved with the environment, society, other persons, and oneself provides one with continuing sources of conflict which must be managed effectively in order to become an actualized, fulfilled, and joyful person.

There are three approaches for differentiating between a constructive and a destructive conflict. The first two involve criteria by which the outcomes of a conflict can be judged to be constructive or destructive. Thus Deutsch (1971) states that a conflict has productive consequences if the participants all are satisfied with their outcomes and feel that they have gained as a result of the conflict; a conflict has destructive consequences if the participants are dissatisfied with their outcomes and feel that they have lost as a result of the conflict; finally, a conflict whose outcomes are satisfying to all of the participants will be more constructive than one which is satisfying to some and dissatisfying to others. Deutsch's approach to defining constructive and destructive conflicts is to focus upon the psychological state of the participants after the conflict is resolved. Another approach is to specify criteria by which the outcomes of conflict can be labeled constructive or destructive; thus, if a conflict resulted in increased commitment to a relationship, in higher self-esteem by the participants, in a closer, more loving relationship, or in greater efficiency in work, the conflict is defined as constructive, while if the conflict resulted in disruption, alienation, separation, and decreased efficiency, it would be defined as destructive. The third approach to determining the constructiveness or destructiveness of a conflict is to apply criteria to the process of handling the conflict before the outcomes are known. Thus, when a conflict becomes a cooperative problem-solving situation characterized by mutual understanding, accurate and complete communication, and a trusting attitude, the conflict is defined as being constructive, when a conflict becomes a win-lose situation characterized by misperceptions, inaccurate and incomplete communication, and distrustful attitudes, the conflict is defined as being destructive.

The Fifth Achievement

Robert R. Blake
Jane Srygley Mouton

A great new challenge to the American way of conducting its national life is taking shape. Conformity with older patterns is breaking down. Yet creative definitions of new patterns are not forthcoming, or at best are coming at a snail's pace. Unless the challenge of finding new patterns that can serve to strengthen society is successfully met, some of the nation's most cherished human values may very well be sacrificed. If we can meet it, however, our deeply embedded beliefs as to the role of men in society may not only be reinforced but may find even richer and more extensive applications in the society of tomorrow.

What is this challenge?

We widely acknowledge the objective of an open and free society based on individual responsibility and self-regulated participation by all in the conduct of national life. That men will differ in the ways they think and act is accepted as both inevitable and desirable. Indeed, this is one hallmark of an open society. Differences are intrinsically valuable. They provide the rich possibility that alternatives and options will be discovered for better and poorer ways of responding to any particular situation. Preserving the privilege of having and expressing differences increases our chances of finding "best" solutions to the many dilemmas that arise in living. They also add the spice of variety and give zest to human pursuits.

When it is possible for a man to make a choice from among several solutions, and when he can make this choice without infringing upon another man's freedom or requiring his cooperation, there is genuine autonomy. This is real freedom.

But in many situations not every man can have his own personal solution. When cooperation and coordination are required in conducting national life — in government, business, the university, agencies of the community, the home, and so on — differences that arise must find reconciliation. A solution must be agreed upon and embraced which can provide a pattern to which those involved are prepared to conform their behavior. Yet efforts to reconcile differences in order to achieve consensus-based patterns of conduct often only serve to promote difficulties. When disagreements as to sound bases for action can be successfully resolved, freedom can be retained and necessary solutions implemented. Dealing with the many and varied misunderstandings that are inevitable in a society dedicated to preserving the privilege of having and expressing differences is the challenge. As individuals, we find this hard to do. As members of organized groups, we appear to find it even more difficult.

FOUR CLASSICAL SOLUTIONS FOR RESOLVING CONFLICTS

In the conduct of society there are at least four major and different kinds of formal, structural arrangements which we rely on for resolving differences. They are the scientific method; politics; law, with its associated police powers; and organizational hierarchy.

Of undisputed value in finding the objective solution to which agreement can readily be given are the methods of science. A well-designed experiment confirms which of several alternatives is the most valid basis of explanation while simultaneously demonstrating the unacceptability of the remaining explanation.

Our political mechanisms are based on the one-man-one-vote approach to problem solving. This provides for the resolution of differences according to a weighting approach, and the basis is usually that the majority prevail. By this means, decisions can be made and actions taken even though differences may remain. Simply being outvoted, however, does not aid those on the losing side in changing their intellectual and emotional attitudes. While it ensures that a solution is chosen, the fact that it is often on a win-lose or a compromise basis may pose further problems when those who are outvoted resolve to be the winners of the future. Often the underlying disagreements are deepened.

Legal mechanisms apply only in resolving differences when questions of law are involved and other means of reaching agreement usually have met with failure. With application of associated police powers, the use of force is available to back up legal mechanisms when law is violated. But this constitutes a far more severe solution to the problem. The ultimate failure of law which invites the use of military power is in effect a court of last resort.

Within society's formal institutions such as business, government, education, and the family, organizational heirarchy, or rank, can and does permit the resolution of differences. The premise is that when a disagreement arises between any two persons of differing rank, the one of higher rank can impose a solution unilaterally based on his position. In the exercise of authority, suppression may also sacrifice the validity of a solution, since there is no intrinsic basis of truth in the idea that simply because a man is the boss of other men he is ordained with an inherent wisdom. While this arrangement provides a basis for avoiding indecision and impasse, it may and often does have the undesirable

consequence of sacrificing the support of those to whom it is applied for the solution of the problem, to say nothing of its adverse effects on future creativity.

These classical solutions to dealing with differences — science, politics, law
and hierarchy — represent real progress in learning to conduct the national life.
Where it can be applied, scientific method provides a close to ideal basis for
resolving differences. That politics, courts of justice, and organizational hierarchy, though more limited, are necessary is indisputable. But that they are
being questioned and increasingly rejected is also indisputable. Even if they
were not, none of these alone nor all of them together provide a sound and
sufficient basis for the development of a truly problem-solving society.

WHAT IS THE FIFTH ACHIEVEMENT?

There is another essential ingredient. It is sharply increased understanding by
every man of the roots of conflict and the human skills of gaining the resolution of differences. The acquisition of such insight and skill by every man
could provide a social foundation for reaching firm and sound understandings
on a direct man-to-man basis of the inevitable disagreements that arise in
conducting the national life. This kind of deepened skill in the direct resolution
of differences could do much to provide a realistic prospect that the antago-
nisms, cleavages, or injustices real and imagined in society today can be
reduced if not eliminated. It offers the promise that the sicknesses of alienation
and apathy, the destructive aggressions, and the organization-man mentality
can be healed.

The Fifth Achievement, then, is in the establishment of a problem-solving
society where differences among men are subject to resolution through insights that permit protagonists themselves to identify and implement solutions
to their differences upon the basis of committed agreement. That men ultimately will be able to work out, face to face, their differences is a hoped-for
achievement of the future. Extending their capacity to do so could reduce the
number of problems brought before the bench or dealt with through hierarchy.
At the same time, scientific and political processes could be strengthened if
progress were made in this direction. Even more important, it could perhaps
lead to the resolution of many conflicts on a local level that block the development of a creative and committed problem-solving community. Success in
meeting this challenge in the period ahead is perhaps the surest way to
preserve and strengthen the values of a free society while protecting and even
strengthening the privilege of having and expressing differences.

HOW TO INCREASE SKILL IN MANAGING CONFLICT

Why do men rely on these other four approaches to conflict settlement while
placing lower value on the resolution of differences in a direct, man-to-man
way? One explanation for this might be that they do not hold in concert a
conceptual basis for analyzing situations of disagreement and their causes. It
should be said that conceptual understanding, while necessary for strengthening behavior, is clearly not in itself a sufficient basis for learning the skills of
sound resolution of conflict. Personal entrapment from self-deception about
one's motivations is too great. Insensitivity about one's behavior and the
reactions of others to it is too extensive. To connect a conceptual analysis to
one's own behavior and conduct in ways that permit insight and change seems
to require something more in the way of personal learning.

Classroom learning methodologies that could enable men to gain insights regarding conflict and acquire skills for resolving it seem to be impoverished. To aid men in acquiring both the conceptual understanding for managing conflict and the skills to see their own reactions in situations of conflict, man-to-man feedback seems to be an essential condition. A variety of situations involving laboratory learning that permit this have been designed (Bach and Wyden 1969; Blake and Mouton 1968; Bradford, Gibb, and Benne 1964; Schein and Bennis 1965). They set the stage for men to learn to face their differences and find creative and valid solutions to their problems.

Success in mastering this Fifth Achievement will undoubtedly require reconception of the classroom in ways that permit the study of conflict as a set of concepts and the giving and receiving of feedback in ways that enable men to see how to strengthen their own capacities and skills for coping with it directly.

CONCEPTUAL ANALYSIS OF CONFLICT

This paper concentrates upon a first step toward this Fifth Achievement by presenting a conceptual basis for analyzing situations of conflict. The Conflict Grid [Fig. 6.9 in the text] is a way of identifying basic assumptions when men act in situations where differences are present, whether disagreement is openly expressed or silently present (Blake and Mouton 1964; Blake, Shepard, and Mouton 1964).

Whenever a man meets a situation of conflict, he has at least two basic considerations in mind. One of these is the *people* with whom he is in disagreement. Another is *production of results,* or getting a resolution to the disagreement. It is the amount and kind of emphasis he places on various combinations of each of these elements that determine his thinking in dealing with conflict.

Basic attitudes toward people and toward results are visualized on nine-point scales. These form the Grid in [Fig. 6.9]. The nine-point scale representing concern for producing a result provides the horizontal axis for the Grid. The phrase "concern for" does not show results produced but rather denotes the degree of emphasis in his thinking that the man places on getting results. The *1* end represents low concern, and the *9* represents the highest possible concern. The same applies on the vertical or concern-for-people axis. Considering the interactions of these two scales, there are 81 possible positions. Each describes an intersection between the two dimensions.

The following pages discuss strategies of managing conflict according to the five basic theories — those appearing at the four corners and the center of the figure. When these basic styles are understood, one can predict for each how a man operating under that style is likely to handle conflict. There are eight additional important theories composed from various mixtures of these five, but basic issues of conflict resolution can be seen in dealing with these "pure" theories.

No one style is exclusively characteristic of one man in comparison with another, although one style may be dominant in a man's actions. Furthermore, even though one may be dominant for a time, it may be abandoned and replaced by another when the first has been ineffective in achieving resolution.

What are some of the ways of dealing with conflict?

Conflict can be controlled by overpowering it and suppressing one's adversary (9,1 in the lower right corner of the Grid). An ultimate expression of this is in the extremes of police power and military action. Extracting compliance by authority-obedience is possible when rank is present. The conflict can be cut off and suppressed in this way, "Yours not to question why!" When rank is not available, a win-lose basis expresses the same set of assumptions. Winning for one's own position predominates over seeking valid solution.

Another strategy is to smooth conflict by cajolery, by letting a man know that with a little patience he will find that all is right (1,9 in the upper left corner). The assumption of sweetness and light often leads to resolution by people's retracting from previously held positions, preferring personal acceptance to solution validity. This can promote accord and harmony, but it sacrifices conviction and insight into differences, while decreasing the likelihood of achieving valid solutions. Staying out of situations that provoke controversy or turning away from topics that promote disagreement represents a set of assumptions about how to live in a conflict-free way (1,1 in the lower left corner). Then one need not be stirred up even though the issue may need resolution. A man can remain composed if he does not let himself be drawn into controversy; he avoids it by remaining neutral. This kind of "see no disagreement, hear no disagreement, and speak no disagreement" represents a withdrawal from social responsibility in a world where the resolution of differences is key to finding sound solutions. It is the ultimate in alienation.

A third set of assumptions leads to a middle-of-the-road solution to differences through accommodation and adjustment. Disagreement is settled through bargaining a compromise solution (5,5). The assumptions underlying compromising of one's convictions are at the root of this approach. It means agreeing so as to be agreeable, even to sacrificing sound action; settling for what you can get rather than working to get what is sound in the light of the best available facts and data.

The mental attitude behind the one-man-one-vote approach often leads to the endorsement of positions calculated to get majority support even though this means giving up a solution of deeper validity. The same assumptions often prevail behind the scenes in out-of-court settlements.

Outside the sphere of industrial management, solutions to major political and international problems of recent years provide classic examples of 5,5 splitting. One is the "separate but equal" approach to solving what is seen as the race problem. The cessation of hostilities in Korea by the establishment of the thirty-eighth parallel as a line of demarcation between North and South in the early Fifties is another. This set a precedent for setting up the "Demilitarized Zone" between North and South Vietnam. The Berlin Wall is probably the most significant symbol of the East-West split. The 5,5 attitude is reflected daily by news reporters and commentators who quote "unidentified but high-level sources" or hide their sources by attributing their facts merely to "usually reliable sources."

Under a 9,9 approach, disagreement is valued as an inevitable result of the fact that strong-minded people have convictions about what is right. A man says, "Nothing is sacrosanct. What are the facts? What are the causes? What are the conclusions?" Reservations and emotions that interrupt agreement based on logic and data are confronted through candid discussion of them directly with the person involved in the disagreement. Insight and resolution are possible but involve maturity and real human skill. This approach may be time-consuming in the short run but time-conserving over the long term. It permits men to disagree, to work out their disagreements in the light of facts, and ultimately to understand one another. Such problem-solving constructiveness in conflict situations is the fundamental basis for realizing the Fifth Achievement.

CONFLICT, CONFORMITY, AND CREATIVE PROBLEM SOLVING

How does effective conflict management interrelate with other social processes of seemingly equal or greater significance in strengthening society? Indeed, it might be maintained that the challenge to society seen today is in nonconformity with its norms, rather than in faulty management of conflict.

In what ways are conflict and conformity interdependent (Blake and Mouton 1961)? Men in everyday life do conform to the expectations of others and the patterns of their institutions. This readiness to conform reduces conflict and is what permits regularity, order, and predictability. To adhere to common norms provides a basis for organized effort. From conformity with conventionalized social and organizational practices can come a sense of identification, belonging, and esprit de corps. On the other hand, failure to conform may stir conflict with one's colleagues and associates so that the nonconformist is rejected. Indeed, anxiety about rejection can be so overwhelming that, for many, conformity becomes an end in itself rather than a means to cooperation through interdependence. Under these circumstances, the capacity to challenge outmoded traditions, precedents, and past practices is lost. With sound ways of approaching and resolving conflict, outmoded patterns can successfully be challenged and upgraded by replacement of them with agreements which themselves can promote problem solving and creativity. In this way, finding new and better ways to accomplish personal, organizational, national, and perhaps even international objectives becomes possible.

Just stimulating people to challenge and contest status quo conformities, however, is likely to do little more than provoke disagreement and controversy, increase polarization, and ultimately end in win-lose, impasse, compromise, or chaos. Yet the status quo requirements must continuously be challenged in a problem-solving and creative way, not in a manner that pits man against man to see who can win or, even worse, in a way that ends in anarchy.

The Conflict Grid is useful in seeing the more subtle connections among conflict and conformity and creative problem solving. Conformity to the 9,1 authority-obedience demands that are involved in hierarchical rank is exemplified by the boss, teacher, or parent who gives the orders to subordinates, students, or children who are expected to obey. The exercise of initiative which produces differences is equivalent to insubordination. Conformity under 9,1 may produce the protocol of surface compliance, but the frustrations of those who are suppressed are often evident. Ways of striking back against the boss, teacher, or parent appear. Such acts may be open ones of resistance and rebellion or disguised ones of sabotage, cheating, or giving agreement without following through. Each of these in a certain sense involves reverse creativity, where ingenuity is exercised in attacking or "beating" the system. It is creativity in resentment of the system, not in support of it.

In another type of conformity, the rules of relationship are, "Don't say anything if you can't say something nice" (1,9). Togetherness, social intimacy, and warmth engendered by yielding one's convictions in the interests of personal acceptance are certainly objectionable solutions in a society where having and expressing differences is relied on as the basis for finding sound courses of action. It can produce a quorum of agreement but smother creative problem solving in sweetness and love. The kind of disagreement that might provoke resentment is avoided. The opportunity for creative problem solving to emerge is absent.

Another kind of conformity relates to adhering to the form and not to the substance of life. Here people conform by going through the motions expected of them, treadmilling through the days, months, and years (1,1). In this way, survival is accomplished by being visible without being seen.

Organization-man conformity (5,5) entails positively embracing the status quo with minimum regard for the soundless of status quo requirements. Yet, even here, as new problems arise, differences appear and disagreements become evident. There are several kinds of 5,5 actions that on shallow estimation may give the appearance of approaching problems from an altered, fresh, and original point of view. Pseudo-creativity may be seen when new approaches, even though they constitute only small departures from the outmoded past, are recommended on the basis of their having been tried elsewhere. Under these circumstances a man is forwarding actions taken by others rather than promoting examination of actions on the basis of his own convictions. In this way, he can suggest, while avoiding the challenge or rejection of his own convictions. Deeper examination of 5,5 behavior leads to the conclusion that imitation rather than innovation is the rule.

In other instances, solutions which are proposed as compromise positions can give the impression of "flexibility" in thought. When adjustment and accommodation, backing and filling, twisting and turning, shifting and adapting take place in the spirit of compromise, the motivation behind them is usually to avoid interpersonal emotions resulting from confrontation. Behaving in this manner is a reaction to disagreement, and it means that personal validity is being eroded.

Flexibility is a highly valued component in mature and effective behavior. But is it not contradictory to advocate flexibility on the one hand and to forewarn against compromise on the other? This question is important to clarify.

Flexibility calls for deliberate examination of options and alternatives. It means having back-up tactics that permit swift resolution of unforeseen circumstances, a climate that permits people to move back and forth and in and out from one situation to another, but based on facts, data, and logic of the situation as it unfolds. These are the characteristics of creative problem solving that permit gains to be made as opportunities arrive; that permit opportunities to be created, threats to be anticipated, and risks that result when people fail to react to be reduced.

Thus there are actions to adjust a difference to keep peace and actions to adjust to altered circumstances for better results. It is most important to distinguish between the two kinds. Flexibility for better results is likely to have a stamp of 9,9 on it; "flexibility" to keep peace by avoiding clash of personalities is in the 5,5 area. One is enlivening and promotes creativity. The other leads to the perpetuation of the organization-man mentality of status quo rigidities.

In the final analysis, conformity is to be valued. The problem is to ensure that the thinking of men conforms with sound purposes and premises. Conformity which means adherence to premises of human logic so that decisions reached are furthering growth capacity in sound and fundamental ways is what every individual might be expected to want. It is what man should want in the underpinnings of his daily interactions. It is conformity at this level that promotes the pursuit of creative and innovative solutions. Only when the values of a nation stimulate experimentation and promote a truly constructive attitude toward discovery and innovation is the full potential from creative efforts available as a source of thrust for replacing outmoded status quo conformities with more problem-solving requirements (9,9).

WHAT MEN WANT — TRANSNATIONALLY

Though varying widely in their ways of *actually* dealing with conflict, studies show that leaders in the United States, Great Britain, the Middle and Far East all indicate that they would *prefer* the 9,9 approach of *open confrontation* as the soundest way of managing situations of conflict, particularly under examination (Mouton and Blake 1970). Though extremely difficult, it appears to be the soundest of several possible choices. This is not to imply that every decision should be made by a leader through calling a meeting or obtaining team agreement. Nor for a crisis situation does it imply that a leader should withhold exercising direction. But a 9,9 foundation of interdependence can build a strong basis for an open, problem-solving society in which men can have and express differences and yet be interrelated in ways that promote the mutual respect, common goals, and trust and understanding they must have to achieve results in ways that lead to personal gratification and maturity.

POSSIBILITIES OF THE FIFTH ACHIEVEMENT FOR STRENGTHENING SOCIETY

This challenge to America, the need for men to learn to confront outmoded status quo requirements and to manage to resultant conflict in such ways as to promote creative problem solving, promises much for the decades ahead, if we can meet and master it.

Consider for a moment the possibility of success in mastering this Fifth Achievement. What might it mean?

1. Enriched family life rather than the steady rise in the divorce rate.

2. Sounder child rearing, evidenced in teen-age youngsters capable of expression and action in dealing in a problem-solving rather than a protest way with adults and the institutions of society who are capable of interacting in an equally sound way.

3. The conversion of academic environments from subject-oriented learning centers to ones that expand the capacity of individuals for contributing creatively to the evolving character of society.

4. The betterment of communities in ways that more fully serve human wants.

5. The more rapid integration of minorities into a more just society, with the reduction and eventual elimination of disenfranchised, alienated segments.

6. Fuller and more creative use of human energies in conducting the organizations that serve society.

7. A greater readiness to support and utilize science for approaching problems when evidence, facts, and data come to have an ever greater value as the bases for gaining insight.

8. A strengthening of politics by readiness to advocate positions on the basis of statesmanlike convictions rather than to adopt positions for political expediency.

9. Reliance on knowledge rather than rank in the resolution of differences and disagreements in organization situations.

10. A stronger basis for mind-meeting agreements rather than resorting to legal actions to force a resolution of disputes.

If erosion of social institutions has not already become too great, all of these aims can perhaps be forwarded over time by our classical institutions for settling conflicts. But surely men capable of resolving their conflicts directly would forward human progress with a dramatic thrust — and on a far more fundamental and therefore enduring basis.

If this Fifth Achievement is to be realized, it is likely that greater use of the behavioral sciences may well lie the key to a more rewarding and progressive society in which men can share and evaluate their differences, learn from them, and use conflict as a stepping stone to the greater progress that is possible when differences can be resolved in a direct, face-to-face way.

Will this challenge be met, or will the cherished freedom of having and expressing differences be sacrificed?

NOTES
Bach, R. R., and Wyden, P. *The ultimate enemy.* New York: Morrow, 1969.

Blake, R. R., and Mouton, Jane S. The experimental investigation of interpersonal influence. In A. D. Biderman and H. Zimmer (eds.) *The manipulation of human behavior.* New York: Wiley, 1961.

Blake, R. R., and Mouton, Jane S. *The managerial grid.* Houston: Gulf, 1964.

Blake R. R. and Mouton, Jane S. *Corporate excellence through grid organization development: A systems approach.* Houston: Gulf, 1968.

Blake, R. R., Shepard, H. A., and Mouton, Jane S. *Managing intergroup conflict in industry.* Houston: Gulf, 1964.

Bradford, L. P., Gibb, J. R., and Benne, K. D. (eds.) *T-group theory and laboratory method: Innovation in re-education.* New York: Wiley, 1964.

Mouton, Jane S., and Blake, R. R. Issues in transnational organization development. In B. M. Bass, R. B. Cooper, and J. A. Haas (eds.) *Managing for task accomplishment.* Lexington, Mass.: D. C. Heath, 1970. Pp. 208-224.

Schein, E. H., and Bennis, W. G. (eds.) *Personal and organizational change through group methods: The laboratory approach.* New York: Wiley, 1965.

7

Consequences

THE TUBBS MODEL OF SMALL GROUP INTERACTION

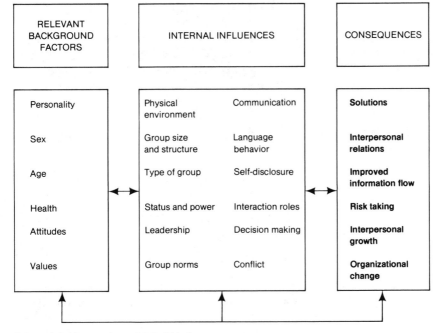

RELEVANT BACKGROUND FACTORS	INTERNAL INFLUENCES		CONSEQUENCES
Personality	Physical environment	Communication	**Solutions**
Sex	Group size and structure	Language behavior	**Interpersonal relations**
Age	Type of group	Self-disclosure	**Improved information flow**
Health	Status and power	Interaction roles	**Risk taking**
Attitudes	Leadership	Decision making	**Interpersonal growth**
Values	Group norms	Conflict	**Organizational change**

Concepts in **boldface** are the emphases of this chapter.

CASE STUDY

Dave King is president of XYZ fraternity, which has 60 members living in the house. The house has room to sleep 75 but membership has declined somewhat in recent years and several rooms in the house are unfilled.

The fraternity house is located near a river that periodically floods its banks. When this happens, one room of the house gets water-soaked. This room has four members residing in it at the present time. These four have put a sign on the door of their room calling themselves the "swamp rats," and labeling the room "the Riverfront Apartment."

Dave and the other fraternity officers (vice-president, treasurer, and house manager) decided in an executive council meeting to use some of the unoccupied rooms in the house by letting the "swamp rats" move to drier quarters. They announced this plan at a chapter meeting on a Tuesday evening. That night, several members went to the "swamp rats' " room to help them move out. The "swamp rats" had barricaded themselves in their room by placing their mattresses against the inside of the locked door. When Dave and the others tried to reason with the "swamp rats" to move out of the water-soaked room, the "swamp rats" opened the door and a fight broke out. The "swamp rats" insisted that they did not want to be evicted from their "riverfront apartment." Now there is a high degree of hard feelings among the fraternity members and two factions have emerged. One group backs the officers, who feel that they were only trying to help. The other group backs the "swamp rats," who feel that the officers are overstepping their authority in trying to move them out of their room.

1. *What should Dave have done differently?*

2. *How would you go about correcting the situation as it now exists?*

W

his case study points to the fact that not all problem-solving attempts have positive outcomes or consequences. Dave King found out the hard way that even well-intentioned leaders sometimes live to see their best efforts backfire. This chapter deals with the potential outcomes or consequences of group interaction. These are sometimes referred to as the *end results*. However, our systems theory perspective reminds us that groups are ongoing and that today's end results are simply the new *inputs* for tomorrow's activities. The consequences of this particular decision eventually led to the deterioration of Dave's effectiveness as fraternity president. The interactions among the fraternity members led to increased polarization between the two factions. This problem eventually resolved itself when the senior class graduated and a river flood control program eliminated the flooding problem altogether. Now the fraternity is troubled with a whole set of new problems, and so it goes with the ongoing cycle of small group events.

After wading through six chapters on small group interaction, you should be able to answer such questions as, "Why use groups anyway? Wouldn't it be easier to just do the job yourself?" Certainly by now you are more aware of the many difficulties and complexities involved with group behavior. Before you throw up your hands and give up, read this chapter. At this time we will begin to elaborate upon the advantages of group interaction by determining the end results or potential consequences of group discussion. In this chapter we will examine six of these end results: (1) solutions to problems, (2) changes in interpersonal relations, (3) improved information flow, (4) increased risk taking, (5) interpersonal growth, and (6) organizational change.

SOLUTIONS TO PROBLEMS

QUALITY OF SOLUTIONS

A clear result of small group research is that groups have the potential to make better-quality decisions than the same individuals would make if working alone. Group performance does not always surpass individual performance, but in those instances, the group process has been counterproductive. This notion has been stated in the following formula (Steiner 1972, p. 9):

Actual productivity = Potential productivity −
    Losses due to faulty process

When the group process is functioning well, group productivity tends to be as good or better than the individuals' productivity.

In an early test, Shaw (1932, p. 492) studied the relative effectiveness of individuals and groups in solving this problem (see if you can solve it):

> On one side of a river are three wives and three husbands. Get them
> all across the river by means of a boat carrying only three at a time.
> No man will allow his wife to be in the presence of another man
> unless he is also there.

Shaw found that 60 percent of her groups were able to determine the correct solution, while only 14 percent of the individuals were able to.

In a related study, Maier and Solem (1952, p. 280) asked individuals and groups to solve this task:

A man bought a horse for $60 and sold it for $70. Then he bought it back for $80 and again sold it for $90. How much money did he make?

About 45 percent of individuals solved the problem, while 72 percent solved it in a leaderless group discussion, and 83 percent solved it in a discussion group with a leader who encouraged discussion and raised questions that promoted the group effort. Thus the study indicated that the groups surpassed the efforts of individuals, and that a leader helped improve the group effectiveness.

In addition to the type of tasks described above, some studies have examined tasks that could be subdivided (for example, assembly line production), tasks that involved guessing the number of objects in a jar, and tasks in which individuals compared the length of lines. Other studies have examined the effect of the presence of onlookers on a person's performance. It was found that some people are encouraged by the presence of others, while others are stimulated negatively, and some are unaffected. It has also been found that groups are better at solving complicated tasks requiring reasoning and elimination of poor solutions. In addition, it would seem that simply having several individuals solving a problem would increase the probability that a good solution would emerge. In other words, "two (or more) heads are better than one." Luft (1970, p. 30) summarizes the issue of group versus individual productivity:

Problems calling for a wide variety of skills and information or the cross-checking of facts and ideas seem to call for a group approach. Feedback and free exchange of thinking may stimulate ideas that would not have emerged by solo effort.

Finally, Collins and Guetzkow (1964, p. 55), summarizing the research on this issue, state:

Group members may collectively achieve more *than the most superior members are capable of achieving alone.* (Emphasis added.)

As we saw in Chapter 6, there are four methods for reaching decisions: (1) railroading, (2) teaming up, (3) majority vote, and (4) consensus. Consensus typically is the best method since it optimizes good-quality decisions as well as a high degree of acceptance.

ACCEPTANCE OF SOLUTIONS

The plant manager of a large manufacturing plant decided that his supervisors were using far too many ink pens, and that this was an unnecessary cost. He wrote a memo to all supervisory personnel indicating that each one would have to turn in a completely empty ink pen to an assistant plant manager in order to get a new pen. The intent was to save money. Actually, the pens cost about 50 cents apiece and the supervisor's salary figured out to about $10.00 per hour, so if a foreman had to spend more than three minutes searching out the assistant plant manager, the cost was actually *greater* than if the foreman had just gotten a new pen from the immediate area. The foremen determined that it usually took them about 30 minutes to find the assistant plant manager. Thus, under the new policy, the cost of replacing the pen had increased by ten times.

An even greater cost was the foremen's loss of positive attitude toward the plant. They felt that they were being treated like children, and several foremen went out of their way to do a poor job in retaliation. After less than one month the plant manager rescinded his new policy in favor of the old practice of replacing pens.

This case illustrates one of the most common problems suffered by organizations: namely, employees rejecting solutions to problems. For solutions to be effective, they must be of high quality and they must be accepted by those who must carry them out. If a solution is weak on either of these two dimensions, its overall effectiveness is reduced. Maier (1963, p. 5) offers the following formula and explanation for determining a decision's effectiveness:

$$ED = Q \times A,$$

where *ED* represents effective decision, *Q* represents quality, and *A* represents acceptance.

Three types of problem situations can be identified from this frame of reference. The first includes problems requiring a high quality but low acceptance. These problems are best solved by persons with a high level of technical knowledge and expertise. They might include important financial decisions involving setting prices, determining expenditures, and so on.

Second, some solutions require high acceptance but low quality. These might include fair ways of distributing new equipment, vacation schedules, undesirable work assignments, new offices or office equipment, or a new vehicle such as a truck. Decisions such as these may include all individuals who may be affected by the results of the decision.

Third, some decisions require both high quality and high acceptance. It would appear that the majority of problems fall into this category. Since this is the case, Maier recommends that problem-solving groups rather than isolated individuals be used, since the acceptance of the solution is likely to be higher when people are involved in formulating a solution, and because we have already seen that groups tend to produce better-quality solutions than individuals.

Participative decision making (PDM) not only can result in high-quality decisions and increased acceptance of the solutions, it may also result in increased levels of satisfaction, commitment, and loyalty to the solution

---

See the article at the end of this chapter in which Norman Maier more fully explains the use of the ED $= Q \times A$ formula. This article also shows the relevance of small group interaction to organizations and their effectiveness.

---

and to the group. Let us return to the ink pen replacement problem. The chances are that if the foremen were made aware of the problem and were asked to help find a way to reduce it, several things would occur. First, they might suggest a good solution. Second, they would be more likely to accept the new solution. Third, they probably would use peer pressure on one another to see that the new solution was followed. In each case, the result might have been better than what actually happened.

During World War II a group of social scientists was assigned to persuade housewives to more frequently serve kidneys, beef hearts, and sweetbreads to their families, thus better utilizing the scarce supply of meat. Six groups of housewives were studied. Three groups heard a persuasive lecture showing how the use of these foods at home would help the war effort and would still be nutritious and tasty for their families. The other three groups were drawn into discussions of the difficulties of using these meats, and ways of overcoming these difficulties. In both sets of groups, the housewives were asked to indicate (by a show of hands) how many thought that they would actually serve these meats in the upcoming week. A follow-up study revealed that 3 percent of the women in the lecture groups actually served the unfamiliar meats, while 32 percent of the discussion-group members actually served the meats (Lewin 1953). Although this study had some methodological defects, it has become a classic in that it demonstrated the dramatic increase in commitment to an action plan that resulted from participating in a group discussion compared to listening to a persuasive speech. Many other studies have confirmed this powerful phenomenon (Tubbs and Carter 1977).

A related study in industry was conducted with an assembly-line operation. Workers were to paint parts of wooden toys and hang them on an overhead conveyor belt of hooks that carried the toys to a drying area. The speed of the conveyor line had been carefully calculated by plant engineers. The employees were paid on the basis of how many toys they painted (piecework). Problems developed in that the job produced high turnover of employees, high absenteeism, and low job satisfaction.

A consultant was called in to arrange a series of meetings between supervisors and employee representatives. As a result, the operators were given permission to vary the conveyor belt speed from "slow" to "medium" to "fast." The results were that employee satisfaction increased, product quality remained high, and overall productivity was higher than before (Whyte 1955).

FRANK AND ERNEST   by Bob Thaves

..AND THAT'S MR. FITZIMMONS ...OUR VICE-PRESIDENT IN CHARGE OF RESISTANCE TO CHANGE.

Reprinted by permission. © 1975 NEA, Inc.

These studies indicate two things. First, people generally are resistant to changes that affect their lives, especially if these changes are initiated by others. Second, group decision making and "people involvement" can be a very powerful asset in increasing satisfaction and overcoming resistance to change. Let us look at each of these in more detail.

Resistance to change is a phenomenon that some would argue begins with the so-called birth trauma in which the fetus resists being plucked from the warm, dark security of the womb only to be exposed to the shock of the cold, bright, noisy world outside. Over time and experience, most of us develop a "separation anxiety" when we are forced to leave (or be separated from) any place or set of circumstances in which we feel comfortable. Each time we move or change schools or jobs, a certain amount of this is experienced. Try to remember how threatening your first day of high school (or college) was, compared to the comfortable security of your immediate past.

Resistance to change is normal, and tends to increase when we do not understand the need for change, or if we are not instrumental in bringing about the change. A good example of such resistance, writes Zander (1961), "was furnished by a farmer in the TVA [Tennessee Valley Authority] area. He assured us that he knew all about contour plowing, the rotation of crops, and the use of what he called 'phosaphate' for improving the soil. He allowed as how these were good ideas. 'But,' he said, 'I don't do it that way.' "

More recently, many major American companies have increased their use of "quality circles" to increase both their product quality and worker involvement and commitment. A quality circle is simply a small group of employees (usually 10 to 15) who get together on company time to talk about how they can do their jobs better. Main (1981, p. 76) quotes one top executive in Westinghouse as saying:

> The point is, we are making much better decisions than before . . . we are getting a contribution and commitment from larger numbers of people. The management team becomes excited and it works. When

participative management catches on, . . . decisions are carried out by enthusiasts who have helped shape them, who feel they "own" the decisions, rather than by unwilling subordinates who have simply been told what to do without really knowing why.

There are several important factors to remember in *overcoming resistance to change*. First, people will accept changes that they have a part in planning. Obviously it is much easier to live through the trauma of going to college if we choose to go and if we like the college or university than if we are forced by our parents to go, or to go someplace we don't like. Second, changes will be accepted if they do not threaten our security. Many office work groups resist innovations such as computer systems for fear that the computer will eventually take away some of their jobs. Third, changes will be more readily accepted when people are involved in gathering facts that indicate the need for change. Farmers who notice decreasing crop yields will be more receptive to farming innovations than those farmers who are prospering. Finally, greater acceptance and commitment will result when the changes are kept open to further revision based on the success or failure of the new procedures. None of us is very enthusiastic about adopting changes for a lifetime. However, if we feel the changes are on a trial basis, subject to modification, we are usually more willing to give them a try. Obviously, to the extent that the above conditions are *not* met, resistance to change will be increased.

CHANGES IN INTERPERSONAL RELATIONS

Probably the most notable difference between a television interview with a professional golfer who has just won a major tournament, and a baseball team that has won the World Series (or a football team that has won the Super Bowl), is the tremendous amount of energy, enthusiasm, and esprit de corps of the group versus the low-keyed response of the lone golfer. The backslapping, hugging, and champagne splashing of the group are some of the most obvious signs that interpersonal relations are an important by-product of group activity. Sensitivity training groups frequently provide powerful emotional experiences for group members. One group participant wrote of his experience (Tubbs and Moss 1974, p. 243):

> I thought we had a good meeting. Afterward several people came up and we walked across campus together, which made me feel that they weren't resentful about my getting emotional. . . . I am feeling happier about myself in the group.

In Chapter 6 we examined the positive and negative aspects of conflict. Group discussion may improve interpersonal relations through the successful resolution of conflict. Conflict may be intragroup or intergroup. In either case, resolving conflict tends to favorably affect interpersonal relations.

A common technique for improving intergroup relations is to have members of each group get together and write down their perceptions of (1) themselves, (2) the others, and (3) how they think the others view them. Production and service groups in manufacturing plants frequently need to have such meetings to coordinate their activities more effectively. The production groups frequently feel that a service department (such as maintenance) does not act quickly enough to get defective machinery working. On the other hand, maintenance people feel as if they are always put under unreasonable pressures, since every time a piece of machinery breaks down, each production supervisor wants immediate attention to his or her problems even though several machines require repair simultaneously.

Meetings designed to share perceptions of one another and to inform each other of particular problems can potentially clear up and reduce areas of misperception and misunderstanding. After one such meeting, one man said to another from a different department, "After drinking coffee with you and hearing your side of the story, it's going to be hard for me to cuss you out tomorrow the way I usually do." This comment is typical of the increased quality of interpersonal relations that can come out of group problem solving conducted in an atmosphere of support and mutual gain. However, if the meetings are conducted in an atmosphere of blame placing and faultfinding, the relations are likely to be even worse than if the meetings had not been held. In other words, the intermediate influences discussed in Chapters 5 and 6 have a significant influence on the end results.

A subset of interpersonal relations is group cohesion. Cohesiveness, according to Schachter *et al.* (1968, p. 192),

has been defined variously as referring to morale, "sticking together," productivity, power, task involvement, feelings of belongingness, shared understanding of roles, and good teamwork.

This definition covers a lot of territory and can be further clarified by the definition offered by Cartwright (1968, p. 91):

Most agree that group cohesiveness refers to the degree to which the members of a group desire to remain in the group.

Group cohesion can also be a by-product or end result of group activity. Generally, a prestigious or successful group is more attractive to belong to and results in higher levels of cohesion. The Cincinnati Reds baseball team and the Los Angeles Raiders football team are two examples of successful groups that could be expected to have high levels of cohesion.

Cohesion is a result of group interaction, but it in turn influences other things. As we saw in Chapter 4, cohesive groups tend to have stricter norms and tolerate smaller amounts of deviance from the group values. Cohesive groups may have high or low productivity, depending on the group norm regarding productivity. Cohesiveness increases the loyalty of each member to that particular group, but frequently breeds deeper cleavages *between* groups. This may become a problem if the groups happen to be part of a single organization in which integration of several groups is necessary.

As with so many topics in this book, cohesiveness has been identified as one type of variable (consequence). However, it also has an influence on other variables. Cartwright (1968, pp. 106-107) describes the complexity of classifying cohesiveness:

> In our attempt to discover some theoretical order among the many findings related to group cohesiveness, we have identified certain factors as determinants and others as consequences of cohesiveness. . . . Factors that increase cohesiveness lead to consequences that, in turn, lead to greater cohesiveness. Several examples . . . come readily to mind. Similarity of beliefs and values tend to generate interpersonal attractions among members, and the resulting cohesiveness gives the group power to influence members toward greater similarity. As a group becomes more cohesive its ability to satisfy the needs of members increases, thereby raising the incentive value of the group. And cohesiveness tends to generate frequent interaction among members, which, under certain conditions at least, heightens interpersonal attraction and thus cohesiveness.

Cartwright goes on to say that the opposite spiral may also occur — that is, negative experience may lead to negative attitudes, which in turn may cause more negative experiences.

In summary, it is important to note that small group interaction has the potential of increasing interpersonal relations and cohesiveness. The great emphasis on "team building" in management training illustrates the usefulness of this concept. In terms of learning theory, the behaviors of talking and cooperating rather than avoiding and competing with one another have been reinforced, and the cooperating behaviors are therefore more likely to occur again. Thibaut and Kelley (1959, p. 12) put it this way:

> The selectivity observed in interaction reflects the tendency for more satisfactory interactions to recur and for less satisfactory ones to disappear. The consequences of interaction can be described in many different terms, but we have found it useful to distinguish only between the rewards that a person receives and the costs he incurs.

The critical element in improving interpersonal relations through group interaction is to make the experience as rewarding as possible.

IMPROVED INFORMATION FLOW

Communication in small groups can also result in an increased knowledge level and increased coordination among group members based on the sharing of information. Information may be distorted severely if passed along serially from one person to the next through ten people. However, the distortion will be significantly decreased if the same ten people hear the information simultaneously in a meeting. In addition, active discussion by participants will help them remember the information better than if they heard an announcement or read it in a memo.

Another factor is the tendency for subgroups to form so that information that passes *between* groups is restricted. This is especially true in complex organizations. Lawrence and Lorsch (1969) have referred to problems of this nature as differentiation-integration problems. On one hand, organizations require specialization (differentiation) in order to operate effectively. Thus different groups become specialists in such departments as production, finance, legal, research and development, data-processing inspection, master mechanics, engineering, accounting, sales, or personnel. At the same time, these groups must cooperate and coordinate their efforts to keep from working at cross purposes and generally harming organizational success. Lawrence and Lorsch (1969, pp. 54-55) summarize the results of one such set of four interdepartmental meetings.

> The managers and scientists were generally enthusiastic about what the program had accomplished. They reported that as a result of the program they had developed a more concerted effort to coordinate all of their research activity. . . . They were also using a new set of decision criteria to evaluate research and development projects. This was a direct result of their effort and according to them had facilitated the resolution of conflict. . . . Finally, the members of the integrating group indicated that they were devoting more time to working with other functional groups, enabling research to get a unified new product effort. According to organizational members, all of this added up to improved organizational integration without sacrificing differentiation.

Coordination problems certainly occur among members of a single group as well as among multiple groups in an organization. Almost invariably groups of students assigned to work on class projects have at least some difficulty in finding (1) each other, (2) a free hour in common in which to meet, (3) the materials necessary to conduct the research for their assignments, and sometimes (4) a suitable place in which to conduct their discussion. In addition, group members may forget that they were supposed to meet, or they may get too busy to adequately prepare for the meeting, and a host of other tangential problems may add to the coordination difficulties. Not all of these problems will be solved by group discussions, but they will probably at least be reduced. In some circles it is known as "letting the right hand know what the left hand is doing."

Likert (1967) also points out that group decision making tends to lead to a different type of solution than person-to-person decision making. In the one-on-one setting, the focus of the solution is on the person perceiving an individual problem. In an organization, this approach frequently solves one person's problem while *creating* new problems for others. Suppose that five supervisors all want to take their vacations in June and July. Assuming that all of them cannot be absent at once, any decision regarding one person's vacation will potentially influence the vacation plans of the others. It may be that one person's plan is flexible and could be modified in light of the situations of the others in the group. The group method then focuses on coordinating the best solution for all, considering the limitations of the job demands.

See the article by Rensis Likert at the end of this chapter for a good explanation of the key role small group interaction plays in running an effective organization. This article and the one by Norman Maier clearly show the practical application of small group interaction theories to a person's career in an organization.

In addition to offering better decisions for more people, the group decision-making method reduces the jealousy and hostility that frequently accompany the person-to-person method. When individuals are awarded decisions in their favor without others knowing the circumstances surrounding the decision, the others frequently feel that "special deals" have been made and the superior is accused of playing favorites. However, this reaction is drastically reduced when all interested parties are witness to the decision and the surrounding circumstances. Although the group method may be time-consuming, the end results of increased knowledge level and increased coordination are frequently worth the time spent. In fact, the total time expenditure may be less, since the related problems of jealousy and resentment do not occur as much and do not have to be solved as offshoots of the orignial problem.

INCREASED RISK TAKING

Imagine the following situation (Wallach, Kagan, and Bem 1962):

> An engaged couple must decide, in the face of recent arguments suggesting some sharp differences of opinion, whether or not to get married. Discussions with a marriage counselor indicate that a happy marriage, while possible, would not be assured.

In deciding questions such as this, as well as those dealing with career choices, decisions in football games, decisions regarding one's health, and other decisions, it has been found that groups tend to take bigger risks than individuals. This concept was first proposed by Stoner (1961) and has become a heavily researched topic known as the "risky shift phenomenon."

GRIN AND BEAR IT   by Lichty & Wagner

Courtesy of Field Newspaper Syndicate.

"I like to be where the action is...on the Budget Committee!"

Several theories have been proposed to account for such an occurrence. The "leadership hypothesis" holds that the influence of the group's leader causes the shift. The "diffusion of responsibility" hypothesis argues that since nobody in the group feels as much personal responsibility or accountability for the decision, more risk is taken. The "rationality hypothesis" argues that greater risk is simply a better choice with a greater likelihood of payoff. The "conformity hypothesis" posits that people take more risk as a result of buckling to pressure from others in the group. Finally, the "risk value" hypothesis holds that risk is generally admired or valued in our culture, and this value is reinforced in the group setting.

There is a great deal of contradictory evidence on each of these hypotheses, but some consistent trends can be identified. First, the risky shift itself is a fairly predictable phenomenon. Teger and Pruitt (1970, p. 72) state that:

> The difference between the mean level of risk taken initially by the individuals and the mean of their later group decisions is termed a "shift." If there is a change toward greater risk, it is termed a "risky shift." A risky shift is almost always found.

Second, the "leadership hypothesis" seems to have at least some limitations, since not all leaders encourage risk, and since some studies show that risky choices are made even before the leader says anything.

The "diffusion of responsibility" hypothesis has the most intuitive appeal for many. It seems that people would feel more security in numbers and less fear of personal harm if they made decisions as part of a group. However, a summary of the literature on this view indicates that the hypothesis has serious shortcomings (Clark 1971).

The "rationality hypothesis" has also been seriously questioned, since several studies have shown what we might intuitively expect, that not all risky decisions are the better rational choices, and in some cases the groups actually choose the riskier choices that lead to worse consequences (Malmuth and Feshbach 1972).

The "conformity hypothesis" has also been criticized due to the fact that not all groups exert pressure toward risk. The "risk value" hypothesis seems to be one of the most popular views. Brown (1965) argues that our culture values risk and that this value causes group members to want to avoid being seen as "chicken," which results in their making riskier choices. However, Clark (1971) has argued that even this is not always the case. There are several other conditions that affect the occurrence of the risky shift. In his summary of the literature (1971, p. 264) he identifies four such conditions. The group must (1) actually discuss risk relevant topics; (2) not have severe consequences for failure; (3) have members who vary in initial riskiness; and (4) have individuals who perceive themselves as being at least as willing to take risks as others in the group.

In your own group experiences you should be aware that groups do tend to cause individuals to take greater risks than they might take as individuals. In some cases this may be good, but in other situations excessive risks might result.

INTERPERSONAL GROWTH

Although we can probably learn to improve our interpersonal skills by observing our behavior and the behavior of others in any group, the encounter group or the sensitivity training group has this as one of its major objectives. Instead of focusing on problem solving (for example, how can we solve the problem of evaluating student performance in a communication course), encounter groups focus on improving interpersonal skills. The Johari window discussed in Chapter 5 is one model used for bringing about greater interpersonal growth.

In order to change a person's interpersonal behavior, a three-phase process must be undertaken. These phases are (1) unfreezing, (2) change, and (3) refreezing (Bennis et al. 1968). In order to better visualize this process let us look at two actual individuals and their experiences in an encounter group.

The Case of Jim
Jim was a 28-year-old man who worked as a statistician in a manufacturing plant. He explained on the first evening of class that he wanted

to be a supervisor and that he wanted a $150,000 home by the time he was 30. He and his wife had no children and lived in an apartment.

In the first class period, the leader stated that the experience would be unconventional and unstructured, with a lot of group discussion and few lectures. Within minutes, Jim began to criticize the leader by asking such questions as, "What are you getting paid for if you aren't going to teach us anything?" and, "Why should we do your job for you?" The leader responded by saying, "I think it is interesting that you feel that learning can occur only if I lecture to the group. Do you think that it is possible for us to learn together rather than me trying to tell you the 'answers'?" A lively discussion followed in which the assumptions of traditional methods of education and leadership were discussed.

Over several weeks Jim criticized each of his bosses and former bosses and indicated that he had a record of quitting jobs due to conflicts with his supervisors. In each case, the problem (according to Jim) was that the supervisor did not adequately recognize his worth. Each week Jim would criticize the leader in class. Criticisms included the following:

> I think you wear striped shirts because you like to get attention.

> When are you going to tell us what we are supposed to be getting out of this class?

> I suggest if Frank won't tell us what to do, we start for ourselves. Let's go around the room and have everybody tell us one observation he has had about this group so far.

Over time, others in the group commented that Jim's criticism of the leader irritated them, and that they thought that the class procedures were worthwhile. Then one night the leader asked, "Jim, do you see any connection between your dissatisfaction with my leadership and your dissatisfaction with each of your bosses on your jobs?" Jim's face lighted up and he said, "I never thought of that!" Over several weeks Jim began to see that he was struggling for control with leaders and vacillated between exerting control (initiating an exercise in group observation skills) and requesting control ("When are you going to tell us what we should be learning?").

Over time, Jim was encouraged to try leadership behaviors in the group and was encouraged not to always expect the leader to have to lead. At the end of the term, Jim told the group that he felt that he had learned a lot about his problems of relating to authority figures and that he even felt more comfortable with his boss at work.

The Case of Wendy

Wendy was a 19-year-old college sophomore majoring in philosophy. On the first day of class she said that she had been valedictorian of her class and was currently into Nietzsche and Nihilism. According to a sociogram taken in class, she was the least popular person in the class. She asked for feedback as to why and she was told that "she seemed too condescending, cold, and generally snotty." She participated in an exercise called the "trust fall" in which she allowed herself to fall into the arms of a circle of her classmates.

Afterwards the exercise was discussed and she said that she felt that she did not have to try to impress everybody with her superior intellect just to be accepted. Over the course of the term, she was gently reminded when she slipped back into her "superiority complex." For several years after the course, I would see her on campus and she seemed to have retained her new warmth and approachability.

Jim and Wendy had different problems, but the same procedures were used to help them learn to improve their interpersonal skills. In both cases, an *unfreezing* occurred in which the assumptions about how to behave were questioned. Jim assumed that a leader had to be perfect and had to be strong and decisive to be of any value. Wendy assumed that she had to impress people with her intellect to be accepted. Both learned through feedback that their assumptions were not always correct.

The *change* phase came when both people were encouraged to adopt new behaviors that they typically would not have been willing to try. Jim tried leading the group himself and Wendy tried to drop her facade and let people accept her for more reasons than just her brains.

The *refreezing* came when the group tried over time to reinforce or encourage Jim and Wendy's new behaviors. This trial and error learning over time, followed by feedback, tends to increase the likelihood that the new behaviors will be retained after the encounter group experience is over.

As we have said, acquisition of these new interpersonal skills follows the sequence of unfreezing, change, and refreezing. Johnson (1972, p. 6) breaks it down a bit more specifically into five steps.

Unfreezing   1. Becoming aware of the need for and uses of a new skill.

Change   2. Identifying the behaviors involved in the new skill.

3. Practicing the behaviors.

Refreezing   4. Receiving feedback concerning how well you are performing the behaviors.

5. Integrating the behaviors into your behavioral repertoire.

It is quite general and vague to say that encounter groups provide an experience for interpersonal growth. Some more specific ways of identifying such growth have been identified by Egan (1973). He states (p. 23), "I grow interpersonally if

- ☐ I am freer to be myself in my interactions with others,
- ☐ I manage interpersonal anxiety more effectively,
- ☐ I learn how to show greater concern for others,
- ☐ I can take initiative in contacting others more easily,
- ☐ I can share myself more openly and deeply with the significant others in my life,
- ☐ I can be less fearful in expressing feelings and emotions in interpersonal situations,
- ☐ I can step from behind my facade more often,
- ☐ I can learn to accept myself and deal with my deficits in the community of my friends more often,
- ☐ Intimacy frightens me less,
- ☐ I can endure concerned and responsible confrontation more,
- ☐ I can learn to confront those who mean something to me with care and compassion,
- ☐ I can come to expect myself and others to work on the phoniness in their lives,
- ☐ I can commit myself more deeply to others without fear of losing my own identity.
- ☐ I can come to know who I am a bit more in terms of my personal goals and the direction of my life.

Although these goals may not be achieved by all encounter-group participants, they are potential outcomes for some.

Numerous studies have been conducted to empirically test the extent to which the goals mentioned above are actually accomplished in encounter groups. An excellent review of these has been published by Cooper and Mongham (1971). Statistically significant positive changes have been documented in a number of studies, including Miles (1965), Bunker (1965), Valiquet (1968), Underwood (1965), Lieberman, Yalom, and Miles (1973), and Burke and Bennis (1961). On the other hand, some writers have shown either no significant changes or some negative changes as a result of encounter groups. Campbell and Dunnette's (1968) well-known article indicates some areas of weakness in encounter group research. They acknowledge the point that studies have shown that encounter groups do seem to bring about generally desirable results in line with their goals.

However, they also point out that more specific behavioral measures should be used to determine success. They call for more research to indicate which *specific* encounter group practices (such as methods of giving feedback) are constructive and which are potentially destructive. They also indicate that encounter groups used for management training do not show any necessary improvement in specific indices of job performance.

Undoubtedly smarting from the sting of such critics as Campbell and Dunnette, Lieberman, Yalom, and Miles (1973) published an extensive volume of encounter-group research. Eighteen different student groups at Stanford were studied in several different varieties of encounter-group experiences, each lasting 30 hours. As a result of the encounter-group experiences, of the total of 206 students who initially participated, 28 changed greatly, 40 changed moderately, 78 were unchanged, 17 changed negatively, 16 were casualties, and 27 dropped out (Lieberman, Yalom, and Miles 1973, p. 118). The results seem to represent moderate support in favor of encounter groups. The 16 casualties were concentrated for the most part in the groups whose leaders were more aggressive and confrontive. Also, the casualties had lower self-esteem and a more negative self-concept prior to the experience.

ORGANIZATIONAL CHANGE

Based on a rapidly increasing rate of change, modern organizations have been put under greater and greater pressure to adapt or go under. Certainly the policies and practices of colleges and universities have to be different today than they were five years ago. Numerous attempts have been made to help "ease the squeeze" felt by organizations. These attempts usually fall under the general label *organization development* (OD), which is another name for planned organizational change.

Over thirty years ago, Kurt Lewin (1951) wrote about the problem of trying to get people to change. He called his analysis "force field analysis," and it states basically that any situation occurs as a result of the combination of various competing forces. If you have ever tried to live up to your New Year's resolutions, you have experienced this. Figure 7.1 illustrates the concept further. Your motivation to live up to your New Year's resolutions represents one of the arrows labeled "driving forces." If you are thinking about exercising more or losing some weight, several arguments can add to your motivations (better-fitting clothes, more dates, better health). The restraining forces would be all the reasons why you don't live up to your resolutions (it's fun to eat, it's too cold to exercise, you hate to exercise alone).

Just as this force field analysis can be applied to individuals, it can be applied to groups and to organizations. In groups, some members may

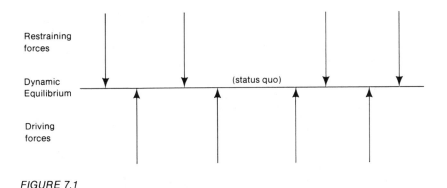

FIGURE 7.1

want to get the job accomplished (task-oriented behavior), while others may be much more interested in socializing with an attractive group member of the opposite sex. In fact, they may have joined the group just to meet that person. How much work actually gets accomplished is the status quo where these competing sets of forces meet. If the socializing couple leaves, the restraining forces will go up. Change can occur through either a reduction in the restraining forces or an increase in the driving forces, or both. Various methods of organizational development are designed to move the status quo in the more positive direction.

While OD methods vary, most writers in the field would agree that various group methods play an important part in the process. Argyris (1962) contends that holding encounter groups with top administrators is the most effective tactic for promoting organizational change. Beckhard (1969) uses small groups as the basis of a "confrontation meeting" in which differing factions within an organization are brought together to resolve their mutual differences. Lorsch and Lawrence (1972) focus their OD attempts on diagnosing the problems within and between groups in their differentiation-integration approach discussed earlier. Likert (1967) has shown that group decision making is one of the basic methods of effective management, and that organization development can occur through the use of small groups discussing survey feedback with their supervisors.

In a study of eleven successful and six unsuccessful change efforts, Greiner (1970) found that the successful efforts involved what he called *shared power approaches* (including group problem solving and group decision making). These were found to be more effective than either the *unilateral approaches* (including change by decree, by personnel replacement, or by structure) or the *delegated authority approaches* (including case discussion and encounter group sessions). Greiner (p. 217) describes the shared power approaches as follows:

More toward the middle of the power distribution continuum, as noted earlier, are the shared approaches, where authority is still present and used, yet there is also interaction and sharing of power. This approach to change is utilized in two forms.

By Group Decision Making Here the problems still tend to be defined unilaterally from above, but lower level groups are usually left free to develop alternative solutions and to choose among them. The main assumption tends to be that individuals develop more commitment to action when they have a voice in the decisions that affect them. The net result is that power is shared between bosses and subordinates, though there is a division of labor between those who define the problems and those who develop the solutions.

By Group Problem Solving This form emphasizes both the definition and the solution of problems within the context of group discussion. Here power is shared throughout the decision process, but, unlike group decision making, there is an added opportunity for lower level subordinates to define the problem. The assumption underlying this approach is not only that people gain greater commitment from being exposed to a wider decision-making role, but also that they have significant knowledge to contribute to the definition of the problem.

Schein and Bennis (1965), in an early work entitled *Personal and Organizational Change through Group Methods,* describe in detail the reasons why groups are so potent in changing organizations. Changes occur in three ways. First, individuals gain an increased *awareness* of problems of which they are a part. This represents an intellectual or cognitive change in their amount of information. Second, there tends to be a change in *attitude* toward the problems. Individuals may be more willing to become a part of the solution rather than expending all their effort trying to place the blame for the problem. This part of the change process is more emotional or gut level. Third, group experiences tend to produce a change in *behavior* that goes beyond the change in knowledge level or attitude. Schein and Bennis (1965, p. 37) refer specifically to these behavioral changes as "increased *interpersonal competence;* i.e., skill in handling interpersonal and group relationships toward more productive and satisfying relationships." It is perhaps this threefold form of individual change that accounts for the tremendous potential that groups have for bringing about organizational change. (See also the Maier and Likert articles that follow this chapter.) Main (1981, p. 93) quotes William Coates, executive vice-president of Westinghouse, as stating that organizational change is best achieved through the group participation method. Although it eats up many hours, Coates says that lost time is recovered later. "We spend a lot of time trying to get a consensus, but once you get it, the implementation is instantaneous." The company has already reduced millions of dollars of expenses that would otherwise have to be added to their product costs.

THE SYSTEMS PERSPECTIVE

This chapter dealt with the consequences of group interaction. In Chapter 1 our model indicated that all of the other variables tend to culminate in these consequences. However, in ongoing groups, the outcomes or consequences of earlier group interactions tend to have a continuing influence on subsequent group activities. Take the fraternity case study at the beginning of this chapter. As a result of the conflict over the "swamp rats," the fraternity developed two subgroups. This cleavage led to a deterioration over time of the entire fraternity's ability to work and play as a team. This example illustrates the systems concepts of *input* and *throughput* resulting in *output* that is fed back into the group as new *inputs,* since many groups represent ongoing *cycles* of events.

In this chapter we looked at six potential consequences of group interaction: (1) solutions to problems; (2) changes in interpersonal relations; (3) improved information flow; (4) increased risk taking; (5) interpersonal growth; and (6) organizational change. Each of these potential consequences may vary considerably depending on the particular combination of the other variables depicted in the model. For example, the quality and acceptance of solutions will vary depending on the degree of group member participation.

A great deal of material has been written about member acceptance of group-derived solutions. The term *consensus* is typically used in this context. Consensus means unanimous agreement with the solution. Conceptually, consensus and acceptance of the solution appear to be roughly equivalent. Gouran (1969) found that consensus is related to fewer opinionated statements (that is, fewer statements that express feeling, belief, or judgment, when the factual basis for the statement is not apparent). Knutson (1972) found that groups containing individuals engaging in "high orientation behavior" will be more likely to reach consensus. Orientation behavior was defined (Knutson 1972, p. 160) as

> behavior which reflected an attempt on the part of the individual to resolve conflict, facilitate achievement of a group's goal, make helpful suggestions, or lessen tension.

Hill (1976) conducted a follow-up study on the question of the relationship of opinionatedness and leadership to group consensus. He found two interesting interrelationships: first (p. 257), that

> leadership behavior characterized by moderately opinionated or unopinionated communication will be associated with groups which

come closer to total consensus than groups with manifestly opinionated leaders.

The second finding was that

group leaders who behave in an opinionated manner will be perceived by their fellow group members as significantly less competent than will be unopinionated leaders, and they will also be perceived as significantly less objective than either moderately opinionated or unopinionated leaders.

All of the studies cited above confirm our thesis that small group interaction must be viewed as a system of interrelated variables in which a change in any one variable creates changes in the other variables in the system.

The second section of this chapter dealt with interpersonal relations. We saw that group member relations may be improved as a result of group interaction. However, groups comprised of members with highly incompatible personalities or value systems may in fact become even more polarized as a result of small group interaction. This outcome would depend on the style of leadership and quality of conflict resolution in the group. Information flow may also be improved as a result of interaction, but with a highly structured communication network and authoritarian leadership, communication flow might actually diminish. Similar points can also be made regarding risk taking, interpersonal growth, and organizational change. Each of these potential consequences depends to a considerable degree on the quality of the mix of other relevant variables in the model.

What we have attempted to do in this chapter and throughout the book is to indicate ways to better understand and improve your functioning in small groups. There are no guarantees that these improved consequences will occur. However, considerable research cited earlier leads us to believe that there is a distinct probability that you can and will become a more effective group participant if you are able to implement the ideas we have discussed.

The readings for this chapter help show how you can improve several small group consequences. Directly or indirectly these articles touch on how to improve all six consequences discussed in this chapter. The article by Norman Maier even suggests a contingency model consistent with systems theory that suggests which types of problems are more likely to be solved using group decisions and which types of problems can be solved by the leader acting alone.

Exercises

1. Getting the Car Home

Divide the class in half. Let one half attempt to solve this problem individually, with no conversation allowed between and among participants. Record the number who solve the problem correctly as well as the average amount of time taken to solve it (sum the times of each person and divide by the number of persons). Have the other half of the class form into groups of four or five people. Record how many groups correctly solve the problem and the average length of time taken per group.

Problem You are stranded with a flat tire. In attempting to change the tire, you step on the hubcap containing the lug nuts (which hold the wheel on) and all five nuts are lost down a storm sewer. How do you get the car home?

2. Personal-Feedback Exercise

On the basis of in-class experiences this term, answer the questions in Fig. 7.2 for each person in the class (while every other person in the class does the same thing). Ultimately you will receive feedback from every other class member. These can be anonymous, or you may sign your name if you wish.

OVERVIEW OF READINGS

Most of us who work in small groups are interested to one extent or another in getting results. In the first article, Norman Maier offers a very practical discussion of the formula $ED = Q \times A$ briefly described in this chapter. This article also bridges the gap between communicating in small groups and applying those concepts and skills to meeting the needs of an organization.

In the final article, Rensis Likert goes still further in describing the crucial role groups play in running an effective organization. He considers Systems 4 management as the most effective management style to employ. This discussion is very much related to the article by Carl Rogers at the end of Chapter 5 in that it emphasizes the importance of establishing a *supportive relationship* between the individuals involved. Both of these articles relate to the discussion in Chapter 3 regarding the work group as one important type of group in which the methods discussed in this book may apply. Note that the causal, intervening, and end result variables discussed in Likert's article are analogous to the system concepts discussed throughout this book, namely, background factors, internal influences, and consequences.

Comments for _

Following are some general impressions I have formed of your performance over the course of the semester.

1. In the *task or problem-solving areas*, you seem to have the following strengths:

    weaknesses:

2. In terms of your ability to *communicate clearly and effectively* on an interpersonal level, you seem to have the following
    strengths:

    weaknesses:

3. In terms of your ability to *work with others on a social-emotional level*, you seem to have the following
    strengths:

    weaknesses:

4. In the following areas you seem to have improved during the semester:

5. Additional comments:

FIGURE 7.2
Personal feedback exercise form.

Improving Decisions in an Organization

Norman R. F. Maier

THE PRAGMATIC TEST OF DECISIONS

Most management situations are sufficiently complex so that solutions to problems or decisions that are to be made cannot be classified into correct and incorrect categories. Rather the alternative possibilities have relative merits, and the standards by which they are to be judged are not agreed upon. Frequently the criteria for judging them are unclear, or there is a lack of agreement on the correct standards to use. People may favor certain decisions because they fit the facts, because they like them, because they get support from those who must execute them, because they are the only ones that came to mind, because making a change in preference may cause them to lose face, because they like the person who suggested a particular decision, because the alternative favored is their brain child, because they participated in reaching it, and for a variety of other reasons. Some of these reasons may be of assistance in the reaching of effective decisions while others may be a hindrance.

Regardless of why people favor certain solutions or decisions over others, the test of a decision's value is quite a different matter. If the pragmatic test is to be used, an effective decision would be the one that produced the desired objectives most completely, achieved the desired objective most efficiently (costwise, energywise, and with the least undesirable side effects), and carried with it the most valuable by-products. These three measures of success might sometimes be in conflict, but in any event they would all be dependent on the outcome of the decision.

From Norman R. G. Maier, *Problem-Solving Discussions and Conferences* (New York: McGraw-Hill, 1963), pp. 1-19. Reprinted by permission of the estate of Norman R. F. Maier.

In other words, decisions can best be evaluated in terms of subsequent events, and unfortunately it is then too late to change the decision. For example, General Eisenhower's decision to invade the French coast at a time when the weather report was doubtful is regarded as a good one because it turned out that the weather did not interfere with the plans. Had the weather turned out to be sufficiently unfavorable and created great losses, his decision would have been open to criticism. In this instance the weather information indicated that invasion was risky on the date set for the invasion. However, the alternative was to set another date and go through the costly preparation process again.

Decisions of this sort may be regarded as lucky, or we might suppose that the decision maker has some kind of intuition, some special wisdom, or some special information that guides him. Regardless of how we view such decisions, the factor of chance plays a part. Some people are wealthy because their ancestors happened to settle along a river bank that later became a thriving city. Even if we view the ancestors as having the intuition to settle at the right place, the payoff on these decisions did not occur in their lifetimes. It seems unlikely that potential real estate values were factors influencing these decisions, and hence it would be more appropriate to attribute the successes of the decisions to luck than to wisdom.

Granting that chance plays a part in successful decisions, we also must concede that some people seem to be lucky more often than others and that the difference exceeds what one would expect from the laws of probability. Some executives seem to have an uncanny way of making decisions that turn out to be highly successful; others may go through several bankruptcies. Although the borderline between luck and decision-making aptitude may sometimes be narrow, it is important to do what we can to reduce the chance factors to their bare minimum if we are to examine the factors that make for decision-making ability.

Since the final evaluation of the decision is only possible some time after the decision has been made, and since the evaluation of alternatives is often not available, we must confine our speculation to the ingredients of decision that have high probabilities for success. In examining alternate decisions we may appraise them from the point of view of their probable effectiveness.

For example, if a first-place baseball team is to play the seventh-place team, an even-money bet placed on the first-place team would be wiser, even if it turned out that the seventh-place team won. One cannot take unknowns into account in appraising decisions before the actual test. However, failure to consider all the factors and influences that are available before the decision is made will reduce its possibility for success. Thus the illness of two star players on the first-place team should not be overlooked.

THE DIMENSIONS OF EFFECTIVE DECISIONS

Two different dimensions seem to be relevant in appraising a decision's potential effectiveness. One of these is the objective or impersonal *quality* of the decision; the other has to do with its *acceptance* or the way the persons who must execute the decision *feel* about it. The usual conception of effective decisions has emphasized the quality dimension. This approach leads to a careful consideration of the facts of the case. The advice is to "get the facts;

weigh and consider them; then decide." It is this emphasis that causes one to assume that there is a correct answer to a problem, a right decision to make. Although this position is sound in technological matters that do not involve people, one cannot assume that it is universally sound. It is this position that causes us to concentrate on getting more information and to assume that when decisions do not work out there must have been some oversight. Thus nations may debate peace plans for the world, attempting to improve the decision, when the fault may lie elsewhere. It is quite possible that any number of plans would be adequate if they received international acceptance. As soon as the behavior of people is involved, opinions and feelings introduce a second dimension.

It is important to clearly separate these two dimensions since, as we shall see, the ways for dealing with them are very different. Failure to differentiate the dimensions leads to complications in discussion because one person may be using terms such as "good" to describe the quality of the decision, another to describe its acceptability; and a third may be thinking in terms of the outcome, which depends on both.

Decisions may have varying degrees of acceptance by the group which must execute them; and it follows that, quality remaining constant, the effectiveness of decisions wil be a function of the degree to which the executors of the decision like and believe in them.

For example, let us suppose that there are four ways to lay out a job and that the quality of these methods, from best to poorest, is in the following order: method A, method B, method C, and method D. Suppose further that the persons who must use these methods have a preference order as follows: method D, method B, method C, and method A. It is conceivable under these circumstances that method B would yield the best results even though it is not the decision of highest objective quality. Naturally one must consider the degrees of difference between each alternative; nevertheless, the fact remains that an inferior method may produce better results than a superior one, if the former has the greater support.

The formula for an effective decision *(ED)* therefore would require consideration of two independent aspects of a decision: (1) its purely objective or impersonal attributes, which we are defining as quality *(Q)*; and (2) its attractiveness or desirability to persons who must work with the decision, which we are defining as acceptance *(A)*. The first depends upon objective data (facts in the situation); the second on subjective data (feelings which are in people). Simply stated, the relationship may be expressed as follows:

$$ED = Q \times A$$

This separation of quality and acceptance somewhat alters the meaning of such expressions as "good" decisions and "correct" decisions. The term "goodness" might be used to describe degrees of quality, acceptance, or effectiveness and hence has little meaning when applied to decisions. The term "correct" similarly has different dimensions and in addition is limited because it is an absolute term and suggests that there are no moderately effective decisions, medium-quality decisions, and partially acceptable decisions.

It must also be recognized that the effect of acceptance on performance will vary from one problem to another. It is clear that when the execution of a decision is independent of people, the need for acceptance is less than when the execution is influenced by the motivations and attitudes of the people who must carry it out. Nevertheless, a respect for acceptance may be a worthwhile consideration in all group problem solving since a concern for a participant's satisfaction may influence his motivations and attitudes, which in turn would influence his contributions. For example, a marketing plan may have high quality and still have poor acceptance by a group of persons involved in designing the visual appearance of a package. Since the execution of the design and its reception by the public are independent of the initial planning group, it can be assumed that the success of the decision will be independent of the degree of acceptance of the decision-making group. However, what effect will such a decision have on a group if it has been railroaded through? If some members of the planning group are dissatisfied with the decision, may not this make them less valuable participants in the future? When we take the long-range point of view, dissatisfaction with a perfectly good decision can depress a group's future performance; whereas, high satisfaction with a decision may serve to upgrade future performance.

If we can assume the position that the acceptance of a decision by the group that must implement it is a desirable ingredient, what are the problem issues? First of all, we must examine how this ingredient is related to the other desired ingredient — quality.

It is one thing to say that in striving for effective decisions two criteria must be satisfied, but can one achieve both of these objectives simultaneously? High-quality decisions, on the one hand, require wisdom, and wisdom is the product of intelligence and knowledge. Decisions of high acceptance, on the other hand, require satisfaction, and satisfaction is the product of participation and involvement in decision making. Thus the method for achieving *quality* differs from the method for achieving *acceptance;* as a matter of fact they are in conflict.

Figure 1*A* describes this basic problem in aiming at two objectives. If we aim for both objectives, we may achieve neither. The traditional leadership approach is to aim for quality first, as in Fig. 1*B*. This means that the man responsible for decisions uses whatever resources he feels are needed in obtaining facts and opinions, and he may make free use of experts or consultants. However, the actual decision-making function resides in the leader who finally weighs the evidence and decides. Once a satisfactory quality has been achieved, the next step in this process is to obtain acceptance of the decision.

Traditional methods for achieving this secondary objective have ranged through (1) imposing the decision on subordinates who must execute it (dictatorial methods, using the motivation of fear); (2) playing the father figure and gaining acceptance through a sense of duty and trust (paternalistic methods, using the motivation of loyalty); (3) using persuasion types of approach which explain the virtues of the decision (selling methods, in which personal gains are stressed); and (4) using participative approaches which encourage discussion of decisions by subordinates but leave the final decisions to the superior (consultative management, in which the motivation is based on a limited degree of participation in which there is opportunity to discuss but no right to make a decision). Although this evolution of the decision-making process reveals improvement, the change has been confined to the aspect that is

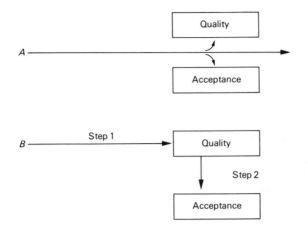

FIGURE 1
Quality and acceptance as targets. (*A*) Aiming at
both objectives achieves neither. This is particularly true when the aim is good. As one moves
from right to left and approaches the objectives,
the directions in which they lie become farther
apart. When one is next to them, they lie in
opposite directions. (*B*) The traditional approach
is to aim at quality and so assure achieving it.
Once this is accomplished, concern turns to
acceptance, which thereby becomes a secondary
objective.

concerned with obtaining acceptance of decisions by subordinates. Throughout
the history of the decision-making process, the quality ingredient has remained
in the hands of the top man or group leader. Management philosophy is that
the person held accountable for the decision should be the one who makes it.
The fact that changes in methods for obtaining acceptance have occurred,
however, suggests that the adequacy of the acceptance ingredient still leaves
something to be desired. Patching up an old method may improve things, but it
lacks elegance.

Suppose for the moment we make a fundamental change in our thinking
and regard acceptance as the initial objective. This approach is shown in Fig. 2.
To ensure success with this objective it is necessary to share the decision
making with the subordinates who must execute the decision. Group decision,
a method in which problems are solved and group differences are resolved
through discussion, now emerges as the appropriate approach. It immediately
becomes apparent that in attempting to be sure of obtaining acceptance, one
risks the ingredient of quality. At least, that is the first concern of leaders and
superiors when the question is raised. This notion of group decision becomes
even more threatening when the leader discovers that he is to be held
responsible for decisions made by his immediate subordinates. It is for this

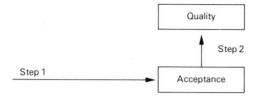

FIGURE 2
Acceptance as primary objective. When
acceptance is the initial target and is
thereby assumed, concern for quality is
the major worry. Will quality suffer if it is
made the secondary objective?

reason that he wishes to retain a veto power; yet such a safeguard tends to
destroy the value of group problem solving. Yes-men are the products of a
superior's tendency to disapprove of decisions made by subordinates.

It appears then that the second objective is endangered whenever the
appropriate method for obtaining the first is used. If this conflict is inevitable, it
may be well to conclude that there is no one best approach to the problem of
effective decision making. Perhaps problems, as well as approaches, should be
analyzed. It is possible that the best approach may be a function of the nature
of the problem.

BASIC DIFFERENCES IN PROBLEMS

Problems may be examined with respect to the degree in which quality and
acceptance are implicated. For example, in pricing a product it is apparent that
a price may be so low that the loss will increase with the volume of business, or
it may be so high that the company will be priced out of business. These two
fates are possible, regardless of how acceptable the price is to the persons
who make or sell the product. Establishing a proper price, therefore, is an illustration of a problem where the quality of the decision is a prime consideration.
Although acceptance may influence the manufacture or sale of the product, it
is quite clear that satisfaction with company decisions would not depend
primarily upon problems of this type.

In contrast, let us select a problem involving the issue of fairness. What is
fair is largely a matter of feeling, and it would be difficult for anyone to find an
objective criterion that would ensure the achieving of fairness in a group. For
example, when a new typewriter is introduced into an office group to replace
an old one, who should get it? Should it be the person whose typewriter is
replaced, the person with most seniority, the person who is most skilled, the
person who is least skilled, the person who does the most work, or should
some other criteria be found? Each member of the group might advocate a
different scale of values, and invariably the criterion proposed is found to favor
the person who advocated it. Thus when people want something, they select
the facts and the values that tend to favor their feelings.

If a problem of this kind were solved by group decision, the supervisor
would hold a meeting and conduct a group discussion to determine the fair
way to introduce the new typewriter into the group. Usually this type of

discussion resolves itself into a reshuffling of typewriters so that several persons stand to gain. Furthermore, different groups will solve the same problem in different ways, and each group will be most satisfied with its own solution. Solutions of this kind cannot be generalized, and their merit lies in the fact that they are tailored to fit the groups who make them.

The question of quality is a minor one in such instances. The supervisor need not be concerned with which of several possible solutions is objectively the best; his primary concern is to have a decision that is acceptable. Future performance of the group will depend more upon the way the members accept decisions on such matters than upon their objective qualities. As a matter of fact, it might be difficult to find measures of quality that would be acceptable to everyone.

If we follow this approach to distinguishing between problems, the first step in decision making is to analyze the problem in terms of the important objective — quality or acceptance. Three classifications of problems would seem to emerge.

HIGH-QUALITY, LOW-ACCEPTANCE REQUIREMENT

These are problems in which the quality of the decision is the important ingredient and the need for acceptance is relatively low. Such problems can be solved effectively by the leader with the aid of experts. The ingredient of acceptance should come up for consideration only after concern with the quality of the decision has been satisfied. Thus the procedure for obtaining acceptance may be regarded as secondary, though necessary.

We shall see later that the quality of decisions often can be improved by the effective use of group participation. This use of the group has additional objectives and raises new problems. For the present we will confine the discussion to the types of problems that can adequately be solved by experts and do not create major acceptance problems. These include:

Decisions regarding expansion, new products, decentralization, plant sites, etc.

Problems concerned with setting prices, determining costs, etc.

Decisions regarding the purchase of materials

Solutions to problems requiring specialized or technical knowledge

Although persons may disagree on the relative importance of the *quality* and *acceptance* requirements, this evaluation must be made by the person who is responsible for the decision. If he feels that a particular decision is required, he is in no condition to permit participation without directly or indirectly imposing his views. In this state of mind he is in a better condition to supply the solution and make acceptance the secondary objective. When the leader strongly favors a particular decision, he is a more effective persuader than conference leader. Thus, regardless of whether quality is the most important factor in a decision or whether the leader thinks it is the most important, the procedure is the same — protecting quality by the effective utilization of the knowledge and intelligence of the decision maker.

Certain decisions that involve acceptance but for which there are no acceptable solutions may also be included in this classification of problems. For example, an airline had the problem of choosing a uniform for stewardesses when the company's new jet plane was introduced. The solution to this problem involves a quality aspect in that the uniform should artistically conform to the design of the plane's interior, and it involves an acceptance decision from the stewardesses, who would have to wear the uniforms. In this instance, the reaction of the stewardesses to the company-imposed decision was quite unfavorable, so that it seemed that the approach used may have been a poor one. On the other hand, could stewardesses have agreed on a solution even if effort had been made to hold group meetings with such a large population?

If we assume that blondes, brunettes, and redheads are favored by different color combinations, it is quite unlikely that all girls would be satisfied with the same uniform, so that any group decision would tend to favor the predominant group. Would such an outcome be a good group decision? Until we know more, it might be best to confine the group decision method to situations that permit a resolution of differences. However, it is important not to assume that all conflicts in a group resist resolution. It is conceivable that if group discussion had been used the girls would have:

1. Evolved a compromise that was artistic

2. Adopted a uniform that permitted variation in some part (such as a scarf) so that complexion differences would have been recognized

3. Been more satisfied because of having had some opportunity to influence the decision

Whether the cost of such meetings would offset the cost of the discontent, which would be temporary, is a decision that the responsible person must make.

HIGH-ACCEPTANCE, LOW-QUALITY REQUIREMENT

These are problems in which poor acceptance can cause a decision to fail and in which the judgment of quality is influenced by differences in position, experience, attitudes, value systems, and other subjective factors. Problems of this type can best be solved by group decision.

An illustration of a problem falling into this group arose when a supervisor needed two of the three girls in his office for work on a Sunday. He asked them individually, and each claimed that she had made a date that she could not break. The fact that Sunday work paid double did not interest them.

He decided to try the group decision method he had just learned about in the company training program. He asked the girls to meet in his office on Friday morning and told them about the emergency job. Since he needed the help of two of them, he wondered what would be the fairest way to handle it. The girls readily entered into the discussion. It turned out that all had dates, but one had a date with some other girls, and all three girls agreed that a date with other girls was not a "real" date. Thus this girl agreed that it was only fair that she should work.

One more girl was needed. Further discussion revealed that one girl had a date with the man to whom she was engaged, and the third had a date with a new boyfriend. All girls agreed that a date with a fiancé was a real date, but it was not a "heavy" date. It was decided that the third girl, who had the date with a new conquest, should be excused from Sunday work. Thus she was not required to work, even though she had least seniority, because this was considered fair.

The quality issue does not enter into this problem for two reasons: (1) All girls were qualified to do the work. Had this not been true, the supervisor might have been more reluctant to try out the method. However, it remains to be seen whether the girls would have placed an incompetent girl on the job. (2) The problem was stated in such a way as to limit it to the matter at stake. Had he posed the problem in terms of whether or not anyone should be forced to work on Sunday, the answer might have been "no." We shall see later that a problem should be so stated as to keep it within the bounds of the supervisor's freedom of action. If he has no authority to set such matters as pay rates, he cannot expect the group to solve this type of problem through group decision.

In using group decision the superior serves as the discussion leader and presents the problem to his subordinates. His objective is to have the group resolve their differences through discussion while he remains neutral. He confines his activities to clarifying the problem, encouraging discussion, promoting communication, supplying information that may be at his disposal, and making appropriate summaries. His objective is to achieve unanimous agreement on a decision that is the product of the interaction in a group discussion.

Problems that fall into the high-acceptance category have to do with:

The fair way to distribute something desirable, be it a typewriter, a truck, office space, office furniture

The fair way to get something undesirable accomplished, be it unpleasant work, unattractive hours or shifts

The scheduling of overtime, vacations, coffee breaks, etc.

The fair way to settle disciplinary problems that involve violations of regulations, lack of cooperation, etc.

HIGH-ACCEPTANCE, HIGH-QUALITY REQUIREMENT

These are the problems that do not fall into the other two categories. At first this may seem to be the largest category of all, so that little seems to have been achieved by extracting the other two. However, in working with group problem solving, it soon becomes apparent that group decisions are often of surprisingly good quality. It is not uncommon for a supervisor to volunteer the information that the group's solution surpassed not only what he had expected, but what he could have achieved by himself. The fear that group decisions will be of poor quality appears to be greater than the hazard warrants. However, if the supervisor is anxious about the outcome, he is likely to interfere with the problem-solving process, rather than facilitate it. For this reason this category of problems should be handled by group decision only when the leader is experienced. Thus it is a category for which either group decision or leader decision is recommended, depending upon the supervisor's skills.

The fears of people frequently determine the motives they ascribe to others, particularly if they are members of an opposition group. For example, if a manager fears a drop in production, he unjustly assumes that his employees are motivated to produce less. Actually the motivational forces in employees form a complex pattern. They include not only what the employees want, but ways of protecting themselves from what they fear management wants to accomplish. With fear removed by the opportunity to participate, the outcome of a discussion often differs greatly from what is anticipated. Obstacles that seem insurmountable frequently disappear in thin air.

THE DYNAMICS OF GROUP PROBLEM SOLVING

In order to illustrate the types of forces at work in a problem-solving interaction, it may be best to describe a case in the use of group decision. Specific incidents serve to bring theories and generalizations in closer contact with reality.

This case is selected because it is characteristic of the manner in which men solve problems involving attitudes toward prestige and seniority rights. At the same time it illustrates how the men on the job are aware of company objectives and do not take advantage of the company or of each other when the need for protective behavior is removed.

The problem arose because repair foremen in the telephone industry had a persistent problem in getting their men to clear "wet-weather drops."[1] A wet-weather drop is a defective line that runs from a pole to a building. These lines have to be replaced from time to time because water can seep through a break in the insulation and create a short. After a heavy rain there are reports of trouble, but since the difficulty is present only when the line is wet, the problem is a purely temporary one. During periods of expansion or when replacement material is at a minimum, many lines suffer from this wet-weather difficulty. If a station is out of order for this reason, the loss of service corrects itself and is not as serious as if the station were completely out of order. Hence the company, as well as the men, regards wet-weather drops to be minor and routine jobs in contrast to emergency jobs. Furthermore, repair men do not like to do this unimportant work, and they feel that anyone can do it without thinking. As a consequence, the men make little effort to get these jobs done. If the foreman decides to pressure men into bringing in a few wet-weather drops, he finds himself at a disadvantage. The men may promise to pick up one or two and then fail to do so. When asked why, they can claim that they ran into extra difficulty on an emergency job and say, "You wanted me to do a good job on the other first, didn't you, boss?" Although the foreman may know the men are shirking, he never knows on what occasion the excuse is justified. It thus comes about that wet-weather drops are a headache to the foreman. When he gets far enough behind, he puts one man on the job full time and lets him clear wet-weather drops. The man in question feels degraded and wonders why he is picked on. To be as fair as possible, this job is usually given to the man with the least seniority. He may complain violently, but invariably the man with least seniority is in the minority. Among supervisory groups this practice is considered the fairest way to handle the situation, and they believe that the men want seniority to be recognized this way. They are completely unaware of the fact that this practice turns an undesirable job into one that has low status as well.

In a particular crew of twelve men the number of wet-weather drops was gradually increasing, and the time was approaching when something would have to be done about the matter. The foreman decided that this was a good problem on which to try group decision. He told his men that he realized no one liked to clear wet-weather drops and that he wanted to have their reactions on how the problem should be handled.

Of interest is the fact that no one in the group felt that the man with the least seniority should do the whole job. The man with most seniority talked against the idea of picking on the fellow with least seniority, saying that he had hated being stuck with the job when he had the least seniority and that he couldn't see why everybody shouldn't do a share of it. It was soon agreed that the job should be evenly divided among the crew. This crew divided up the job by assigning a work area for each man. In this way each man was to be responsible for the wet-weather drops in his area, and he was to be given a list of those. Each morning the local test desk was to designate for each man the wet-weather drop most in need of replacement. It was understood that he was to clear this one, if at all possible. This condition took care of clearing up the drops that were most essential from the point of view of the office. In addition, all agreed that each man should clear as many additional drops as his load permitted. However, when a man had cleared up all the wet-weather drops in his area, it was specifically understood that he should not be asked to help out another. This last condition clearly reveals an attitude built up over the years. It is evident that the reluctance to clear wet-weather drops hinged on the idea that when a man was conscientious, advantage was taken of him. Soon he got to be the "sucker" in the group or perhaps the foreman's pet. It was evident that all men were willing to do their parts but they did not wish to run the risk of being made a sucker. (Other foremen have testified that this defensive reaction made sense from the manner in which the job is frequently handled. The foreman wants to get the job done, and he begins to rely on those individuals who have cooperated in the past. Soon these men find they are doing all the undesirable jobs. It is just a matter of how long it takes a man to find out that he is losing out with the group.)

The results of this solution were immediately apparent. During the three-month period previous to the discussion, a total of eighty wet-weather drops had been cleared; during the week following the discussion, seventy-eight wet-weather drops were cleared and without any letup on the rest of the work. Within a few months the problem was practically nonexistent. The reaction of the men also bore out the effectiveness of the decision. Men discussed the number of drops they had cleared and showed a friendly competitive spirit. They discussed the time when they expected to be caught up and would only have to take care of wet-weather drops as they arose.

It should be noted that the men's notion of fairness was quite different from what the supervisor had anticipated. Although men strongly urge seniority privileges, they do not wish to give junior men a hard time. Rather, advantage is taken of junior men only when seniority rights are threatened. It is of special interest to note the protective reactions against the possibility that cooperation will lead to abuse. Once the protection was ensured, the men considered customer service. This recognition of the service is apparent from the fact that the crew wanted to clear the drops in the order of their importance. With defensive behavior removed, it is not uncommon for good quality solutions to emerge.

DEPENDENCE OF THE SOLUTION'S QUALITY ON THE LEADER'S SKILLS

The quality of group decisions can further be enhanced by improving the skills and the attitude of the discussion leader. Even with a minimum of skills the group decision approach can be effective with problems such as the following:

Setting standards on tardiness and absenteeism

Setting goals for production, quality, and service

Improving safety, housekeeping, etc.

Introducing new work procedures, changing standards, introducing labor-saving equipment, etc.

It is apparent that both quality and acceptance are needed in solving problems of this type, and for this reason they are the areas of greatest conflict in labor-management relations. However, the requirement of skill is more than methodology because it is something that cannot be decided, adopted, or purchased. It requires additional training in conference leadership, and this means an increase in a company's investment in management talents.

CONCLUSIONS

Problems may be divided into the following three types:

Type 1. Q/A problems: those for which the quality of the decision is clearly a more important objective than its acceptance. These may be successfully solved by the leader.

Type 2. A/Q problems: those for which acceptance of the decision is clearly a more important objective than its quality. These may be successfully handled by the group decision method in which the decision is made by the subordinates with the superior serving as a discussion leader.

Type 3. Q-A problems: those for which both quality and acceptance of the decision become major objectives. These problems may be handled in either of two ways, each requiring a different set of skills on the part of the leader. The alternatives are as follows:

Leader decision *plus* persuasive skills to gain acceptance or

Group decision *plus* conference leadership skills to gain quality.

The emphases in this book are on the second alternative because conference skills permit the effective use of a greater range of intellectual resources, thereby achieving high-quality decisions as a by-product.

NOTE

1. Taken from N.R.F. Maier, *Principles of Human Relations*, Wiley, New York, 1952.

The Interdependent, Interacting Character of Effective Organizations

Rensis Likert

In this article we shall examine the effect on performance of three basic concepts of System 4 management: (1) the use by the manager of the principle of supportive relationships, (2) his use of group decision making and group methods of supervision, and (3) his high performance goals for the organization.

The principle of supportive relationships is a general principle which the members of an organization can use to guide their relationships with one another. The more fully this principle is applied throughout the organization, the greater will be the extent to which (1) the motivational forces arising from the noneconomic motives of members and from their economic needs will be harmonious and compatible and (2) the motivational forces within each individual will result in cooperative behavior focused on achieving organizational goals. The principle is stated as follows:

> The leadership and other processes of the organization must be such as to ensure a maximum probability that in all interactions and in all relationships within the organization, each member, in the light of his background, values, desires, and expectations, will view the experience as supportive and one which builds and maintains his sense of personal worth and importance.

In applying this principle, the relationship between the superior and subordinate is crucial. This relationship, as the principle specifies, should be one

From Rensis Likert, *The Human Organization* (New York: McGraw-Hill, 1967), pp. 47-52, 71-77. Reprinted by permission.

which is supportive and ego-building. The more often the superior's behavior is ego-building rather than ego-deflating, the better will be the effect of his behavior on organizational performance. In applying this principle, it is essential to keep in mind that the interactions between the leader and the subordinates must be viewed in the light of the subordinate's background, values, and expectations. The subordinate's perception of the situation, rather than the supervisor's, determines whether or not the experience is supportive. Both the behavior of the superior and the employee's perceptions of the situation must be such that the subordinate, in the light of his background, values, and expectations, sees the experience as one which contributes to his sense of personal worth and importance, one which increases and maintains his sense of significance and human dignity.

It is possible to test readily whether the superior's (and the organization's) behavior is seen as supportive by asking such questions as the following: (If the principle of supportive relationships is being applied well, the subordinate's answer to each question will be favorable to the superior or to the organization. The following questions are equally applicable to both.)

1. How much confidence and trust do you feel your superior has in you? How much do you have in him?

2. To what extent does your boss convey to you a feeling of confidence that you can do your job successfully? Does he expect the "impossible" and fully believe you can and will do it?

3. To what extent is he interested in helping you to achieve and maintain a good income?

4. To what extent does your superior try to understand your problems and do something about them?

5. How much is your superior really interested in helping you with your personal and family problems?

6. How much help do you get from your superior in doing your work?
   a. How much is he interested in training you and helping you learn better ways of doing your work?
   b. How much does he help you solve your problems constructively — not tell you the answer but help you think through your problems?
   c. To what extent does he see that you get the supplies, budget, equipment, etc., you need to do your job well?

7. To what extent is he interested in helping you get the training which will assist you in being promoted?

8. To what extent does your superior try to keep you informed about matters related to your job?

9. How fully does your superior share information with you about the company, its financial condition, earnings, etc., or does he keep such information to himself?

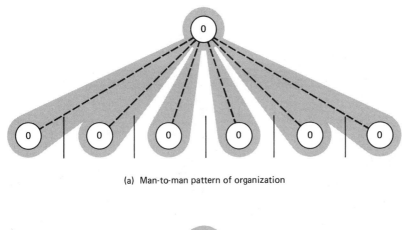

(a) Man-to-man pattern of organization

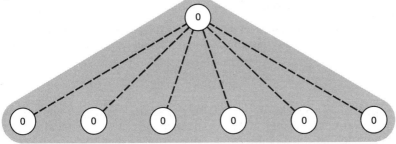

(b) Group pattern of organization

FIGURE 1
Man-to-man and group patterns of organization. (From Rensis Likert. *New Patterns of Management.* New York: McGraw-Hill, 1961. By permission of the publisher.)

10. Does your superior ask your opinion when a problem comes up which involves your work? Does he value your ideas and seek them and endeavor to use them?

11. Is he friendly and easily approached?

12. To what extent is your superior generous in the credit and recognition given to others for the accomplishments and contributions rather than seeking to claim all the credit himself?

GROUP DECISION MAKING AND SUPERVISION
The use by the superior of group decision making and supervision in the management of his work group is the second fundamental concept of System 4 whose effect of performance we shall examine in this article.

The traditional organizational structure (Systems 1 and 2) does not use a group form of organization but consists of a man-to-man model of interaction,

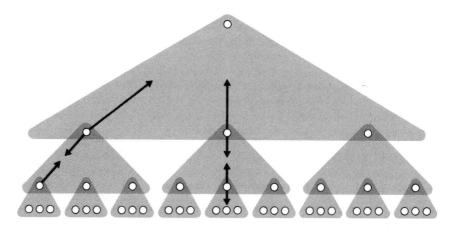

(The arrows indicate the linking-pin function)

FIGURE 2
The linking pin. (From Rensis Likert. *New Patterns of Management.* New York: McGraw-Hill, 1961. By permission of the publisher.)

i.e., superior-to-subordinate (Fig 1a). In this model, starting at the top of the firm, the president has full authority and responsibility. He delegates to each vice-president specific authority and responsibility and holds each accountable. Each vice-president in turn does the same with each of his subordinates, and this continues down through the organization. The entire process — stating policy, issuing orders, checking, controlling, etc. — involves man-to-man interaction at every hierarchical level.

System 4 management, in contrast, uses an overlapping group form of structure (Fig. 1b) with each work group linked to the rest of the organization by means of persons who are members of more than one group. These individuals who hold overlapping group membership are called "linking pins" (Fig. 2). The interaction and decision making relies heavily on group processes. Interaction occurs also, of course, between individuals, both between superiors and subordinates and among subordinates. At each hierarchical level, however, all subordinates in a work group who are affected by the outcome of a decision are involved in it. (A work group is defined as a superior and all subordinates who report to him.)

When the group process of decision making and supervision is used properly, discussion is focused on the decisions to be made. There is a minimum of idle talk. Communication is clear and adequately understood. Important issues are recognized and dealt with. The atmosphere is one of "no nonsense" with emphasis on high productivity, high quality, and low costs. Decisions are reached promptly, clear-cut responsibilities are established, and tasks are performed rapidly and productively. Confidence and trust pervade all aspects of the relationship. The group's capacity for effective problem solving is maintained by examining and dealing with group processes when necessary.

It is essential that the group method of decision making and supervision not be confused with committees which never reach decisions or with "wishy-washy," "common-denominator" sorts of committees about which the superior can say, "Well, the group made this decision, and I couldn't do a thing about it." Quite the contrary! The group method of supervision holds the superior fully responsible for the quality of all decisions and for their implementation. He is responsible for building his subordinates into a group which makes the best decisions and carries them out well. *The superior is accountable for all decisions, for their execution, and for the results.*

HIGH PERFORMANCE ASPIRATIONS

The third concept whose influence on organizational effectiveness will be considered deals with performance goals. Many studies show that employees rather generally want stable employment, job security, opportunities for promotion, and satisfactory compensation. They also wish to be proud of the company they work for and of its performance and accomplishments. Since these needs and desires are important to the members of the organization, the principle of supportive relationship requires that they be met. This can be done best by an organization which is economically successful. A firm must succeed and grow to provide its employees with what they want from a job: pride in the job and company, job security, adequate pay, and opportunities for promotion. Economic success is a "situational requirement" which can be met only when the organization, its departments, and its members have high performance goals.

Superiors in System 4 organizations, consequently, should have high performance aspirations, but this is not enough. Every *member* should have high performance aspirations as well. Since these high performance goals should not be imposed on employees, there must be a mechanism through which employees can help set the high-level goals which the satisfaction of their own needs requires.

System 4 provides such a mechanism through: (1) group decision making, and (2) multiple, overlapping group structure. As a consequence, System 4 organizations set objectives which represent an optimum integration of the needs and desires of the members of the organization, the shareholders, customers, suppliers, and others who have an interest in the enterprise or are served by it. Since economic and status needs are important to the members of an enterprise, the goal-setting processes of System 4 necessarily lead to high performance goals for each unit and for the entire firm. Any time these high performance aspirations do not exist, there is a deficiency in the interaction processes of the organization and a failure to recognize the situational requirements.

FINDINGS FROM 78 SALES OFFICES

My colleagues have extended their study of the 40 sales offices whose data we have been examining to include an additional 38 sales units whose performance covered more of the total range from best to poorest. In reporting their findings for the 78 offices, they propose four dimensions of leadership and then compare the relationship of these dimensions with the performance of the sales office. Their four leadership dimensions are:

1. *Support* — behavior which serves the function of increasing or maintaining the individual member's sense of personal worth and importance in the context of group activity.

2. *Interaction Facilitation* — behavior which serves the function of creating or maintaining a network of interpersonal relationships among group members.

3. *Goal Emphasis* — behavior which serves the function of creating, changing, clarifying, or gaining member acceptance of group goals.

4. *Work Facilitation* — behavior which serves to provide effective work methods, facilities, and technology for the accomplishment of group goals (Bowers and Seashore 1964, p. 2).

Their analysis is based "mainly upon an inspection of the intercorrelation matrix for these variables, and secondarily upon partial and multiple correlation procedures designed to assess the joint and separate effect of various combinations of leadership dimensions." The following comments indicate their interpretation (Bowers and Seashore 1964, pp. 5-6):

1. Our data sustain the idea that group members do engage in behavior which can be described as leadership, and that in these groups, it appears likely that the total quantity of peer leadership is at least as great as the total quantity of supervisory leadership. The groups varied greatly from one another with respect to the degree and the pattern of emphasis in peer leadership behavior.

2. The four dimensions of leadership developed initially for the description of formal leaders appear to be equally applicable to the description of leadership by group members.

3. The supervisor's pattern of leadership (i.e., relative degree of emphasis on each of the four dimensions) tends to be replicated in the leadership behavior of his subordinates; that is, the subordinates tend to provide leadership in much the same way as does the formal leader. This correspondence of pattern, however, is not so great as to preclude the possibility that some compensatory member leadership is occurring. Proof is lacking on this point. The joint effects of peer and supervisory leadership are mixed, with some instances of an additive relationship, some of substitution. None of the tested cases appears to involve a multiplicative relationship.

4. With respect to the issue of relative potency, the peer leadership variables are at least as potent as supervisory leadership variables, and possibly more so, in predicting group achievement of goals.

5. Selective impact on performance clearly occurs. Each of the peer leadership variables and each of the supervisory leadership variables appears to be selective in its impact. For example, the variable "peer goal emphasis" relates significantly to group cost performance, to the group's style of business (larger items, sold to more affluent clients, etc.) and to member satisfaction with fellow salesmen, but it does not rate significantly to such

performance variables as volume of business, business growth rate, satisfaction with job. Peer goal emphasis appears in the case of these groups to play a central role, as it is either the best single predictor, or is a significant additive predictor in relation to a majority of our criteria of group performance.

With regard to point 4 in the above conclusions, it is possible that when another variable — time — is considered, supervisory leadership will prove to be the more potent.

Irrespective of the influence of time, however, the analysis by Bowers and Seashore provides impressive evidence of the substantial contribution to organizational success of the leadership provided by the nonsupervisory members of an organization. To find that differences in peer-leadership activities among the office contribute to the differences among them in their performance is all the more surprising when the character of the product is considered. As was pointed out previously, these salesmen are in competition with each other to sell the same product to the same total group of prospects in the same market. They are compensated on a straight commission basis so that any time taken to coach peers or engage in other leadership processes is taken from what would otherwise be time available for income-producing selling for themselves. Nevertheless, time spent on peer leadership yields a more successful sales office and greater income to the salesmen than time spent on selling without such activity.

These findings of Bowers and Seashore are important for another reason. A large number of studies, starting with the famous Western Electric Hawthorne project, have provided extensive evidence to show that "informal organization and leadership" are present in most enterprises and, as a rule, cause costly reductions in organizational performance because of the restriction of output. Very few studies are available which demonstrate that these peer-leadership processes can result equally well in increased rather than restricted production. Three studies which do so are the Coch and French (1948) experiment, the clerical experiment (Likert 1961, Chap. 5; Morse and Reimer 1956), and the study by Patchen (1960). The Bowers and Seashore study adds important evidence to show that peer leadership can contribute substantially to high performance and should be used positively for this purpose rather than being permitted to restrict production through the use of System 1 or 2 management.

PEER COMPETITION MAKES INADEQUATE USE OF A STRONG MOTIVE
The data from the 40 sales offices, examined at some length in this article, along with the additional findings from Bowers and Seashore help to clarify the nature of System 4 management and reveal the sophisticated and effective use that science-based management can make of powerful human motives in addition to the economic needs. The data are particularly valuable in providing an important insight into how the drive for a sense of personal worth can be used more effectively than at present in achieving organizational success.

As a general practice, sales management relies heavily on the economic needs as a source of motivation. This is the case in all of the 100 sales offices of the company in which this study was conducted. The plan of compensation used by all of these offices is the same and is designed to make the most effective use of economic needs. The men are paid on a straight commission basis. But, as the data from these 40 sales offices show, reliance on the economic needs alone yields only mediocre results.

Another widespread practice among sales managers is to seek to reinforce the motivational forces from the economic needs by adding to them those forces which status and recognition can create. Contests and similar competitive procedures are used in an attempt to capitalize on each salesman's drive for a sense of personal worth. The data from these 40 sales offices, as well as results from other studies, demonstrate that this use of the drive can and often does yield high levels of motivation and quite good sales productivity but does not yield the highest levels of motivation or sales performance. There are serious "side effects" from this use of one of man's most powerful drives which are costly to the organization in its efforts to realize its objectives.

These adverse side effects are the motivational forces created among the salesmen in an office to engage in behavior which will help only themselves and to avoid helping those with whom they are competing. Forces are created, for example, against sharing new information with the other salesmen, against telling them of better appeals, better answers to objections, better sales strategies, new markets, etc. These motivational forces also act to restrain each salesman in other ways. If he sees one of his office mates wasting time with "busy work," he is delighted. He does *not* encourage him to get out and make the calls that yield sales. Similarly, neither he nor his fellow worker feels any motivation to help the other on a tough sales problem or to ask for help. Competitive procedures pit salesman against salesman and reward each economically and with status for keeping what he knows to himself.

Although these negative forces arising from competition often may have their full impact tempered, because most members of an organization like to receive warm, friendly, supportive reactions from their colleagues, this tempering is not sufficient to yield the high levels of cooperative motivation which can be attained from making a more sophisticated use of the drive for a sense of personal worth.

The findings in this article show that the most successful sales managers are discovering and demonstrating that the drive for a sense of personal worth and importance when used to create competitive motivational forces yields productivity and sales performance appreciably short of the best. The best performance, lowest costs, and the highest levels of earnings and of employee satisfaction occur when the drive for a sense of personal worth is used to create strong motivational forces to *cooperate* rather than *compete* with one's peers and colleagues. The use of this motive in ways which yield cooperative rather than competitive relationships appears to yield stronger motivational forces oriented toward achieving the organization's objectives and is accompanied by positive rather than negative side effects. Subordinates aid each other and share leadership tasks rather than putting immediate self-interest ahead of long-range self-interest and organizational success.

The strong motivational forces created by competition can be used without incurring its negative consequences when the enterprise operates under a System 4 model. For example, the individual can compete with his own past record or with "par for the course." Even better, the entire sales office can

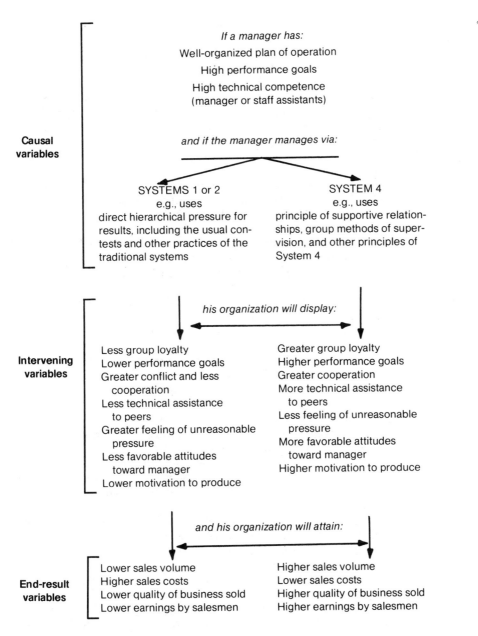

FIGURE 3
Sequence of development in a well-organized enterprise, as affected by use
of System 1 or System 4. After Rensis Likert, "New Patterns in Sales
Management," in Martin R. Warshaw (ed.), *Changing Perspectives in
Marketing Management.* Ann Arbor, Mich.: University of Michigan Bureau of
Business Research, 1962. By permission of the publisher.

compete with its own past record and with current goals the group has set for itself.

All that has been said in the preceding paragraphs about the motivation of salesmen is, of course, equally applicable to sales managers. Contests and the pitting of office against office, district against district, or region against region are all less sophisticated ways to apply the drive to achieve and maintain a sense of personal worth and importance and yield, on the average, poorer performance than applying this basic motive through science-based methods of decision making and managing.

SUMMARY

The findings presented in this article are from a sales organization. They are consistent with data from many other studies. The overall consistency in the general pattern of findings indicates that the conclusions as to the nature of System 4 management have wide applicability. The nature of the specific procedures for applying System 4 management in a particular firm will vary depending upon the nature of the work and the traditions of the company. The basic principles of System 4 management, such as those examined in this chapter, are the same, however, for all situations.

The interrelationships among some of these key variables can be portrayed graphically in a useful although oversimplified form, Fig. 3. The three kinds of variables shown in this figure are the causal, intervening, and end-result variables.

The causal variables have two essential characteristics: (1) they can be modified or altered by members of the organization; i.e., they are neither fixed nor controlled by external circumstances; (2) they are independent variables; i.e., when they are changed, they cause other variables to change, but they are not, as a rule, directly influenced by other variables.

The level or condition of the intervening variables, as shown in Fig. 3, are produced largely by the causal variables and in turn have an influence upon the end-result variables. Attempts by members of the organization to improve the intervening variables by endeavoring to alter these variables directly will be much less successful, usually, than efforts directed toward modifying them through altering the causal variables. Similarly, efforts to improve the end-result variables by attempting to modify the intervening variables will usually be less effective than changing the causal variables.

The end-result variables reveal the final outcome and reflect the influence of the intervening variables upon them.

Figure 3 indicates direction of causality and the influence of an especially important variable, time. The great impact of this variable has been largely ignored by both operating managers and social scientists, with unfortunate consequences both for company operations and for the development of organizational theory.

References

Adams, W. Clifton, 1972. The interrelationship among need for social approval, persuasibility, and activation. *Central States Speech Journal* **23:** 188-192.

Adler, Alfred, 1956. *The individual psychology of Alfred Adler.* Heinz and Rowena Ansbacher (eds.). New York: Basic Books.

_____, 1964. *Superiority and social interest by Alfred Adler.* Heinz and Rowena Ansbacher (eds.). Evanston, Ill.: Northwestern University Press.

Adorno, T. W., Else Frenkel-Brunswik, Daniel Levinson, and R. Nevitt Sanford, 1950. *The authoritarian personality.* New York: Harper & Row.

Allport, Floyd, 1924. *Social psychology.* Boston: Houghton Mifflin.

Allport, Gordon W., 1967. Attitudes. In Martin Fishbein (ed.), *Readings in attitude theory and measurement.* New York: Wiley, pp. 3-13.

Altman, Irwin, 1975. *The environment and social behavior.* Monterey, Calif.: Brooks/Cole.

Applbaum, Ronald, Edward Bodaken, Kenneth Sereno, and Karl Anatol, 1974. *The process of group communication.* Palo Alto, Calif.: Science Research Associates.

Argyle, Michael, 1967. *The psychology of interpersonal behavior.* Baltimore: Penguin.

_____, and J. Dean, 1965. Eye-contact, distance, and affiliation. *Sociometry* **23:** 289-304.

Argyris, Chris, 1962. *Interpersonal competence and organizational effectiveness.* Homewood, Ill.: Irwin.

Aronoff, Joel, and Lawrence A. Messe, 1971. Motivational determinants of small-group structure. *Journal of Personality and Social Psychology* **17:** 319-324.

Aronson, Elliot, 1973. The rationalizing animal. *Psychology Today* **6:** 46-52.

————, and Judson Mills, 1959. Effect of severity of initiation on liking for a group. *Journal of Abnormal and Social Psychology* **59:** 177-181.

Asch, Solomon, 1952. *Social psychology.* Englewood Cliffs, N.J.: Prentice-Hall.

————, 1955. Opinions and social pressure. *Scientific American* **193:** 31-35.

————, 1956. Studies of independence and conformity: a minority of one against a unanimous majority. *Psychological Monographs* **70:** No. 9 (Whole No. 416).

Atkinson, John W., 1966. Notes concerning the generality of the theory of achievement motivation. In John W. Atkinson and Norman T. Feather (eds.), *A theory of achievement motivation.* New York: Appleton-Century-Crofts, pp. 163-168.

Bach, George, and Peter Wyden, 1968. *The intimate enemy.* New York: Morrow.

Bales, Robert F., 1950. *Interaction process analysis.* Reading, Mass.: Addison-Wesley.

————, 1954. In conference. *Harvard Business Review* **32:** 44-50.

————, 1970. *Personality and interpersonal behavior.* New York: Holt, Rinehart and Winston.

————, and Fred Strodbeck, 1951. Phases in group problem solving. *Journal of Abnormal and Social Psychology* **46:** 485-495.

Barnlund, Dean, 1962. Consistency of emergent leadership in groups with changing tasks and members. *Speech Monographs* **29:** 45-52.

————, 1968. *Interpersonal communication: survey and studies.* Boston: Houghton Mifflin.

————, and Franklyn Haiman, 1959. *The dynamics of discussion.* Boston: Houghton Mifflin.

Bass, B, C. Wurster, P. Doll, and D. Clair, 1953. Situational and personality factors in leadership among sorority women. *Psychological Monographs* **67:** No. 16 (Whole No. 366).

Batchelor, James, and George Goethals, 1972. Spatial arrangements in freely formed groups. *Sociometry* **35:** 270-279.

Bauduin, E. Scott, 1971. Obscene language and source credibility: an experimental study. Paper presented at the annual conference of the International Communication Association. Phoenix, Arizona.

Bay, Christian, 1967. Political and apolitical students: facts in search of a theory. *Journal of Social Issues* **23:** 76-91.

Beckhard, Richard, 1961. The confrontation meeting. In Warren Bennis, Kenneth Benne, and Robert Chin (eds.), *The planning of change.* New York: Holt, Rinehart and Winston, pp. 478-485.

Benne, Kenneth D., and Paul Sheats, 1948. Functional roles of group members. *Journal of Social Issues* **4:** 41-49.

Bennis, Warren, 1961. Interpersonal communication. In Warren Bennis, Kenneth Benne, and Robert Chin (eds.), *The planning of change.* New York: Holt, Rinehart and Winston.

————, and Herbert Shepard, 1948. A theory of group development. *Human Relations* **1:** 314-320.

————, and Herbert Shepard, 1961. Group observation. In Warren Bennis, Kenneth Benne, and Robert Chin (eds.), *The planning of change.* New York: Holt, Rinehart and Winston, pp. 743-756.

_____, Edgar Schein, Fred Steele, and David Berlew, 1968. Personal change through interpersonal relationships. In *Interpersonal dynamics: essays and readings on human interaction.* Homewood, Ill.: Dorsey, pp. 333-369.

Berelson, Bernard, and Gary Steiner, 1964. *Human behavior: an inventory of scientific findings.* New York: Harcourt, Brace and World.

Berg, David, 1967. A descriptive analysis of the distribution and duration of themes discussed by task-oriented small groups. *Speech Monographs* **34:** 172-175.

Berg, I. A., and B. Bass (eds.), 1961. *Conformity and deviation.* New York: Harper & Row.

Berne, Eric, 1964. *Games people play.* New York: Grove.

Bilodeau, J., and H. Schlosberg, 1959. Similarity in stimulating conditions as a variable in retroactive inhibition. *Journal of Experimental Psychology* **41:** 199-204.

Bird, G., 1940. *Social psychology.* New York: Appleton-Century-Crofts.

Bird, Lee, 1974. The Nixon years. *Flint Journal,* August 18: D1-D2.

Bittel, Lester R., 1956. Brainstorming. *Factory Management and Maintenance* **114:** 107.

Blake, Robert, and Jane Mouton, 1970. The fifth achievement. *Journal of Applied Behavioral Sciences* **6:** 413-426.

Bloom, Benjamin S., and Lois J. Broder, 1961. Problem-solving processes of college students. In Theodore L. Harris and Wilson E. Schwahn (eds.), *Selected readings in the learning process.* New York: Oxford University Press, pp. 31-79.

Bormann, Ernest, 1969. *Discussion and group methods.* New York: Harper & Row.

_____, 1970. The paradox and promise of small group research. *Speech Monographs* **37:** 211-216.

Bostrom, Robert, 1970. Patterns of communicative interaction in small groups. *Speech Monographs* **37:** 257-263.

_____, and Charles Rossiter, 1969. Profanity, justification, and source credibility. Paper presented at the annual conference of the International Communication Association, Cleveland, Ohio.

Braybrooke, David, and Charles E. Lindblom, 1963. *A strategy of decision.* New York: Free Press.

Brilhart, John, 1974. *Effective group discussion.* (2nd ed.) Dubuque, Iowa: Wm. C. Brown.

Brock, A. J. (trans.), 1952. Galen, On the natural facultires. In R. M. Hutchins (ed.), *Great books of the Western World.* Chicago: Encyclopaedia Britannica **10:** 163-215.

Brown, Roger, 1965. *Social psychology.* New York: Free Press.

Bruskin, R. H., 1973. Fear. Reported in *Spectra* **9:** 4.

Bunker, Douglas, 1965. Individual applications of laboratory training. *Journal of Applied Behavioral Science* **1:** 131-147.

Burgoon, Michael, 1971. Amount of conflicting information in a group discussion and tolerance for ambiguity as predictors of task attractiveness. *Speech Monographs* **38:** 121-124. (a)

_____, 1971. The relationship between willingness to manipulate others and success in two different types of basic speech communication courses. *Speech Teacher* **19:** 178-183. (b)

_____, Gerald R. Miller, and Stewart L. Tubbs, 1972. Machiavellianism, justification, and attitude change following counterattitudinal advocacy. *Journal of*

Personality and Social Psychology **22:** 366-371.

Burke, Richard, and Warren Bennis, 1961. Changes in perception of self and others during human relations training. *Human Relations* **14:** 165-182.

Bynner, Witter (trans.), 1944. *The way of life according to Lao-tzu.* New York: John Day, Saying 17.

Campbell, John, and Marvin Dunnette, 1968. Effectiveness of T-group experiences in managerial training and development. *Psychological Bulletin* **70:** 73-104.

Cartwright, Dorwin, and Alvin Zander, 1953. *Group dynamics: research and theory.* New York: Harper & Row.

———, 1968. The nature of group cohesiveness. In D. Cartwright and A. Zander (eds.), *Group dynamics.* (3rd ed.) New York: Harper & Row, pp. 91-109.

Champness, Brian, 1969. Communication: what's in a glance? *Time,* October 17, p. 74.

Christie, Richard, and Florence L. Geis, 1970. *Studies in Machiavellianism.* New York: Academic Press.

Clark, Russell, III, 1971. Group induced shift toward risk: a critical appraisal. *Psychological Bulletin* **76:** 251-270.

Collins, Barry, and Harold Guetzkow, 1964. *A social psychology of group processes for decision making.* New York: Wiley.

Cooley, Charles, 1918. *Social process.* New York: Scribner's.

Cooper, Gary, and Iain Mongham, 1971. *T-groups: a survey of research.* New York: Wiley-Interscience.

Couch, A., and K. Keniston, 1960. Yeasayers and naysayers: agreeing response set as a personality variable. *Journal of Abnormal and Social Psychology* **60:** 151-174.

Crane, Loren, Richard Dieker, and Charles Brown, 1970. The physiological response to the communication modes: reading, listening, writing, speaking, and evaluating. *Journal of Communication* **20:** 231-240.

Crockett, Walter H., and Thomas Meidinger, 1956. Authoritarianism and interpersonal perception. *Journal of Abnormal and Social Psychology* **53:** 378-380.

Crowne, D. P., and D. Marlowe, 1964. *The approval motive.* New York: Wiley.

Crutchfield, Richard, 1959. Personal and situational factors in conformity to group pressure. *Acta Psychological* **15:** 386-388.

Culbert, Samuel A., 1968. *The interpersonal process of self-disclosure: it takes two to see one.* New York: Renaissance Editions.

Dance, Frank E. X., 1972. The centrality of the spoken word. *Central States Speech Journal* **23:** 197-201.

———, and Carl E. Larson, 1972. *Speech communication: concepts and behavior.* New York: Holt, Rinehart and Winston.

Delbecq, André L., Andrew H. Van de Ven, and David H. Gustafson, 1975. *Group techniques for program planning: a guide to nominal group and Delphi processes.* Glenview, Ill.: Scott, Foresman.

Deutsch, Morton, 1969. Conflicts: productive and destructive. *Journal of Social Issues* **25:** 7-43.

———, 1971. Toward an understanding of conflict. *International Journal of Group Tensions* **1:** 42-55.

———, and Leonard Solomon, 1959. Reaction to evaluations by others as influenced by self-evaluations. *Sociometry:* 93-111.

Dewey, John, 1910. *How we think.* New York: Heath.

Edwards, Allen, 1953. *The Edwards Personal Preference Schedule.* New York: Psychological Corporation.

_____, and L. E. Acker, 1962. A demonstration of the long-term retention of a conditioned galvanic skin response. *Psychosomatic Medicine* **24:** 459-463.

Egan, Gerard, 1973. *Face to face: the small group experience and interpersonal growth.* Monterey, Calif.: Brooks/Cole.

Ehninger, Douglas, and Wayne Brocriede, 1963. *Decision by debate.* New York: Dodd, Mead.

Ehrlich, H. J., and Dorothy Lee, 1969. Dogmatism, learning, and resistance to change: a review and a new paradigm. *Psychological Bulletin* **71:** 249-260.

Etzioni, Amatai, 1964. *Modern organizations.* Englewood Cliffs, N.J.: Prentice-Hall.

_____, 1968. *The active society.* New York: Free Press.

Ewbank, Henry, and Jeffrey Auer, 1946. *Discussion and debate.* New York: Crofts.

Exline, Ralph, John Thibaut, Carole Hickey, and Peter Gumpert, 1970. Visual interaction in relation to Machiavellianism and an unethical act. In Richard Christie and Florence L. Geis, *Studies in Machiavellianism.* New York: Academic Press, pp. 53-75.

Faris, Ellsworth, 1932. The primary group: essence and accident. *American Journal of Sociology* **28:** 41-50.

Festinger, Leon, 1954. A theory of social comparison processes. *Human Relations* **7:** 117-140.

_____, 1957. *A theory of cognitive dissonance.* Stanford, Calif.: Stanford University Press.

_____, and Elliot Aronson, 1968. Arousal and reduction of dissonance in social contexts. In Dorwin Cartwright and Alvin Zander (eds.), *Group dynamics: research and theory.* (3rd ed.) New York: Harper & Row, pp. 125-136.

Fiedler, Fred, 1967. *A theory of leadership effectiveness.* New York: McGraw-Hill.

_____, and Martin Chemers, 1974. *Leadership and effective management.* Glenview, Ill.: Scott, Foresman.

Filley, Alan C., 1975. *Interpersonal conflict resolution.* Glenview, Ill.: Scott, Foresman.

Fisher, B. Aubrey, 1970. Decision emergence: phases in group decision making. *Speech Monographs* **37:** 53-66.

_____, 1974. *Small group decision making: communication and the group process.* New York: McGraw-Hill.

_____, and Leonard C. Hawes, 1971. An interact system model: generating a grounded theory of small groups. *Quarterly Journal of Speech* **57:** 444-453.

French, John, and Bertram Raven, 1959. The bases of social power. In Dorwin Cartwright (ed.), *Studies in social power.* Ann Arbor: Institute for Social Research, pp. 150-167.

Freud, Sigmund, 1960. The psychopathology of everyday life. In the *Complete Works,* Vol. 6. London: Hogarth Press.

Gardner, Eric, and George Thompson, 1956. *Social relations and morale in small groups.* New York: Appleton-Century-Crofts.

Geier, John, 1967. A trait approach to the study of leadership. *Journal of Communication* **17:** 316-323.

Gibb, Jack, 1961. Defensive communication. *Journal of Communication* **11:** 141-148.

Giffin, Kim, and Kendall Bradley, 1969. Group counseling for speech anxiety: an approach and rationale. *Journal of Communication* **19:** 22-29.

————, and Shirley Masterson Gilham, 1971. Relationship between speech anxiety and motivation. *Speech Monographs* **38:** 70-73.

————, and Bobby Patton, 1974. *Personal communication in human relations.* Columbus, Ohio: Charles Merrill.

Goffman, Erving, 1961. *Encounters.* Indianapolis: Bobbs-Merrill.

Goldberg, Alvin, and Carl Larson, 1975. *Group communication.* Englewood Cliffs, N.J.: Prentice-Hall.

Goldhaber, Gerald, 1971. Communication and student unrest. Unpublished report to the President of the University of New Mexico.

————, 1974. *Organizational communication.* Dubuque, Iowa: Wm. C. Brown.

————, et al., 1979. *Information strategies: new pathways to corporate power.* Englewood Cliffs, N.J. Prentice-Hall.

Goldhamer, E., and E. Shils, 1939. Types of power and status. *American Journal of Sociology* **45:** 171-182.

Golembiewski, Robert, and Arthur Blumberg, 1970. *Sensitivity training and the laboratory approach.* Itasca, Ill.: Peacock.

Gordon, Thomas, 1955. *Group-centered leadership.* Boston: Houghton Mifflin.

Gouran, Dennis, 1969. Variables related to consensus in group discussions of questions of policy. *Speech Monographs* **36:** 387-391.

————, 1973. Group communication: perspectives and priorities for future research. *Quarterly Journal of Speech* **59:** 22-29.

————, 1974. *Discussion: the process of group decision making.* New York: Harper & Row.

Greiner, Larry, 1970. Patterns of organizational change. In G. Dalton, P. Lawrence, and L. Greiner (eds.), *Organizational change and development.* Homewood, Ill.: Irwin, pp. 213-229.

Gross, Bertram M., 1964. *Organizations and their managing.* New York: Free Press.

Gulley, Halbert, 1968. *Discussions, conferences, and group processes.* New York: Holt, Rinehart and Winston.

Hailey, Arthur, 1971. *Wheels.* New York: Doubleday.

Haiman, Franklin, 1963. Effects of training in group processes on open-mindedness. *Journal of Communication* **13:** 236-245.

————, 1951. *Group leadership and democratic action.* Boston: Houghton Mifflin.

Hain, Tony, 1972. *Patterns of organizational change.* Flint, Mich.: General Motors Institute.

Hall, Edward T., 1959. *The silent language.* New York: Doubleday.

Halpin, A. W., and J. Winer, 1957. A factorial study of the leader behavior description questionnaire. In R. Stogdill and A. Coons (eds.), *Leader behavior: its description and measurement.* Research Monograph No. 88, Columbus, Ohio: Bureau of Business Research, Ohio State University, pp. 6-38.

Haney, William V., 1973. *Communication and organizational behavior.* (3rd ed.) Homewood, Ill.: Irwin.

Hare, A. Paul, 1962. *Handbook of small group research.* New York: Free Press.

————, and Robert Bales, 1963. Seating position and small group interaction. *Sociometry* **26:** 480-486.

Harnack, Victor, and Thorrel B. Fest, 1964. *Group discussion, theory and technique.* New York: Appleton-Century-Crofts.

Harris, Thomas A., 1967. *I'm OK—you're OK.* New York: Harper & Row.

Hart, Roderick P., and Don M. Burks, 1972. Rhetorical sensitivity and social interaction. *Speech Monographs* **39:** 75-91.

———, William F. Eadie, and Robert E. Carlson, 1975. Rhetorical sensitivity and communicative competence. Paper presented at the annual convention of the Speech Communication Association, December, Houston.

Harvey, Jerry, and C. Russell Boettger, 1971. Improving communication within a work group. *Journal of Applied Behavioral Science* **7:** 1964-79.

Harvey, O. J., and C. Consalvi, 1960. Status and conformity to pressures in informal groups. *Journal of Abnormal and Social Psychology* **60:** 182-187.

Hatvany, Nina, and Vladimir Pucik, 1981. Japanese management practices and productivity. *Organizational Dynamics,* Spring: 5-21.

Hayes, Donald, and Leo Meltzer, 1972. Interpersonal judgments based on talkativeness: fact or artifact? *Sociometry* **35:** 538-561.

"He who runs may read," 1975. *Notes and Quotes,* July-August.

Hearn, G., 1957. Leadership and the spatial factor in small groups. *Journal of Abnormal and Social Psychology* **54:** 269-272.

Heider, Fritz, 1958. *The psychology of interpersonal relations.* New York: Wiley.

Hersey, Paul, and Kenneth H. Blanchard, *Management of Organizational Behavior.* (4th ed.) Englewood Cliffs, N.J.: Prentice-Hall, 1982.

Hill, Timothy, 1976. An experimental study of the relationship between opinionated leadership and small group consensus. *Communication Monographs* **43:** 246-257.

Homans, George C., 1961. *Social behavior: its elementary forms.* New York: Harcourt.

Howell, William, and Donald Smith, 1956. *Discussion.* New York: Macmillan.

Huse, Edgar F., and James L. Bowditch, 1973. *Behavior in organizations: a systems approach to managing.* Reading, Mass.: Addison-Wesley.

Janis, Irving, 1971. Groupthink. *Psychology Today,* November, pp. 43-46.

———, 1972. *Victims of groupthink.* Boston: Houghton Mifflin.

Jennings, Helen Hall, 1950. *Leadership and isolation: a study of personality in interpersonal relations.* (2nd ed.). New York: Longmans, Green.

Johnson, David W., 1972. *Reaching out: interpersonal effectiveness and self-actualization.* Englewood Cliffs, N.J.: Prentice-Hall.

———, 1973. *Contemporary social psychology.* New York: Lippincott.

Jones, Richard P., 1981. Nude sunbathing. *Flint Journal,* September 6, p. c6.

Jourard, Sidney M., 1964. *The transparent self: self-disclosure and well-being.* Princeton, N.J.: Van Nostrand.

Karrass, Chester L., 1970. *The negotiating game.* New York: T. Crowell.

Kast, Fremont E., and James E. Rosenzweig, 1970. *Organization and management: a systems approach.* New York: McGraw-Hill.

Katz, Daniel, and Robert Kahn, 1966. *The social psychology of organizations.* New York: Wiley.

Kearney, William, and Desmond Martin, 1974. Sensitivity training: an established management development tool? *Academy of Management Journal* **17:** 755-760.

Keltner, John, 1970. *Interpersonal speech communication.* Belmont, Calif.: Wadsworth.

Kendon, A., 1967. Some functions of gaze-direction in social interaction. *Acta Psychologica* **26**: 22-63.

Keniston, Kenneth, 1967. The sources of student dissent. *Journal of Social Issues* **23**: 108-137.

Kepner, Charles H., and Benjamin B. Tregoe, 1965. *The rational manager: a systematic approach to problem solving and decision making.* New York: McGraw-Hill.

Kibler, Robert, and Larry Barker, 1969. *Conceptual frontiers in speech communication.* New York: Speech Association of America.

———, Larry Barker, and Donald Cegala, 1970. Effect of sex on comprehension and retention. *Speech Monographs* **37**: 287-292.

Kiesler, Charles, and Sara Kiesler, 1969. *Conformity.* Reading, Mass.: Addison-Wesley.

Kinch, John W., 1974. A formalized theory of the self-concept. In Jean Civikly (ed.), *Messages: a reader in human communication.* New York: Random House, pp. 118-126.

Kinkade, Kathryn, 1973. Commune: a Walden-two experiment. *Psychology Today,* January **6**: 35-38.

Kinzel, Augustus, 1969. Toward an understanding of violence. *Attitude,* Vol. 1.

Kline, John, 1970. Indices of orientation and opinionated statements in problem-solving discussions. *Speech Monographs* **37**: 282-286.

Knapp, Mark L., 1972. *Nonverbal communication in human interaction.* New York: Holt, Rinehart and Winston.

Knutson, Thomas J., 1972. An experimental study of the effects of orientation behavior on small group consensus. *Speech Monographs* **39**: 159-165.

Korda, Michael, 1975. *Power! How to get it, how to use it.* New York: Random House.

Korzybski, Alfred, 1948. *Selections from science and sanity: an introduction to non-Aristotelian systems and general semantics.* Lakeville, Conn.: Institute of General Semantics.

Kretch, D., R. Crutchfield, and E. Ballachey, 1962. *Individual in society.* New York: McGraw-Hill.

Kriesberg, M., 1950. Executives evaluate administrative conferences. *Advanced Management* **15**: 15-17.

Lakin, Martin, 1972. *Interpersonal encounter: theory and practice in sensitivity training.* New York: McGraw-Hill.

Larson, Carl E., 1969. Forms of analysis and small group problem solving. *Speech Monographs* **36**: 452-455.

———, and Robert D. Gratz, 1970. Problem-solving discussion training and T-group training: an experimental comparison. *Speech Teacher* **19**: 54-57.

Lawrence, Paul, and J. Lorsch, 1969. *Developing organizations: diagnosis and action.* Reading, Mass.: Addison-Wesley.

Leary, Timothy, 1957. *Interpersonal diagnosis of personalty.* New York: Ronald Press.

Leathers, Dale, 1969. Process disruption and measurement in small group communication. *Quarterly Journal of Speech* **55**: 287.

_____, 1970. The process effects of trust-destroying behaviors in the small group. *Speech Monographs* **37:** 180-187.

_____, 1976. *Nonverbal communication systems.* Boston: Allyn and Bacon.

Leavitt, Harold, 1951. Some effects of certain communication patterns on group performance. *Journal of Abnormal and Social Psychology* **46:** 38-50.

_____, 1964. *Managerial psychology.* (2nd ed.) Chicago: University of Chicago Press.

Lefkowitz, M. R. Blake, and J. Mouton, 1955. Status factors in pedestrian violation of traffic signals. *Journal of Abnormal and Social Psychology* **51:** 704-706.

_____, 1938. The conceptual representation and measurement of psychological forces. *Contributions to Psychological Theory* **1,** No. 4: 62.

Lewin, Kurt, 1948. *Resolving social conflicts.* New York: Harper.

_____, 1951. *Field theory in social science.* New York: Harper & Row.

_____, 1953. Studies in group decision. In Dorwin Cartwright and Alvin Zander (eds.), *Group dynamics.* Evanston, Ill.: Row, Peterson.

_____, Ronald Lippitt, and Ralph White, 1939. Patterns of aggressive behavior in experimentally created "social climates." *Journal of Social Psychology* **10:** 271-299.

Lieberman, Morton, Irvin Yalom, and Matthew Miles, 1973. *Encounter groups: first facts.* New York: Basic Books.

_____, Irvin Yalom, and Matthew Miles, 1972. The impact of encounter groups on participants: some preliminary findings. *Journal of Applied Behavioral Science* **8:** 29-50.

Likert, Rensis, 1961. An emerging theory of organization, leadership, and management. In Luigi Petrutto and Bernard Bass (eds.), *Leadership and interpersonal behavior.* New York: Holt, Rinehart and Winston, pp. 290-309.

_____, 1961. *New patterns of management.* New York: McGraw-Hill.

_____, 1967. *The human organization.* New York: McGraw-Hill.

Lomranz, Jacob, Martin Lakin, and Harold Schiffman, 1972. Variants of sensitivity training and encounter: diversity or fragmentation. *Journal of Applied Behavorial Science* **8:** 399-420.

Luchins, A. R., 1942. Mechanization in problem solving. *Psychological Monographs* **54:** No. 6 (Whole No. 248).

Lorsch, Jay, and Paul Lawrence, 1972. *Managing group and intergroup relations.* Homewood, Ill.: Irwin.

Luft, Joseph, 1969. *Of human interaction.* Palo Alto, Calif.: National Press.

_____, 1970. *Group processes: an introduction to group dynamics.* (2nd ed.) Palo Alto, Calif.: National Press.

McClelland, David C., 1961. *The achieving society.* Princeton, N.J.: Van Nostrand.

_____ (ed.), 1955. *Studies in motivation.* New York: Appleton-Century-Crofts.

_____, J. W. Atkinson, R. A. Clark, and E. L. Lowell, 1953. *The achievement motive.* New York: Appleton-Century-Crofts.

McCroskey, James, 1971. Human information processing and diffusion. In Larry Barker and Robert Kibler (eds.), *Speech communication behavior: perspectives and principles.* Englewood Cliffs, N.J.: Prentice-Hall, pp. 167-181.

_____, Carl Larson, and Mark Knapp, 1971. *An introduction to interpersonal communication.* Englewood Cliffs, N.J.: Prentice-Hall.

_____, and David W. Wright, 1971. The development of an instrument for measuring interaction behavior in small groups. *Speech Monographs* **38:** 335-340.

McGrath, Joseph E., and Irwin Altman, 1966. *Small group research: a synthesis and critique of the field.* New York: Holt, Rinehart and Winston.

McKeachie, W., 1952. Lipstick as a determiner of first impressions of personality: an experiment for the general psychology course. *Journal of Social Psychology* **36:** 241-244.

McLaughlin, David, and Jay Hewitt, 1972. Need for approval and perceived openness. *Journal of Experimental Research in Personality* **6:** 255-258.

Maier, Norman R. F., 1963. *Problem-solving discussions and conferences.* New York: McGraw-Hill.

————, and A. R. Solem, 1952. The contributions of a discussion leader to the quality of group thinking: the effective use of minority opinions. *Human Relations* **5:** 277-288.

Main, Jeremy, 1981. Westinghouse's cultural revolution. *Fortune,* June 15, pp. 74-93.

Malmuth, Neil M., and Seymour Feshbach, 1972. Risky shift in a naturalistic setting. *Journal of Personality* **40:** 38-49.

Maslow, Abraham, 1970. *Motivation and personality.* (2nd ed.) New York: Harper & Row.

————, and N. Mintz, 1956. Effects of esthetic surroundings: I. Initial effects of three esthetic conditions upon perceiving "energy" and "well-being" in faces. *Journal of Psychology* **41:** 247-254.

Mayo, Elton, 1933. *The human problems of an industrial civilization.* New York: Macmillan.

Mead, Margaret, 1935. *Sex and temperament in three primitive societies.* New York: Dell.

Meerloo, Joost, 1956. *The rape of the mind.* New York: Grosset and Dunlap.

Mehrabian, Albert, 1956. Significance of posture and position in the communication of attitudes and status relations. *Psychological Bulletin* **71:** 359-372.

————, 1971. Nonverbal betrayal of feeling. *Journal of Experimental Research in Personality* **5:** 64-73.

Mikol, Bernard, 1960. The enjoyment of new musical systems. In Milton Rokeach (ed.), *The open and closed mind.* New York: Basic Books, pp. 270-284.

Miles, Matthew B., 1965. Changes during and following laboratory training: a clinical-experimental study. *Journal of Applied Behavioral Science* **1:** 215-242.

————, 1967. *Learning to work in groups.* New York: Teacher's College Press, Columbia University.

Milgram, Stanley, 1974. *Obedience to authority: an experimental view.* New York: Harper & Row.

Miller, Gerald R., and Paula Bacon, 1971. Open and closed-mindedness and recognition of visual humor. *Journal of Communication* **21:** 150-159.

Mills, Judson, and Elliot Aronson, 1965. Opinion change as a function of the communicator's attractiveness and desire to influence. *Journal of Personality and Social Psychology* **1:** 73-77.

Mills, Theodore, 1967. *The sociology of small groups.* Englewood Cliffs, N.J.: Prentice-Hall.

Morris, Charles, and J. Richard Hackman, 1969. Behavioral correlates of perceived leadership. *Journal of Personality and Social Psychology* **13:** 350-361.

Mortenson, C. David, 1970. The status of small group research. *Quarterly Journal of Speech* **56:** 304-309.

Moseley, Ray, 1974. Soviet monkey business: aping American execs. *Flint Journal* January 13, p. A-8.

Mosvick, Roger, 1971. Human relations training for scientists, technicians, and engineers: a review of relevant experimental evaluations of human relations training. *Personnel Psychology* **24:** 275-292.

Myers, Gail E., and Michele Tolela Myers, 1973. *The dynamics of human communication.* New York: McGraw-Hill.

Murray, Henry, 1938. *Explorations in personality.* New York: Oxford University Press.

Nadler, E. B., 1959. Yielding, authoritarianism, and authoritarian ideology regarding groups. *Journal of Abnormal and Social Psychology* **58:** 408-410.

Newcomb, Theodore, 1943. *Personality and social change.* New York: Dryden.

_____, 1963. Persistence and regression of changed attitudes: long-range studies. *Journal of Social Issues* **19:** 3-14.

Nye, Robert, 1973. *Conflict among humans.* New York: Springer.

Ober, Nelson, and Fred E. Jandt, 1973. Students self-concepts and evaluations of discussion instruction. *Speech Teacher* **22:** 64-66.

Ogden, Charles K., and I. A. Richards, 1946. *The meaning of meaning.* New York: Harcourt, Brace.

Osborn, Alex, 1953. *Applied imagination: principles and procedures of creative thinking.* New York: Scribner's.

Osgood, Charles, 1969. Calculated de-escalation as a strategy. In D. G. Pruitt and R. C. Synder (eds.), *Theory and research on the causes of war.* Englewood Cliffs, N.J.: Prentice-Hall, pp. 213-216.

Parkinson, C. Northcote, 1957. *Parkinson's law: and other studies in administration.* Boston: Houghton Mifflin.

Patton, Bobby, and Kim Giffin, 1973. *Problem-solving group interaction.* New York: Harper & Row.

Payne, Sam, David Summers, and Thomas Stewart, 1973. Value differences across three generations. *Sociometry* **36:** 20-30.

Petelle, John, 1964. The role of conflict in discussion. *Speaker and Gavel* **2:** 24-28.

Pettinger, Robert, 1964. *The first five minutes.* Itasca, N.Y.: Peacock.

Pfeffer, Jeffrey, 1981. *Power in organizations.* Marshfield, Mass.: Pitman.

Pfeiffer, J. William, and John Jones, 1969. *Structured experiences for human relations training.* Iowa City: University Associates.

Phillips, J. D., 1948. Report on discussion 66. *Adult Education Journal* **7:** 181-182.

Psychology Today, 1970. Del Mar, Calif.: CRM Publications.

Quinn, Robert, 1973. *Job satisfaction: is there a trend?* Washington, D.C.: United States Department of Labor.

Rarick, David, Gary F. Soldow, and Ronald S. Geizer, 1976. Self-monitoring as a mediator of conformity. *Central States Speech Journal* **27:** 267-271.

Regula, C. Robert, and James Julian, 1973. The impact of quality and frequency of task contributions on perceived ability. *Journal of Social Psychology* **89:** 112-115.

Ringwald, Barbara, Richard Mann, Robert Rosenwein, and Wilbert McKeachie, 1971. Conflict and style in the college classroom: an intimate study. *Psychology Today*, February, pp. 45-47, 76-79.

Roberts, W. Rhys, 1941. Rhetoric. In Richard McKean (ed.), *The basic works of Aristotle*. New York: Random House, pp. 1318-1451.

Robinson, F. P., 1961. *Effective study.* New York: Harper & Row.

Roethlisberger, Fritz, and William Dickson, 1939. *Management and the worker.* Cambridge, Mass.: Harvard University Press.

Rogers, Carl R., and F. J. Roethlisberger, 1952. Barriers and gateways to communication. *Harvard Business Review* **30:** 48.

Rogers, Everett, and Dilip K. Bhowmik, 1971. Homophily-heterophily: relational concepts for communication research. In Larry Barker and Robert Kibler (eds.), *Speech communication behavior: perspectives and principles.* Englewood Cliffs, N.J.: Prentice-Hall, pp. 206-225.

———, and F. Floyd Shoemaker, 1971. *Communication of innovations.* (2nd ed.) New York: Free Press.

Rokeach, Milton, 1948. Generalized mental rigidity as a factor in ethnocentrism. *Journal of Abnormal and Social Psychology* **43:** 259-278.

———, 1954. The nature and meaning of dogmatism. *Psychological Review* **61:** 194-204.

———, 1960. *The open and closed mind.* New York: Basic Books.

———, 1968. *Beliefs, attitudes, and values.* San Francisco: Jossey-Bass.

———, 1971. Long-range experimental modifcations of values, attitudes, and behavior. In William A. Hunt (ed.), *Human behavior and its control.* Cambridge, Mass.: Schenkman, pp. 93-105.

———, 1973. *The nature of human values.* New York: Free Press.

Rosenfeld, Howard, 1965. Effect of approval-seeking induction on interpersonal proximity. *Psychological Reports* **17:** 120-122.

———, 1966. Instrumental affiliative functions of facial and gestural expressions. *Journal of Personality and Social Psychology* **4:** 65-72.

Rosenfeld, Lawrence B., and Gene D. Fowler, 1976. Personality, sex, and leadership style. *Communication Monographs* **43:** 320-324.

———, and Vickie Christie, 1974. Sex and persuasibility revisited. *Western Speech* **38:** 244-253.

———, and Kenneth Frandsen, 1972. The "other" speech student: an emprical analysis of some interpersonal relations orientations of the reticient student. *Speech Teacher* **21:** 296-302.

Ross, Edward, 1920. *The principles of sociology.* New York: Century.

Ross, Raymond, 1970. *Speech communication fundamentals and practice.* Englewood Cliffs, N.J.: Prentice-Hall.

Ruben, Brent, 1972. General system theory: an approach to human communication. In Richard Budd and Brent Ruben (eds.), *Approaches to human communication.* New York: Spartan, pp. 120-144.

———, and John Y. Kim (eds.), 1975. *General systems theory and human communication.* Rochelle Park, N.J.: Hayden.

Ruch, Richard S., 1972. An analysis of the Freudian slip and errors in speech communication. *Journal of Technical Writing and Communication* **2:** 343-352.

Runyan, Kenneth, 1973. Some interactions between personality variables and management styles. *Journal of Applied Psychology* **57:** 288-294.

Russo, N. F., 1967. Connotations of seating arrangements. *Cornell Journal of Social Relations* **2:** 37-44.

Sattler, William, and N. Edd Miller, 1968. *Discussion and conference.* Englewood Cliffs, N.J.: Prentice-Hall.

Schachter, Stanley, 1951. Deviation, rejection, and communication. *Journal of Abnormal and Social Psychology* **46:** 190-207.

_____, Norris Ellertson, Dorothy McBride, and Doris Gregory, 1968. An experimental study of cohesiveness and productivity. In D. Cartwright and A. Zander (eds.), *Group dynamics.* (3rd ed.) New York: Harper & Row, pp. 192-198.

Scheidel, Thomas, 1970. Sex and persuasibility. *Speech Monographs* **37:** 292-387.

Schein, Edgar, and Warren Bennis, 1965. *Personal and organizational change through group methods.* New York: Wiley.

Schelling, Thomas C., 1960. *The strategy of conflict.* Cambridge, Mass.: Harvard University Press.

Schneider, Frank W., and James G. Delaney, 1972. Effect of individual achievement motivation on group problem-solving efficiency. *Journal of Social Psychology* **86:** 291-298.

Schutz, William C., 1958. *FIRO: a three-dimensional theory of interpersonal behavior.* New York: Holt, Rinehart and Winston.

_____, 1967. *Joy: expanding human awareness.* New York: Grove.

_____, 1971. *Here comes everybody: bodymind and encounter culture.* New York: Harper & Row.

Seiler, John A., 1967. *Systems analysis in organizational behavior.* Homewood, Ill.: Irwin-Dorsey.

Sereno, Kenneth, and Edward Bodaken, 1975. *TRANS-PER: understanding human communication.* Boston: Houghton Mifflin.

Shaw, Marjorie, 1932. A comparison of individuals and small groups in the rational solution of complex problems. *American Journal of Psychology* **44:** 491-504.

Shaw, Marvin E., 1964. Communication networks. In Leonard Berkowtiz (ed.), *Advances in experimental social psychology.* (Vol. 1) New York: Academic Press, pp. 111-147.

_____, 1981. *Group dynamics: the psychology of small group behavior.* (3rd ed.) New York: McGraw-Hill.

Sheldon, William, 1940. *The varieties of human physique.* New York: Harper & Row.

_____, 1942. *The varieties of temperament.* New York: Harper & Row.

_____, 1954. *Atlas of man: a guide for somatotyping the adult male of all ages.* New York: Harper & Row.

Sherif, Muzafer, 1963. *The psychology of social norms.* New York: Harper & Row.

_____, Carolyn Sherif, and Roger Nebergall, 1965. *Attitude and attitude change: the social judgment-involvement approach.* Philadelphia: Saunders.

Shils, Edward, 1951. The study of the primary group. In Harold Lasswell and Daniel Lerner (eds.), *The policy science.* Stanford, Calif.: Stanford University Press, pp. 44-69.

Simmel, George, 1955. *Conflict.* Translated by K. H. Wolff. Glencoe, Ill.: Free Press.

Smith, David C., 1974. WAW adds its selections to '75 model name parade. *Ward's Auto World* **10:** 13.

———, 1975. The new small Seville: Cadillac's king-size gamble. *Ward's Auto World* **11:** 23-28.

Sommer, Robert, 1959. Studies in personal space. *Sociometry* **22:** 247-260.

———, 1965. Further studies of small group ecology. *Sociometry* **28:** 337-348.

———, 1969. *Personal space: the behavioral basis of design.* Englewood Cliffs, N.J.: Prentice-Hall.

South, E. B., 1927. Some psychological aspects of committee work. *Journal of Applied Psychology* **11:** 348-368, 437-464.

Stein, Carroll, 1973. Group grope: the latest development bromide. *Personnel Journal,* January, pp. 19-26.

Steiner, Ivan D., 1972. *Group process and productivity.* New York: Academic Press.

Steinmetz, Lawrence, 1969. *Managing the marginal and unsatisfactory performer.* Reading, Mass.: Addison-Wesley.

Steinzor, B., 1950. The spatial factor in face-to-face discussion groups. *Journal of Abnormal and Social Psychology* **45:** 552-555.

Stogdill, Ralph, 1948. Personal factors associated with leadership. *Journal of Psychology* **25:** 35-71.

———, 1974. *Handbook of leadership: a survey of theory and research.* New York: Free Press.

Stoner, J. A. F., 1961. *Comparison of individual and group decisions involving risk.* Unpublished master's thesis, Massachusetts Institute of Technology, School of Industrial Management.

Streigel, Quincalee Brown, 1975. Self-reported behavioral and attitudinal changes by participation in a women's consciousness-raising group. Paper presented at the annual convention of the Central States Speech Association, April, Kansas City, Missouri.

Strodbeck, Fred, and L. H. Hook, 1961. The social dimensions of a twelve-man jury table. *Sociometry* **24:** 397-415.

Strongman, K., and B. Champness, 1968. Dominance hierarchies and conflict in eye contact. *Acta Psychologia* **28:** 376-386.

Symington, James W., 1971. *The stately game.* New York: Macmillan.

Tannenbaum, Robert, Irving Weschler, and Fred Massarik, 1961. *Leadership and organization: a behavioral science approach.* New York: McGraw-Hill.

———, and Warren Schmidt, 1972. How to choose a leadership pattern. In Jay Lorsch and Paul Lawrence (eds.), *Managing group and intergroup relations.* Homewood, Ill.: Irwin, pp. 188-200.

Tavris, Carol, 1974. Women in China: they speak bitterness revolution. *Psychology Today,* May 7, pp. 43-49.

Teger, Allan I., and Dean G. Pruitt, 1970. Components of group risk taking. In R. Cathcart and L. Samovar (eds.), *Small group communication: a reader.* Dubuque, Iowa: Wm. C. Brown, pp. 72-81.

Terman, L., and C. Miles, 1936. *Sex and personality: studies in masculinity and femininity.* New York: McGraw-Hill.

Thayer, Lee, 1968. *Communication and communication systems.* Homewood, Ill.: Irwin.

Thelen, Herbert, and Watson Dickerman, 1949. Stereotypes and the growth of groups. *Educational Leadership* **6:** 309-316.

Thibaut, John W., and Harold H. Kelley, 1950. An experimental study of the cohesiveness of underprivileged groups. *Human Relations* **3:** 251-278.

———, and Harold H. Kelley, 1959. *The social psychology of groups.* New York: Wiley.

Time, January 19, 1976, pp. 55-56. Groupthink.

Time, July 23, 1973, pp. 31-32. The return of the gang.

Time, January 14, 1974, p. 58. The impressario of the brain.

Thornton, G., 1944. The effect of wearing glasses upon judgments of personality traits of persons seen briefly. *Journal of Applied Psychology* **28:** 203-207.

Tillman, R., Jr., 1960. Problems in review: committees on trial. *Harvard Business Review* **47:** 162-172.

Toulmin, Stephen, 1958. *The uses of argument.* Cambridge: At the University Press.

Triandis, Harry C., 1971. *Attitude and attitude change.* New York: Wiley.

Tubbs, Stewart L., 1976. The transactive nature of therapeutic communication. Paper presented at the annual convention of the Speech Communication Association, San Francisco, December.

———, and John Baird, 1980. *Self-disclosure and interpersonal growth.* Columbus, Ohio: Special Press.

———, and Robert M. Carter, 1977. *Shared experiences in human communication.* Rochelle Park, N.J.: Hayden.

———, and Sylvia Moss, 1974. *Human communication: an interpersonal perspective.* New York: Random House.

———, and Sylvia Moss, 1983. *Human communication: an interpersonal perspective.* (4th ed.) New York: Random House.

Tuckman, Bruce, 1965. Developmental sequence in small groups. *Psychological Bulletin* **63:** 384-399.

Tuddenham, R. D., 1961. The influence upon judgment of the apparent discrepancy between self and others. *Journal of Social Psychology* **53:** 69-79.

Underwood, W., 1965. Evaluation of laboratory method training. *Training Director's Journal* **5:** 34-40.

Unger, Mark, 1974. Unpublished behavioral science term paper. Flint, Mich.: General Motors Institute.

Valiquet, M. I., 1968. Individual change in a management development program. *Journal of Applied Behavioral Science* **4:** 313-326.

Viscott, David, 1972. *The making of a psychiatrist.* Greenwich, Conn.: Fawcett.

Von Bertalonffy, Ludwig, 1968. *General system theory.* New York: George Braziller.

Wahlers, Kathy J., and Larry L. Barker, 1973. Bralessness and nonverbal communication. *Central States Speech Journal* **24:** 222-226.

Wallach, Michael A., Nathan Kagan, and Daryl J. Bem, 1962. Group influence on individual risk taking. *Journal of Abnormal and Social Psychology* **65:** 77.

Walker, E. L., and R. W. Heynes, 1967. *An anatomy for conformity.* Belmont, Calif.: Brooks/Cole-Wadsworth.

Walster, E., V. Aronson, D. Abrahams, and L. Rohmann, 1966. Importance of physical attractiveness in dating behavior. *Journal of Personality and Social Psychology* **4:** 508-516.

Warschaw, T., 1980. *Winning by negotiation.* New York: McGraw-Hill.

Watzlawick, Paul, Janet Beavin, and Donald Jackson, 1967. *Pragmatics of human communication.* New York: Norton.

Weaver, Richard, 1971. Sensitivity training and effective group discussion. *Speech Teacher* **20:** 203-207.

White, Ralph, and Ronald Lippitt, 1968. Leader behavior and member reaction in three social climates. In D. Cartwright and A. Zander (eds.), *Group dynamics.* (3rd ed.) New York: Harper & Row, pp. 318-335.

Whyte, William F., 1943. *Street corner society.* Chicago: University of Chicago Press.

———, 1955. *Money and motivation.* New York: Harper, Chapter 10.

Widgery, Robin, 1974. Sex of receiver and physical attractiveness of source as determinants of initial credibility perception. *Western Speech* **38:** 13-17.

———, and Bruce Webster, 1969. The effects of physical attractiveness upon perceived initial credibility. *Michigan Speech Journal* **4:** 9-19.

———, and Stewart L. Tubbs, 1972. Machiavellianism and religiosity as determinants of attitude change in a counterattitudinal situation. Paper presented at the annual convention of the International Communication Association, April, Atlanta.

Wilmot, William, 1975. *Dyadic communication: a transactional perspective.* Reading, Mass.: Addison-Wesley.

Wilson, Paul, 1968. Perceptual distortion of height as a function of ascribed academic status. *Journal of Social Psychology* **74:** 97-102.

Wolfe, T., 1979. *The right stuff.* New York: Farrar, Straus & Giroux.

Wong, H., and W. Brown, 1923. Effects of surroundings upon mental work as measured by Yerkes' multiple choice method. *Journal of Comparative Psychology* **3:** 319-331.

Zajonc, Robert, 1966. *Social psychology: an experimental approach.* Belmont, Calif.: Brooks/Cole.

Zalenik, Abraham, and David Moment, 1964. *The dyanmics of interpersonal behavior.* New York: Wiley.

Zander, Alvin, 1961. Resistance to change: its analysis and prevention. In Warren Bennis, Kenneth Benne, and Robert Chin (eds.), *The planning of change.* New York: Holt, Rinehart and Winston, pp. 543-548.

Zimbardo, Philip, 1972. Pathology of imprisonment. *Society* **9:** 4-8.

Index